The Shape of Reason

The Shape of Reason
Argumentative Writing in College

THIRD EDITION

John T. Gage

University of Oregon

Contributing Editors:

Carolyn Bergquist
Brad Hawley
Julia Major
Mary Peters
David Sumner
Kenneth Wright

Allyn and Bacon
Boston   London   Toronto   Sydney   Tokyo   Singapore

Vice President: Eben W. Ludlow
Series Editorial Assistant: Grace Trudo
Executive Marketing Manager: Lisa Kimball
Production Editor: Christopher H. Rawlings
Editorial-Production Service: Omegatype Typography, Inc.
Composition and Prepress Buyer: Linda Cox
Manufacturing Buyer: Suzanne Lareau
Cover Administrator: Linda Knowles
Electronic Composition: Omegatype Typography, Inc.

Between the time website information is gathered and published, some sites
may have closed. Also, the transcription of URLs can result in typographical
errors. The publisher would appreciate notification where these occur so that
they may be corrected in subsequent editions.

Library of Congress Cataloging-in-Publication Data
Gage, John T.
    The shape of reason : argumentative writing in college / John T. Gage.—
3rd ed.
        p.   cm.
    Includes index.
    ISBN 0-205-31927-0
    1. English language—Rhetoric.   2. Persuasion (Rhetoric).   3. Report
writing.   I. Title.

    PE1431 .G34 2001
    808'.042—dc21

                                                             00-028849

Printed in the United States of America
10 9 8 7 6 5 4 3 2 1   05 04 03 02 01 00

Credits appear on pages 360–361, which constitute an extension of the
copyright page.

This edition of *The Shape of Reason*
is dedicated to some of the pioneers

Wilma Ebbitt
Albert R. Kitzhaber
William J. Brandt
Arthur Quinn

CONTENTS

Argumentative writing is writing that reasons its way to a conclusion. It addresses ideas that the writer takes seriously enough to want to explore and support with good reasons. This book is about this process: writing as reasoned inquiry.

You are invited to engage in this process by responding critically to the ideas of others and by writing about your own ideas in such a way that you try to earn the understanding and assent of your audience. In this way, you are invited to use writing to enter an intellectual dialogue that should be a central part of your experience in college. This approach has some consequences in the way I have written this book.

First, I have tried to challenge you to think about ideas and about writing. I want you to make up your own minds about everything in this book.

Second, this book treats the writing process as moving from a sense of the whole argument to the discovery of specific parts, rather than building separate "skills" in isolation from complete writing intentions. This mean that you will not be asked to produce writing merely for the sake of practicing some part of a whole composition (such as sentences or paragraphs), although you will be asked to write thesis statements that represent the whole intention of an essay and the line of reasoning that it will develop.

Third, this book treats the form of an essay as something that is *generated* by the writer rather than as something *imposed* on the writer. I want you to generate the structures that give your essays their own unique shape based on your ideas, rather than try to fill up "empty forms" imposed from outside. Form follows function. Ideas come first.

Fourth, I have placed the process of reasoning through an argument and generating the structure of an essay within the context of critical reading. Critical reading underlies the process of inquiry, which requires some kind of response to others' ideas and some basis of knowledge from which to respond. So, I have treated argumentation here as a matter of inventing and shaping the best possible reasons to earn your reader's understanding and assent, and not as a matter of trying to "win" your case by overpowering the "opposition." I have tried to underplay persuasion, as your aim, in favor of inquiry. Critical reading is a kind of prerequisite to inquiry, because it challenges us with ideas we may not have thought about, and provides us with whatever we need to know to be sure we are responding and inquiring responsibly.

Finally, I have tried to be honest with you about why I think argumentative writing matters. Thinking and writing are not processes that you can ever expect to "master." By doing them you learn the rewards of intellectual accomplishment as well as experience the limits of human understanding. Thinking is an adventure that requires risks. It always balances certainties with uncertainties. By facing both, we learn to live with our own uncertainties and to be more tolerant of the beliefs of others.

So, I urge you to treat this book and the writing that it invites you to do as an adventure in thinking. We are all in this together. The possibilities are endless.

In *The Shape of Reason,* I have presented argumentative writing as a large enough category to contain the kinds of intellectual and compositional skills that students should be practicing in college. Argumentative writing, for me, does not focus on one mode of developing ideas to the exclusion of another. The process of coming to conclusions may engage the writer in every possible kind of compositional pattern, depending on the nature of the issue and the writer's situation. I have presented argumentation as a process of inquiry into questions at issue that is best pursued if guided by principles but not governed by rules. Consequently, I have adapted the classical rhetorical concept of the enthymeme as the central basis for the invention and structuring of arguments, an approach that blends classical insights about rhetorical reasoning with contemporary understandings of the composing process as generative and organic, situated within discourse communities. This helps to remove logic from the sometimes rigid realm of disabling rules and formulas by treating reasoning as a natural and informal process.

I have included other features in the book that I hope will make the approach more effective. Extended discussions of important terms, such as *dialectic, structure, thesis, enthymeme,* and *style,* show how these concepts are flexible and shaped by the purposes to which we, as writers, put them. Each chapter ends with "Questions for Thought, Discussion, and Writing" that call for independent evaluation of the ideas in the chapter, often in relation to readings collected at the end of the text.

Instructors familiar with the second edition might be interested in the most significant changes that I have made in this third edition.

1. In order to emphasize the generative and collaborative nature of the enthymeme as an informal guide to reasoning, I have removed discussions of formal logic. Formal logical categories can be useful in this approach to teaching writing, at times, to enable students to see the dynamics of the enthymeme more clearly, yet they can also suggest a more prescriptive and formulaic model for reasoning than I think is necessary to engage students in serious, practical reasoning. Teachers interested in including formal logic in connection with their teaching of informal, practical reasoning will find this discussion moved to the new *Instructor's Manual* for this edition prepared by Margaret Johnson.

2. Similarly, a comparison between the enthymematic approach to invention and the "Toulmin model" for analyzing arguments has been deleted,

but made available in the *Instructor's Manual* to those teachers who wish to make such a comparison.

3. I have added a new chapter on dialectic in order to deepen our students' understanding of the linguistic and communal origins of the very human act of argumentation, and to develop further the crucial difference between argument as an intellectual journey into the realm of ideas and argument as verbal aggression.

4. Based on the responses of many teachers and students, I have chosen a number of new readings for this edition, while keeping those that have proven most successful in teaching this book. The readings are now arranged at the end of the book in a sort of mini-anthology, organized around a range of questions at issue. As before, *The Shape of Reason* may be taught as a stand-alone text or together with a separate anthology. I hope by this new arrangement of readings to illustrate the dynamic nature of responses to questions at issue, which do not fit neatly into "pro" and "con" positions, and to further this idea the readings now include three different forums, or selections of texts that were specifically written in response to each other, including a short Internet colloquy. To further illustrate the dynamics of informal reasoning, I have included works of fiction and personal narrative among the readings. A new section on arguments in and about fiction has been added to Chapter 4.

5. Instead of modeling at great length the processes of thought and revision that lead to a reasoned thesis and from that thesis to a fully conceptualized structure, I have offered only general advice on these processes to students and included in the new *Instructor's Manual* more explicit advice to teachers on how to conduct workshops in class in which students can engage directly in revising enthymemes and developing structures. I hope this change streamlines students' reading of the text and allows my advice to be related more directly to their own ideas for writing.

6. Discussions formerly found in several chapters dealing with the research process have for this edition been consolidated into a new Chapter 8 in order to focus more direct attention on research methods. The chapter does not provide a complete guide to research writing, but is intended to draw out and apply the implications for research of the specific approach to argumentative writing taken in *The Shape of Reason*.

7. Finally, I have sought, without in any way reducing the challenge to students that I hope this book presents, to revise the text in those places where it needed to be made more accessible. Everything I say in this book as advice to students applies to my own writing, and that includes always being open to the possibility of making it better, knowing that perfection is probably unattainable.

The approach to writing taken in *The Shape of Reason* will work best if students discuss ideas freely and write essays that respond honestly to the issues and arguments that develop during such a discussion. It invites and enables you to respond to students' ideas and writing as a critical thinker and writing consultant. It is in this way that I hope the book serves to enliven teaching as well as learning. This process is one from which both instructors and students never cease to learn.

I urge you to discuss your discoveries and questions about this approach with your colleagues, and thereby to form a discourse community of your own about your mutual insights and concerns. The *Instructor's Manual* for the book can provide a basis for such discussions as well as specific advice about teaching the book.

The third edition of the *Instructor's Manual* has been prepared by Margaret Johnson, based on Kathleen O'Fallon's revisions for the second edition of my original version. These experienced teachers of the book have provided different perspectives from mine, and our collaborations have led to a more useful guide to teaching argumentative writing than I could have produced on my own.

ACKNOWLEDGMENTS

I have been assisted in preparing this edition of *The Shape of Reason* by a group of contributing editors whose outstanding knowledge of the book and the theory behind it, and whose extraordinary talents as teachers and editors, have been invaluable to me. I consulted this group collectively about changes that would improve the book, and many of the ideas for this edition came out of these discussions. Each also helped me with specific revising tasks, contributing new material and rewriting when it was needed: Carolyn Bergquist contributed to the revising of Chapters 5 and 6; Brad Hawley drafted material on the teaching of argument using fiction and helped with the selection of appropriate works of fiction for the readings; Julia Major researched and selected new readings and contributed to the revision of Chapter 7; Mary Peters helped me to revise Chapter 4 and collaborated on the new Chapter 8; David Sumner helped me to revise Chapter 2 and also collaborated on the new Chapter 8; and Kenneth Wright researched and selected new readings and contributed to the revision of Chapter 8. For some who have taught *The Shape of Reason* in the past, this new edition has been a long time coming; without the assistance of these six expert teachers, it would have been much longer. Our work was made easier and better by the excellent advice of the following consultants who provided extensive suggestions for the third edition and commented helpfully on our proposed changes: Victoria Aarons, Trinity University; Suzanne Bordelon, University of Alaska–Fairbanks; Julie M. Farrar, Fontbonne College; Martin J. Jacobi, Clemson University; and Charles Paine, The University of New Mexico.

In the first and second editions of this book, I acknowledged my debt to my own teachers, to friends and colleagues, and to those who have influenced my thinking from Aristotle to Wayne Booth. Since then, many teachers and students have told me about their experiences with this book, and I am grateful to all of them for helping me think about revising it. I am especially indebted to the following people for specific suggestions, exemplary teaching of this book, and other forms of help and support during the long gestation period of this new edition: David Bartholomae, Holly Bauer, Margaret Bayless, Peter Blakemore, James Boren, Grant Boswell, Gideon Burton, Michael Bybee, Laird Christensen, Suzanne Clark, Keith Comer, Tom Conley, James Crosswhite, Joel Davis, Richard Dickson, Mary Lynn Diggs, Ann Dobyns, Georgiana Donavin, Alexis Easley, Barry Eckhouse, Barbara Emmell, David Esselstrom, Rick Filloy, Karen Ford, Bill Gholson, David Gilcrest, George Gopen, Lawrence D. Green, Anita Helle, Kathleen Horton, Rob Howard, Diane Hunsaker, Claudia Ingram, Kevin Jefferson, Ann Johns, Wendy Johnson, Keiko Kagawa, Perrin Kerns,

Melody Kilcrease, Peter Kittle, Ron Ladau, Jameela Lares, Anne Laskaya, Creighton Lindsay, Sherry Little, Yameng Liu, Dennis Lynch, Peter Mack, Joan Mariner, Jeff McCarthy, Glen McLish, Linda Mitchell, Candace Montoya, Erik Muller, Roark Mulligan, Laurence Musgrove, Kathleen O'Brien, Cezar Orna-towski, Carol Poster, Tison Pugh, Ellen Quandahl, Bart Queary, Marilyn Reid, Eric Reimer, Amy Ross, Mariolina Salvatori, Mike Snell, Melissa Sprenkle, Richard Stevenson, Kathleen Stradley, Ernie Stromberg, Carol Sweedler-Brown, Russ Tomlin, Lynn Tullis, Jeffrey Walker, John O. Ward, Molly West-ling, Brian Whaley, and of course all my Writing 121 and 122 students at the University of Oregon.

As always, Robin and Molly Gage contributed beyond measure.

JTG

The Shape of Reason

The Shape of Reason

chapter

1

Writing and the College Community

Discourse Communities

All of us are individuals, but we coexist with other individuals in communities. We belong to, or interact with, a variety of communities, each of which makes different demands on us, and which we, in turn, affect in different ways. As a member of your generation you are part of one kind of community, as a college student you are part of another, as a family member you belong to another sort of community, and as a person who holds certain political beliefs you are part of another sort of community. Such a list of examples could go on practically indefinitely: different communities for different aspects of our lives. Each of us belongs to a large number of overlapping communities.

Although we share some characteristics with the other members of each community we belong to, as individuals we are also unlike those members in other ways. A community is defined by some characteristic that unites its members, but diversity among people is present in every community. Diversity of opinion may be set aside to one degree or another for the good of the community, or it may become an obstacle to cooperation. Communities are dynamic things in which the members are always seeking cooperation but not at the expense of loss of individuality.

Some communities may be called **discourse communities.** A discourse community is any kind of community in which the members attempt to achieve cooperation and assert their individuality through the use of language. We are all members of a variety of discourse communities, each of which uses language in different ways. Family communities have their own ways of using language, some of which you use only when you are among family members (and some of which you may try to avoid). Political communities have their own ways of using language. Communities of natural scientists use language in some ways unique to them, as do communities of artists, athletes, businesspeople, farmers, and others. Language, because it is adaptable to any purpose, takes on characteristics that help the community to achieve its goals. Communities define themselves to a greater or lesser degree by the way in which they use language.

The uses of language in any discourse community go beyond specialized vocabularies. Yes, certain communities may have words that only members of those communities know or use. Such words are called jargon—words that you know by virtue of being part of some discourse community, words that nonmembers of that community do not know. But, more importantly, each community differs (more or less) in other ways in its use of language: Different forms of language (such as oral or written, spoken or sung, formal or informal, letters or essays, and so on) may predominate in the discourse of a group; language may be valued differently (language has a different value in the discourse of visual artists, say, than it does in the discourse of newspaper journalists); the purposes of language may vary (such as selling merchandise, persuading voters, praying, reporting information, telling jokes, telling stories, or telling lies). Such differences also overlap from community to community.

As a college student, you are a part of several discourse communities, each of which values language differently and uses it for different purposes. The language used in your biology and math classes will differ from the language used in your history and English classes. It will differ in vocabulary as well as in style. Short answers, lab reports, and factual questions may be more appropriate to some kinds of disciplines, whereas whole essays, speculative questions, and discussions may be favored in others.

Despite such differences, these discourse communities are also part of a larger discourse community: the college community itself. Like any other community, the scholarly community of the college has goals that in part determine how it uses language.

The purpose of the scholarly community is to inquire and to share with others the products of inquiry—understanding and knowledge. This is the central purpose that unites its members and that motivates them to cooperate with each other, despite differences among individuals. **Inquiry,** seen as the active search for answers to questions, suggests certain values and uses that language has in such a community. If language is used in such a community to inquire and to share knowledge, it will be used in certain ways, not ways that are necessarily better or worse than other ways but that are more suited to these goals. Language is valued in such a community for its ability to aid inquiry and to share understanding and knowledge honestly and precisely.

Diversity of point of view is not only respected in a college community, then, but it is actively sought. A community in which all members think alike on the most important questions is unlikely to inquire into those questions, because there will be no alternative points of view. Diversity of opinion is a prerequisite to inquiry and should be valued as such. This is why a scholarly community is one that seeks to open issues of any kind to further questioning by seeking other points of view, rather than to close off questioning by failing to listen to the challenging ideas of others who differ.

As college students, you are invited to join a community of inquiring minds. As learners, you are expected to do more than receive information passively. Like all other members of this discourse community, you are expected to participate actively in the open questioning of that information, listen to all sides, make judgments, and present those judgments to others coherently. The activities you are asked to go through in college—reading, discussion, writing, research, experiments, and so on—have a purpose beyond the acquisition of information in each class. They are meant to help you become better able to cope with the intellectual demands of a complex world, a world in which you will frequently be called upon to make independent decisions among competing ideas in the interest of one or another community to which you belong. Such decisions have to be made on the basis of reasoned thought, not by flipping a coin or following the crowd or a charismatic leader. An education prepares you to exercise judgment.

Perhaps it seems strange to you to hear education described in terms of an old-fashioned-sounding word, *judgment,* at a time when we are said to be experiencing a revolution in our ability to store and rapidly retrieve *information.* The twenty-first century promises to be the so-called information age, and as a student you are often exhorted to prepare yourself for living in a time when the amount of information and speed of accessing it made possible by computers and the Internet will continue to grow. But it is this exponentially rapid increase in the sheer amount of information available to us that will make the quality of judgment even more important to our lives, insofar as we will constantly have to adapt to change, to new information, and to new ways of processing that information. And we will constantly be faced with the necessity to make decisions *about* the information so plentifully available to us. But how does this apply to you as student writers?

Judgment and Writing

Judgment applies to all those occasions when we must decide what to do with information in its raw form. Do we accept it or deny it? How do we measure its significance or value? How should we use it? How does it relate to other bits of information? If people did not exercise judgment, their knowledge would be a useless hodgepodge of unrelated and equally significant bits of information. No educated person can do without the quality of judgment that enables her or him to make sense of all those bits. Yet there are no rules or procedures that can be followed to learn to exercise it. Judgment is learned only by practicing it. It is the act of judiciously appraising, discriminating, sorting, adapting, transforming, and applying ideas. Inasmuch as all of these actions require choice, judgment is learned best when one is faced with alternative answers.

Writing argumentative essays in college—a community of inquiring minds—is an opportunity to practice and improve this kind of judgment. If you choose ideas for your essays that are worth writing about, in response to problems that require careful reasoning to solve, you will be challenging yourself on many levels to exercise your best judgment. Writing is not simply an act of finding the right words; it involves looking at issues from different points of view, examining different positions and potential reasons for holding them, and thinking about potential structures and ways of presenting ideas to a reader. In performing such mental acts, you will be enhancing your understanding of the ideas you write about and your ability to reason while you improve as a writer.

It is important to remember that no writing class by itself can teach you to write at your best. All writers, even if they seem to write effortlessly, learn to write better each time they take on and complete a new writing challenge. Each new writing task is a challenge of its own, and the best a writing class can do is to create situations that will allow you, or invite you, to meet the challenge. If you are thinking about these challenges, you may not always feel your writing is improving when in fact it is. As you improve as a writer, you will naturally take on slightly more challenging writing tasks and find yourself writing about somewhat more difficult issues. As you respond to new writing situations, you may feel inadequate, simply because they will require you to go beyond what you already know how to do. A feeling of inadequacy (which you share with all writers, whether they will admit it or not) is therefore nothing to worry about. It is the way you should feel if you are learning.

Writing, as this book stresses, is a process of finding and structuring reasons. When we face a writing task, and when that task emerges from our attempts to find cooperation in a community of diverse opinions, writing becomes more than an attempt to put the right words in the right order. It becomes a search for reasons. It is in this way that the serious attempt to compose your thoughts in writing will often lead you to the very important discovery of what you think and why you think it.

Thus, writing is at the very center of what you do as you participate actively in a discourse community of inquirers. Any college student in any class can read, listen, take notes, pass objective tests, and even think deliberately about what it all means. But writing about the information with which you are presented in college has an effect that none of these other activities alone can produce. Writing causes you to clarify the information and the problems that come with it, to work out positions for yourself, and to explore reasons for holding those positions. Writing, because it is undertaken to communicate, must be clear. But if writing is also undertaken to influence the discourse community's thinking, that is, to be understood and believed, then it requires more than clarity. It also requires us to find the best reasons we can. Any act of writing that does not stop with the mere assertion of unrelated bits of information will engage the writer in a search for good reasons, and in that process the writer's judgment, as well as the writer's composing skills, is being exercised. Judgment and skills grow together.

This Book and You

The assumptions I have made about the importance of writing in college have led me to approach reason and structure as the main elements of good writing. This book is intended to guide you through a process of thinking and composing that will result in thoughtful, well-structured essays about ideas that matter to you.

The chapters are organized to focus on aspects of this process, but you will find as you compose essays that these aspects are not as separate as the parts of the book suggest. Books about writing must inevitably make distinctions among principles and stages of composing that are arbitrary and artificial in order to spread them out into a sequence of chapters. Ideas and choices that may occur to a writer in any order or all at once must be taken apart and given the appearance of a necessary order. In this book, the order will be as follows.

Chapter 1 looks at how our purposes as writers are connected to a community of inquiring minds in college and how our responsibilities as members of such a community affect how we conduct argumentative writing. Chapter 2 will help you become a more critical reader of others' arguments. Chapter 3 will explore ways in which language functions to generate the terms of our thinking. Chapter 4 will give you some advice for finding a meaningful idea to write about in response to questions at issue. Chapter 5 will discuss the process of finding adequate support in the form of reasons, and Chapter 6 will discuss how to use reasons as a basis for structuring your writing. Chapter 7 will give you some guidelines for revising your writing and making stylistic choices. Chapter 8 will explore the implications of these discussions for research writing.

Although abstract, this arrangement is meant to represent a process that is intuitively followed by every writer: being confronted with the conflicting ideas of others, responding with ideas of one's own, and developing one's reasons into a form and into language that will enable them to be understood and believed by others. As you give each stage your conscious attention, you can experience a process of thinking from which to draw as you compose, even though your actual acts of composing will never be completely self-conscious or neatly divided into stages.

The readings found in Part II are not meant to serve as models for you to imitate as you compose essays. There are no ideal models for a well-reasoned, well-structured essay, because no two pieces of writing arise from the same situations or need to satisfy the same conditions. They are meant instead to have two other functions. The first is to help you to investigate and assess how other writers have faced the challenge of inquiry, reasoning, and writing that the chapters discuss. As you analyze them, you can see more deeply into the process of thinking and writing that you will follow, in your own way, as you compose essays that respond to the unique circumstances of your own thinking. The second function of these readings is to confront you with the ideas of others, ideas that may challenge you to argue for your own. The authors of these readings, in this way, will become part of the larger discourse community in which you participate as you use writing to explore your own thinking on similar issues. These readings can become the beginning of an intellectual inquiry that takes you into further exploration of your own and others' arguments.

Ideally, as you use this textbook, you are engaged in active, open, reasonable discussion with others about the ideas in this book and in any other reading you may be doing for your writing class. Ideally, the members of the class will form a discourse community of inquiring minds, people who engage in an exchange of ideas and who will attempt to offer each other reasonable grounds for changing each others' minds. Ideally, the members of this community, who share your concern about the issues you discuss but who may not share your responses to those issues, will become the audience to whom you write. And you, in turn, will become part of the audience they need to address. In such a class, the activities of thinking, discussing, writing, and judging will not be separate. They will merge and reinforce each other.

My purpose in this book is to invite you to struggle with and find your way among real ideas, ideas that matter. The positions you forge for yourself will be your own positions, reasoned about and structured in such a way that you will feel a sense of achievement in each essay that you write. If you enter the process of reasoning and writing discussed in this book in a willing and thoughtful way, you will be writing essays that represent your best thinking on issues that are important to you.

Writing classes should be just as concerned with the important issues of a complex world as is any other college class. Students who are asked to write about the teacher's favorite idea just to practice writing or who churn out empty-headed compositions on prefabricated topics, such as "My Favorite Movie" or "How to Change a Tire," are doomed to write boring stuff for an already bored teacher. And they are cheated of the opportunity to use writing to learn what they really think and why. So, let's get real. I want you to learn to write, but I also want you to write to learn. It's my intention to enable you to use writing to learn where you stand in the ongoing discussion of ideas that demand serious attention from thinking people. Serious does not mean solemn, though. I also hope you will find the process interesting and fun.

Purpose and Design

As an active participant in the discourse communities of your college and your classroom, you will have two main purposes: to find your own way among the ideas of others as you read and listen to them, and to present the result of your inquiry in writing. Finding out what you think is what enables you to know what purpose will guide your writing. In saying this, however, I do not mean that writing comes only after thinking. The search for ideas, the process of inquiry itself, can and should go on during the activity of writing. Writing itself can generate ideas and is often the way we find our meanings. Consequently, this book will ask you to write at every stage of your thinking and to rewrite at every stage as well. But before we get to that, we should talk about the idea of purpose and how it is a guide to writing, even though in the process of writing new purposes may be discovered.

The shape that any piece of writing takes on results from the writer's overall sense of purpose. If we think of that shape as the progress from part to part in a composition, it may become easier to see that some sense of a destination, a goal to be reached, is what gives the writer—and the reader—a sense that the parts are held together in meaningful ways. We feel, as we read, that each new part is somehow justified by what went before it and that together they are progressing toward some conclusion. You have probably encountered writing that lacked this quality, and your response was to wonder, at some point as you slogged through it, "How did I get here?" "Where am I going?" You had this experience because the writer had somehow failed to connect the parts in a way that suggested forward progress. Thus, both the reader's sense of progress and the writer's control of this quality come from the same source: a clear sense of an intention that accounts for the necessity of each of the parts and their relations.

That thought reminds me of an episode in *Alice's Adventures in Wonderland,* when Alice encounters the Cheshire Cat sitting goodnaturedly in a tree. She asks the Cat:

> "Would you tell me, please, which way I ought to go from here?"
> "That depends a good deal on where you want to get to," said the Cat.
> "I don't much care where—" said Alice.
> "Then it doesn't much matter which way you go," said the Cat.
> "—so long as I get *somewhere,*" Alice added as an explanation.
> "Oh, you're sure to do that," said the Cat, "if you only walk long enough."

Lewis Carroll is having fun here with an idea that is central to an understanding of human actions of all kinds, including writing. That idea may seem self-evident, but it sometimes escapes us: Intention determines choice. When we face a choice of one or another way of acting, it is our intention that guides us. Sometimes, of course, we are not certain whether one or another way will, in fact, serve our intention, but the kind of deliberation that we enter into in that case still concerns the relationship of means to ends. What Carroll illustrates is that if we have no intended *end,* then the *means* that we choose hardly matters, In reference to the way in which we shape writing, we might say that if we have no destination to guide us, it hardly matters what parts we choose to put in or leave out. If we have no end in mind to use as a reference point for decisions along the way, any shape will do as well as another.

Whole compositions have unique shapes, or structures, then, because they have unique intentions. Generating the unique structure for your own composition must start with some degree of clarity about your own intentions. The self-evident relation between means and ends in composing gives you three principles to help ensure that the writing you create will present the reader with functionally related parts:

1. Try to be as clear as possible about what purpose you want your writing to achieve.
2. Use your intended purpose as the test for deciding whether any given part is necessary and whether any additional parts are needed.
3. Make your own sense of your purpose clear to the readers too, so that they can follow the parts and the transitions between them as they progress through the writing.

The purpose of a composition is its *whole* purpose, the sum of its parts. Its *structure* is the way in which those parts are held together to achieve that purpose. The purpose of a whole piece of writing is best described as an idea. Of course, compositions contain more than one idea, but they must all somehow relate to each other because they serve an overall idea of some kind.

Earned Conclusions

The overall or central idea that holds the parts of a composition together is sometimes called a **thesis.** Later, I will discuss thesis statements more fully and their role in helping you to generate structure. Now it is enough to say that the purpose of any piece of nonfiction prose writing is to provide the audience with sufficient ideas within its structure to enable them to understand and to accept its main idea.

We can speak of many different kinds of actions that ideas perform within a composition, such as *to show, to explain, to illustrate, to develop,* or *to support.* But one kind of action takes in all such particular actions and makes them necessary; that action is *to earn.* Whatever else the ideas in a composition do, they are there in order that the writer can earn the reader's attention or assent. It is one thing to assert an idea. It is another to earn it.

It may sound strange to you to hear the word *earn* applied to a reader's response to your ideas. Why have I chosen it? Consider another situation in which we usually apply this word, other than when we are referring to being paid for work: We sometimes speak, for instance, of earning someone's respect. We apply the term *earning* to human relationships, metaphorically, because we know that another's respect is not automatically given; it cannot be assumed. It is not owed to us. And we also know that whether we deserve respect is up to us and depends on how we act toward that person and how those actions are perceived. So, if we want that respect, we need to accept the responsibility to act in such a way that it will be given. Similarly, the sharing of ideas is like building a respected relationship. We cannot assume that we will automatically be listened to or believed. Readers or listeners are not compelled to hear us out, to pay attention, or to accept what we say just because we say it. Whether our ideas are listened to attentively and taken seriously depends on the quality of our communication. Thus, if we wish to be listened to, taken seriously, and believed, we must accept the responsibility of creating earned assent.

So, I have chosen this word *earn* to characterize the act of developing ideas in writing because it suggests that writing to be believed is an ethical act. *Ethical* suggests fairness and respect toward the reader. But even more, when a writer has an idea that she or he wishes to put forth for others to understand and accept, the word *earn* brings with it a sense of responsibility to make the writing do justice to that idea. A thesis is not just any idea, picked out of thin air for no other reason than to have something to write about. A thesis is a special kind of idea, one that you choose because you feel a sense of investment in it and want others to feel that same sense. It is such a sense of investment that makes composing seem worth the effort. If you were to compose without caring about the central idea, you would be in Alice's predicament of not knowing which way you ought to turn because you don't much care where it is you go. When you care about an idea, you have a reason to enter the process of searching for other ideas to use to earn that idea.

At one time or another, all writers have the experience of writing like Alice, lost in a confusing wonderland of words, thinking, "If only I write long enough I'm bound to get *somewhere.*" In fact, you may have found that writing can lead you into unexpected and interesting discoveries when you let yourself explore ideas freely. I hope you, like many students, have experimented with freewriting in which you "just wrote" without knowing, or without caring, where you would go in the end. In the process, you may have stumbled onto a new thought that seemed very interesting or a purpose that you didn't know you had. There are many ways of coming upon ideas and purposes, and freewriting can certainly be one of them. If you have had the experience of discovering what you wanted to say *as* you were engaged in writing, you were open to new ideas. But the experience didn't end there. You probably also realized that once you made the discovery you became responsible for doing something with all your freewriting to tie it somehow to that new idea, that new conclusion. Once the new idea was there, new responsibilities came along. Unless you were writing in the form of free association, as in a journal, you realized that the writing you did to stimulate this new idea could not necessarily stand as a composition *about* that idea. This awareness came from a feeling that once you knew just what you wanted to say you somehow accepted the responsibility of making sure that everything else you wrote was relevant to that thought. Your journal entry, for instance, may have generated the thought, but then the thought had to generate the composition.

Either way, writing is an act of inquiry. Once you know what it is you want to write about—and this decision will involve much more than freewriting, but include reading and discussion, too—inquiry becomes a process of looking into the implications of your idea and potential means of supporting it. It is in this way that having one idea leads to the discovery and testing of other ideas. Having taken responsibility for earning your main idea, you begin to see that there are many, too many, possible things to say *about* it, and you have to begin testing some of those things to see whether they are worth putting into your writing or leaving there. Writing is a process of accepting and rejecting many possible ideas, in light of the overall idea they are meant to support. As you decide which ideas to include, you are judging the quality of your own thoughts.

Questions for Thought, Discussion, and Writing

1. Think about your own attitudes toward your education and honestly ask yourself whether you generally seek challenges on your own or whether you mostly look for an easy way out of an assignment. Perhaps you can describe situations of each kind. What made the difference?

2. Think about an experience you have had in which you felt that what you already knew was adequate to solve a significant problem. Think about another experience in which your knowledge was not adequate to solve such a problem. Then compare what you learned from these two experiences.

3. Describe an experience in which you came to a clarification of your own thinking through writing.

4. Before reading any further in this book, describe the approach to writing you expect it to take. What *responsibilities* will you be asked to take as a writer? What do you feel about taking them?

5. Have you ever discovered your own intention in a piece of writing after you had begun to write? What did you do as a result of this discovery?

6. What does it mean to you to hear that you should be conducting genuine *inquiry* into your ideas as you write? What does *earning* your ideas mean to you?

7. As you read a selection from the writings in Part II, or any reading you may be doing for another class, identify the main idea, or thesis, and then identify other ideas that the writer uses to *earn* that thesis. In each case, try to ask yourself how the ideas are structured to make a whole: What makes each part of the essay necessary? Why are they arranged in this order? Having identified what you think are the supporting ideas, try to assess whether they provide you with sufficient grounds for accepting the conclusion. By what means do you judge whether they do?

2

Critical Reading

How We Read

In this chapter, I want to go into the question of what it means to believe what we read. Why is it that we sometimes think ideas are obvious whereas at other times we do not want to believe them? We understand ideas in relation to all of the ideas that surround them in any given piece of writing that we read, and we somehow adjust our beliefs to fit what we already know. The act of believing is the result of a decision, and we can decide how *much* belief to give to any idea based on how well it connects to other ideas and to what we know independently. The process of giving and withholding belief can be carried out in a rational or an irrational way. We are rational when we adjust our belief based on reasons. Each time we see a reason, we have to figure out whether it is a good one. So, reading is a process of making our way between the extremes of too much unreasonable belief (when the reasons to believe aren't good enough) and too much unreasonable doubt (when the reasons to *dis*believe are not good enough). Keeping this delicate balance is much easier said than done.

At least two kinds of beliefs are asked of us when we read. We are asked to believe the *information* presented by the writer, and we are asked to believe the *ideas* that are asserted about that information. In both cases, we read with some awareness that we do not *have* to believe something just because a writer says it. The question is: What kind of mental process do we go through to help us decide whether to believe the information and ideas we read?

Whether we are habitual readers, casual readers, or infrequent readers, we are all readers, and a lot of what we know and think has been the result of *how* we have read whatever we happen to have read. *Somebody* must be reading all those ads for exercise in a bottle or fat vanishing cream with guileless innocence, even if *we* all know not to believe them. And somebody, similarly, must be reading the front page of the *Washington Post* as if it were part of a well-orchestrated conspiracy. We change our reading habits to fit the nature of the reading matter and our reasons for reading it. It would be silly to adopt the same guarded stance when reading the Sunday comics that we might adopt when reading the advertisements. But might the comics ever be trying to sell us anything? Are they not sometimes asking for our belief in certain ideas? You bet they are. We might change our reading habits to fit the occasion, and we should, but we might not want to give up our ability to think critically about what we read.

Whether rightly or wrongly, we must often rely on reading when we need information. We may not believe everything that we read, but we nevertheless know that if we are to have reliable information, we probably ought to seek it in a reliable written source. Part of becoming educated is learning to distinguish among sources of information. We have all learned that some sources of information are more reliable than others. The *New York Times* is usually going to be more reliable than the *National Enquirer.* I say usually because when dealing with questions of belief there are always exceptions. There are probably examples of some fact being reported in the *National Enquirer,* denounced in the pages of the *New York Times* as a lie, and then discovered independently to be correct. There are certainly many examples of facts reported in the *New York Times* that have turned out to be wrong. Most of us have surfed the Web enough to know that the reliability of information varies greatly on the Internet. Because of our easy access to a wide range of Web sites and the sometimes ephemeral quality of those sites, the integrity and authority of the information we find on the Internet may be more difficult to assess than when we read well-established printed sources.

When considering different sources, we have also learned that the reliability of a source may depend on the type of information we are seeking. If we want to learn about the possible benefits of nuclear power, for instance, we may seek information from the nuclear power industry rather than from an environmental group; but if we want to learn about the possible dangers of nuclear energy, we will go first to the environmental group instead. Yet this convenience in finding appropriate information is also a hazard: Each of these kinds of resources may have built-in biases that affect the reliability of its information.

Examples like these raise questions about how to weigh information in order to know what facts to trust and whether to make up our minds based on them. To what extent should we rely on reading as a source of information? What tells us whether a source is reliable? By what means do we decide that a given piece of information is to be trusted? Let's consider another example, in more detail.

A Case in Point

In 1996, the Oakland, California, school board adopted a policy that proved to be very controversial. In that policy, African American Vernacular English, also called Ebonics, is treated as a language separate from English for certain purposes. This decision to classify Ebonics as a language generated a considerable amount of commentary in the national press from a wide range of points of view. My point here is not to judge the merits of the Oakland school board's decision, but rather to ask you to think about reading. When such a controversy erupts in our lives, we generally read about it first in journalistic reports. As you read the following newspaper article, which appeared in the *New York Times* at the time of this decision, think about how the school board's policy is being portrayed.

Jackson Says Black English Isn't a Separate Language

Neil A. Lewis

Washington—The Rev. Jesse Jackson said Sunday that the school board in Oakland, Calif., was both foolish and insulting to black students throughout the nation when it declared that many of its black students speak a language distinct from traditional English.

Speaking on the NBC News program *Meet the Press,* Jackson did not hesitate to wade into the explosive racial and educational issue thrust into prominence this week by the Oakland school announcement. "I understand the attempt to reach out to these children, but this is an unacceptable surrender, borderlining on disgrace," he said. "It's teaching down to our children."

Jackson's comments were seconded by the other guests, former Education Secretary William Bennett, a frequent commentator on contemporary culture, former New York Gov. Mario Cuomo and Sen. Joseph Lieberman, D-Conn.

Wednesday, the Oakland school board declared that many of its 28,000 black students, who make up a little more than half the district's pupils, did not speak standard English. Rather, they conversed in a distinctive language spoken by American blacks called *Ebonics,* a name taken from the words *ebony* and *phonics.*

In making the decision, the board effectively equated students speaking *Ebonics* with other students whose first language is Chinese or Spanish.

Jackson said the Oakland school board had become a national laughing stock, and he urged its members to reverse their decision, which he said was a misguided attempt to win extra federal money.

He said that black youths in Oakland and around the nation need to be challenged to speak proper basic English. Without that challenge, he said, they will not, "get in the University of California. They cannot get a job at NBC or CBS or ABC unless they can master this language, and I'll tell you they can master it if they are challenged to do so."

Oakland Schools Superintendent Carolyn Getridge has said the board's resolution was an effort to acknowledge that "African-Americans have a different language system and we want to recognize that and build on that."

Jackson compared the move to lowering the height of basketball rims. "We demand that the goals be 10 feet high and the rims have the same circumference," he said. "We're not going to teach basketball down and don't teach English and science and literature down."

If this were the only thing you had ever read about the Oakland school board's decision, how would you characterize the policy the board adopted? It seems, based on the information presented in the article, that Oakland's policy is to instruct African American children in Ebonics rather than in Standard English. Jesse Jackson complains that such instruction will not prepare those children for good universities and good jobs. Yet, is this an accurate description of what the Oakland school board intended by the policy? Should we trust this article? After all, it is published in the *New York Times*. It cites a respected authority on African American issues, Jesse Jackson. In other words, all the evidence seems to indicate that we should be getting truthful information here, even if we may reserve judgment on whether to agree with the policy. Especially if this issue is important to us—say, we have children in the Oakland schools or we ourselves have struggled with Standard English in our education or we are concerned about the implication of educational trends—we need to know whether the information is reliable before we can form our opinion about it. We may want to seek other sources on the topic. Among those sources, we might come across this document, issued by the Oakland school board itself.

Synopsis of the Adopted Policy on Standard American English Language Development

Oakland Unified School District

On December 18, 1996, the Oakland Unified School District Board of Education approved a policy affirming Standard American English language development for all students. This policy mandates that effective instructional strategies must be utilized in order to ensure that every child has the opportunity to achieve English language proficiency. Language development for African American students, who comprise 53% of the students in the Oakland schools, will be enhanced with the recognition and understanding of the language structures unique to African American students. This language has been studied for several decades and is variously referred to as Ebonics (literally "Black sounds") or "Pan-African Communication Behaviors" or "African Language Systems."

This policy is based on the work of a broad-based Task Force, convened six months ago to review the district-wide achievement data (see Appendix 1) and to make recommendations regarding effective practices that would enhance the opportunity for all students to successfully achieve the standards of the core curriculum (see Appendix 2). The data show low levels of student performance, disproportionately high representation in special education, and underrepresentation in Advanced Placement courses and in the Gifted and Talented Education Program. The recommendations (see Appendix 3), based on academic research, focus on the unique language stature of African American pupils, the direct connection of English language proficiency to student achievement, and the education of parents and the community to support academic achievement.

One of the programs recommended is the Standard English Proficiency Program (S.E.P.), a State of California model program, which promotes English-language development for African American students. The S.E.P. training enables teachers and administrators to respect and acknowledge the history, culture, and language that the African American student brings to school. Recently a "Superliteracy" component was added to ensure the development of high levels of reading, writing, and speaking skills. The policy further requires strengthening preschool education and parent and community participation in the educational processes of the District.

The recommendations of the Task Force establish English language proficiency as the foundation for competency in all academic areas. Passage of this policy is a clear demonstration that the Oakland Unified School District is committed to take significant actions to turn around the educational attainment of its African American students.

Oakland's Standard: English

The Board of Education adopted a policy on teaching English, not Ebonics. Unfortunately, because of misconceptions in the resulting press stories, the actions of the Board of Education have been publically misunderstood.

Misconceptions include:

- Oakland School District has decided to teach Ebonics in place of English.
- The District is trying to classify Ebonics (i.e., "Black English") speaking students as Bilingual.
- OUSD is only attempting to pilfer federal and state funds.
- OUSD is trying to create a system of perverse incentives that reward failure and lower standards.
- Oakland is condoning the use of Slang.
- Oakland has gone too far.
- Ebonics further segregates an already racially divided school district.
- There is no statistical evidence to support this approach or that this approach will improve student achievement.

Nothing could be further from the truth.

1. The Oakland Unified School District is not replacing the teaching of Standard American English with any other language. The District is not teaching Ebonics. The District emphasizes teaching Standard American English and has set a high standard of excellence for all its students.
2. Oakland Unified School District is providing its teachers and parents with the tools to address the diverse languages the children bring into the classroom.
3. The District's objective is to build on the language skills that African American students bring to the classroom without devaluing students and their diversity. We have directly connected English language proficiency to student achievement.
4. The term *genetically based* is synonymous with genesis. In the clause, "African Language Systems are genetically based and not a dialect of English," the term *genetically based* is used according to the standard dictionary definition of "has origins in." It is not used to refer to human biology.

Appendix 1: Findings

- 53% of the total Oakland Unified School District's enrollment of 51,706 is African American.
- 71% of the students enrolled in Special Education were African American.
- 37% of the students enrolled in GATE classes were African American.
- 64% of students retained were African American.
- 67% of students classified as truant were African American.
- 71% of African American males attend school on a regular basis.
- 19% of the 12th grade African American students did not graduate.
- 80% of all suspended students were African American.
- 1.80 average GPA of African American students represents the lowest GPA in the district.

Appendix 2: Core Curriculum Standards at Benchmark Grade Levels

- Grade 1: All students will read and perform mathematics at grade level.
- Grade 3: All students will read at grade level, have mastery of mathematical operations, and compose written works on a computer.
- Grade 5: All students will meet or exceed the fifth grade standards for the core curriculum in Language Arts, Mathematics, Science, and Social Science.
- Grade 8: All students will be able to read and engage with complex and diverse literature, conduct a research project and write a scholarly paper on that research, perform mathematics at a level required to enroll in Algebra, organize and participate in community service and social events, and utilize technology as a tool for learning and work.

- Grade 10: All students will successfully complete college required coursework in English, Math, and Science, and will enroll in a career academy or program.
- Grade 12: All students will successfully complete courses required for entrance into a college or university, meet the requirements for an entry level career position, and develop and defend a senior project.

Appendix 3: Overview of Recommendations

The recommendations, based on identified conditions and outcomes, are aligned with the Content Standards adopted by OUSD, prekindergarten–12th grades, 1996–1997.

It is the consensus of the African American Task Force that the African American students' language needs have not been fully addressed.

This report addresses the language needs of African American students as one of the nine major areas of recommendations to be implemented by OUSD.

1. African American students shall develop English language proficiency as the foundation for their achievements in all core competency areas.
2. All existing programs shall be implemented fully to enhance the achievements of African American students.
3. The Task Force on the Education of African American Students shall be retained in order to assist OUSD in developing workplans and implementation strategies.
4. Financial commitments shall be made to implement the Task Force on the Education of African American Students recommendations during the current fiscal year.
5. The district's identification and assessment criteria for GATE and Special Education Programs shall be reviewed.
6. The community shall be mobilized to partner with OUSD to achieve recommended outcomes.
7. OUSD shall develop a policy which requires all categorical and general program funding to be used to ensure access to and mastery of the core curriculum.
8. All resources of the district shall be applied and used to ensure that these recommendations be implemented.
9. OUSD shall develop recruitment procedures that facilitate the hiring of administrators, teachers, counselors and support staff that reflect the culture of African American students' composition of the student population.

"Black children are the proxy for what ails American education in general. And so, as we fashion solutions which help Black children, we fashion solutions which help all children."

This document gives a different picture. After reading it, we can see that Jesse Jackson, William Bennett, and others cited in the first article were apparently responding to the school board's policy without a full understanding of what it actually said. There are many controversial points in the policy, but nowhere does it advocate teaching Ebonics as the language students should learn instead of Standard English. Rather, the policy advocates recognizing Ebonics as a second language in order to better teach Standard English to African American children. In all fairness, Jesse Jackson realized that he had spoken without understanding the policy and later changed his position. However, the question for us is about reading and belief. In reading accounts such as Lewis's article, we may think, as many did, that the school board was advocating abandoning Standard English in favor of teaching Ebonics. The Lewis article does not read in a way that would make us suspect it as a biased source, and yet we could be seriously misled in our attempt to make up our minds if we trusted it uncritically. The article is from a generally reliable source and does not seem to have a political axe to grind. The people cited in it are experts. So there must be a way to measure one's belief when reading even the most apparently credible sources, such as, for instance, this book! Is there a process we can go through as readers to measure our belief in the facts we read?

What sort of process am I talking about? Not one, I assure you, that will prevent you from ever being duped or that will tell you when a thing is true. Critical reading can do no more than keep you asking about potentially good or bad reasons, so that when you face the question of whether to agree or disagree, you will be able to make a qualified decision based on your understanding of the quality of the reasons given. **Critical reading is the conscious act of adjusting the degree of one's agreement with any idea to the quality of the reasons that support that idea.** People who believe without caring about the quality of the reasons, as well as people who disbelieve without caring about the quality of the reasons, no matter *what* they believe, are, by this definition, uncritical. All of us are uncritical sometimes. We are more or less critical at different times. When we are reading, however, we should try to read as critically as we can. If we don't, we risk being misinformed and possibly coming to conclusions we cannot support.

When writers write, they do not simply string together sentences that all directly assert some information. As we have seen in Chapter 1, writing takes its shape from the writer's intention. That is, writers want people to believe something. They write with an idea in mind, therefore, but their choice of things to say in addition to that idea depends on what they think people need to hear in order to believe it. Writing is purposeful and *strategic*. Writing that contains information, then, will also contain something put there in order to help you or encourage you to believe that that information is true.

A critical reader must, therefore, pay attention to more than *what* a piece of writing says. A critical reader must also consider *how* information is presented, and in what context. This is because a writer who thinks strategically is mindful of the *means* that is necessary to reach the *end* that he or she has in mind. This does not mean that writers cheat or want to deceive us. It simply means that writers intuitively understand that they must convince readers to believe them, and they make use of available means of persuasion accordingly. Information by itself is rarely the *end* of a piece of writing, even in news stories such as the Lewis piece. Lewis is true to the facts in one sense: He has quoted Jackson accurately (I presume). However, the placement of these facts can make a difference in how we interpret them. For example, Lewis briefly defines Ebonics and then writes, "In making the decision, the board effectively equated students speaking Ebonics with other students whose first language is Chinese or Spanish." Is Lewis stating what the policy does, or is he interpreting the policy for us at this point? His way of phrasing this statement might suggest that he intends us to see the definition as ridiculous. He uses this to support Jackson's position implicitly, rather than to investigate whether Jackson's view might itself be based on a misunderstanding. He does not report the school board's reasoning. Would a critical reader at this point be cautious of quickly agreeing with Lewis or Jackson? If we were reading critically (and some may want to know whether we can read everything too critically), only further exploration of the issue, and a wider range of opinion, could provide adequate grounds to move us one way or another in our belief.

The process of finding out more and hearing a wider range of points of view is potentially endless, but even to begin it one must be motivated by a sense of the importance of making up one's mind based on the *best* reasons. For example, one might read the school board's policy and at least have a better informed view of what the board meant and why, but that in itself would not suffice to answer certain kinds of questions about the accuracy of the board's definition of Ebonics. One might then seek a different kind of information and discover, for example, Carolyn Temple Adger's account of the controversy from the point of view of the study of linguistics. (Her article and other texts related to this controversy are provided in the readings in Part II of this book.) While reading her argument, we may also become aware that the school board amended its initial policy decision, and then we may want to seek the amended resolution. In the end, though, it will be up to us to seek different relevant views and then to evaluate those views according to the quality of the reasons they give in support of their conclusions, and not on the basis of the credibility of the source or the authority of the writer alone.

Reading and Belief

Some people are accustomed to think that facts must be either believed or disbelieved—as if belief were like a light switch with only two positions, on or off. My use of the Ebonics controversy is intended to illustrate that belief does not have to operate as a simple yes or no choice, all or nothing. Belief can be more conditional; it can be something that we decide to have up to a point or to a degree. And so, the question we might ask ourselves while reading does not have to be "Should I believe it or not?" but instead "How seriously should I entertain this possibility?" This latter question implies that the belief we have in any given fact, or in any given idea, is not determined by whether it sounds right or whether the source is an authority. It means that our beliefs are determined by the reasons that justify them. Belief is not a mechanical action, brought about by invariable rules of nature. It is a human activity, the exercise of judgment.

The process of weighing beliefs against the quality of reasons is one that you already go through all the time, whether you are aware of it or not. We all do. The practice of critical reading is the exercise of this kind of judgment on purpose. By doing it, we protect ourselves from being led into belief for inadequate reasons, but at the same time we open up our minds to the possibility of arriving at belief for adequate ones. If we decide to grant or withhold assent based on the quality of the reasons that we are given, we admit at the same time that two things are possible: We admit that we might assent less in the future if we discover that the reasons are not so good after all; and we admit that we might assent more if we are ever presented with better reasons than we had formerly known. This attitude is not pure skepticism any more than it is pure credulity. It is somewhere in between. It is the attitude of an open-minded thinker, of someone who wishes to be responsible for deciding for herself or himself what to believe. This attitude also implies a willingness to question one's own beliefs while at the same time remaining open to new and different ideas.

The practice of critical reading, then, can do more than protect us from jumping too quickly to conclusions. Because it is a process of examining reasons and measuring conclusions against them, it can provide us with a way to learn to live with uncertainty. Living with uncertainty is one of those skills we need to get along in this world, but it is also a skill that people do not talk about much. We have just seen that certainty is not easy to come by. It requires that we assume some responsibility for questioning what we read, which might entail a search for more information and better reasons than we are given in a single source. In other words, it requires independent inquiry and thought, which are carried out not only because we want to know what to believe but also because each of us alone must make up his or her own mind.

If absolute, permanent belief is not available about many matters that concern us, we must adjust to this situation and accept it. It can be a situation to be enjoyed, not lamented, because it is what makes thinking and learning an adventure. More inquiry is always possible. New ideas or new reasons may turn up. This keeps our minds alert and active. It makes us want to continue to learn because we are more able to accept new ideas. It makes us less susceptible to the tactics of people who would like to do our thinking for us. Instead of the easy convictions that come from narrow-mindedness, this process offers us the possibility of continuing to think about things that matter to us.

Critical reading, then, is something we practice in order to acknowledge that we belong to a "community of inquiring minds," as I called it earlier—a discourse community in which inquiry and argument are valued for their ability to keep us thinking and talking to each other.

Some Considerations for Critical Reading

The preceding section has offered you some philosophical ideas about reading and writing, about education, on which this book is based. You are free, in fact encouraged, to question them. But now we must get practical in our thinking about critical reading.

Here are some questions that a critical reader might consider in order to arrive at an adequate basis for deciding how much to give or withhold assent. Asking the questions will not, of course, guarantee answers. It can only serve to guide further thinking.

1. *What is the writer's purpose?* What is this writer trying to do to the reader? What is the single most important idea in the writing, the one that makes everything else in it necessary? This central idea (or thesis) may or may not be stated explicitly by the writer. It may or may not be obvious.

2. *What question does the writing answer?* The writer's intended audience is assumed to share a concern for some question, which the essay serves to answer in some way. The question may or may not be explicit or obvious. Do I share this concern? Should I?

3. *Why does the writer think this question is important?* There must be some reason the writer has chosen this question to answer. What difference does it make to the writer that the question be resolved? What about the writing tells me this?

4. *How persuadable am I?* Do I already have my mind made up on this question? How willing am I to listen to another point of view? If I agree with the author, can I maintain some critical distance and not agree with the reasons just because I already agree with the conclusion? What untested reactions do I have to the writer's thesis?

5. *What are the writer's reasons?* What ideas does the writer advance in defense of the thesis? What ideas are advanced in defense of *those* ideas?

6. *Where does the reasoning stop?* What reasons are asserted as if they are self-evident? Although some reasons are supported by a further line of reasoning, it is impossible for all of them to be. If the reasoning depends on these ideas being believed without further support, do I believe them?

7. *Are the reasons adequate?* Not all reasons actually support the conclusions they seem to support. What actually connects the reasons to the conclusions?

8. *What responsibility does the writer take for the verifiability of information?* If the writer cites facts, studies, experiences, or sources, is there an adequate basis for checking up on them, or does the writer expect us simply to take his or her word for them?

9. *What has the writer done to put the reader in a receptive frame of mind?* Not all parts of a writing have the strictly logical function of supporting a thesis. Some aspects of the composition, especially its style, will function to create confidence in the writer or a special bond between the writer and the reader. How do I react to these features?

10. *What am I going to do about it?* If a critical reader is engaged in measuring assent, then I should know how I might be changed by having read and thought about these ideas. To what extent must I adjust my thinking? Do these ideas have relevance to my thinking about other questions? Are there connections between these ideas and other things I believe? What are the consequences or practical effects for me of believing or doubting?

Perhaps you ask yourself many of these questions anyway when you read, even if you never become self-consciously deliberate about doing so. They are not intended as a checklist, to proceed through in mechanical fashion. They are not, as you will see, quite as separate as a numbered list might suggest. Use them as a basis for more thought, that's all.

Questions for Thought, Discussion, and Writing

1. Have you ever had the experience of believing something you read and then discovering later that it was not true? What did this experience teach you about reading?

2. Have you ever read something that someone told you was bad for you? Was it? How do you know? How about something that someone said would be good for you?

3. Can you think of any ideas that you agree with only to a certain degree? What has your agreement to do with the quality of the reasons you have heard in support of these ideas?

4. In general, how would you define a "good reason"? Find some examples of good reasons and bad ones to illustrate what you mean. Does everyone agree with your examples?

5. Read the forum on Ebonics contained in Part II (beginning on page 265), and continue the analysis of the reliability and credibility of these sources begun in the discussion in this chapter. How does the expansion of your reading on this issue affect the degree to which you are able to assent to the school board's policy? What questions remain unanswered for you

that need to be answered in order for you to make up your mind? Where might you go for reliable answers to those questions?

6. As you read other selections in Part II, or any other reading you are currently doing, use the ten questions at the end of this chapter to guide your critical reading. For a particular reading, write short answers to each of the ten questions. Does your conscious attempt to apply these critical reading questions provide you with ideas for an essay of your own? Do they open up areas in which you wish to conduct further inquiry?

3

The Deep Structure of Reasoning

On Dialectic

Where do arguments come from? One answer to this question is that arguments are generated by ideas in opposition. Before we go on to talk about ideas and how they form the basis for structuring argumentative writing, let's consider the idea of opposition itself. Where does opposition come from? Perhaps, the answer that comes most readily to mind is that it comes from differences or conflicts among people, but let's consider for a moment the way that differentiation and opposition are deeply embedded in language, providing the basic material out of which all arguments arise. Meaning itself would be impossible without differentiation; a word names one thing, not another. The word *table* has meaning because it distinguishes one kind of furniture from other kinds.

Opposition is a special form of differentiation. Let's consider it more fully.

The poet Richard Wilbur writes about a family word game in which someone says a word and another has to make up an opposite for that word. Wilbur then makes poems out of the words:

What is the opposite of *hat*?
It isn't hard to answer that.
It's *shoes,* for shoes and hat together
Protect our two extremes from weather.

The opposite of *doughnut*? Wait
A minute while I meditate.
This isn't easy. Ah, I've found it!
A cookie with a hole around it.

The opposite of *spit*, I'd say,
Would be *a narrow cove or bay.*
(There is another sense of spit,
But I refuse to think of it.
It stands opposed to *all refined
and decent instincts of mankind*!)

The fun of this game is in thinking up a reason that something can be seen as the opposite of something else. Play the game yourself. What is the opposite of *chair?* Hmm. It depends. Is it *couch?* Or is it *floor?* Or is it *bicycle?* Whatever it is, it would have to be a joke, like Wilbur's opposites, because *chair* belongs to a category of words that do not have opposites, in the ordinary sense. Nouns that name concrete things don't generally have opposites, even though they can be contrasted with other words for things:

> *tree*   in contrast to   *bush*
> *lumber*
> *building*

These contrasting words could be seen in opposition to the word *tree* in different circumstances. *Tree* and *bush* might be seen in opposition in the context of landscaping. *Tree* and *lumber* are opposed in the context of raw material versus product. *Tree* and *building* might be said to be opposed in the sense that one is natural and the other artificial. In each case, it's the qualities assigned to the tree, or the context in which it is seen, that are opposed to other qualities, not the tree itself.

Opposition, then, is not really a condition of specific things, or words for specific things, but of abstract concepts that might be applied to things. Some nouns that name things do seem to have opposites, such as:

> *circle*   *square*
> *land*   *ocean*
> *city*   *countryside*

Yet in such cases, these are not concrete things so much as they are qualities of concrete things. At yet a higher level of abstraction, words, unlike the nouns used to name specific things or qualities of things, name concepts, like *love.* Such concepts are understood not because we can point to them but because we can name and define them in terms of other concepts. Opposition is inherent in abstract terms because for any such term naming a concept there is a term that may be used potentially to name its negation or absence, like *hate* in relation to the concept *love.*

A few more examples would be:

> *motion*   *stillness*
> *sound*   *silence*
> *beauty*   *ugliness*
> *intelligence*   *stupidity*
> *grace*   *clumsiness*
> *wealth*   *poverty*

Abstract terms seem to come to our minds and exist in our awareness already paired with opposing terms. Such pairs of terms are used to define each other. They are known to us because we understand them in terms of the opposite concepts with which we pair them. Such pairings may be called **dialectical oppositions,** when we understand one of the terms by defining it in opposition to the other term, as in, for example:

deep	*shallow*
joy	*sadness*
sacred	*profane*
lost	*found*
large	*small*
clear	*obscure*
loyalty	*betrayal*
sharp	*dull*
power	*weakness*
friend	*enemy*
pleasure	*pain*

We understand each term only in relation to the other: *Deep* is understood relative to *shallow,* or *clear* relative to *obscure,* and so forth. The meaning of the term is somehow not inherent in the term itself without the contrasting term to define it by comparison or negation. Language seems to have an infinite number of dialectical oppositions, pairs of words that are understood as opposed concepts. If you look up an abstract word in the dictionary, it will often be found to have several opposites, called antonyms. Dialectical opposites are those antonyms we understand through negation, each word forming a necessary part of the definition of the other. In the previous examples, *power* is defined as the absence of weakness and *weakness* as the absence of power. We know something to be large when we compare it dialectically to something small, and vice versa. Something that is sharp cannot be said to be dull at the same time, because each of the two concepts is understood as the quality of not being the other.

We often associate dialectical pairings with qualities of "good" or "bad," which is, of course, a basic dialectical opposition itself. Sometimes such positive and negative associations are purely cultural, as in the following oppositions:

rich	*poor*
introversion	*extroversion*
beauty	*ugliness*
conflict	*agreement*

To see how we tend to associate positively and negatively with such oppositions, try putting each pair into these sentences:

> _____   is better than   _____ .
> _____   is worse than   _____ .

In most cases, one sentence or the other will feel right. But think about circumstances in which reversing the terms in the sentence might be closer to the truth.

Certain philosophical pairings of words in our language do not have inherent or cultural negative and positive poles. It is impossible to say of these that one "is better than" the other, apart from their application to particular conditions. Here are some examples of what I mean by such dialectical pairs:

nature	*nurture*
society	*individual*
reason	*emotion*
past	*future*
active	*passive*
natural	*artificial*
plain	*ornate*
essential	*accidental*
general	*abstract*
means	*ends*
cause	*effect*
part	*whole*
subjective	*objective*
theory	*practice*
central	*marginal*
universal	*particular*

Only a particular application of these terms to a circumstance will tell us whether one or the other half of such a pair seems to be better than the other. For example, even though neither *objective* nor *subjective* seems inherently better, I may think that it's important to be subjective when judging a painting I might choose to buy but objective when judging candidates for whom to vote. In such a case, either term can carry the quality of good or bad depending on the situation.

Assigning value to dialectical oppositions is a basic precondition to the formulation of arguments. Such pairings orient us to ideas: When ideas are in conflict, it is generally because underlying those ideas there is a dialectical opposition of some kind, and when we choose one idea over another conflicting idea, it is because we have placed a positive or negative value on the terms of that opposition. In a given circumstance, we associate ourselves, orient our thoughts, with one term or the other of a dialectical pairing.

What I have said up to this point might give you the impression that dialectical terms lead us to think of argument as on either one "side" of an issue or another. I do not mean to give you that impression. We think in terms of dialectical oppositions, but we employ them to serve a wide range of different positions, and it is the range of oppositions we have to choose from and the way we associate them (as in the following discussion) that permits any number of different positions to be possible. In any argumentative situation, a wide spectrum of potential positions might be taken, not just the choice of one side or its opposite. I am talking about the dialectically opposed terms we use to construct a position, not opposed positions as such. We make use of dialecti-

cal terms freely to construct positions. For instance, I may see a particular issue in terms of the dialectical opposition between *justice* and *injustice* and that
will define my position, but on the same issue I might take a different position
by framing it in terms of the dialectical opposition between *justice* and *mercy*
instead. In one set of circumstances, *beauty* may be opposed to *ugliness* but in
a different circumstance it may be opposed to *truth*. One's position is not predetermined by dialectical oppositions, only made possible by them.

Let me illustrate dialectical oppositions at work in an argument that addresses a complex issue and can't be reduced to a simple "side."

If you have not read Martin Luther King, Jr.'s famous "Letter from Birmingham Jail" (found on page 173), please do so at this point. In this letter King
makes use of a number of fundamental dialectical pairings, including the distinction between *justice* and *injustice*, as in his references to *just* and *unjust*
laws. This dialectical opposition comes to our minds already associated with
a positive and a negative polarity. King makes use of this ready-made preference for justice over injustice in his argument that his direct actions in the
Birmingham demonstrations, even though against the law, were necessary
and therefore right. The dialectical distinction he creates between *direct* action
and *indirect* action becomes linked to these values and the idea of direct action
is thereby associated with the value of justice. The situation in which King
found himself helped define for him the opposition between direct action and
indirect negotiation, but this pairing is not necessarily already associated with
a positive or negative quality: In some situations negotiation is better than direct action; in others direct action is better. King must ally himself with one or
the other, in his present circumstance, and he does so by linking the opposition between *direct* action and *indirect* negotiation with the opposition between *justice* and *injustice*. That is, he argues that direct action is necessary in
this situation in order to create justice. Notice how in this argument King must
also reduce our sense of a strict dialectical opposition between *legal* and *illegal* acts. Also notice that in taking a position against the eight clergy who
wrote him the letter to which he responds based on the dialectical opposition
between legal and illegal acts, he takes a position with them in his belief that
their motives are *sincere*, as dialectically opposed to *insincere*, and in his appeal
to shared faith in God.

These are not just word games; King provides the reasons for these associations and disassociations, which are important to his thinking about civil
rights issues. But without the oppositions already provided by the dialectical
nature of abstract language, he could not provide those reasons in order to get
his beliefs across.

In the writings by Plato, Thoreau, the eight Birmingham clergy, King,
Bari, Van Dusen, and Barrett I have clustered together in Part II, all of which
address the question of whether and in what circumstances one is justified in
breaking the law, similar oppositions precondition the development of the argument. Obeying the law and disobeying the law are dialectically opposed

concepts, and the ways these writers argue for different ways of understanding these concepts, and for choosing one in preference to the other, are by linking them to other dialectical oppositions, such as:

freedom	*slavery*
the good of the society	*the good of the individual*
the good	*the expedient*
ends	*means*
violence	*nonviolence*
wisdom	*foolishness*
body	*mind (or soul)*

Notice the way some of these terms shift in value when Bari, in her argument, links them to the dialectic of gender: *male/female*.

The argumentative process of making such distinctions and using them to debate conflicting ideas is itself often called **dialectic,** the process of reasoning from basic distinctions. Dialectical argument is often seen as a process that involves reasoning about the consequences of making certain distinctions, and it was practiced most famously by the philosopher Socrates in the writings of Plato. You can see this method at work in the Platonic dialogue I have included for your reading entitled "Crito" (found on page 145). Because Plato wrote his arguments in the form of dramatic dialogues, dialectical reasoning and the form of dramatic dialogue are historically related to each other. One can practice dialectical reasoning without putting it in the question-and-answer form of dialogue that Plato uses, but something about the form of dialogue is particularly appropriate to the presentation of dialectical argumentation. That something is the human element of dialectic: Reasoning from basic distinctions implies a kind of interior dialogue, the ability to pursue an idea by asking and answering questions about it. Dialectical reasoning pays attention to the arguments made on different sides of any question. It seeks the best reasons, not just those that support one side. This kind of internal debate is a quality of all argumentation, as I am using that term in this book (based on a dialectical opposition between *inquiry* and *fighting*). We engage in reasoned inquiry in the presence of opposing views, or with an imaginary other who challenges our thinking by representing a different dialectical preference.

In this sense, as this book will show in different ways, reasoning is itself a communal process, not just because we reason together but because we reason in response to others' views. These views are both opposed and not opposed to our own. Our ability to imagine what ideas might oppose our thinking is what motivates us to reason, whereas our knowledge of what ideas might agree with our thinking enables us to know where our reasoning must begin and end. Thus, dialectic somehow operates in the very fabric of our thinking. And both agreement and disagreement (one of the basic dialectical oppositions on which this book is based) are necessary to generate the thinking we do.

The Interplay of Dualisms

To explore further how we make distinctions and link them to dialectical pairings, let's go back briefly to Richard Wilbur's game of opposites. As we have already seen, when we make up opposites for words that are not dialectical, words that do not naturally have opposites, we find that our choice is somehow affected by context or perspective. For example, if I ask, "What is the opposite of *shirt*?" a variety of answers are possible depending on the context in which the nondialectical term *shirt* is considered. In the context of pickup basketball games, the opposite of *shirt* is *skin*. In the context of an individual's apparel, the opposite of *shirt* might be *pants*. In the context of boy's and girl's clothing, the opposite of *shirt* might be said to be *blouse*. From the perspective of one's choice of a particular garment, the opposite of *shirt* might be *tank top*. Notice that in each case the very meaning of *shirt* is slightly different. Our understanding of the term changes when we see it in relation to these other terms.

Here's another example. This time ask yourself what context or perspective determines whether each potential opposite seems appropriate.

The opposite of *photograph* is   *painting*
movie
negative
interpretation
memory
hearsay
postcard

When you imagine a context in which each of these terms might be opposed to *photograph*, you are, in effect, constructing an argument about what the term means. Try playing this game with other nondialectical terms.

In the case of dialectical terms, where opposites are somehow paired in our minds, context may also affect our understanding of the meaning of one or the other term. Let's consider, for example, the meaning of the term *freedom*. *Freedom* is paired conceptually with its opposite: *bondage* or *constraint* or *limitation*—terms that themselves are defined as a lack of freedom of some kind. But what kind? In what contexts might different terms be appropriately said to be the opposite of *freedom*? What, for instance, is the opposite of *free* in each of these sentences or expressions?

Here is your free gift.
You are free to choose only from the items on the menu.
You have ten minutes of free time.
Freedom ends where responsibility begins.
"Free at last, free at last, thank God Almighty, I'm free at last."
"Freedom's just another word for nothin' left to lose."

You are pretty free with your criticism.

He believes in free love.

He's a free agent.

I'm free and easy.

I'm home free.

Do you have a free hand?

In each case, does the meaning of *free* change? Is *freedom* the opposite of *responsibility* or are they part of each other? Whole philosophical or political systems are built around different answers to this question. *Freedom* means one thing when contrasted to the literal condition of slavery, another when contrasted to social or economic oppression, something else when contrasted with a lack of opportunity or means to take a certain action, and another thing when contrasted to lack of permission to use the car on Saturday night. It seems then as if the answer to the question "What is freedom, really?" might be that it depends on what you mean by the opposite of *freedom*.

Dialectical oppositions may themselves provide the context from which we view the meaning of other oppositions, as we saw in the case of King's letter. In such a way, dialectical oppositions form perspectives. Take, for example, the dialectical pair *intellect/emotion*. How does your understanding of the relationship between these concepts change when you look at the distinction in terms of other dialectical pairs, such as the following?

science	*religion*
objectivity	*subjectivity*
male	*female*
art	*craft*
fact	*value*

Linking one side of such an opposition with either intellect or emotion creates an association and signifies a preference. From such linkages, if you feel drawn to them, positions follow that give rise to arguments. You can see this by playing with the word *mere* in sentences that combine such dialectical terms:

Science requires intellect, whereas religion is mere *emotion.*

Religion values emotion over mere *intellect.*

True art derives from emotion; a craft is the exercise of mere *intellect.*

Art comes from feeling, not mere *intelligence.*

Facts must be true, not merely *believed.**

Arguments are built on the basis of a process similar to this; each of these stated preferences could be supported with further evidence. For example, my dis-

*This exercise is adapted from *Modern Dogma and the Rhetoric of Assent* by Wayne C. Booth, The University of Chicago Press, 1974, pp. 17–18.

cussion of critical reading in the preceding chapter relied on certain associations deriving from paired opposites. When I argued that reported facts are not necessarily to be trusted, I developed my discussion by drawing on distinctions between *critical* and *uncritical* thinking, *understanding* and *misunderstanding*, and *reliable* and *unreliable* sources. I could have, but did not, base that argument on reasons that followed from the distinction between *telling the truth* and *telling lies*. (Can you imagine why not?) When I argued that to be open-minded it is necessary to look beyond conclusions to the reasons, I built my case for this out of associations among the distinctions I made use of: *open-mindedness / prejudice, conclusions / reasons*. Again, the presence of these oppositions in the language form the precondition to my being able to construct these arguments, as well as the precondition for your being able to accept or dispute them.

Many of the most difficult and divisive arguments that take place around us derive from the association of one set of dialectical terms with another set of irreconcilable dialectical opposites. For instance, *evolution* and *creation*, as pure concepts, may not be necessarily opposed to each other, but looked at from the perspective of the dialectical pair *science / religion*, they are put into seemingly irreconcilable opposition. Similarly, *electric chair* and *lethal injection* are not opposites when they are seen as both on the same side of the opposition between *death* and *life* sentences. But when seen in the context of the dialectical pair *humane / inhumane*, they can be put into opposition. *Capital* and *corporal* punishment are put into seemingly irreconcilable opposition when associated with the dialectical pair of *revenge / mercy*. Can you think of other examples of terms that are put into opposition by framing them in the context of dialectical pairs?

There is a kind of free play among dialectical pairs if they are considered only in the abstract. But when we encounter them in the context of serious debates about matters that are important to us, a great deal is at stake when we create, use, and assign value to distinctions based on dialectical oppositions. We make such associations freely and without rules to guide us. The dialectical oppositions of language are available to be used by all of us, no matter what so-called side we take in any conflict of ideas. And we cannot avoid using them.

To return to the *evolution / creation* opposition that is so intractably part of our cultural debates, I recently read an exchange in the letters to the editor in our local newspaper in response to articles about the debate over a school board's adoption of science textbooks. One writer tried to make his audience believe that the opposition between creationism and evolutionary theory in this debate is a false distinction because the two can be seen to be compatible if only we make another distinction: between *how* and *why*. Science deals with how questions, this writer argued, whereas religion deals with why questions. If seen this way, he wrote, science and religion do not conflict because each deals with different questions. But in a few days, another letter appeared in answer to this letter, saying that the distinction between *how* and *why* is itself a false distinction because when looked at from the point of view of complete understanding, as opposed to partial understanding, the two questions are not opposed but part of the same whole. Thus, the first writer used a distinction between knowing *how* and knowing *why* to undo a previous distinction, whereas the second writer used a distinction between *complete* knowledge and *partial* knowledge to undo that one.

It's interesting, and sometimes frustrating, to see distinctions arise and collapse in association with various dialectical oppositions. Argument, the process of trying to find the best reasons to support an idea, cannot do without distinctions of this kind, and underlying all arguments, at some level, are various dialectical oppositions. The term *opposition* itself—which is the opposite of . . . what? *harmony? oneness? sameness?*—might suggest to you that arguments always break down into one side or the other. But the interplay among dialectical oppositions of all kinds makes it possible for there to be many sides to any question, not just two, based on the ways one ascribes qualities to or sees things in terms of many kinds of dialectical relationships. We find ourselves in agreement with an argument when we identify with all of the choices made by a writer in putting dialectical pairings together. We find ourselves in disagreement with some part of it when we cannot identify with the way any or some of those distinctions and associations are made.

Some debates in our society, such as the evolution versus creation controversy I discussed above, seem unable to find common ground because the most basic dialectical oppositions on which the arguments are constructed cannot be shared. For example, debates about abortion are notorious for sometimes failing to make sense to people who disagree: The so-called right-to-life argument sees the issue in terms of the opposition *life* and *death* of another human, or between *God's* authority and *humans'*, whereas the so-called freedom-of-choice argument sees the issue in terms of an opposition between *freedom of choice* and *lack of control* over one's own body, or between an *individual's* authority and the *government's*. In order to find any shared ground of agreement from which to conduct mutual inquiry—as opposed to totally missing each other's point—such oppositions have to be reassociated with other sharable oppositions that change the values identified with those terms. This is an especially difficult process when beliefs are attached to the language's most fundamental dialectical pairings, such as *good/evil, right/wrong, appearance/reality.**

I have argued in this chapter that all arguments rely on distinctions, and choosing among distinctions depends on associations with underlying dialectical oppositions. Where do arguments comes from, then? In one sense, they come from conflicts that are already present among words in our language. Such conflicts generate arguments in the sense that they give rise to the way distinctions are created. But it's people, of course, who associate themselves

---

*If you wish to pursue this idea further, I recommend Chaim Perelman's discussion of "The Dissociation of Ideas," in *The Realm of Rhetoric* (Notre Dame, IN: University of Notre Dame Press, 1982), p. 126 ff., as a good place to begin.

with one side or another of dialectical oppositions. So, of course, arguments come from people too. But people who disagree do so because language makes it possible, by providing them with dialectical terms that function in their thinking. If these oppositions already exist in language, it's possible to say that although we use language to make arguments, it is also the case that language uses us. That is, ready-made oppositions exist in language that can seem so natural and commonsensical that we are not even aware of them. Thinking about how language itself is the source of argument helps, then, to see that our struggle to make a case is not a struggle *against* other people, but a struggle to get control of the language—to be able to think with it and about it, rather than to have it do our thinking for us.

Even though this is not an easy goal, or even one that we can hope to achieve in every case, it is possible to become more conscious of the role dialectical oppositions have in our thinking. In this way we might also gain more control of the distinctions we make use of when we compose a reasoned argument. So now we need to return to consideration of the basic structural elements of arguments: questions, answers, and reasons. As we do so, think about how the arguments you read as examples, and even the arguments I make *about* argument, rely on fundamental distinctions and associations with dialectical opposed pairs of terms.

Questions for Thought, Discussion, and Writing

1. Make a list of dialectical oppositions that have not already been cited in the chapter. Can you link or associate these pairs with other dialectical oppositions? What perspectives or ideas are suggested by these associations?

2. Choose a piece of argumentative writing you have encountered in this book, in your reading of a newspaper or magazine, or in another class, and try to analyze the way its reasoning is based on dialectical oppositions or fundamental distinctions. How does the reasoning also link those distinctions to others? What happens to your understanding of or agreement with that reasoning if you imagine that those associations are reversed or replaced by others?

3. Write a dialogue between two (or more) characters engaged in a campus or civic controversy. Identify the dialectical oppositions that you want to use to develop the conversation between them. Do you find it difficult to give each participant an equally reasonable voice? Also ask yourself whether your characters are engaged in mutual inquiry or whether they seek to outmaneuver and defeat each other's argument.

4. What dialectical opposition is implied by the last sentence in Question 3? How does that opposition function in the way you are invited to engage in argumentation in this book?

4

Asking Questions, Generating Ideas

An Idea Worth Writing about

Individual members of a discourse community (such as college or your writing class) agree about many issues but also disagree about other issues of mutual interest. When there is mutual interest, when members of the community care about whether an issue is resolved, disagreement is what creates the need to look for and use ways to cooperate, and the need to reason toward the best possible answer to shared questions. You are engaged in such an inquiry whenever you talk to anyone about a problem you share and try to reason together toward a solution. You are engaged in argumentative writing whenever you use writing to respond (whether formally or informally) to a difference of opinion, trying to find support for what you think is a good answer.

The word *argument* itself can be an obstacle to engaging in the process of reasoned inquiry I am inviting you to practice in this book, because that term is also used to identify a cultural phenomenon that emphasizes emotional and threatening debate over rational dialogue. In her book, *The Argument Culture: Moving from Debate to Dialogue,* Deborah Tannen argues that a warlike atmosphere in our culture leads us to see all issues in terms of polarized sides, or strictly pro and con positions.* This tendency produces an adversarial frame through which ideas are debated. We are all familiar with programs in which representatives of opposing viewpoints shout their conclusions at each other, not listening to each other's arguments and, indeed, not really offering arguments, just declarations. Whether on radio or television, in print, or over the Internet, we have seen debates take the form of verbal violence. And we often talk as though our debates are violent by definition: the war on drugs, the battle of the sexes, the cable wars. Complex issues of public concern are often reduced

---

*For an in-depth look at these ideas, see Deborah Tannen's *The Argument Culture: Moving from Debate to Dialogue* (New York: Random House, 1998).

to only two sides, each of which is seen as trying to destroy the other. The common assumption informing this phenomenon, Tannen argues, is that opposition is seen as the best way to get to the truth. But, as Tannen explains, this oppositional frame can pose problems when it becomes interpreted in terms of winning and losing. Victory over the opposition becomes more important than mutual understanding and collaborative inquiry. When argument is more about winning than about seeking solutions to problems, Tannen argues, everyone loses. In her book, Tannen advocates a change in cultural values, placing the value of engaging in dialogue over the value of winning a debate.

I certainly agree with Tannen's attempt to redefine what the term *argument* suggests when we hear it used in public forums. It is important to our culture to seek dialogue to get at the truth, and opposition is not the best way to do it if the word *opposition* is associated dialectically with *war* or *violence*. But in another sense opposition is a vital part of our diverse society, and in our debates *is* the best way to get at the truth, because without opposition there are no questions to be answered or differences to be resolved. We cannot do away with opposition, nor would we want to in a tolerant society. We must engage it. But *how* we respond to opposition and use it in our communication with each other is up to us. When I described the interplay of dualisms in my discussion of dialectic in Chapter 3, I was not referring to armies of opposed thinkers using words as weapons to destroy each other, but to the way we must use language creatively to construct bridges to agreement. The word *argument* in the context of argumentative writing in college does not mean a verbal battle between opponents, each of whom desires to silence the other. It means, instead, the search for reasons that will bring about cooperation among people who differ in how they view ideas but who nevertheless need to discover grounds for agreement. Argumentative writing, then, may be seen as a process of *reasonable inquiry into the best grounds for agreement between a writer and an audience who have a mutual concern to answer a question.*

This definition is not confined to the academic essay, of course. You have probably written arguments in letters or other informal situations whenever you felt the need to explain or support your ideas. The argumentative **essay** (the word comes from the French for "attempt") is a more formal composition that attempts to deal reasonably with significant ideas. It is the form that college writing usually takes, simply because in an essay a writer encounters ideas directly, for the sake of coming to a new understanding. By writing essays, you can explore significant ideas for the sake of coming to earned conclusions. But this process goes on in college for the sake of a larger aim: to help you deal reasonably with diverse ideas wherever you may encounter them.

A significant idea is not necessarily any idea that you happen to come up with. Some ideas are so conventional that they cannot be said to be ours. Some are trivial. Some might seem like good ideas for a moment but turn out to be silly after a bit of thought. Ideas of these kinds occur to everyone. But when we set out to *write* about an idea, it is generally not one of these. We write because we have an idea that is worth writing about. Such an idea is one that the writer thinks should matter to other people and that the writer cares enough about to discuss. This means that the writer also thinks that others can be led to share the idea and that the writer, therefore, accepts the burden of communication. If an idea is worth writing about, it must be worth communicating effectively.

Ideas in Context: Audience

Ideas worth writing about do not exist in a vacuum: Writing—even in a diary—is meant to be read, and writers imagine their words entering into dialogue with readers when they sit down to write. As I type these words, I focus on the question that governs the beginning of any writing process: Who is my audience and what is our shared concern? You know that in order to communicate an idea effectively, you need to consider your audience. But have you ever thought about the possibility that you need to consider your audience in order to know what your ideas *are*?

Any idea you choose to argue is to some degree determined by your audience, those members of your discourse community whom you are addressing in your writing. The intention of any piece of argumentative writing combines what the writer has to say and what the audience needs to hear. What is at issue for the audience and the writer both? You are free, of course, to choose to argue anything you like, in an absolute sense, but it is only when you find your audience that you really face the necessity of reasoning well. If I were to argue that "A moon colony should be used for the purpose of manufacturing perfect golf balls" to an audience that in no way cares whether I am right or wrong, then it would hardly matter whether I based my case on good or bad reasons. (Remember Alice and the Cheshire Cat?) But if I argue it in a situation where some people believe that moon colonies should not be used for commercial purposes or that perfect golf balls are a useless commodity, then the reasons I choose will make all the difference in whether I am listened to or not.

Your knowledge of your audience can never be complete, of course. Not only does an audience usually consist of more than one person having more than one set of interests and beliefs, but audiences may also consist of people who are entirely unknown. The question of who constitutes an audience is not a simple one, nor should it be made to seem simple. It is one of those matters about which you need to make a judgment, using whatever knowledge there is, without being able to arrive at certainty. You do not have to think of your audience as particular people with individual characteristics, nor do you have to invent imaginary readers who function as mere "straw men" to be blown over by incomplete reasoning. You can write, instead, to a more general audience, assumed to be made up of people who share your argumentative situation, who share the question at issue, and who are capable of reasoning in response to your assertions. Whether you think of this general audience as an extension of the beliefs of a particular person or as a composite of possible points of view, the relevant characteristics of that audience are characteristics that somehow make a difference for how the argument is conducted. If you were arguing about your right-to-life stance, for instance, you would probably not think about the relevant characteristics of your audience in terms of hair color or nationality, but you might think of your readers in terms of religious beliefs or social class.

When you write for an audience, you take on a kind of obligation to that audience that does not exist if you write simply for yourself or if you write just for your instructor or for a grade. We have all done this kind of writing, and it can be valuable—but to write without an audience can often feel as though you are writing without a purpose. Once you have an audience in mind, your purpose is clear: You write for an audience that shares your concerns (but perhaps not your views).

Writing in the context of a discourse community is a social act: You use language to explore issues of common concern and to share the results of your inquiry into those issues. In this sense, the audience is really the invisible component to a well-formed argument, because the concerns and commitments of the audience determine the kind of question you will address. In a discourse community, ideas are put forward in response to questions that arise for that community.

Stasis

It may seem strange to think about a thesis as a response to a question, but if you think about writing as a social act, as a way of entering into discussion about an issue, then the idea that a thesis responds to a question may begin to make more sense. As members of any number of discourse communities, we constantly face questions which we must think about before we respond. The questions we confront as members of communities take many shapes: Is assisted suicide really murder? Does bilingual education slow the process of assimilation for non-English-speaking public elementary students? Should property taxes be raised to fund higher education? Is Hamlet's decision to avenge his father's death a good one? These are not simple questions by any means, but they are worth writing about when they reflect the concerns of particular communities.

Questions like these do not have ready (or easy) answers: They require careful (and sometimes difficult) thought from the members of the communities to which they are posed. Clearly, not all community members would respond to these questions in the same way. As a property owner, I may not like the idea that my taxes could be raised to support local schools. If I have children who attend those schools, my attitude may be different. And what if I am a teacher in a public school? As you can see, a single question may lead me to consider several positions from within my own discourse community, questions that ultimately will help shape my response to the question, Should property taxes be raised to fund higher education?

Questions like these are said to be *at issue* because to answer them requires inquiry into grounds for shared assent. Different kinds of questions call for different kinds of answers and for answers that take different shapes.

Stasis: Kinds of Questions at Issue

The kind of thesis that you compose and use as the basis for your essay will depend on the kind of question that is at issue for you and your audience. Whether a question is at issue depends on the particular situation you are in when you feel compelled to state your case. To understand this situation, it helps to know what sort of question really separates you and your audience, because if the situation calls for you to answer one kind of question and you answer another kind instead, you may not be successfully addressing the audience you mean to address.

Questions at issue may be seen as one or another of these six basic kinds:

- **Questions of fact** *arise from the reader's need to know "Does this [whatever it is] exist?"*

- **Questions of definition** *arise from the reader's need to know "What is it?"*

- **Questions of interpretation** *arise from the reader's need to know "What does it signify?"*

- **Questions of value** *arise from the reader's need to know "Is it good?"*

- **Questions of consequence** *arise from the reader's need to know "Will this cause that to happen?"*

- **Questions of policy** *arise from the reader's need to know "What should be done about it?"*

These are sometimes called stasis questions. The **stasis** of any argument is the specific point on which the controversy rests, that point on which one person says "yes" but another says "no" or "I'm not sure." You have often discovered such points when you have listened to someone else's argument and found yourself in agreement with some parts of it but not others. You might have said "Yes, but . . ." and pursued your disagreement in the context of other parts of the argument where you already agreed. The question on which you found yourself doubting was the stasis question, or the **question at issue.**

In any particular argumentative situation, questions of one kind or another will be at issue while others may not be. In a discussion of civil disobedience, for instance, controversy may arise over the meaning of the term itself—or it may not. A writer may misjudge the issue by choosing a definitional thesis (such as "Civil disobedience applies only to laws that are unjust," or "Any law is unjust that imposes the will of a minority on the actions of another minority") in a situation where a question of consequence is what, in fact, divides the audience. In his essay "Resistance to Civil Government" (found on page 156) Henry David Thoreau wrote:

> Unjust laws exist; shall we be content to obey them, or shall we endeavor to amend them, and obey them until we have succeeded, or shall we transgress them at once?

By putting the question in this way, Thoreau assumed that the question of definition (what makes a law unjust?) and the question of value (is an unjust law good?) were not at issue, but that the question of policy (what should we do about unjust laws?) is the one that needed his attention.

More than one kind of question may be at issue, of course, in a particular argumentative situation, and questions of one kind may have to be answered before one can ask questions of another. But the writer who wishes to make a genuine contribution to an inquiry may be aided by thinking about the kind of question that defines the situation. "What is really at issue here? Are we questioning how to *define* a concept or whether an idea (or action) is *good* or whether a certain consequence will *result* or what we *should do* about it?" Trying to place the question in this way is one means by which the writer may meet the audience. Answering the wrong kind of question in any situation will lead to missing the audience—talking at cross-purposes or saying the obvious. You don't want your readers to say, "Sure, but so what?" Ultimately, the question you decide to respond to gives you and your audience a sense of where your essay is headed and what to expect along the way. Once you know what the question is, you'll begin to have a sense of how to remind your audience that you are addressing an idea of importance to them by raising that issue in terms you know they will respond to readily.

Kinds of Inquiry

Different kinds of stasis questions represent different argumentative situations and call for different kinds of inquiry. When **questions of fact** are at issue, it generally means that readers need to be given information or that they require a demonstration that some fact is "in fact" the case. The arguments of science are often of this kind. "At what temperature does water freeze?" is a question of fact, as is "Will this antifreeze work in my car over the winter?" Situations in which questions of fact are at issue are those in which there is an unknown to be discovered.

When was Othello *first performed?*
Who discovered X rays?

Is it possible to build a bridge here?

What was the final vote on Measure 6?

Such questions have in common the determinacy of their possible answers. In each case, the answer is a matter of verifiable fact. If the answer could not be verified somehow, then the question must remain unanswered. The answers to questions of fact are either correct or incorrect, true or false, yes or no. Such questions will be more or less interesting—either important or trivial—depending on the subject matter.

There is no absolute test of whether a question of fact is worth pursuing for its own sake. In matters of literature, say, or political science, such questions may have less inherent interest than they would in matters of, say, chemistry. I might find an answer to any of these questions and then find myself asking, "So what?" At that point I would have discovered that the question I had been pursuing was only a doorway into a question of larger significance, a question of a different sort.

When **questions of definition** are at issue, it generally means that readers do not accept a particular meaning for a word or concept. Although it might seem as if such questions are easily answered by consulting the dictionary, many questions of definition are not answered so easily if they are actually at issue. Definitions may separate people who know what the dictionary says but who must inquire into shared meanings that no dictionary can contain. For instance, if I do not know what *law* means, I can look it up. But if I ask, "What are the different meanings of *law* in Martin Luther King, Jr.'s letter?" the answer can be discovered only by examining instances of the word in the text itself, which may not define the word for us. Arguments sometimes hinge on definitions that cannot be resolved by verification in the dictionary.

Is Chuck Yeager an astronaut?

Is this film pornographic?

Is abortion murder?

In such cases, the answer lies not only in the meanings of the words but also in the dialectical oppositions the words may imply and on whether certain circumstances match those meanings and oppositions. Such questions may hide deeper issues. Like questions of fact, questions of definition may be ends in themselves or may lead to different kinds of questions.

Questions of definition and questions of interpretation are similar and often overlap. When **questions of interpretation** are at issue, it means that more than the meaning of a word is in doubt but that the significance of something needs explaining. Interpretations may apply to the meaning of many words or the significance of events, actions, structures, or concepts. Interpretations can never be answered by consulting a reference work because they refer to what something means to the interpreter.

Is Othello an Aristotelian tragic hero?

Will this new bridge represent the concern of our community for the environment or will it show others how wasteful we are?

Does the result of this election signify a mandate for all of the candidate's policies?

Does this film advocate the use of violence as a means of social change?

Questions of interpretation generally are at issue when there is a difference in point of view. Interpretations involve looking at a phenomenon from a particular perspective, or through the lens of a particular dialectical opposition. Hence arguments about interpretation often require that the point of view itself be articulated or defended.

Questions of interpretation arise in most fields, especially when the subject of inquiry is discourse or human action. That Hannah Arendt called evil a "banality" is a fact I can verify by citing her work. What she meant, however, is a question with which historians and social theorists have had to struggle. Anthropologists may seek to interpret a ritual act or a social relationship. Sociologists may seek to interpret data collected in surveys. Questions of interpretation result whenever the significance of a word, an idea, an event, or a fact is not self-evident.

Does the potential uncertainty of questions of interpretation make them less important than questions of fact? We have seen just the opposite. Questions of interpretation often attempt to answer the "So what?" questions that matters of fact can raise. Yet, they seem equivocal because they cannot be answered with the certainty of questions of fact. An idea can often have more significance to our understanding as it becomes less certain. As we attempt to go beyond facts and to establish interpretations, we are dealing with our own relation to the subject matter as much as we are with the raw data. What we learn about when we interpret is twofold: We learn about the subject and we learn about ourselves.

Questions of value are similar to questions of interpretation. When questions of value are at issue, it generally means that people agree on the meaning of something, but differ on whether it is "good" or "bad." Like interpretation, then, value depends on one's point of view or the system of values that informs one's judgment. Some standard of good is used as the measure; thus arguments about questions of value often require one to articulate standards. "Is this essay worth an A?" The answer obviously depends on whose standards of judgment are being used. Yours may differ from your teacher's and each of you will judge accordingly. Any argument about the issue will have to address both those standards and the features of the essay that they apply to, a question of interpretation. Questions of value nearly always depend on answers to questions of interpretation.

Although some standard of good and bad is at issue in value questions, other words are generally used to communicate a sense of value. **Value terms** are words that already imply a judgment of good and bad. Thus, the assertion "*Huckleberry Finn* contains only racist stereotypes," although offered as a neutral interpretation, would generally imply that "racist stereotypes" are not good. The statement "This film is not pornographic, it is erotic"—although seeming to answer a question of interpretation or definition—invokes a dialectical opposition based on value. Questions of definition and interpretation can be questions of value in disguise.

There are those who believe that questions of value depend so much on subjective criteria that they cannot really be argued. Yet all but the most factual kinds of questions are subjective to a degree, and those kinds of questions are the very ones we do not have to argue, because we can demonstrate them. Nearly all real questions at issue require acts of judgment and interpretation, and thus subjectivity alone is not a reason to rule a question out of bounds for inquiry. If we limit argument to questions that are objective, we might find ourselves unable to decide what to do with the information we have gathered, because that decision must result from our own interests, perspectives, and concerns. We must be careful not to associate objectivity dialectically with good argument and subjectivity with bad argument. It is possible to have good or bad arguments of either kind, if that means careful or sloppy, thorough or perfunctory. The idea that objective argument is somehow better may be the result of applying the standards of scientific judgment to all realms of knowledge, but this is risky. There are many kinds of knowledge, some wholly objective, some wholly subjective, and some a mixture of the two.

Questions of consequence are at issue when people find themselves disagreeing or wondering about cause and effect. Answering questions about what causes some occurrence or what result some event will have requires interpretation. "This bridge will help the economy of our city by encouraging more construction of homes across the river." This statement makes two *causal* interpretations. Causality is subject to varying degrees of certainty. "Will the bridge encourage more home building?" is a question that might not be as difficult to answer, or be as likely to be at issue, as the question "Will more homes across the river help or hurt our city's economy?" Answering either question will require argument about causes and their probabilities.

> *Do opinion polls discourage people from voting?*
>
> *What is the effect of too much television on children?*
>
> *Will tax exemptions on capital gains stimulate investments?*
>
> *Can the slaughter of elephants be stopped by banning the sale of all ivory?*

Speculations, rather than controlled experiments, are necessary to determine reasonable answers to such questions. Yet, like scientific experiments, those speculations must consider which variables make the difference. Thus, most speculations about cause and effect will be conditional: "It depends on . . ." or "Yes, if . . ." Arguments about probable causes generally acknowledge that certain conditions must prevail and seek to demonstrate that they do. For instance, to argue that the banning of the sale of ivory would end the slaughter of elephants, you would have to show a causal link between the sale of ivory and this slaughter. *If* ivory comes only from the illegal slaughter of elephants, and *if* that is the only reason elephants are slaughtered, then banning the sale of ivory might have this effect. In making this case, it would be your responsibility to show that these conditions were the case.

Because most questions of consequence, unless strictly scientific, can be answered only conditionally, it might seem as if they are useless to argue. Think, however, of the vast number of questions of consequence that must be argued if we are to know how to solve important problems in our lives and in society. We seek to solve such problems using the best reasoning we can construct, even if it does not constitute absolute certainty.

When **questions of policy** are at issue, it generally means that readers differ on whether, or how, to take a particular action. Such questions are answered with a recommendation, a prescription, or a preference for some action. Questions of policy thus arise from situations in which alternative actions are possible, and the problem confronting those for whom such questions are at issue is which of the alternatives is best. You can see why such answers also are conditional, because they depend on acknowledging that the action will achieve its end (a question of consequence) and that the end is desirable (a question of value).

> Should television networks voluntarily refrain from announcing voting results in the East until the polls close in the West? Should Congress vote to force them to do so?
>
> Should this bridge be built? Should property taxes be used to pay for it?
>
> Should the school board remove Huckleberry Finn from the school library? How should we respond to this action?
>
> How should AIDS prevention information be distributed to children? What form should it take?

Policy questions, like questions of consequence, must be answered conditionally. If the action will bring about a specific result, and if that result is desired, then it follows that the action should take place. But it does not necessarily follow absolutely. Who should perform it? Will negative results accompany the positive one? Are there other, better, ways to achieve the same end? Such considerations always complicate policy issues.

As we have seen, questions of fact, definition, interpretation, value, consequence, and policy are interrelated. No argument is likely to be confined to only one kind of question. Arguing for an answer to one kind of question can imply that other kinds of questions are already answered. In any argumentative situation, some questions will not be at issue while others will define the stasis of the argument. This is why it is helpful to ask what *kind* of question is really at issue.

For instance, if you chose to argue that "The university should send AIDS information to all students," your thesis would answer a question of policy. But it would also presuppose that your audience shared that kind of question with you and that other kinds of questions were not at issue. The discourse community might be divided, not on the policy question, but on a question of consequence, such as "Will this particular piece of information be effective in educating students about AIDS?" You may not be in agreement with your audience on a question of interpretation, such as "Is the university responsible for AIDS education?" or of value, such as "Is AIDS education important enough to justify the expense?" Questions of fact may need to be settled first, such as "Can the university afford this?" or "Do the students already know everything the information provides?" And so forth. Knowing whether a particular kind of question is at issue requires an understanding of what the people in the discourse community are actually saying to each other, what they already agree about, and what they desire to find agreement about. The complex network of issues and stances that characterizes any real controversy is a little easier to understand by thinking about the kind (or kinds) of questions that are actually at issue.

What a Thesis Does

Responding to a significant question at issue confronts a writer with certain responsibilities: to be sure that sufficient reasons exist for believing an idea and to be sure that those reasons are able to be understood by others. These responsibilities are present throughout the writing process. They begin when one thinks about composing a thesis.

A thesis is an idea, stated as an assertion, that represents a reasoned response to a question at issue and that will serve as the central idea of a composition.

After the previous discussions, this definition should come as no surprise. Let's take a closer look at it, to determine what you need to think about when trying to come up with a thesis that will provide the best basis for composing an essay. Each of the terms of this definition has special significance for the process of composing a good argumentative essay.

A thesis is an idea. . . . Some people use the word *idea* to mean something like topic or subject, phrases that indicate an *area* of potential interest, such as "economics" or a "cure for cancer" or "my first encounter with Professor Smith." These phrases might be said to be broad or narrow subjects, but they are not yet ideas because they do not say anything *about* economics or *about* a cancer cure or *about* the first time I met Smith. Perhaps you have had a teacher who was fond of telling you to narrow your subject. Such advice misses the point, unless that teacher also pushed you to come up with an idea by saying something about your subject. The noun *economics* is not an idea. The narrowed (or focused) noun phrase "economic conditions in South Africa in

1875" is still not an idea. "Economics is bull" *is* an idea—although, of course, not a very good one. The difference between noun phrases that are not ideas and statements that are ideas lies in the verb. Ideas are sentences; they complete a thought by connecting a verb to the noun phrase. Saying something *about* a subject requires making some kind of connection between it and something else. It isn't the size of the noun phrase that matters; it's what you have to say about it—and this will be found in the verb that you connect to it. Any noun phrase, no matter how broad or narrow, might become the basis of many different ideas, even totally contradictory or incompatible ones. "Economics is my best class" is a very different idea from "Economics is bull," and yet both apparently share the same subject.

A thesis is . . . stated as an assertion. Not all ideas are stated with the intention of asserting something to be the case. Even though an idea must be a complete sentence, not all sentences are uttered for the purpose of asserting a proposition. "Go away" is certainly a sentence that communicates, but it does not seem to be proposing anything as true. It expresses a desire but does not put forth a claim. "I guess I'll take a walk." "What a day for baseball!" "Please tell me how to get to the geology building." "Gimme a break!" Sentences, ideas, can perform many other actions besides asserting.

To assert is to claim that some condition is the case. Each of the nonassertions above could be made into assertions by making them into such claims. "A walk would be good for me right now." "Sunny days are best for baseball." "Geology is to the left of Art." Assertions propose ideas to which one might respond, "No, that's not the case," or "Yes, that is the case." As you can see, making assertions implies that one believes in what one has just said. To seem to assert without belief would be a different kind of action: to lie or to joke. Assertions imply a willingness to defend an idea against the possibility that it might not be the case.

A thesis . . . represents a reasoned response to a question at issue. An assertion is worth writing about when not everyone already believes it and when people should care whether to believe it or not. A thesis answers a question, in other words, that people are really asking because they do not already share the answer. As we have seen in the previous section, all assertions answer a stasis question of some kind. Not all assertions answer a question at issue. Consider these assertions and the questions to which they are answers:

It's raining.	*Is it raining?*
Today is election day.	*Is today election day?*
You should vote "no" *on Measure 6.*	*Should I vote "yes" or "no"* *on Measure 6?*
Measure 6 will violate your *constitutional right to* *own a handgun.*	*Will Measure 6 violate my* *constitutional right to own* *a handgun?*
The Constitution does not make *handgun ownership a right.*	*Does the Constitution make handgun* *ownership a right?*

Are the questions to which these assertions respond *at issue*? You're right if you answer "it depends." It depends on who is asking them and why. It depends on the context in which the question is asked. A thesis is a response to a *situation,* which includes a community of people who, for their own reasons, are addressing certain questions. There are situations in which these questions might constitute questions at issue, and there are different situations in which they would not. The difference is whether the answer calls for argumentation. Is there some doubt whether the answer should be believed? If I assert that "It's raining" in a situation where the question is not at issue—where no one cares whether it's raining or not or where everyone is satisfied by my mere assertion—then there is no issue to be argued. If I assert that "Today is election day" in a situation where everyone already knows it, then there is no issue. In this case, however, the question at issue might become "What, then, should we do about it?" and argument might ensue over whether it's worth going out in the rain to vote. Then, again, it might not, if that question is not at issue. If I am talking to some friends who have already decided to vote against Measure 6, then my statement that "You should vote 'no' on Measure 6" would not be at issue, although my statement that "Measure 6 will violate your constitutional right to own a handgun" might be at issue if those friends were divided on *why* Measure 6 should be defeated. If I were addressing an audience of uncommitted voters, my assertion that "Measure 6 will violate your constitutional right to own a handgun" might address a question at issue. But if that audience happened to believe that the Constitution does not provide citizens with such a right, then I would have missed them with my arguments because I chose to address the wrong question. I would have to back up and address the question of whether there is, in fact, such a right. Only by finding the question at issue and arguing for an assertion that answers it do I find my audience.

The judgment of whether you have focused on such a question must be made by thinking about your audience. What do they already believe? What answers do they share with you? On what issue are you divided? To what assertions of yours will they say, "Yes, but . . ."? Such questions help you decide whether to argue this assertion or that one, and the decision can change from situation to situation, from audience to audience.

As a reasoned response to a question at issue, a thesis cannot be taken for granted. It is determined by a process of inquiry into the question. A stance that does not emerge from inquiry is sometimes called a "knee-jerk response" to indicate that it is formed as a reaction without thinking. Keeping a critical reader in mind is one way to be sure that you give a thesis adequate consideration before asserting it unequivocally. And then you may find that a qualified assertion is better than an unqualified one.

A thesis . . . will serve as the central idea of a composition. This final part of the definition points us forward, toward the process of development by which a thesis becomes an essay. The last two parts of the definition, one pointing backward and one pointing forward, suggest that a thesis has two functions, which stand at the center of your thinking about what you will write. It represents the result of a process of inquiry, and it represents the beginning of a process of putting together sentences and paragraphs to make a whole essay. As a beginning, a thesis provides a basis for any further thinking that you must do to produce a fully developed argument. If a thesis is reasonable in the sense that it emerges from your deliberations about what assertion to argue, it should also be reasonable in the sense of being able to be supported by reasons.

We have already seen how the thesis stands for the whole composition, in a way, and represents its overall intention. This means that the parts of a composition are, in some sense, implicit parts of its thesis. As a complete idea, a thesis will have several parts, and identifying them will become a basis of planning what the essay must say and how it must say it.

For example, suppose I have decided to argue that:

Hydroelectric power provides an acceptable alternative to nuclear energy in supplying present power needs.

Assuming that the assertion satisfies the definition of a thesis in other ways (although it may not), consider how it points forward to an essay. Its parts must become parts of that essay, because that essay would not be complete without satisfying certain demands that the thesis makes. The thesis calls for the essay to describe hydroelectric power and nuclear energy, and also to compare them according to how each satisfies "present power needs," which must also be described. Finally, the essay must make the essential connection that is asserted in its verb phrase: "provides an acceptable alternative to." This will necessarily entail a discussion of *how* hydroelectric power is preferable to nuclear power, probably by showing that it has some benefit that nuclear power lacks or that it avoids some risk that nuclear power creates, or maybe both. There are further parts that this essay might contain, of course, but these constitute the essential elements that an essay written from *this* thesis must contain in order to be complete. (This process is the subject of Chapter 6.)

This example illustrates that any thesis statement creates responsibilities and provides the basis for fulfilling them. You are free to choose your thesis or to change it at any time, but having done so you become responsible for somehow developing the essential parts of your thesis and for *earning* it. There are limitless kinds of possible thesis statements, but all will have essential parts that must be developed and connections that must be made.

Knowing precisely what your thesis is will help you think about what to include and what not to include in your essay. It will help you to distinguish between details that are necessary and those that are superfluous. Of course, no rule will tell you exactly what details are necessary and sufficient to make a complete essay, because every thesis will make its own unique demands. But a precise thesis will make the choices easier to recognize.

The Need for Precision

In the stasis section of this chapter, we saw that different ways of asking a question can lead to different kinds of inquiry. Likewise, the way a thesis is phrased can be very important. Different ways of asserting the same stance can lead to different ways of developing an essay. Hence, you should be ready to ask yourself "Is this precisely the question?" and "Is this precisely what I want to say?" You should be concerned about the precision of your language as you think about questions at issue and thesis statements.

Let's look at a couple of the examples I used to illustrate questions of consequence and see how they might be rephrased more precisely. The question "Do opinion polls discourage people from voting?" seems very general, not because the issue itself is a large one but because the terms are imprecise. Anyone seriously asking such a question would probably intend it to refer to a specific context in which certain kinds of opinion polls occur. But it's hard to tell what is meant when the question remains so vaguely worded. Changing the wording to make it more precise would change the nature of the issue, as in the following possibilities:

> *Does the early publishing of exit poll results discourage people from voting?*
>
> *Do people think that opinion polls accurately predict the outcome of elections?*
>
> *Do opinion polls actually change public opinion?*
>
> *Do opinion polls encourage a bandwagon effect that makes it impossible for an underdog to win?*

Other ways of stating the question are possible. Each of them implies a different meaning for the original question. Any of them could have been intended by the original question. So, until a more precise form of the question is found, it isn't clear exactly what the issue is.

Similarly, the question "What is the effect of too much television on children?" is imprecise. Some people would call this a loaded question because the answer is implied: "Too much television" is already a bad thing, and bad effects are what "too much television" must have. But to make a distinction, the issue probably depends instead on saying what the effect of a precise amount of television is. The inquiry might in fact need to address the kind of television and not just its sheer quantity. Also, the issue may need to be defined in terms of some children (i.e., preschoolers) and not others. It all depends on what the members of the discourse community are actually trying to decide. Thus any of these rephrasings, and others, are possible:

> *Does lengthy exposure to violent programming cause antisocial behavior in preteens? (What is "lengthy exposure"? What does* violent *mean? What is "antisocial behavior"? Which "preteens"—in which social conditions? . . .)*

Do cartoons about consumer products confuse children about the difference be-
tween advertising and entertainment? (All such cartoons or those of a certain
kind? What does confuse *mean here? What is "the difference between adver-*
tising and entertainment"? . . .)

My further questions about each of these rephrasings indicate that precision is
a relative matter. Readers can always ask for clarification. The wording of a
question or a thesis statement is precise enough when both you and your
reader understand it to mean the same thing. You can't know with certainty,
of course, when this will be, so you have to anticipate as many questions as
possible and clarify as necessary. When you are part of an argumentative situation that will call for you to write what you think, the effort of drafting and
redrafting possible questions at issue and thesis statements for precision will
be worth it in helping you think clearly about your argument.

Generating Stasis Questions about Fiction

For this course, you will read mostly nonfiction argumentative essays and develop questions at issue in response to those essays. But how do we understand
an author's argument when it is presented through a fictional text? Asking this
question assumes that fictional works—short stories, novels, plays, poems, and
films—actually do convey arguments. Remember that even though you are
writing academic essays to make your arguments, all writing is an act of communication intended to have an effect on an audience. This means that all writing, even fiction, conveys a kind of argument.

The best way to understand the arguments made in fiction is to consider
one of the main differences between essays and stories: Whereas a nonfiction
essay presents an argument that is given *directly* to the audience, a fictional
story presents a plot with characters to whom we respond and through whom
a complex argument is made *indirectly*. This indirection makes the arguments
presented in fiction harder for us to respond to because we usually can't locate
claims or infer a thesis. We respond sympathetically or unsympathetically to
characters and their actions rather than to reasons.

This difference between fiction and nonfiction will lead us to different
kinds of questions at issue. Because we can't be said to agree or disagree with
a plot, because it makes no claim, these questions will be based on what Wayne
C. Booth, a rhetorical critic, calls understanding and overstanding. Questions
of *understanding* will get us to ask how an author presents his or her arguments
through fiction. Such questions are questions of interpretation. There are often
disagreements about how to understand a fictional argument. For example, in
the course of a story we may begin to care about a character who eventually goes
off to fight in a war. One reader might make an assertion about the novelist's

argument: "This author is glorifying war because she gets us to care about a character and, as a result, we respect his decision to go to war." Another reader might object with a more convincing argument, pointing out aspects of the story the other reader has failed to consider: "No, the author doesn't glorify war because the author lets us see that the character is thinking negatively about war at the same time as he goes. In other words, the author is critiquing war because he's showing how strong the pressures are on an individual if they can make someone who is opposed to war decide to fight despite those objections."

These assertions could be developed in an essay with a close look at the elements of the story: How do we know that we are supposed to respect one character and not another? How does the author guide us to have these reactions and feelings? How is the argument complicated when an author leads us to care equally about two characters who disagree in a story? Answering these questions will help guide these two readers in supporting their assertions about the argument conveyed in the novel. The question at issue for these two readers is based on *understanding* because both share a common concern. They both want to answer the question "What argument about war is being made by the author of this novel?" But what if our second reader convinces the first reader that the novel does actually critique the war? If they agree on an understanding of the novel, then they might move to a question at issue based on what Booth calls *overstanding*.

A question at issue that leads to *overstanding* must be based on a shared common ground of understanding: In this case, our readers agree that the author of the novel is critiquing war. At this point, they can move from questions of interpretation to questions of value, consequence, definition, or policy. A possible question at issue in terms of overstanding might be asked in this way: "Is the argument made as convincingly as it could be?" In answering this question, our two readers might again disagree. One might argue that even though the critique is clear, it isn't as convincing as it could be because the character doesn't die in the war. The reader might argue, "If the author wants to critique war, that critique is limited because the main character we care about lives. As a result, we never have to experience the emotions of sorrow and despair that real people experience when they lose someone they care about."

This reader's argument is based on the idea that emotions must be appealed to in a way that corresponds with emotional responses to similar events in the real world. Our second reader might respond in several ways arguing that the novel does effectively critique war. First, he could argue that other characters we do care about in the novel do die and as a result, we experience the necessary emotions of revulsion to war. This argument would be based on the shared assumption that those emotions are necessary for the argument to be effective. The question at issue is whether the novel appeals to those emotions in the reader. However, our second reader might question this concept itself by agreeing that those emotions are never invoked in the reader while arguing that the author doesn't need to use this emotional appeal to make his argument.

We can consider another type of question that involves overstanding—"*Should* the author be making this argument?" This question leads us to evaluate a fictional argument even if we agree that the argument is well made. For example, we might agree that a novelist is advocating the use of violence. And we might agree that the argument is conveyed as well as possible. Still, we might want to overstand by pointing out the ethical problems with writing novels that make this kind of argument. On the other hand, we might argue that a novel critiques war but doesn't make that critique as well as it could. Still, we could argue that flawed arguments such as this one are better than convincing arguments that we find ethically wrong.

Stasis questions that come from reading fiction can lead not only to interpretive papers but also to engaging discussion and argumentative essays about issues that are important to our discourse community, a community that includes readers of novels and stories and viewers of fictional works in movies and other forms. These kinds of arguments affect how we respond to ideas as much as direct arguments do, and we can think about them in the same ways.

Revising a Thesis

The process of rethinking and redrafting a thesis is important because it helps you to confront questions in your thinking while changes still can be easily made. It is much easier to rephrase a thesis statement until it works than it is to try to revise a whole essay that has gone off in a confusing direction because it is based on a poor thesis. You cannot predict every feature of an essay in advance, of course, but you can at least have the advantage of thinking through potential directions that an essay might take. Revising a thesis carefully can help you to avoid premature commitments to ideas that may not work out.

You can use these questions as a guide to revising possible thesis statements:

1. Is it an *idea*? Does it state, in a complete sentence, an *assertion*?
2. Does it answer a question that is really *at issue* for the audience? (What *kind* of question is it?)
3. Does the thesis say exactly what I mean? Are the terms I use precise and clear?
4. Has it developed out of a process of reasoning? Have I considered each side of the issue adequately?
5. Can it be developed reasonably?

Having a thesis that satisfies these conditions will help you to see clearly what responsibilities you must meet as you compose an essay in support of it.

Attempting to revise your thesis using these questions will have its pay-off in a more coherent, better-argued essay. But it will also prove to be difficult if you feel locked into your ideas and can't change your mind. We feel close to our own ideas, and it's hard to think of them as things to be manipulated and fiddled with, like a clay sculpture. It helps to remember that just because they sound clear and convincing to us, a reader will not necessarily come at them with the same familiarity. So, I recommend going over these questions with a friend in your class, or as part of a workshop in class where others ask these questions about your thesis statement and you ask them about theirs. Get others' points of view. Try out suggestions. Change the wording just to see how it sounds. Let yourself play with the idea in order to get used to feeling less locked into the version of your thinking that emerged on the first attempt.

Nothing can guarantee that you will come up with a good thesis even by working at it. Some people have no trouble coming up with good ideas, whereas others must struggle to find them. (Most of us experience both, at different times.) Having good ideas is simply part of the intuitive mystery of the mind, and no rules can be written to account for it. But trying out a thesis and then thinking about rewriting it—with the five criteria in mind—is one way to keep your thinking alive and focused in a productive direction. It's like giving inspiration a boost.

Questions for Thought, Discussion, and Writing

1. What kind of stasis question is each of the following? How do you know? Under what circumstances might each be at issue? What related kinds of questions might also be at issue in each case?
   a. Are groups that use dangerous drugs in religious ceremonies exempt from laws against use of those drugs?
   b. Do college administrations have the right to censor the contents of student newspapers?
   c. Is marriage outmoded?
   d. Are scientific experiments that cause pain to animals necessary?
   e. Do grades inhibit learning?
   f. Does the widespread practice of repeating "urban legends" indicate that people are willing to believe anything as long as it sounds probable?
   g. Is mandatory drug testing for athletes wrong?

2. Say whether you think the following statements fit the definition of a thesis. Why or why not? If they could be improved, what would the writer have to think about?
   a. I want to write my paper about sports and society and how it should be changed.
   b. Some people just don't know how to take a joke.
   c. I wish people would stop bugging me about what I'm going to do with my life, so I can find out.

  d. The escalation of defensive weapons into space will make a nuclear war more likely.
  e. The use of *he* and *man* to refer to both men and women is sexist.
  f. *The Federalist Papers* should be read by all students before they graduate from high school.
  g. All teaching will someday be done by computers, leading to a more effective education for all students.

3. What responsibilities does a writer accept in choosing any of these statements as a thesis? What parts would an essay about each of them have to contain to be complete?
  a. Legalization of marijuana would give young people greater confidence in government.
  b. Procrastination, more than any other cause, leads good students to perform badly on assignments.
  c. Belief in a CIA conspiracy to murder President Kennedy has led critics of the Warren Report to misinterpret its findings.
  d. Overpopulation is a greater threat to world peace than nuclear proliferation.
  e. Eradicating cigarette smoking by the year 2020 should be a priority of the U.S. government.
  f. A clear conscience is not necessary for happiness.

4. Read one of the sections of readings in Part II that includes a work of fiction (e.g., by Barrett or Butler), and consider the ways in which the fictional work addresses issues and constructs arguments. Compare these ways to one of the nonfiction writings. What kinds of questions do these different kinds of writing address? Construct a thesis about the work of fiction that attempts to *understand* that work, and then construct a thesis that represents an attempt to *overstand* it. How would you argue either thesis?

5. After you have discussed an issue in class, construct a thesis that represents your response to that discussion; that is, something you have to say that addresses some question that was at issue for the class. Considering the five criteria on page 53, revise that thesis until you think it would provide you with a good basis for writing what you have to say in the form of an argumentative essay. Then show that thesis to other members of the class for whom the question was also at issue, and see whether their responses lead you to want to make further revisions.

5

Giving Reasons

What a Reason Does

A reason is any idea that functions to support another idea. It is nothing more than the answer to an implicit question, "Why?" It invites the reader to agree with one statement by linking it to another statement that explains why it is true. A reason, then, is anything one might say after *because* or before *therefore*. Reasons, of course, do not have to be connected to conclusions by such words. They can imply such a relationship simply by being asserted along with the conclusion.

> *The present arms control negotiations do not go far enough.*
>
> *These negotiations do not include discussion of biological and chemical weapons.*

These two assertions are connected by an implicit *because*. If they were presented in reverse order, they would seem to be connected by an implicit *therefore*. Any assertion can function as a reason.

> *The current administration is not really serious about arms control.*
>
> *The present arms control negotiations do not go far enough.*

Here, the same assertion that functioned as a conclusion has taken on the role of a reason when put beside a different assertion.

No idea is necessarily a reason or a conclusion until it is put into relation with another idea. *Reasoning is a process of creating relationships between ideas in such a way that belief in one is intended to follow as a consequence of belief in another.*

Before going any further into the question of how reasons work, I want to clarify one possible confusion that results from the ambiguity of the word *reason*. The word can refer to an explanation of cause or motive, or it can refer to a statement that argues for belief. This distinction is important, because in talking about reasoning in this chapter I am focusing on the second meaning.

Statements that explain why without actually arguing in support of another statement are also called reasons. For instance, if I said, "I want to go to the mountains for my vacation *because* I have hay fever and need to get away from the grass seed pollens," I would have explained my reason, but I would not have given a reason to believe that it is in fact the case that "I want to go to the mountains." Of course, no such argument is needed in this case; an explanation will suffice. But there are many instances in which this distinction might be crucial. Here is an assertion:

> *The Supreme Court has made it harder for African Americans to achieve representation in Congress.*

If I responded to this assertion by asking "Why?" I might be asking either for an explanation or for a reason to believe the assertion. In answer to my questions, I might get answers of either sort:

> *Because the Court is inherently racist.*

or

> *Because the Court has repealed voter's rights legislation.*

The first reason answers the question "Why has the Court made it harder for African Americans to achieve representation?" or "What are its motives?" The second reason answers the question "Why should I believe that assertion is true?" Both of these are reasons. Each is potentially important. But only the latter reason argues directly for the assertion to be believed. So when I said that "Reasoning is a process of creating relationships between ideas in such a way that belief in one is intended to follow as a consequence of belief in another," I did not use *reasoning* to refer to the kinds of explanations we often introduce with the word *because*. I am referring to those *because* statements that answer the implicit question, "Why should I believe that that assertion is the case?"

In this sense any assertion can function either as a conclusion or as a reason, because any assertion that is used to substantiate another (answering "Why is it true?") can also be substantiated by another reason. Here, for instance, is a paragraph in which some of the sentences seem to have this dual function:

> Ours is a paradoxical world. The achievements which are its glory threaten to destroy it. The nations with the highest standard of living, the greatest capacity to take care of their people economically, the broadest education, and the most enlightened morality and religion exhibit the least capacity to avoid mutual destruction in war. It would seem that the more civilized we become the more incapable of maintaining civilizations we are.*

This writer has made a series of assertions, without labeling them as reasons or conclusions by adding connective phrases. But we experience the sentences as functioning logically anyway, simply by understanding what one sentence

---

*F. S. C. Northrop, *The Meeting of East and West* (New York: Macmillan, 1946), p. 1.

has to do with another. After analyzing these relationships, we could make them explicit (at the expense, perhaps, of the dignity of the author's prose):

> Ours is a paradoxical world. *How do I know this? Because* the achievements which are its glory threaten to destroy it. *I think this is the case because* the nations with the highest standard of living, the greatest capacity to take care of their people economically, the broadest education, and the most enlightened morality and religion exhibit the least capacity to avoid mutual destruction in war. It would, *therefore,* seem that the more civilized we become the more incapable of maintaining civilization we are.

The first sentence is supported by a reason in sentence two, which in turn becomes the conclusion of another, more detailed reason in sentence three. The last sentence is a conclusion based on the reasons offered in sentences two and three, which is itself a reason explaining the general assertion in the first sentence. People often speak of writing as having a "line of reasoning" because the sentences of prose are often held together in this way; one reason gives rise to the need for another. Reasoning is the glue that holds the ideas together.

As this example also illustrates, any reason, because it is an assertion, can be supported by another. But a writer cannot keep supporting reasons with reasons forever. This passage comes at the beginning of a book that offers much more specific support for these general claims as it goes along. But, however much support is given, it must stop somewhere. At some point, the writer must decide to stop answering the question "Why?" A line of reasoning must result from consideration of what assertions to support and what reasons to develop, because it cannot, obviously, support and develop all potential lines of reasoning that might be followed. Of all the potential reasons for asserting that "Ours is a paradoxical world," this writer had to choose those he thought best, based on his sense of his audience. The reasoning available to be used always exceeds the scope of a piece of writing. Once he chose a line of reasoning, the author had to decide how far to pursue it. Writers make such decisions by asking themselves what makes a good reason and how far it must be developed. In order to pursue one line of reasoning, we have to give up the pursuit of some other. Our problem as writers of arguments is to decide which of many possible lines is worth pursuing and which are not. This consideration, in relation to a thesis, will be what determines the shape, or structure, of the composition.

The Enthymeme: Connecting Reasons and Conclusions

At this point, we need a name for the relationship created between a reason and a conclusion. I will call this combination of assertions an **enthymeme,** a term adopted from classical rhetoric. It is more open and flexible than any of the terms I might have adopted from formal logic. For many people, *logic* suggests mathematical formulas and rules that must be followed. For the purpose of gaining more control of the logical process that underlies our writing, it is sufficient to think of reasoning as a creative, generative process rather than following a system of prescribed rules and formulas. We reason all the time, without trying to follow any rules or fit our thoughts into predefined patterns or stopping to consider whether those connections conform to logical models. I will use the term *enthymeme* to refer to any combination of ideas in which a conclusion of any kind is supported by a reason.

Enthymemes occur throughout our discourse whenever we connect ideas in this way:

>Idea 1   *because*   Idea 2

or

>Idea 1   *therefore*   Idea 2

In the first case, Idea 1 is the conclusion. In the second case, Idea 2 is the conclusion. The following pairings of ideas are each enthymemes because they connect a conclusion to a reason:

>*The toxic waste disposal business is a noble career goal, because a healthy environment in the future will depend on proper elimination of harmful chemicals.*
>
>*Free the monkeys now! (We need the laughs.)*
>
>*We have to win this election. So vote early and vote often!*

As the examples show, the conclusion–reason model by itself does not guarantee that an enthymeme makes connections that are reasonable. Some ideas can be put into such a relationship and seem unreasonable whereas others seem reasonable. What makes the difference? What makes some enthymemes seem compelling? What makes a conclusion seem to follow?

Connecting the Enthymeme and Audience

The relationship created between a reason and a conclusion is not self-contained. It makes implicit reference to other ideas that help to bind the reason to the conclusion, making it seem to follow. Before discussing serious examples of this process, let me give you a nonsense one, just to show how it works:

Suppose two moms are talking about the man their daughter is dating. One says, "That boy Jason, he stays out too late at night." The other replies, "And that's why he'll never be wealthy." Has the second parent jumped to a conclusion? Well, that depends. It depends on whether the two ideas these two moms have asserted are connected by a third idea, which neither of them actually said. Of course, that idea is, in this case, the proverb "Early to bed, early to rise, makes a man healthy, wealthy, and wise." If these parents both believe that proverb is true, then the second mom may not be jumping as far as it first seemed. She asserted a reason, but it seems like a reason only if we perceive and accept that connecting truth. The second mom's statement assumed that this truth was shared between the two of them. She didn't have to say it out loud. It was implicit in her reasoning.

So, the inferential process at work in the second mom's thinking is something like this:

Stated reason: *Jason stays out late at night.*

Unstated assumption: *Early to bed, early to rise, makes a man healthy, wealthy, and wise.*

Stated conclusion: *Jason won't ever be wealthy.*

As long as this unstated assumption is a matter of agreement, the reason will seem like a reason. As soon as that assumption is denied, or if it is not shared at the outset, then the reason seems like no reason at all.

When enthymemes are asserted, they imply more than they say because reasons somehow appeal to assumptions that constitute the given condition behind the reasoning. Enthymemes therefore can be said to derive from beliefs that the particular audience is assumed already to have accepted as given. The choice of one reason or another to support a conclusion results from an understanding of what sorts of agreements can be assumed in one's audience.

If I were to argue, for instance, that "America is in great shape," I could draw on a wide variety of potential reasons to use as support for this assertion. If I chose to support it by saying "because hamburger consumption grows by 10 percent every year," I would be making a very risky assumption (as well as imagining a very uncritical reader who would share it). I would be basing my reasoning on the implied precondition that consumption of hamburgers is an index to a country's well-being. If I chose to support the assertion by arguing "because our products set the trends in international markets," I would be assuming my reader already believed that "Any country that sets the trends for other countries' markets must be in great shape," also a risky assumption. If I chose to argue the assertion by saying "because national unemployment has fallen to 6 percent," I might be basing my reasoning on an assumption that is somewhat more likely to be acceptable to a critical audience, that falling rates of unemployment signify national health. This is not a complete argument, of course, but it is on somewhat firmer ground.

Here is an example of enthymemes used in an actual argument, in a brief passage from Martin Luther King, Jr.'s "Letter from Birmingham Jail."

> A law is unjust if it is inflicted on a minority that, as a result of being denied the right to vote, had no part in enacting or devising the law. Who can say that the legislature of Alabama which set up the state's segregation laws was democratically elected? Throughout Alabama all sorts of devious methods are used to prevent Negroes from becoming registered voters, and there are some counties in which, even though Negroes constitute a majority of the

population, not a single Negro is registered. Can any law enacted under such circumstances be considered democratically structured?

Having already seen that certain dialectical oppositions are at work here (in Chapter 3), let's now consider the logic of King's case. King's reasoning supports the conclusion that Alabama's segregation laws are unjust. This conclusion is itself unstated, but we perceive it because the reasoning makes it seem to follow. That reasoning depends on enthymemes that also work on the basis of assumptions, either stated or unstated:

Conclusion: *Alabama's segregation laws are unjust.*

Reason: *Those laws are inflicted on a minority that had no role in enacting them.*

Assumption: *Any law that is inflicted on a minority that had no role in enacting it is an unjust law.*

The reason here is itself the conclusion of another enthymeme:

Conclusion: *African Americans had no role in enacting Alabama's segregation laws.*

Reason: *African Americans were prevented from voting for the state legislature.*

Assumption: *Anyone prevented from voting for the legislature has no role in enacting laws passed by that legislature.*

Real arguments, like King's, are often hard to reduce to the underlying enthymemes from which they derive their reasoning. But such enthymemes are there, nevertheless, providing the basis on which the argument's actual sentences are formed. The enthymemes represent the reasoning of the argument, even though that reasoning may be explicit or implicit, directly or indirectly conveyed in the language of the argument.

I have thus far talked about enthymemes as a basic structure of reasoning. I have distinguished three kinds of statements that make up enthymemes: conclusion; stated reason; and unstated reason, or assumption. In the sections that follow, I will explain how principles of informal reasoning can help you think about selecting a line of reasoning, and then how you can test its logic.

Informal Reasoning

In our various discourse communities we rarely demand a standard of proof as rigorous as that which pertains in science and mathematics. Some people think that we ought to demand such a standard, but they are not always able to define it. The mathematical truth that $9 + 5 = 14$ is expressed in symbols that are assumed to mean exactly the same thing to everyone. The quantities referred to by the numbers and the operations referred to by the symbols are said to come very close to this degree of certainty: "Water is wet." Obviously. But the statement is self-evident; that is, it needs no evidence other than itself. It is so obvious that no one would argue with it. And if anyone did decide to argue with it, testing its self-evidence, they would begin by asking "What do these words mean?" This is one of the ways that lawyers are taught to think of the so-called self-evident in language. It seems self-evident that, if there is a law against spitting on the sidewalk, and if somebody spits on the sidewalk, he or she has broken that law. Yet this person's lawyer might ask us to ponder the unpleasant (and deceptively simple) question "What is spit?" before rendering judgment. We might, in the process, discover that what seemed obvious is not.

So when we reason about ideas that are not self-evident and when we use ordinary language (rather than mathematical symbols) to do it, we must think of reasoning as an activity *guided* by a sense of probability but not *governed* by rules of valid inference. In other words, rather than mathematical formulas to tell us whether our reasons lead to true belief in our conclusions, we rely instead on our sense that they *seem* to support conclusions with more or less certainty. Although rules guide our sense that $9 + 5 = 14$, no such rules are available to us to account fully for our belief in (or disbelief of) statements about most actual questions at issue, statements such as "Computer simulations can replace tests on live animals in medical research" or "Politicians' private conduct is an important measure of their suitability for public office." In the world of real issues that demand real answers from us, we must settle for agreement based on the best available reasons rather that expect perfectly reliable methods of reaching conclusions.

To summarize before moving on, here are two key points about the enthymeme and informal reasoning:

1. Enthymemes express what we think here and now, and why we think so, rather than permanent, stable, unambiguous truths. They express our reasoning concerning questions of interpretation, value, consequence, and policy in the absence of a mathematically perfect system of logic to apply to such questions.
2. Enthymemes are not, therefore, to be judged according to a mathematical standard as either valid or invalid. They make more or less adequate, weaker or stronger, arguments relative to the knowledge and beliefs of the intended audience.

All real arguments probably seem somewhat sloppy compared to the elegant and strict proofs of geometry. But this does not mean that we cannot talk with some precision about how they work, and apply some standards to how we judge them. These standards will be matters of judgment. We have already applied one such standard in the preceding chapter: An argument must address a question that is actually at issue or it will not seem relevant to its intended audience.

Exploring the Audience Connection

Another kind of informal connection between reasoning and its audience is the direction in which the reasoning moves, up or down a ladder of abstraction. Does it move from the general to the particular or from the particular to the general? Neither way is better nor will yield more reliable conclusions. Different circumstances might call for one or the other kind of reasoning. If members of the discourse community are connected by the assumption of certain general principles, then those principles can be used as a basis for reasoning toward more specific conclusions. If specific facts or details can be taken for granted by the members of a different discourse community, then those may be used as a basis for reasoning toward more general principles. The choice depends on what one thinks the audience already knows.

It is possible for a reason to be stated in the form of a general principle, from which a more specific conclusion is derived. Or it is possible for a reason to be stated in the form of a specific instance, from which a more general conclusion follows. In these examples of each kind of enthymeme, consider what the audience is assumed to believe already that might have helped to determine the direction the enthymeme moves:

From General to Specific:

1. *Grades should be abolished, because the purpose of education is to teach people, not to rank them.*
2. *Handguns should not be outlawed because the Second Amendment of the U.S. Constitution establishes the right to bear arms.*
3. *War would be less likely if women outnumbered men in the Senate, because women seek compromise more readily than men do.*

From Specific to General:

1. *Grades do not accurately assess what students have learned because test scores reveal only a small part of the knowledge a student may have.*
2. *Handgun ownership should be unregulated because many people have protected themselves from violent assault using unlicensed handguns.*
3. *More women need to be elected to the Senate because 95 percent of women in state legislatures voted pro-choice.*

Of course, *general* and *specific* (a dialectical pair) are relative to each other. No statement is inherently either general or specific, although it may seem so when compared to another statement. Thus, the conclusion that "The Olympic Games promote world peace" could be said to be general in relation to this reason:

> *because countries with incompatible types of government must learn to compete in athletics using the same rules.*

but specific in relation to this one:

> *because world peace is made more likely whenever countries cooperate to bring about international events.*

You may already have noticed from these enthymemes that when specific reasons are stated, general principles tend to be assumed, and vice versa. Here's a simple example:

Conclusion: *Rap music is designed to shock parents . . .*

Stated reason: *. . . because its lyrics advocate teenage sexuality.*

Assumption: *Parents are shocked by lyrics that advocate teenage sexuality.*

This argument is based on the specific kinds of lyrics contained in the songs and would be developed by showing how those lyrics do in fact advocate teenage sexuality. The audience does not need any more evidence that such lyrics are shocking to parents. But this emphasis assumes a certain kind of audience. Consider the difference if the stated reason is changed from the specific one to the general one:

Conclusion: *Rap music is designed to shock parents . . .*

Stated reason: *. . . because parents are shocked by lyrics that advocate teenage sexuality.*

Assumption: *Rap lyrics advocate teenage sexuality.*

This argument assumes an audience that already knows what the lyrics advocate but does not already agree about what does and does not shock parents. Thus, some reasons might need to be developed whereas others can be allowed to remain undeveloped because they are assumed. This decision depends on whether the audience is most likely to agree on the general principle or on the specific facts. Of course, developing both kinds of reasons is often necessary.

When it is the general principle that can be assumed and the specific reason that must be developed, the reason is sometimes said to define the **burden of proof.** The term probably brings to mind a courtroom because in court settings the law itself is not on trial and forms the general principle of most arguments, so that the facts and whether they fit the general law must be argued:

Conclusion: *Sidney S. must pay child support to Sylvia R.*

Stated reason (burden of proof): *Sidney is the natural father of Suzie R., Sylvia's two-year-old daughter.*

Assumption: *The law requires men to pay child support to mothers of children they father.*

If Sylvia's lawyer can establish that Sidney is the natural father, the conclusion will follow. If Sidney's lawyer can show that fact to be wrong, the conclusion will not follow. Neither spends any time arguing that the assumption is or is not true. (They will leave that argument for an appeal to the Supreme Court.)

The concept of burden of proof functions in other kinds of arguments, too, even though the proof called for may not be a factual kind.

Conclusion: *State education money should not be used to fund intercollegiate athletics . . .*

Stated reason (burden of proof): *. . . because intercollegiate athletics has a negative effect on the education of the students.*

Assumption: *State education money shouldn't pay for anything that has a negative effect on the education of students.*

In any real situation in which this argument would be proposed, the stated reason would have to be developed and the assumption would probably need no further explanation. (Once again, this depends, of course, on the audience.) But although this reason establishes the burden of proof, the statement cannot be proved except to offer more reasons. *Burden of proof* can simply mean the responsibility to develop the argument further. In the following section, I want to consider some of the ways in which this responsibility may be met. Conclusions are reached by means of reasons that are meant to *appeal* to the audience.

Kinds of Appeal

When we talk about wanting to reach an audience with our argument, we sometimes say we want to appeal to them. Another way to discuss informal, practical reasoning is to distinguish reasons according to the *kind* of appeal that they make. Now that I have talked about the role that assumptions play in making our reasons sound like reasons, let's explore what kind of reasons are available to us.

In general, we can distinguish three kinds of appeal:

1. The appeal to authority
2. The appeal to emotion
3. The appeal to the logic of the case

The first kind seeks to establish belief in an assertion by referring the audience to the credibility of a source. Appeals of this kind range from the writer's establishment of his or her own expertise to citations from others who are assumed to be believable on a given subject. It is a common form of reasoning, and it takes its power from our willingness to grant superior credibility to others based on their credentials. Such appeals depend on our willingness to accept an idea based on *who* says so.

The second kind of reason, the appeal to emotion, seeks to establish belief in an assertion by referring somehow to the reader's desires. Appeals of this kind can range from the writer's outright manipulation of the reader's feelings to the construction of reasons out of shared moral principles such as justice or mercy. This is also a common form of reasoning, and it takes its power from our willingness to grant superior credibility to ideas that corre-spond to our preference for what ought to be true.

The third kind of reason, the appeal to the logic of the case, seeks to establish belief in an assertion by showing it to be a necessary consequence of belief in some other idea or ideas. Appeals of this kind can range from the use of proven experimental data to the suggestion that one idea follows di-rectly from the acceptance of another one. This common form of reasoning takes its power from the sense of necessity that accompanies logical infer-ences. Such appeals differ from the first and second kinds in that the conclu-sion seems to follow and to remain valid, no matter who says it or whether we wish it were true.

It might seem from this description that the third kind of reasoning is the best. To be sure, it seems to be the purest kind of reasoning, insofar as it does not depend on the seemingly irrelevant considerations such as accepting au-thority or submitting to emotion. But these considerations often enter into our reasoning, to a greater or lesser degree depending on the kind of conclusion we are arguing. One could probably not persuade a mother and father that their love for a child is irrelevant to their reasoning about the child's education. An art critic could probably not be persuaded that emotion is irrelevant to his or her reasoning about the qualities of a painting. And although we may all want to question authority at times, we all probably accept it as reasonable at other times, as when we admit someone else's expertise. Even arguments that seem purely logical often seem to deserve more or less belief based on their source or on how well they accord with our desires.

Perhaps the best way to demonstrate how these appeals work is to dis-cuss a few examples of enthymemes of each kind.

Appeals to Authority

Appeals to authority establish an idea based on the credibility of its source. Thus each of these examples, in its own way, is an appeal of this sort:

> *An exciting game of tennis relieves stress because it works for me.*
>
> *An exciting game of tennis relieves stress because it says so in Dr. Merit's* How to Relieve Stress.
>
> *An exciting game of tennis relieves stress because several studies have shown it.*

Here are three reasons put forth in support of the same assertion. These lines of reasoning might be developed further. Each suggests a different kind of dis-cussion, however, and we must decide initially whether the basic reasoning underlying that potential development is sound. If we were to make this deci-sion on the principle that appeals to authority are never sound, none of the ex-amples could be said to provide a good reason for believing the conclusion. But, in fact, they provide adequate reasons for accepting the conclusion in cer-tain circumstances.

If, for instance, the question at issue is whether tennis ever relieves stress, the testimony of a single individual that it does, as in the first example, would be one way of answering that question convincingly. Once that testimony had been given, who would dispute the fact that, for that individual, the claim holds true? This issue would be better supported by the reasoning in the first example than the reasoning established in the second example, because the best judge of whether one's own stress has been relieved is oneself, not the writer of a popular self-help book. But Dr. Merit's authority to make a general claim about the value of tennis for others may be greater than the authority of any single amateur based on a few Sundays on the court. If the issue is how best to relieve stress, the reasoning in the second example might be more adequate than in the first. This would depend, of course, on how credible Dr. Merit is. Why should I take his word for it? Because he signs himself "Dr."? Certainly not. I should take his word for it based only on what he has to say for himself. If all Merit has to say is that he has enjoyed many rousing tennis games and felt better afterward, then he could hardly be trusted as an authority on what other people ought to do. But if Merit's reasoning proceeds along the lines suggested in the third example, his authority might become more credible—as credible, at least, as the authors of the studies he cites.

Anyone can *say* that something is true "because several studies have shown it," but the speaker's authority is then only as good as the authority of those studies, whatever they are. Sloppy studies, based on inconclusive samples or weighted by inappropriate assumptions, need not *show* any such thing, even if that is what they conclude. Here, then, is an appeal to authority that is appropriate only if the studies themselves are reliable. Such an argument would have to depart from its appeal to authority and talk about the nature of the studies themselves. Studies can be used as appeals to authority or they can be used as appeals to the logic of the case. As mere authorities, studies will generally provide weak support. As a context for discussing the reasons that the studies themselves offer in support of a conclusion, their use can be quite appropriate.

The appeal to authority provides appropriate or inappropriate reasons, depending on whether someone's special knowledge, or testimony, is relevant to the issue. Some issues will call for such reasoning. It is important to consider, however, whether a conclusion would continue to be true no matter who asserted it—and if that is the case, authority might provide relevant reasons that are nevertheless insufficient. Suppose I were to argue, for instance, that

U.S. foreign policy is inconsistent. My political science professor said so.

I could in that statement be said to have chosen a more appropriate appeal to authority than if I had chosen to argue the same conclusion by saying "Julia Roberts said so." My political science professor can probably be expected to know more about the subject than Julia Roberts does. But the appeal to authority is not my only choice and probably not the best one. The issue underlying the assertion is not one that calls for anyone's testimony. It calls for an explanation of what it is *about* U.S. foreign policy that makes it inconsistent, independent of what my professor or anyone else might say. If I can read the newspaper, chances are I can offer this explanation without having to find an expert to agree with me.

Appeals to Emotion

We are sometimes taught that reason and emotion are opposites, and indeed they can function as dialectical pairs, as I illustrated in Chapter 3. By contrasting emotion with reasoning, the emotional appeal can be made to seem unreasonable. There's an old joke ridiculing emotional appeals: A man accused of murdering his mother and father asks the count for mercy *because* he is an orphan. But emotional appeals may be a perfectly legitimate form of reasoning. After all, it is possible to argue reasonably that mercy is justified. Emotion, in this context, refers to a range of human responses that is much broader than what we might mean in casual utterances such as "stop being so emotional." In the case of issues having to do with what is right and just, appealing to emotion is unavoidable, because our sense of right and justice is a feeling as well as an abstract belief. Our feelings inevitably, and properly, enter into our sense of what we *should* believe. Some value statements may legitimately function to arouse our consciences. We rarely respond well to arguments that seem to us cold and objective, or devoid of human feeling.

So, appeals to emotion provide appropriate reasons in certain circumstances. But, like appeals to authority, they do not generally offer the best support available unless the issue specifically makes the reader's desires relevant. Here are three examples of different reasons offered in support of a single conclusion:

> *Students should support the clerical workers' strike by boycotting classes because only scabs will go to class during the strike.*
>
> *Students should support the clerical workers' strike by boycotting classes because joining just causes shows courage.*
>
> *Students should support the clerical workers' strike by boycotting classes because the clerical workers are underpaid.*

In different ways, each of these reasons appeals to the reader's desire. The first example is a kind of threat, and it appeals to the reader's desire not to be thought of as a scab. This kind of name-calling would probably not be effective, but there is a power, nonetheless, in reasons that act on the fears of the audience. "You should not go into Kasstle Park alone at night because if you do you may be a victim of a mugger." This is not an unreasonable statement, even if it uses a strategy similar to the scab argument. What makes that argument seem inappropriate, however, is that the issue—whether students should boycott classes—is not answered by such a threat, the way the issue of whether one should venture alone into Kasstle Park at night is answered by noting the potential danger. *Victims* is a term applied to people who are mugged, whereas *scab* is a label that is used to denigrate people who disagree. No one would choose to be a victim, but people can decide for reasons of their own not to participate in the boycott.

Just as the first example appeals to emotion by threatening the reader with a derogatory label, the second example works by flattering the reader with a positive image. The reasoning connects a desired image on the part of the reader with a desired action on the part of the writer. As a reason for believing that students should join a boycott of classes, however, the appeal is weak. It may flatter the reader into thinking that he or she can be a courageous defender of a just cause, but it does not provide support for the justice of the cause itself. The reader is asked to take part in a cause to be courageous, as if any cause would do. This answers the question of why students might *want* to join the clerical workers, but it does so in a way that serves the appearance of the students more than the cause itself.

In the third example, unlike the second, the reasoning answers the issue by referring to the needs of the workers. Hence, the third example seems to contain reasoning that is more relevant to the issue. The justness of the cause, not the reader's desire to escape or to acquire a particular image, is the basis of the appeal. However, that reasoning is also based on an appeal to emotion, because it arouses the reader's sympathy. Why, in other words, is the fact that the workers are underpaid a good reason to support them? It is a good reason because we desire that people should not be underpaid; we want fairness. Thus, although the reasoning seems more logical, it nevertheless depends on the reader's sense of compassion and a preference for fair treatment of the clerical workers. It may not be as blatant an appeal for sympathy as arguing that the workers cannot afford to feed their families, but it is the same kind of appeal.

Appeals to the Logic of the Case

Appeals to the logic of the case derive one idea from another independent of the writer's authority and the reader's sympathy. The use of this kind of reason does not guarantee that the specific reason chosen will be appropriate, of course. Although no such guarantee exists, one can test the logical adequacy of a reason by looking at its relevance and connection to the claim. You may already have encountered this kind of testing in the logic of a valid syllogism. However, because of the kinds of questions the enthymeme addresses, we are interested here more with the relative strength and weakness of lines of reasoning than we are with the kind of strict mathematical validity sought by formal systems of logic.

Actual discourse rarely comes in the neat categorical statements of formal logic (even though such logic may underlie the reasoning). The principles for exploring the logic of a case that we will use are relevance, connectedness, relative precision, and circularity. In each case it is the relation of the unstated assumption to the reason and conclusion that is being explored. As readers and arguers, we usually understand such assumptions based on our intuitive sense that our conclusions are connected to our reasons by the bridge of obvious truths. Yet, as you have seen in the discussion of dialectic in Chapter 3, much of what underlies our reasoning is not obvious to us. Being as precise as possible about the way the unstated assumption is working will make your reasoning clearer to you and to your audience. The following four techniques for evaluating the logic of an enthymeme are not meant as formulas for mechanically processing your arguments, but rather as considerations that may help you explore the implications of your own reasoning and revise your thinking.

Relevance and Connectedness

It is possible for a line of reasoning to contain true or acceptable claims and yet fail because those claims do not connect with each other. Here is an obvious example:

> *Lambs are not good pets because people eat meat.*

The difficulty is that the reason and the conclusion seem to address different issues. The reason says nothing about the qualities important in a good pet, but rather about people's culinary preferences. Although the two might be related within the broad topic of people's relation to animals, they lack direct relevance to each other.

Most arguments in actual discourse are less obvious than this nonsensical example. Here is a realistic example of an enthymeme in which a lack of relevance makes the relation between the reason and conclusion seem too remote:

> *Commercial television threatens to diminish the intellectual standards*
> *of American society because most people would rather watch television*
> *than read.*

The conclusion says that the threat to diminished intellectual standards is television. The reason given does not say anything about why television is such a threat. The question at issue answered by this enthymeme would be: What threatens the intellectual standards of American society? If commercial television is the answer, then the reason must be about television as well. The stated reason is about how most people prefer one kind of activity or another, not what television does. Although that reason is related to the topic, it is not directly relevant to the question at issue or to the conclusion. After all, if these same people read nothing but magazines about celebrities and trendy fashions, their intellectual standards might be as low or lower than if they watched television.

Here is a revision of the television enthymeme that attempts to make a more relevant connection between reason and conclusion, but that may not yet be adequate:

> *Commercial television threatens to diminish the intellectual standards of American society because it portrays people who value only money and status.*

The reason does address the nature of television and therefore has more relevance to the issue, although the way it makes the connection may still be too remote. The reason and conclusion share a term, so that there is an assumption linking them: Things that portray people who value only money and status diminish intellectual standards. Yet the connection between the reason and conclusion could be stronger. If it is the case that television portrays people who value only money and status (and, of course, such a generalization is itself too sweeping), this by itself has no obvious relevance to television's threat to intellectual standards. The conclusion is about what television does to intellectual standards. The reason is about what television portrays. But the enthymeme does not make a connection between portrayals on television and the effect upon intellectual standards. The unstated assumption may be clearer, but the causal connection could still be made more explicit.

This next revision of the television enthymeme attempts to improve the connection between reason and conclusion:

> *Commercial television threatens to diminish the intellectual standards of American society because it demands no thought from the viewer.*

This example uses a reason with more potential to explain why the effect of television on the viewer is a threat to intellectual standards; it seeks to connect the conclusion not only to the nature of television but also to the nature of television's audience. It thus provides a better reason than the first two because its relevance is direct and apparent. If it were to be developed by showing how television places no demand on thought and by showing how this affects intellectual standards, then this reason might provide the basis for a reasonable argument about the effects of television on society. It is an argument that you may have heard in one form or another. It is one that a few authorities have used to convince people, emotionally, of television's dangerous qualities. It may be an argument that contributes to making television better. At any rate, although it may have all of these functions, it is an argument based on the logic of the case, independent of who says it or whether we want to believe it. This argument will be convincing or not depending on how well each of the aspects of its logic can be developed.

Relative Precision

Unintentionally ambiguous language is a great source of humor, as for instance in those lists of allegedly real headlines that circulate on the Internet:

> *Grandmother of Eight Makes Hole in One*
> *Experts Say School Bus Passengers Should Be Belted*

Court to Try Shooting Defendant
Man Sent Back to Jail for Not Finishing Sentence

Words that may be taken more than one way can also create unintentional misunderstanding.

"Shall we eat at Chez Ray tonight?"
"I have no reservations."
"Well, then, I guess we'll have to go somewhere else."

You know a lot of jokes based on these kinds of ambiguities. The kind of misunderstanding we need to be concerned with in argumentative writing is that which comes from reasoning in language that is simply too broad to allow the writer's explicit meaning to come through. For instance, if someone wrote this enthymeme

Student protesters should be expelled because they disrupt the
educational process.

we would probably object that the reasoning should not apply to all student protesters because most acts of protest do not have such an effect. The term is too broad to specify which acts of protest are at issue. And we might go on to object to such an argument by saying that for us the educational process should include exposure to protests and even participating in them. The term *student protesters* is too general, and the term *educational process* too vague.

Let's return briefly to the revised enthymeme about television and ask whether its terms are precise enough to communicate a specific argument.

Commercial television threatens to diminish the intellectual
standards of American society because it demands no thought
from the viewer.

As potential members of the audience for this argument, we might ask: What are these intellectual standards? There are different kinds of intellectual processes, from those measured by IQ tests or SAT scores to more practical kinds of intelligence about health, financial management, and human relationships. Anytime anyone says something like, "Wow, that was a dumb thing to do," or "I wish I'd thought of that," that speaker is actually applying an intellectual standard. But it may not be similar at all to what the writer of the enthymeme has in mind. That writer may have a specific kind of intellectual standard in mind, but the language in the enthymeme is so broad that the audience cannot know what that is. In the absence of more specific language, the audience has to fill in that space with a specific standard that may or may not be what the author has in mind.

Overgeneralization can also be a problem when particular characteristics are misapplied to a larger group. Consider the group "American society" in the commercial television enthymeme. This group of people is so large as to be difficult to make any specific claim about, and formulating an accurate description of such a large number of people would be very difficult to do. Many kinds of people watch commercial television. How likely is it that all those watching will bring to their viewing the same expectations or be affected by it in the same way? The experiences of people of different ages, socioeconomic groups, and educational backgrounds are likely to be different. Lumping a variety of people together in a category that is so large that relevant differences are ignored weakens the claim.

The misapplication of particular characteristics to a large group is often the basis of prejudicial thinking, whether the characteristic is a positive or a negative one. When forming a claim about a group of people, examine carefully who it is that comes to mind. Are there exceptions in the group that could undermine the claim about them?

The assumption that links reason and conclusion can also be overgeneralized to the point that its application is too broad. Here's an enthymeme I once read in a campus newspaper:

> *Beer should be sold in our student union because it will provide additional revenue for the student body.*

The assumption linking the reason and conclusion seems to be this: Anything that will provide additional revenue for the student body should be sold. Examples that could be used to challenge the validity of this assumption come to mind easily: Should cocaine or marijuana be sold too? They would also provide revenue. The assumption connecting the reason and conclusion cannot be applied as a principle in this argument without committing the writer to unintended positions. What qualifications or distinctions might make this enthymeme more appropriate? The language has to become more precise in order for the logic to work as the writer intends.

The implied assumption underlying any given piece of reasoning may itself be too sweeping and require qualification. Another example I encountered recently is this argument from a letter to the editor written in support of the mandatory teaching of creation theory in biology classes:

> *Evolution can only be considered a theory and not a proven fact, because no one was there to witness it.*

The assumption underlying this reasoning seems to be something like this: Nothing can be considered a fact if no one was there to witness it. How many exceptions to this idea could a critical reader come up with? Would they include creation itself? At any rate, the assumption is so general and vague that it seems a weak foundation for the argument. Revising the reasoning would be a matter of qualifying the language of the stated reason until it rested on firmer shared ground. In order to make such a revision of your own reasoning, you have to consider carefully the potential applications of the implied assumption on which your enthymeme is based.

Circular Reasoning

Circular reasoning, also known as a *tautology,* appears to be reasoning when in fact it is only the repetition of the same idea in both reason and conclusion. Circular enthymemes end up exactly where they began, usually because they contain terms that are no more than redefinitions:

> *Weapons of mass destruction should be banned because they are used to kill a lot of people at once.*

The reason is not actually a reason because it merely redefines the term *weapon of mass destruction* without offering support for the claim. The assumption is nothing but a restatement of the same thing also: Whatever kills a lot of people at once should be banned. We aren't getting anywhere with this logic.

When an enthymeme has this kind of circularity, the cause is often the presence of a definition in the reasoning rather than a new claim that adds a different term to the reasoning.

> *French cooking is high in fat because it uses a lot of sauces made with butter.*
> **Implied assumption:** *Butter is fat.*

This is not actually reasoning as much as it is explaining, and the implied audience is not in need of a reason (there is no question at issue), but an explanation.

Circularity often results from the use of the verb *to be*, because that verb asserts equivalency or definition. Consider this nonsensical circular enthymeme:

> *Time is the root of all evil because it is money.*

The terms in this enthymeme are all interchangeable, because underlying the logic is no more than the proverbial equations: Time is money; money is the root of all evil. There is no line of reasoning to connect one idea to the next that is more than a restatement of the equivalency of two of the terms.

In circular reasoning, then, the reason simply reproduces the claim in one form or another:

> *The accountant is a crook because he embezzled money.*
>
> *This agency's practices will harm the environment because its emissions standards contribute to air pollution.*
>
> *Lack of regular raises will lower the worker's morale because staying at the same pay makes people discontented.*

As with the nonsensical example, the terms all redefine each other and could be interchanged.

To revise an enthymeme that seems to be circular is easier if you are aware of the possibility that some of the terms may simply be redefinitions. If the reason and the conclusion actually state the same thing in different language, then the enthymeme is incomplete, and the support for one's idea is lacking. If that seems to be the case, rewrite the enthymeme so that only one claim is made, and then write a new because clause that answers the question "Why should I believe that that claim is true?"

Questions for Thought, Discussion, and Writing

1. In the following passages, which sentences are reasons and which are conclusions? Do some sentences have both functions? Which ones that you describe as reasons offer explanations of the conclusion, and which offer justifications for believing the conclusion?
    a. I like reading detective novels. They keep me looking for interesting possibilities, like a game of chess. I never can guess the right solution, though. The writers are clever. I'm also too gullible. But it's fun to be fooled. It wouldn't be a challenge if I always knew "whodunnit."
    b. The narrator of "The Turn of the Screw" is unreliable. It isn't possible to tell whether to trust what we are told. Henry James seems to want his reader to wonder whether the events really happened or whether they occur only in the minds of the characters. But which characters? The reader must be meant to wonder which of the characters can trust their own impressions. I think it's a story about the ambiguity of appearance and reality.
    c. Sixty-seven percent of the people surveyed said that they are not influenced by advertising with irrelevant sexual content. This does not, however, mean that such an influence is not more common. If we accept the possibility that there is a subliminal appeal in advertising, some of those who say that they are not influenced might be influenced without knowing it. Survey techniques alone cannot test hypotheses about subconscious knowledge.

2. What kinds of appeal are being made in each of the reasons offered here? How appropriate is the choice of each kind of appeal? Why?
    a. Salaries for state employees should be based on comparable worth, because women workers on the average earn lower wages than men.
    b. A recent study showed that cocaine users are no more likely than anyone else to experiment with heroin. But only a fool would accept this as a "green light" to use coke.
    c. When you consider the extent to which the computer will be used in all parts of our lives in the near future, it becomes obvious that computer literacy should be taught in elementary grades.
    d. We need leaders who are not afraid to tell the truth. Without them, this country is doomed.
    e. The newspaper decided to print pictures of men who went into adult bookstores in our town, hoping to humiliate them into staying away and by this means force the stores to close. The question is whether the newspaper is guilty of invasion of privacy or whether freedom of the

press can include this kind of action. I think the paper has the right but would be wise not to use it. The public's trust in the press is undermined when it abuses its freedoms, just as the booksellers lose respect when they take the First Amendment too far. In both cases, the First Amendment is pushed far enough to risk a backlash that could destroy it.

3. Reconstruct the assumptions that connect the following reasons and conclusions.
   a. The student union should be allowed to sell beer because this would create more revenue to support student activities.
   b. Boxers frequently suffer permanent injury as a result of the impact of brain tissue hitting the inside of the skull. Yet some people continue to call this a "sport." It's not a sport; it's a brutal entertainment spectacle. It should be outlawed.
   c. As long as the nation's laws are written and voted on by a majority of whites, the laws that send minorities to prison in greater numbers than whites are political laws. This makes political prisoners out of people who have done no more than follow their consciences in matters that they have not been able to change with their votes.
   d. The only way a politician can get elected is by telling people what they want to hear. No honest person can win enough votes to get into office.
   e. If the Constitution hadn't guaranteed people the right to pursue happiness, Americans might not be as selfish as they are.

4. Having decided on a thesis for your next essay, turn it into an enthymeme by adding a because clause that you might offer as a major reason for justifying that thesis. If, in the process of doing so, you find that you need to revise the thesis itself, go ahead. After you have composed this enthymeme, bring it to class for a discussion of the reasoning it uses, according to any of the concepts in this chapter.

5. Having read one of the essays in Part II, or one from another source, consider the following questions:
   a. What enthymemes does the writer use?
   b. Can you identify appeals to authority, emotion, and the logic of the case? Does the reasoning tend to move from specific to general or from general to specific, or does it stay on the same level? How are these kinds of reasoning combined?
   c. Has the author overgeneralized from the evidence, made use of overly general assumptions, or fallen into circular reasoning?
   d. What do such analyses tell you about the author's view of the audience for which the essay is composed?
   e. Finally, are you convinced by the writer's reasoning? What *about* that reasoning has succeeded or failed to change your mind?

6

Developing Structures

The Structural Enthymeme

A thesis statement in the form of an enthymeme can provide you with a bridge between the process of thinking about your argument and the process of developing it into the parts of an essay. It can help you to think about and to revise the whole argument in advance. An enthymeme composed to represent the whole argument (the conclusion and the major reason chosen to argue it) will not only help to ensure that the reasoning is adequate to your argumentative situation but also point the way toward structural possibilities in the essay itself.

Once you have discovered a thesis that represents the conclusion of your essay, you can begin to think about potential reasons. Obviously, many reasons are possible. What you seek at this point is a reason that might function as the central or main rational basis for arriving at the conclusion. Putting that reason together with the thesis will make the whole thesis statement into an enthymeme. So now, the whole essay, rather than being based on an assertion alone, can be said to be based on reasoning that you have already developed in response to a question at issue for your audience. If the assumption underlying that reasoning is an idea that you judge your audience as willing to accept without further argumentation, then your essay will also have the advantage of developing out of common ground between you and your audience. So let's now consider the enthymeme as a *generative* principle that can help you to give shape to an entire essay.

A thesis statement in the shape of an enthymeme will have the following very basic but elastic form:

Assertion 1 (thesis)   *because*   Assertion 2 (reason)

Each of these assertions will be a complete idea. The first one will be your conclusion and the second one will be the main reason you have chosen in support of that conclusion. I will call Assertion 2 a *because clause* since together the two assertions can be phrased as a single sentence. If the thesis statement is in this form, you should be able to reconstruct the assumption and by that means ensure that you have thought about the potential connection that your reasoning makes to the beliefs of your readers. As we have seen in the previous chapter, that assumption will be there whether you write it out or not. But it is necessary for you to know what it is if you want to be sure that your reasoning, as well as the issue, finds the audience.

The task, simply stated, is to find the best reason you can to support your idea. I don't mean that there is only one "best" reason for every idea, but our choice of reasons determines the directions in which our thoughts move. The because clause, then, should provide a clear direction in answer to the question "Why should my reader believe that my thesis is true?" Of course, an honest search for such an answer might result in the need to rethink the thesis itself. In fact, it often does. We view our ideas more critically when we carry out a sincere search for good reasons.

The task can be guided by some criteria for an adequate because clause, like those presented in Chapter 4 to help guide the search for an adequate thesis (see page 53). Once you have used those criteria to help you decide on a thesis, the following considerations can guide your search for a because clause:

1. Is the because clause a complete, precisely stated idea?
2. Does it represent a central reason for answering the question "What makes the thesis true?"
3. Is the implied assumption one that my audience can be expected to accept without further argument? (This means, of course, the same audience for whom the question answered by the thesis is at issue.)
4. Have I explored the adequacy of my reasoning in terms of the relevance and connectedness of the because clause, the relative precision of all the terms, and the need to go beyond circular reasoning?

These four criteria do not guarantee an airtight argument, of course. In practical, informal argumentation about the kinds of issues that call for our best reasoning, there may be no such thing as proof beyond doubt. But the conscious attempt to apply these criteria to your own enthymeme can help you to create a more fully developed line of reasoning designed to meet the needs of your intended audience. Having satisfied yourself that the enthymeme you have written and revised meets these criteria, you can then begin to explore ways in which you might expand the elements of that reasoning into a more fully developed essay.

Using these criteria as a basis for revising your enthymeme will pay off in the process of drafting an essay that moves in the directions your reasoning establishes. The application of these questions to your own reasoning can help you from being too easily satisfied with your thinking, which is important because if you write for critical readers they will give your reasoning the same kind of close attention. Your application of these criteria doesn't have to follow a prescribed order. They are considerations for you to use, when they apply, as you revise an enthymeme. It also helps to have others' views in this process, because sometimes it is hard for us to see critically into our own reasoning, which always seems obvious to ourselves. For this reason, your teacher may schedule thesis workshops in class or otherwise have you look at enthymemes written by classmates. If not, you can do this yourself with the help of a friend whom you know to be a good critical reader.

From Enthymeme to Structure

Let's examine in more detail how a thesis statement, in the form of a well-thought-out enthymeme, provides you with the major parts that will hold the structure of your composition together. By thinking through the enthymeme, you will have given yourself a basis for thinking about structure. The shape that your essay will take will, therefore, be the shape of your reasoning, a structure that you have generated to fit the argument that you have chosen to develop. You need rely on no model essay form to find that shape. Your reasoning will generate the shape of your essay.

In the broadest sense, the parts of the enthymeme can be thought of as the largest units of an essay's structure. They can be diagrammed as follows:

Enthymeme		*Structure*
(question at issue)	→	*beginning*
(assumption) *because clause*	→	*middle*
assertion	→	*end*

The enthymeme, having emerged from thinking about your ideas and reasons, can now be looked at as the source for the specific functions of these large structural parts—specific because each enthymeme will have its own requirements. These requirements can be understood by thinking of the structure of an essay as the fulfillment of the logical relationships in the enthymeme:

Beginning: *The reader is introduced to a problem that is of interest because it requires a solution.* The question at issue.

Middle: *The solution to the problem depends on the reader and writer sharing a common understanding.* The assumption.

Given this understanding, an answer to the problem can be developed if a condition can be shown to be the case. The because clause.

End: *Given the assumption and the condition just developed, the solution follows.* The assertion; the thesis.

Needless to say, these parts can be as long or as short as the specific case requires. They do not correspond to paragraphs; this could be the structure of an essay, a chapter, or a book. Within these parts, many kinds of sentences and transitions can occur, as they are called for. But these basic functions are common to essays that *take a reader through a developing line of reasoning toward an earned conclusion.* These elements will in turn help you select and order other elements of thought.

The actual order of these elements will grow out of what you have to say. The enthymeme can therefore help to guide this growth, but it does not determine what form the essay must take. The enthymeme suggests structural possibilities because it connects ideas through reasoning. Consequently, any enthymeme may give rise to different structures for essays, depending on the writer's choices and how the writer sees those connections.

An actual essay will have many more parts than the enthymeme from which its structure derives. This is because as the essay moves through the reasoning of the enthymeme other things must happen. Terms may need to be explained. Distinctions may need to be offered. Further reasons may need to be gone into. Examples may need to be used for clarity. Transitions may need to be composed. At any point that a reader may be expected to question, to object, or to be confused, the writer may find a way to help the reader along. Such considerations arise when the writer attempts to develop the basic reasoning of the enthymeme in such a way that a reader will be able to follow that reasoning clearly.

Outlines of Ideas

An enthymeme can help you to guide the development of your essay's structure by suggesting an outline of ideas. I do not mean an outline having blank spaces with labels such as I.A.b. and to be filled in with a few words—an outline with subdivisions and brief headings. I mean, rather, a sequence of sentences that represents the progress of thought in the essay, the ideas in the order in which they will arise in the essay. Having produced such an outline of ideas, you can use it to help define further responsibilities that you might face as the essay unfolds.

There is no single way of generating a structure of ideas from the parts of an enthymeme, and there is no formula that tells you how to do it. You can learn it only by doing it. But to help make this process clearer, I will give some examples of possible structures that might be generated from an enthymeme. This will also help to give you some sense of the range of possibilities implicit in the enthymeme. The enthymeme is not meant to restrict thought to a narrow linear chain, but to help stimulate thought. In each case, I will illustrate the structure of the essay as an outline of ideas.

Suppose I have composed the following structural enthymeme to represent my argument:

> *The study of myths helps us to understand the social roles of women in history*
>
> *because*
>
> *it reveals how the myths of the past have molded the attitudes of successive generations and preserved social order.**

---

*This basic reasoning, though not the structures or examples that follow, has been adapted from Sarah B. Pomeroy, *Goddesses, Whores, Wives, and Slaves* (New York: Shocken Books, 1975).

This reasoning implies a question at issue and an assumption, both of which connect it to its intended audience. The question at issue (a question of consequence) might be stated this way:

> *Can the study of myths help us to understand the social roles of women in history?*

The assumption that holds the reasoning together might be stated like this:

> *The study of whatever has molded the attitudes of successive generations and preserved social order will be helpful in understanding the social role of women in history.*

Writing out the enthymeme, the question at issue, and the assumption is useful in trying to make decisions about structure. Having written them out, I can ask myself: "Does the assumption need to be included and explained or can it remain unstated?" In the present case, I might well decide that the assumption does not need to be put into the essay at all. I can also ask myself: "Should the question at issue be stated? Should it be developed? Is it obvious to the reader why it is at issue? Should I start with it?" In this case, I might think that it needs to be explained and that it might make a good place to start. Furthermore, I can (and should) ask myself: "What parts does an essay need to have in order to earn this thesis by means of this reasoning?" In this case I might sketch out a small list.

> *The essay must*
> — *show some myths.*
> — *show how those myths molded the attitudes of successive generations.*
> — *show how those myths preserved social order.*
> — *connect those attitudes to the social role of women in history.*
> — *show that those attitudes are preserved as part of the social order.*

My choice to argue this enthymeme and not some other has made me feel responsible to do these things. Of course, my list of responsibilities might be longer. But any structural enthymeme will contain such responsibilities, and they will consist of explaining the parts of the enthymeme and connecting them. Furthermore, I can ask myself: "Should I put the conclusion at the beginning of the essay or should I save it for later?"

Considerations of this sort will enable me to make some structural decisions. I can see that several potential structures are implicit in this enthymeme. The following three outlines of ideas might result from such considerations.

Outline 1

Our understanding of the social roles of women in history can be enhanced by the study of myth.

. . .

How? By seeing first that myths of the past molded the attitudes of successive generations.

. . .

For example, in the myth of Atalanta, her father abandoned her in the forest because he wanted a son.

. . .

This myth suggested that female children were less desirable than male children.

. . .

Also, in Homer, female goddesses direct the actions of the men at war.

. . .

These stories allow men to blame their actions on women.

. . .

These attitudes are reflected in the historical role of women as both socially inferior to men and the cause of men's misfortunes.

. . .

Second, we can see that myths of the past also preserved the social order that such attitudes created.

. . .

For example, Athena was the goddess of wisdom, peace, and war. She was worshiped, and the city of Athens was dedicated to her.

. . .

She was part of the religion, and civil order was seen as part of a sacred order.

. . .

Social roles could not be questioned without questioning sacred order.

. . .

Consequently, we can see how the social role of women in history was so difficult to escape. It was seen as divinely ordered. Men had an excuse to maintain the role of female inferiority and did not have to take the blame themselves.

Outline 2

Women feature prominently in ancient myths.

. . .

For example, the myth of Atalanta . . .

. . .

The goddesses in Homer . . .

. . .

The worship of Athena . . .

. . .

What attitudes toward women do these myths teach?

. . .

That they are inferior to men.

. . .

That they are to blame for men's actions.

. . .

That the civil order was seen as part of a sacred order.

. . .

What do these myths have to do with the continuation of social roles for women in later history?

. . .

They serve to instill these attitudes.

. . .

They preserved the social role of women by connecting those roles to religious beliefs.

. . .

From this we see that the study of myth can help us to understand the social roles of women in history.

Outline 3

In history women were held in high esteem, but they also were kept in subordinate social roles.

. . .

This is a paradox that is hard to understand.

. . .

Perhaps one way to understand it is to look at the function of myth in creating and preserving those roles.

. . .

Myths mold the attitudes of successive generations.

. . .

They do this by giving examples of people that one is supposed to admire.

. . .

The heroes of Greek legends, for instance, illustrate the virtues of brave and noble behavior.

. . .

Myths also preserve social order.

. . .

They do this not only by defining roles according to the attitudes they create about virtuous behavior but also by suggesting that these roles in civil society fit into a divine plan.

. . .

Myths about the gods show them to be very human in their actions, and they not only control but also model how human mortals should behave in society.

. . .

How do these observations about myth help us to understand the social roles of women in history? Let's look at some myths about women in these terms.

. . .

Myths that molded attitudes toward women include the myth of Atalanta and the myths of Homeric goddesses.

. . .

These suggest the attitudes that women are inferior to men and that they control men's actions.

. . .

Myths that preserve social order include the worship of Athena in Greek society.

. . .

This myth suggests that attitudes toward women in society are in accord with divine order and cannot change.

. . .

Therefore, we can see that the study of myths can help us to understand the social roles of women in history and why those roles have been hard to change.

. . .

Perhaps by understanding how myth functions to create and perpetuate women's roles in history we can begin to see how those roles can change in the future.

The basic reasoning in the enthymeme has been used to generate each of these structural outlines, and others could be generated from that same reasoning. None of these outlines is complete, of course. Each of the ideas that will make up parts of the essay must themselves be developed further, as the ellipses indicate. But each of these outlines might form the basis of a well-structured essay, one in which the structure develops out of the reasoning.

If the basic reasoning is the same in each case, then how do these three structures differ? Outline 1 starts out with the thesis itself. Next it asserts and illustrates the first part of the because clause, and then the second part, using each example to explain the implications of the because clause. When the explanation of the reasoning is complete, so is the essay, because the conclusion has already been asserted at the outset.

Outline 2, however, does not assert the conclusion until the end of the essay. It begins, instead, with the examples, as if teasing the reader with these interesting details but not saying what their significance is until the reader is well into the essay. After the examples have gotten the reader's interest, the essay asks a question about them that is designed to lead into the reasoning of the because clause. The question at issue is then posed, and the reasoning that has been developed is used to answer it in the form of a concluding assertion.

Outline 3 begins with statements that are intended to show why the question at issue is important, to raise the issue in such a way that the problem being solved is immediately clear. The essay then explains each part of the because clause, and only after that does it go into any examples. The examples are used to further explain the because clause, and the conclusion is asserted. A further consequence of the reasoning (one that was not necessarily explicit in the enthymeme) is then asserted, as a way of ending the essay on a strong note.

My choice of which structure to use, or whether to think of another, would depend on which parts of the reasoning needed the most emphasis, on what kinds of information I wanted to include, on what I imagine to be my reader's needs and interests in this issue, and on what kind of effect I wanted to create for the reader. Any essay structured in each of the above ways would differ slightly in emphasis, in detail, and in both its initial impact and its final effect on the reader.

In each of the structures, the enthymeme also led me into further reasoning. Often new reasons had to be developed to support the explicit parts of the enthymeme. In this case some of those reasons were inductive (the actual myths that enabled conclusions to be drawn about the function of myth in general). As in any inductive argument, the number of examples was limited somewhat arbitrarily. Any of these structures could have contained further examples. The adequacy of the examples, the amount of development each one needs, and the range of my knowledge or research could affect the decision to use more or fewer examples. The idea outline generated by the enthymeme is like an accordion file: It expands to fit what needs to go into it at any point. If details or examples are added to such a structure, the writer knows where they belong.

As the reasoning of the enthymeme expands to become a structure, further needs may arise. In the example, the reasoning depended on assertions that themselves required support. An essay contains more complex lines of reasoning than can be contained in the initial enthymeme. One reason becomes a minithesis that requires support in the form of another enthymeme. This is why I call the thesis statement a structural enthymeme, to distinguish it from all the other enthymemes that any essay might contain as parts of its reasoning. The structural enthymeme contains the whole argument and consequently generates the needs for subarguments, minitheses, and other local enthymemes. The result is an embroidery of reasons, stitched to form the overall design only sketched by the thesis statement and outline of ideas.

Among the needs that may arise as an enthymeme is expanded into a structure may be the need for examples, the need for definitions, the need for qualifications, the need for factual evidence, the need for explanations (perhaps by way of analogy or anecdote), the need for authoritative testimony, or the need to acknowledge or to refute potential counterarguments. It is impossible to say in advance whether an essay must respond to any of these needs, because they arise as the essay unfolds in relation to the nature of the case being made and the audience.

I will illustrate how another enthymeme may generate different structures, this time showing how such needs might be addressed in different places. Suppose I have drafted this enthymeme to represent the argument I wish to make:

> *Education about date rape would reduce the incidence of rapes on college campuses*

> *because*

> *informing students that all forced sex is rape would make them less likely to force an acquaintance or date to have sex against her will.*

I have based my reasoning on an assumption something like this:

> *Anything that would make students less likely to force an acquaintance or date to have sex against her will would reduce the incidence of rapes on college campuses.*

That assumption is one that I may or may not be able to take for granted, depending on my audience.

Here is one way I might develop this reasoning into a structure:

Outline 1

What is rape?

. . .

The law defines it as "the forcing of sexual intercourse upon a person against that person's will or without that person's permission."

. . .

The law does not say that it's a rape only if there is a gun or knife, or a threat of physical violence. It does not limit rape to the case of a deranged pervert breaking into a stranger's apartment.

. . .

The law does not say that it isn't rape if the man is the woman's husband or if he has bought her dinner or if he has been to bed with her in the past.

. . .

In fact, as many as 80 percent of the rapes reported to police have been committed by someone the woman knows, often someone whom she knows very well. Experts call this "date rape" or "acquaintance rape."

. . .

But many women do not report such rapes because they do not believe that what their friend or lover has done is the same as rape. They suffer in silence and do not get help.

. . .

And many men say they do not believe that the use of some force with a woman who says "no," or sex with a woman who has had so much to drink that she cannot resist, is rape.

. . .

This ignorance—of the law and of what women and men should expect from each other as equal partners in sexual decisions—is the cause of many rapes.
. . .

These are rapes that could be avoided if education informed people of the law and changed people's way of thinking about sexual relationships.

Here is a structure that begins with a question of definition that is part of the overall attempt to answer a question of policy. The definition is needed because it is what the term *education* in the thesis refers to. The essay need not have started with that definition, but it is an effective way to work into the development of the because clause. The structure also incorporates several other parts that were not part of the enthymeme but turn out to be needed as the reasoning develops. Facts, of course, are introduced to support and to clarify the premise asserted in the because clause. Authorities are cited to add credibility to the facts. When the essay turns toward showing that women and men are ignorant of those facts, further opportunities arise. To show that the assertions are true, the writer could add the authority of surveys or more experts. Or, to give the reader a sense of the immediacy of the assertions and to illustrate just how often women or men misunderstand what rape is, the writer could add anecdotes or examples of events that illustrate rapes of these kinds.

A writer's structural choices may depend on the audience. In a different argumentative situation (as perceived by the writer), the same enthymeme could generate a very different structure and a very different kind of essay.

Outline 2

We have a serious problem on this campus.
. . .

Here are some documented cases of rape on this campus in the previous two months, told to me by the head counselor.
. . .

Tell about Bud expecting to have sex with Miriam because he bought her an expensive dinner. She said "no," but he convinced her that she "owed" it to him. She blames herself.
. . .

Tell about Jesse getting drunk and passing out at the party, when house members then had sex with her. She is about to sue the fraternity and the university.
. . .

Tell about Edna who has finally sought counseling to get out of an abusive marriage. Her husband frequently threatens her with more violence if she does not have sex, but she says she doesn't think this is rape.
. . .

Tell about Teri who resisted when her date got a little rough and who was then raped. She didn't seek help for three weeks because her friends told her it happens all the time and she should toughen up. But she was too distressed about it to study.

. . .

These are just four of ten similar instances.

. . .

Here are statistics showing that for every rape reported to anyone, ten go unreported.

. . .

That means that there were probably twenty such rapes on this campus in the last two months.

. . .

So, as college deans, you must begin the date rape education campaign now or you will not be acting responsibly toward our women students.

Here is a situation (an exhortation to the college deans) in which all that needs to be done in the essay is to demonstrate the scope of the problem and its seriousness. Most of the actual reasoning, which is implicit, is undeveloped in relation to the citation of case histories and expert testimony. The deans do not have to be told that these are cases of rape according to the law's definition. They are presumed to know that. They do not need to be told that education is needed to overcome the ignorance of those who commit such rapes or fall victim to them. But they do need to be exhorted to act, and the structure is designed to have that effect.

A third possible structure based on the reasoning of this enthymeme follows.

Outline 3

In a recent case reported in the news, a jury acquitted a man of rape on the grounds that the woman was dressed provocatively and was therefore "asking for it."

. . .

Such a case illustrates that attitudes toward rape are slow to change. Some people still think that a woman can be blamed when a man forces her to have sex.

. . .

Even the widespread success of the feminist movement has not changed many people's minds.

. . .

This is clear from the fact that most rapes are committed by acquaintances, and even dates. Contrary to public opinion, rapes are most likely to be committed by the nice young man next door and not the armed stranger in the night. Attitudes in society, not deranged individuals, seem to be the cause.

. . .

*One reason seems to be that young men and women practice courtship in
ways that enforce the attitude that rape is an accepted form of sex.*
. . .

*Men are traditionally the aggressors in courtship situations, whereas women
are passive.*
. . .

Men spend their money whereas women are supposed to be grateful.
. . .

Men believe that women who say they do not want sex don't really mean it.
. . .

*Of course, it is true that not all men believe such things. But enough do to
make the problem widespread, and even those who don't often find that peer
pressure to "score" is too strong to resist.*
. . .

*Such beliefs result in some men forcing women to have sex because the men
think it is consistent with male/female roles.*
. . .

Beliefs are not inevitable. They can be changed.
. . .

*College is one place where young men and women can be asked to confront
their attitudes and change them.*
. . .

*Therefore, our campus is an appropriate place to conduct an educational
campaign to reduce the number of rapes committed by men who do not believe
that forced sex in some circumstances is rape.*
. . .

*Maybe then some of society's attitudes will change more quickly than they
seem to have done.*

This structure may be more suited to an audience of peers who may not consider acquaintance rape to be rape. Because this essay plan develops the idea
of attitudes (or the "belief" term of the because clause), it can begin with a more
indirect anecdote and it need not offer as many examples. Other ways of raising the issue of people's attitudes are possible. The essay will also contain one
section that qualifies its statements about the beliefs of men, to try to answer a
potential reader's objection that the generalizations are too large and sweeping. The essay later raises the issue of education (and college) to offer a positive solution to the problem for this audience.

The purpose of these examples is to show how an enthymeme can
guide the writer in developing a structure for an essay. But the enthymeme
does not predetermine the structure. As the essay must somehow fulfill the

basic reasoning of the enthymeme, it must have certain parts. But the order they come in and anything else the writer might choose to include to develop the reasoning are still up to the writer, based on the perceived needs of the audience. Such decisions will differ from argument to argument. No model can tell you in advance what parts your essay must have and what order they must go in. Because the enthymeme stands for the specific argument you wish to make, you can use it to guide your thinking about the specific decisions you face when structuring the parts of an essay. A structure generated by the conditions of a well-reasoned enthymeme will be more likely to move the reader from beginning to end than one that is based on a prefabricated form or one that develops aimlessly.

From Structure to Essay: An Analysis

The kind of inquiry that has enabled you to compose a sound enthymeme that represents what you want to say will also have provided you with many ideas for your essay, and those ideas will find a place within the structure you have generated. The words of the sentences also will follow from the clear sense of purpose and structure that you have discovered in this process, although you may sometimes have to struggle to find them. No principles or rules can account for how the right word suddenly enters your mind. If your mind is focused on what you want to say at any given point of your essay, you will find the words.

To review the process of moving from structural enthymeme to idea outline to fully developed essay, let's look at the decisions that seem to have been made by a student who wrote an essay about the ethical responsibilities of scientists. Let's assume that class discussion of issues about science (such as those found debated in the bioethics controversies in Part II, beginning on page 287) turned to the question of whether scientists are morally responsible for bad uses of their research, and if so how scientists ought to be educated. Some students in class thought scientists could not be held responsible, and that led one student to write an enthymeme in response to that discussion:

> *Scientists are responsible for the bad effects of their research, because they ought to be able to predict those effects.*

That enthymeme was discussed in a thesis workshop in class, and other students objected that it did not seem to follow; why does being able to predict a result make one responsible for it? The assumption did not seem to provide the necessary common ground. The student decided that the only way to get scientists to think about their responsibility for effects they can predict is to provide scientists with an ethical education. Rethinking his enthymeme, he came up with this one, trying to address the question of consequence that seemed to him to be at issue:

> *Ethics classes for scientists will teach them to weigh potentially*
> *harmful effects of their research against the potential good because*
> *raising questions of right and wrong in such classes will provide an*
> *alternative perspective.*

Another revision seemed necessary; this enthymeme does not seem to be precise enough. The student thought about exactly what he meant by "alternative perspective," and then rewrote the enthymeme again:

> *Ethics classes for scientists will teach them to weigh the potential*
> *harmful effects of their research against the potential good, because*
> *raising questions of right and wrong in relation to science will confront*
> *them with the compassionate feelings of other people.*

The process of revision that the student went through was based on many considerations, prompted perhaps by the criteria on pages 53 and 78, but motivated by the felt need to get the ideas just right for the audience of classmates with whom he had engaged in discussion. Feeling that this reasoning said just what he wanted to say, and what his audience needed to hear, he decided to try out a possible structural outline based on this enthymeme.

An essay structured according to the logic of this enthymeme might begin by conveying to the reader that there is a problem to be solved. The question at issue is implicit in the thesis, but it requires explanation nonetheless. What makes the issue an issue? Such a consideration seems to provide the best place to start. Thus, the first thing the essay might do is to state the problem in such terms. Here's the outline the student began:

> *The problem of whether scientists should be ethically responsible for the*
> *harmful applications of their research is one that concerns us all.*
> . . .
>
> *Even if someone else makes the application, the scientist is responsible*
> *to some degree if he or she is aware of the possibility of harmful*
> *effects. Thus, one aspect of the problem is to find a way for*
> *scientists to consider their options by weighing harmful effects*
> *against beneficial ones.*
> . . .
>
> *It should not be assumed that scientists, schooled in objective methods*
> *of research, necessarily know how to do this.*
> . . .
>
> *Thus, it may be a question of how scientists are taught. Might the*
> *addition of ethics classes for scientists enable them to learn how*
> *to weigh harmful and good effects, as a way of thinking about*
> *their responsibilities?*

As part of the introduction to an essay (the student didn't know yet how many sentences or even paragraphs that introduction might take), these ideas function to develop the need for the thesis and to promise an answer. He next considered how to connect this to the terms of the because clause:

> *The answer depends on understanding what kind of knowledge is required to be able to weigh harmful effects against good ones.*
> . . .
> *What does* harmful *mean in this case? It means effects that hurt people.*
> . . .
> *Thus, if scientists are to weigh the harm done to other human beings, they must be able to feel compassion for others' suffering. Feeling compassion is what makes it possible for one to know how harmful an effect might be.*

At this point, the assumption implicit in the enthymeme has been proposed. The structure now requires linking this assumption with the remaining terms of the because clause. So the student continued the outline:

> *How do people become aware of their compassionate feelings for others? If people are confronted with their feelings about the welfare of others, they cannot help but think about the extent of their compassion. What kind of activities bring about this confrontation?*
> . . .
> *Asking questions of right and wrong. Questions that require a choice between a right course of action and a wrong one will involve one in examining compassionate interest in the welfare of others.*

At this point, he saw that the enthymeme was pointing him to his conclusion, and his outline took this step:

> *Raising such questions of right and wrong about matters of science would be the aim of an ethics class for scientists.*
> . . .
> *Such a class would, therefore, enable scientists to learn to weigh potential harmful effects against potential benefits of their research and help to make them see their responsibilities.*

The enthymeme has helped this writer generate an outline of ideas that progresses from problem to solution. This basic line of reasoning resulted from introducing the terms of the enthymeme and making connections among them, in an order that the reader might be expected to follow.

This idea outline does not yet constitute the prose of an essay. The outlined statements merely represent a rational backbone for an essay, yet to be fleshed out with further connections, further development, and further support. The outline of ideas that is generated by the enthymeme must now generate an even more thorough treatment, in the actual prose of the essay, according to the needs of the reader.

What does the reader need to know at each point in order to understand, to follow, and to agree? The writer must provide the answers—by imagining potential responses that readers might make as they read from sentence to sentence. A writer might decide to provide a definition, to explain a concept, to provide an illustrative example, to cite the writing of others, or to bring in additional reasons in support of some claim. All such additions to the basic structure might be provided in response to a reader's potential needs, at points where the reader might be imagined to ask "What's that mean?" or "Can you show me an example?" or "Why should I believe that?" Anticipating such questions, when they are reasonable, is one way in which the writer can decide whether any of the innumerable "things to be said" should be said in *this* essay, and if so, where those things should go. The writer is responsible to try to see his or her own argument from the point of view of a reader who may not already agree with it and to consider whether good reasons may also be found to support opposing ideas. This consideration helped the writer to develop a reasonable thesis in the first place. It can now help the writer to develop a better essay, by enabling him or her to deal with objections as they arise within the essay's developing structure.

Based on such considerations, and following the outline of ideas generated by the enthymeme, the student composed an essay. A few rough drafts later, it looked like this:

THE NEED FOR AN ETHICAL EDUCATION FOR SCIENTISTS

1   Scientists are taught to discover "truth" by conducting experiments in an objective manner, without allowing personal feelings to affect the outcome. Yet this view of science has often come under attack, when the possibility exists that objectivity may do more harm than good. When the application of scientific knowledge creates harm, many are willing to blame the scientists, or at least to argue that the scientist shares in the ethical responsibility for these applications.

2   It would be ridiculous to assume that all scientists share in this responsibility equally. Sir Isaac Newton, for instance, cannot be blamed for the applications that the scientists and technicians who developed the first atomic weapon made of his basic laws of physics. It is interesting, though, that Albert Einstein, who built his theories on the basis of Newton's, expressed regret about his contribution to the atomic age. The scientists who worked on the Manhattan project have recently expressed even more sense of responsibility for their more direct contributions to atomic weaponry. Thus, the question of responsibility seems to be a matter of degree, depending on the closeness of the scientist to the application itself. It seems reasonable to think that scientists share a greater burden of ethical responsibility if they are more able to predict the specific harmful application and its likelihood. Newton thought he was disclosing the wonders of God's creation. But the Los Alamos scientists were fully aware that they were working on a bomb.

3   These scientists faced a choice. They could contribute their knowledge to uncovering the secrets of the atom, or they could withhold their support for this project. Some chose to participate because, as scientists, they desired to increase knowledge, while others were motivated by the patriotic goal of winning the war by any means. Some chose to stay home, or even to protest

the activities of the Los Alamos scientists. These scientists all made ethical decisions because they knew that their research could lead to specific harmful applications.

4   Although responsibility must be shared with those who choose to make the application, it does seem that scientists who make a choice to conduct research in full knowledge of the potential beneficial and harmful applications have accepted some ethical responsibility for themselves. They have made their choice by weighing the beneficial applications against the harmful ones, by deciding to risk the possibility of one outcome against the likelihood of another. This kind of decision does not depend on how much one understands about science—although scientific knowledge does help one to predict the likelihood of a result—as much as it depends on being able to determine right and wrong. Scientists have ethical responsibility not as scientists, but as human beings with consciences. They are no more or less able to know what is morally right than anyone else. Yet, because of the power given to scientists by virtue of their ability to create knowledge, they seem to have a special obligation to choose whether to conduct certain kinds of research.

5   Modern society invests scientists with this power, yet it does not seem to do anything special to teach them how to exercise it conscientiously. Vast resources are used to ensure that scientists are good at practicing science, but very little is done to ensure that they become better at making ethical choices. In a world in which the impact of science on the quality of people's lives is enormous, and especially after recent history has shown us how scientists do make ethical choices, it seems obvious that thought should be given to how a scientific education might prepare future scientists for making ethical decisions.

6   Although ethics classes for scientists seems like a good idea, it isn't necessarily clear how such classes might actually make scientists better able to decide whether or not to conduct research based on weighing potentially harmful effects against beneficial ones. A commitment to the idea of adding ethics classes to the scientific curriculum would be easier to make if we were sure that such classes would succeed in making future scientists more capable of thinking about their ethical responsibilities. The question then becomes how such classes would make a difference: Would ethics classes for scientists teach them to make ethical choices?

7   To answer this question, we might consider what kind of knowledge is required by anyone who is able to weigh harmful effects against beneficial ones. How does one learn to think about the relative importance of good and bad outcomes, when both might result? This is a difficult problem, and I cannot solve it to my own complete satisfaction. I think there is a way to begin thinking about it, however, by asking what we mean in this case by *harmful* and *beneficial*.

8   *Harmful* and *beneficial* must refer to effects that hurt or benefit people. They are terms that refer to what people feel about their own conditions. Now, it may be possible to try to measure those conditions by some scientific means, but such efforts will always impose an outside view on feelings that only an individual can really know. What I mean is that *harmful* and *beneficial* could

be defined so that they refer to statistical conditions: Society is harmed if unemployment rates rise, or society is benefited if the gypsy moth is eradicated. These are ways of thinking about harm and benefit as objectively measured characteristics, and by using such definitions, people's actual feelings are abstracted out of the picture. But another way of approaching *harm* and *benefit* is to see them as matters of personal suffering or personal satisfaction. Each person's actual suffering as a result of unemployment will be different; each person's actual benefit as a result of employment will be different, too. Eradicating the gypsy moth may save an industry, but the degree of actual suffering caused by the elimination of that industry is different from the amount of money gained or lost in the process.

9   This distinction helps us to see that scientific methods, such as the study of gain and loss in statistical terms, might provide one way of weighing harm and benefit, but this way does not necessarily produce the ability to measure harm in terms of human suffering. The way in which suffering is really known is not through statistics and balance sheets, but through compassion. Compassion—perhaps an old-fashioned-sounding word to some—is the ability to feel another's hurt or pleasure and to understand it from the inside. If an action results in suffering for individuals, the actual degree of its harmfulness will be unknown to anyone who cannot feel that suffering by empathizing compassionately with the victim.

10   If scientists are to learn to weigh the harm done to other human beings as a foreseeable result of the application of their research, they must be able to feel other's suffering compassionately. This sounds self-evident, but it is easy to forget that scientists may be more inclined than others, because of how they are trained, to view suffering from the objective, "bottom line" perspective. But they need not be. Scientists can become aware of their feelings for others in the same way nonscientists do, by being confronted directly with their feelings for others. Science education doesn't necessarily create this kind of confrontation, but other kinds of learning situations do. This sort of confrontation exists whenever students are asked to choose between right and wrong actions in particular situations where harm and benefit would result. In such situations, more than the likelihood of a specific outcome is at stake; one must also determine how much suffering one is willing to tolerate in exchange for how much benefit.

11   Consider this example: If I am invited to go cycling with a friend, I might object to her refusal to wear a protective helmet. I would face an ethical decision. Should I refuse to go along unless she agrees to wear one? It's her own business to make up her mind, but it's my business whether to encourage her to risk hurting herself. She might say that the risk of having an accident is very slight. That's true, but the suffering that might result for her could be horrible. I have read about such accidents. My ethical responsibility, if that suffering were to result, would be great, I feel, because the suffering would be great. Thus, my decision would be based on three factors—my ability to foresee the possibility of an accident, the likelihood of that possibility, *and* my compassionate understanding of the potential suffering. We all face similar decisions all the time—whether to let a friend drive drunk, for example, or whether to insist that our passengers use seat belts.

12   An education in science would presumably enable scientists to consider the first two factors, because scientific thinking can be applied to predicting effects and their likelihood. But an ethical education of some kind is necessary to enable one to consider the third.

13   Ethics classes for scientists could present such choices in relation to actual kinds of research. Issues in medicine, for instance, such as whether certain kinds of human experimentation should be used, or issues in genetic engineering, would present students with the kinds of confrontation that I have described. Presented with a choice of actions, students would have to examine their own compassionate feelings in order to answer the question of whether the suffering would be worth the benefits. Scientists would not learn that the answers are easy, but they might come to a greater understanding of the kinds of ethical choices they will face in their research careers. This may not prevent harmful effects from occurring, but it might enable scientists to recognize their individual ethical responsibilities. In a society in which scientific knowledge is necessary to solve problems created by science, this is the least that we must hope for.

You may think this is a good argument or a poor one, but at this point let's suspend that judgment and ask *how* this student got from the sketchy structure generated earlier to this more fully developed essay.

Analyzing What the Writer Did

Writing is a process of discovery, and discovery happens within constraints. Writing combines freedom and control. The student's essay illustrates this, even though we do not see what actually went on as the drafting progressed. As the student's thinking developed from enthymeme to structure and from structure to essay, new discoveries resulted at each stage, and they were prompted by the new kinds of questions that each new task presented. In the process of trying to develop the smaller units of the composition out of a clear understanding of the larger units, the writer discovers new possibilities and new challenges. This is inevitable, because a writer cannot conceive of a complete, fully developed essay all at once; an essay must be built up part by part. The process of determining the reasoning and the structure before drafting is not meant to reduce the writer's freedom. Nothing could do that; there are always new possibilities to be discovered. It is meant to direct the necessary choices toward a consistent and intelligent end.

In going over the essay, in comparison with the outline of ideas, we can see where some of these challenges occurred and how the student responded to them. Notice first of all that the essay takes four paragraphs at the beginning to get through the first two structural steps, introducing the problem of whether scientists should be ethically responsible as a subject for inquiry. Why? The writer probably had to back up so far because the *nature* of that problem has to be understood in a certain way in order to prepare for later elements of the essay. The first paragraph not only introduces and explains the general problem but also speaks of it in terms of what the scientist is "taught," which will be a matter of concern later in the essay, as will the idea of "objectivity." Notice how this paragraph introduces dialectical distinctions that are needed for this discussion: *objective/subjective, harm/good, knowledge/application, blame/exoneration.*

The second paragraph attempts to clarify the kind of responsibility under discussion by using examples that also serve to introduce the need to solve the general problem. A new distinction is introduced into this paragraph, one the outline had not specifically required, but that the progression of the prose now seems to call for: Not only is responsibility said to be a matter of degree, as in the second step of the structural plan, but degree itself is determined by the scientist's closeness to the application. This detail occurs, we presume, not only to explain why the writer thinks it is a matter of degree but also to answer a potential objection, which the writer has anticipated: How can a scientist like Newton be responsible at all, even if he could imagine some kinds of applications?

Certain details of these paragraphs are included to clarify the writer's purpose to the reader. The whole of the third paragraph seems to have resulted from the writer's sense that the idea of ethical choice may not be clear to the reader. Thus, the writer feels a need to expand on the example of scientists who did know what the consequences of their research might be. This example demonstrates for the reader that the problem is not a simple one of choosing between good and evil, because it involves scientists who had to weigh their choice between conflicting goods. Thus, the writer has prepared the reader to accept the next part of the structure, the idea that a way must be found for scientists to "consider their options by weighing harmful effects against beneficial ones." This idea is made explicit in paragraph five, but is implicit nonetheless in three and four. The writer has, in fact, departed from the order of the ideas in the outline, because new relationships among thoughts developed as the writing unfolded. The outline would call for saying at this point that "objective methods of research" do not necessarily teach scientists how to make this choice, but the writer has already made us aware of this and, in paragraph four, the writer goes into a variation on this idea:

> This kind of decision does not depend on how much one understands about science— although scientific knowledge does help one to predict the likelihood of a result—as much as it depends on being able to determine right and wrong. Scientists have ethical responsibility not as scientists, but as human beings with consciences. . . . Yet, because of the power given to scientists by virtue of their ability to create knowledge, they seem to have a special obligation to choose whether to conduct certain kinds of research.

Here, the writer has developed new ideas, within the structure as planned and even *because* of the demands created by that structure. The writer is still thinking about the argument, and these new ideas emerge as a result. The new dialectical distinction between using scientific knowledge to determine the likelihood of a result and using some other kind of knowledge to weigh good and harmful results is not part of the logic of the enthymeme, and it is not an element in the idea outline. But it is to become a major feature of the essay as it progresses, one that supports the line of reasoning.

In the fifth paragraph, the idea of the scientist's "power" becomes a transition to the need for education, returning to the structure of the idea outline. This helps the writer make a transition from the question at issue to the writer's initial discussion of the thesis, but it also functions to add an emotional appeal. Note the special appeal to the quality of our lives and how that appeal is strengthened by the writer's understated return to the earlier example of "recent history," reminding us of the nuclear threat without hitting us over the heads with it.

The sixth and seventh paragraphs follow the structural outline and move the argument forward. In explaining the next stages of the line of reasoning, these paragraphs also attempt to respond to a critical reader's potential doubts. They are functional paragraphs, leading the reader to the next crucial step in the logic, but they also defend the need for going on to that step. "A commitment to the idea of adding ethics classes to the scientific curriculum would be easier to make if. . . ." This prepares the reader for an answer at the same time that it asks the reader to speculate along with the writer before rejecting the possibility. In the seventh paragraph, the writer sees a need to make a confession.

> *This is a difficult problem, and I cannot solve it to my own complete satisfaction. I think there is a way to begin thinking about it, however, by . . .*

The writer has become aware of the possibility that a reader might say something like this: "Who are you to be answering a question that has confused people for centuries? It's not as simple as you think." And the writer wants the reader to know that he is speculating, not trying to cram his belief down anyone's throat.

It is in paragraphs eight and nine that the new dialectical distinction between what can and cannot be known by scientific means becomes part of the writer's logic. (A reader of the essay would be surprised to learn that this distinction was not planned, but emerged during the composition, as the necessity for it arose.) The distinction works within the writer's logic by helping to explain what *harmful* and *beneficial* mean—a predetermined move on the writer's part, but one not fully thought-out when the structural outline was written. It also smooths the way for the introduction of an important new term: *compassion*. The structural outline introduced this term abruptly; the essay makes its introduction seem more natural. The distinction between what scientific methods can teach and what they cannot is brought forward again, in paragraph ten, as a way of returning to the question of education, and the next term in the logical structure, *confrontation,* is addressed.

When paragraph ten ends, the writer seems to sense the reader's potential confusion. *Confrontation* is a pretty abstract word here, and the reader may feel that it needs clarification. Paragraph eleven attempts to bring the essay back down to earth a bit and to make the meaning of *confrontation* come alive.

The writer creates a believable example of everyday confrontation with a question of right and wrong. The bicycle example also clarifies the writer's earlier dialectical distinction between scientific and ethical ways of knowing.

> *Thus, my decision would be based on three factors—my ability to foresee the possibility of an accident, the likelihood of that possibility, and my compassionate understanding of the potential suffering.*

The example also takes us back to earlier parts of the essay. It reminds us that in being able to predict the outcome, we are more like the Los Alamos scientists than we are like Newton—"closer" to the outcome and hence responsible to a greater degree. In being able to calculate the likelihood of an accident, we are thinking like a scientist. In having compassion, we are able to confront the ethical nature of the decision most fully. Paragraph twelve explicitly connects the example with those principles. Thus, the writer's case has been well served by an example at this point. It adds reality to the abstract reasoning.

The last paragraph completes the logic of the enthymeme and the structure of the argument. Further examples are brought in to show the reader that the thesis is applicable to a variety of specific issues. The logic is summarized, but in the process the writer introduces a qualification that is once again not present in the idea outline. The writer is again reminding readers of the complexity of the issue and putting the thesis into that context: "This is not the final solution," it seems to say, "but a path to follow." To prevent the reader from leaving the essay with a false impression, the writer adds a final sentence that goes beyond the thesis and yet shows how the thesis might apply to our thinking about the issue. "Don't get me wrong," it seems to say, "I don't think science is bad. We need science. But we need ethics, too, if we are to make science succeed." The writer's final idea—thought up in the process of composing—helps to make the thesis believable, not by continuing to give reasons for believing it, but by relating it to the hope for a better future that the writer and the reader are assumed to share.

This analysis isn't meant to explain why this writer included every sentence or every word. No analysis could explain how a writer makes such decisions. Sometimes the answer to why a writer has done it one way and not another is simply "because it felt right." The best basis for making such a judgment, as this book has argued, is your own clear sense of your intention: what you want to say and how you plan to support it; what you want the reader to understand and how you plan to take the reader there. The thesis, the enthymeme, and the outline of ideas that you work out for this purpose will not guarantee answers or make composing easier. But they will bring the process under greater control than would otherwise be the case.

Although we could measure the success of this essay according to some absolute scale of quality and find it lacking, we can also see it as the result of a writer's struggle to come to a significant understanding and to structure and clarify that understanding for others. This process often leads to a new understanding by the writer, too. From here, the student might reconsider the issue, rethink the thesis, restructure the argument, or simply revise the prose, and produce a better essay on the same subject; or he might use everything learned in the process of writing this essay—much of it unconsciously—to face the challenges of a new one.

Questions for Thought, Discussion, and Writing

1. If you have written a structural enthymeme to use as the basis for your next essay, use the criteria on p. 78 to revise it, if necessary.

2. Having done so, list some of the things that an essay written for this enthymeme makes you responsible to do. Then write an outline of ideas that develops the reasoning contained in the enthymeme. The sentences in this outline should represent the stages in the reasoning suggested by your enthymeme, covering the terms and the relationships you have asserted among them.

3. Where in the developing reasoning might your argument require, or be improved by, any of the following?
   a. further reasons
   b. dialectical distinctions
   c. examples/illustrations
   d. data
   e. qualifications
   f. acknowledgments of counterarguments
   g. analogies
   h. descriptions
   i. anything else?

4. Based on this planning, draft your essay. Don't be afraid to change any part of the plan if you discover a better way while you are composing. Don't be afraid to try out anything that seems right; you can delete, tear up, rewrite, or move anything you want to.

5. After reading an argumentative essay, in Part II or in some other source, try to reconstruct the structural enthymeme that represents the main line of reasoning developed in the argument: the conclusion and the major reason (or reasons) offered to support it. Based on that enthymeme, how does the structure of the writing correspond to parts of that enthymeme? What accounts for the order in which the parts of the essay are arranged? Are there unnecessary parts? Are necessary parts missing? Try to analyze the author's choices in terms of the needs of the audience, as we did in the analysis of the student essay in this chapter.

Revising and Editing

Revision and Style as Rethinking

All writers revise. If writing is a process of discovering ideas, then we change what we have written for the same reasons that we sometimes change our minds: New ideas alter our way of thinking about old ideas. But even if a draft of an essay does not lead to different ways of viewing the subject, revision is still necessary because, after honest reflection, the way in which our writing emerges is not necessarily the way we would like it to appear. In this sense revision occurs throughout the process of writing; even rewriting one's enthymeme to make it work better is revision, and so is rethinking what one wants to argue. Revision takes place as soon as one has an idea and begins to think about it.

So, even though I have waited to discuss revision more fully until Chapter 7 of this book, it is misleading to think of revision as the last stage of the writing process, because writers revise continuously. Revision takes place whenever a writer replaces one phrase or sentence with another, adds a word or phrase or sentence or paragraph, cuts out some part of a composition, or moves writing from one part of an essay to another. These actions can take place at any time during composing, or as a separate activity after a draft is completed. Revision is recomposing, and as such it is simply a matter of changing one's mind about any aspect of the writing. There is no "right" time for changing one's mind; it can happen at any time the writer discovers a better way.

Rethinking your choices may lead to the discovery of new ones. If writing is an act of taking responsibility for ideas, then revising acknowledges that responsibility as an ongoing obligation. Once a word or sentence or whole essay is committed to paper, you assume the responsibility of reassessing, and changing if necessary, what is written. Where does this responsibility come from? In the terms of my discussion in Chapter 1, the need for revision is linked to one's membership in a discourse community. The need to advance understanding within such a community brings with it the responsibility to earn one's conclusions, and this is possible only if those conclusions, and the reasons that support them, are communicated to other members of that community with as much clarity and effectiveness as the writer can create. Clarity and effectiveness require accommodating one's sentences to the reader's needs, just as reasoning requires accommodating one's argument to the reader's assumptions. Both careful reasoning and careful revising are an attempt to base understanding on the common ground between a writer and the community of inquirers to which the writer feels responsible.

If revision is always possible, it's fair to ask: When is a piece of writing ever finished? A time must come, of course, when a deadline is reached, an assignment is due, or a piece of writing is simply abandoned in favor of something else. In that sense, writing is finished when it is submitted to its intended audience. Often, someone has imposed a deadline or a due date. Of course, the final product ought to be as good as you can make it, given the time available, but this does not mean that the final product is finished, in the sense of no longer having room for improvement. Writing may never reach that mythical point of perfection, simply because it is always subject to change. Thus, the decision to stop revising may be somewhat arbitrary, based on your sense that further change would not substantially improve the writing. There comes a time when it is more important to get the writing into the hands of its audience than to continue to tinker with it.

As I said earlier, writing itself encourages discoveries. This means that revision is necessary to be sure that all parts of a composition continue to work together, to satisfy your purpose, as that purpose refines itself during writing. Writers frequently discover that after they have finished a draft of a composition, they must return to the beginning, to change aspects of the writing to fit a new sense of purpose that has evolved. This does not necessarily mean that the thesis itself has changed, but that the writer's attitude, or even degree of conviction, may have changed the writer's approach to that thesis. Revision enables you to consider whether the whole essay, as written, consistently satisfies the needs of its thesis.

Obstacles to Revision

Revision is difficult without **critical distance**, the perspective required to see writing *as writing* and separate from one's self. Revising may sometimes seem harder than writing because we cannot separate ourselves from our thoughts enough to know whether they would be clear to someone who encounters them only through the words that we have written. Our own words seem clear to us because they are intimately related to the thoughts we had while composing them. We may miss many opportunities to improve our own writing simply because as we reread it we are engaged in the same mental process we went through as we wrote it. Yet a reader lacks this intimacy with the mental process that led to those words. Therefore, it is necessary to achieve distance from the writing, somehow, to see it *as if* for the first time. Of course, our own words can never be entirely new to us as we reread them. What, then, can you do to achieve as much distance as possible?

The best source of distance is time. If it is possible to return to a piece of writing after a long period of time, its faults become more obvious. Allowing yourself the leisure to forget how the sentences sound, to let the words slip out of the mental grooves that they have forged in the short-term memory, enables you to read them more critically. There is no better source of critical distance than a desk drawer, where a draft can be put away and returned to after enough time has gone by. But no one has enough time, of course, to make this practical. There is a lesson in this, however, that all writers can apply, even when the time available for composing is short: Don't procrastinate. No matter how much time is available, you should take advantage of all of it, and this means a certain amount of time between drafts to let the distance between you and your words increase. Returning to a draft of an essay after having done something else for a day or two—or a week or two, if possible—can provide just enough critical distance to make revision effective.

Lacking time, you can create other sources of distance. Writers are known to do some wacky things just to alienate themselves from their own prose so that they can revise it from a new point of view. I heard about one writer who tapes his manuscript to a distant wall and revises while reading it through binoculars. A friend of mine revises by turning her manuscript upside-down to read it. Another reads her writing in a mirror. I don't advise any of these tactics; these writers obviously worked them out to suit their own needs. But I can suggest two practices that are less extreme but effective: First, *read your writing to yourself out loud.* Just the sound of the words is often enough to reveal flaws that you might otherwise miss. The rhythm and balance of your sentences can often be improved after you have heard them. Second, *have someone else read your writing out loud while you listen.* This not only will allow you to hear what you have written, but also will reveal trouble spots wherever the reader stumbles or gets the intonation of your meaning wrong.

A second obstacle to revision is an unwillingness to allow anyone to see our writing until it is finished. Perhaps we fear the possibility of negative judgments. Perhaps we want others to read what we have written only so that they will praise us. But such attitudes are not helpful to a writer. It is especially important to develop a positive attitude toward the honest criticism of others. By seeking this criticism, we learn new things about our writing, and thereby learn how to make it better.

Most writers rely on a circle of trusted readers who will comment on their drafts. These test readers can often ask questions or make observations that the writer had not thought about. To have the benefit of a critical reader's response is enormously helpful to writers who wish to revise thoughtfully.

Choose your readers carefully, therefore. Friends who will only flatter you or readers who do not know how to read critically will be of no help. This raises a third potential obstacle to effective revision.

To revise well, try to take criticism without offense and to be willing to make critical judgments about your own writing without damage to your ego. Yes, writing does come from the depths of our minds and hearts, but it is also separate from ourselves once it is on the page, and we can approach it *as writing*, words on paper that can be changed and played with freely. Thus, to revise well, you must be able to separate the personality in your writing from your own personality. This is especially important in college, and in a writing class in particular, because teachers and other members of the class must be able to talk about your writing without making judgments about you as a person.

In reading others' writing, and in accepting the comments of others about your own, the golden rule should apply: Comment about others' writing as you would have them comment about your own; accept the comments of others as you would have them accept yours. If we could accept all advice about our own writing as if it were given solely for the purpose of helping us to write better, we would be fortunate. But advice, like other aspects of human relations, can come with hidden intentions and can be defended against by rationalization— sometimes beyond our conscious control. It is necessary, therefore, to make a real effort to accept criticism gladly and to respond to it thoughtfully.

Responding to Your Teacher's Comments

It's one thing to revise in response to the criticisms of a friend, classmate, or peer, but responding to the criticism of your teacher is more difficult. Your teacher is indeed a member of your intended audience and should therefore function as a critical reader, responding to your ideas just as she or he might respond to the ideas in others' writing. But, let's face it, your teacher is also the person who will judge your performance and whom you would like to please. More importantly, as the person whose responsibility is to help you become a better writer, your teacher will comment on your writing with that end in view. Because you may often be revising your writing in response to your teacher's comments, or writing new essays with those comments in mind, the question of how to take them is worth considering at this point.

Students are certainly justified in their concern for the grade that each assignment receives, but if this concern overshadows their assessment and application of the teacher's critical comments, they have not learned all that they can from the teacher. Although a grade determines what kind of credit you receive for the assignment, it says nothing about how you have written, or might write again. A grade is a kind of conclusion, and comments are the reasons that support it. Like any conclusion, a grade is only as good as the line of reasoning that justifies it. To understand the grade, you must understand the basis on which the teacher determined it. For this reason, many teachers, especially writing teachers, choose not to include a final grade on the returned essay itself, but to communicate the grade separately later. This is an attempt to ensure that students will not read the comments in a defensive or perfunctory way, as they sometimes do when their knowledge of the grade may already have prejudiced their reaction to the comments, for better or worse.

Many students do not respond to grades in this way, of course. You will have to examine your own experience to know whether any such "typical" way of responding applies to you. Whether it does or not, some considerations about how to apply critical comments can lead to making the best use of them.

The way in which you should respond to comments will differ depending on whether the teacher expects the essay to be revised or not. Some teachers like to comment on drafts of a composition and require a revision. Other assignments are, in effect, finished after the teacher has evaluated them. If a teacher expects revision, you have an opportunity to respond *directly* to the comments, by applying the teacher's specific advice about a particular essay to continued work on that same essay. If no revision is required, however, the teacher's comments can be applied only *indirectly* to future essays. The direct application of comments is perhaps the easiest kind. If the teacher has pointed out stylistic infelicities, you can follow the teacher's specific advice. If the teacher has commented that a particular passage is unclear or in need of further support, you can attempt to clarify or explain or add reasons to that portion of the essay. And, if the teacher has made general comments about the logic or the structure of the argument, you can rethink those aspects of the essay.

Direct responses to comments in revision, because they are guided by the teacher's observations, can also be the most perfunctory kind—for the student who is content to do the minimum that a teacher asks for. It is always tempting to respond to a teacher's specific comments without understanding fully why those comments are there or what difference the revisions actually make to the quality of the essay. It is too easy, in other words, to make changes just to satisfy the teacher. A teacher's comments are meant to guide you in rethinking what you have done, and if you respond by automatically doing whatever the teacher asks for you have not taken the opportunity to use those comments to your best advantage. A teacher's comment is not a commandment; it is a suggestion. Only you can decide whether the comment will lead to a better way of writing, and only the thoughtful application of that suggestion can produce a change that will benefit you in the future.

So, if revision is required based on your teacher's comments on a draft of an essay, you are not meant to change the essay only in ways that the teacher has suggested and in no other, nor are you meant to adopt the teacher's suggestions without thinking about their effect on the rest of the essay. Comments are meant to nudge you into further thought. The outcome of that thought should be a revision that goes beyond the teacher's suggestions. It may even be a revision in which some of those suggestions are not adopted. The important thing is not to make every change the teacher says, but to know why such changes are necessary. At times, they may not be. Teachers are human; as they read your essays, they respond in different ways, just as any member of your audience might. This doesn't mean that teachers are "unfair" if you disagree with them. If you choose not to follow a teacher's specific advice—assuming you have understood both that advice and your own reasons for doing it your way—you might want to explain why to your teacher, who may be more impressed finally by how thoughtfully you approach writing than by how slavishly you follow instructions.

If a teacher's comments are expressed in ways that you do not understand, it becomes your responsibility to consult with the teacher, to be sure that you and the teacher are reading your essay in the same way. I'm not talking about arguing with the teacher over your grade, but seeking to understand the intention and the source of whatever troublesome comments the teacher may have made. Most teachers respond positively to this kind of inquiry, even if they may not, understandably, respond favorably to complaints about grades. Make it clear that what you want is a genuine understanding of your own writing. A good deal of the learning that takes place in a writing course can happen in the teacher's office during such conferences.

It helps, further, to remember that comments differ in degree of importance. Typically, a teacher's comments will follow the structure of the essay, usually because it is most convenient to write them in the margins alongside the relevant passage in the essay. (Some teachers have their own methods of making comments, such as putting them all at the end of the composition, or using one form of comment to talk about mechanics and another form to talk about ideas.) Comments that appear side by side are not necessarily equally significant. A teacher may mark a split infinitive in one of your sentences and observe that the logic of the next sentence needs to be stronger. Your response to those comments would necessarily be of a different order. On the one hand you need only make a simple correction. On the other hand you would have to reconsider what you mean and how you might best argue it. The change you are expected to make in the first instance is predictable, but in the second case the teacher has no "right response" in mind other than that you should look critically at your reasoning. The first is a mechanical correction and relatively trivial, the second may be crucial to the success of your argument.

In revising an essay, your attention should be on the nature of the case you are trying to make and the structure of the argument first, letting matters of lesser significance have your attention only when those are under control. You should determine which of the teacher's comments address the most basic aspects of the essay—its reasoning and structure—so that you can respond to those comments before editing the essay.

It may be that a teacher's comments suggest problems with the thesis itself or with the general approach you have taken in arguing it. In that case, an appropriate response would lead you to reconsider the thesis and the logic, which might result in a revised essay that has a different argument and structure from the original. If what is most in need of revision is the thesis of your essay, your revision may well turn out to be a wholly new composition based on a revised intention.

Some students assume that writing teachers should respond only to form and have no right to criticize students' ideas. A writing teacher is not simply an editor, whose job is to make sure that all formal aspects of the writing are under control. He or she is also part of the community of critical, inquiring minds to which your essay is addressed. As an expert on matters of usage and structure, a writing teacher may help you to learn about writing from a formal point of view. But as a critical reader, one who responds intelligently to ideas and their support, a teacher also helps you to learn about your thinking. The two are inseparable, and it is unreasonable to expect a writing teacher, as a thinking person, to ignore ideas for the sake of teaching form alone. If a teacher makes a comment about an idea that he or she thinks is not well argued, it isn't because he or she disagrees with that idea but because it needs further thinking. Your teacher cannot ignore that good writing requires well-reasoned ideas as much as it requires effective and correct composition.

It isn't necessary to revise each essay in order to get the benefit of a teacher's evaluation. But a somewhat different strategy for applying comments is necessary, if you aren't going to revise, because you have to apply concepts that you derive from the comments to new writing situations. Although comments that refer to particular aspects of one essay may not apply to another essay, *principles* derived from those comments can still be applied to any new composition. It is necessary for you to derive those principles yourself.

One specific practice may help you to do this most effectively. When you read a teacher's comments, keep a record of the kinds of problems your teacher has found in your writing. Say, for instance, that your teacher has marked sentence fragments or suggested that in several places in your essay you have not supplied a clear transition. On a separate page, in a note intended only for yourself, you might write: "Watch for fragments," or "Concentrate on clear transitions." (It would be best to have separate pages for different kinds of problems—one for words you have misspelled, another for grammar, another for more general concepts—tailored to your own needs.) These notes, no matter what kinds of advice they contain, will be invaluable to you as you revise your next essay by providing a guide for focusing on problems that you especially need to work on. You can add new features to the list as you receive comments on each essay you hand in, and over the course of time you will find yourself gaining more control of most of the writing problems that your teacher has pointed out to you. If you simply read comments once and make no such attempt to remember and apply them, you will probably not be learning what your teacher is trying to teach you.

Style and Attitudes

Up to this point we have discussed revision in general as applying to any aspect of the writing, at any stage. One aspect of writing that we haven't discussed is style. Anything you write will have some kind of style, and paying too much attention to it as you compose may result in distracting you from your ideas. But paying attention to style during revision is very important.

Style is the "texture" of the writing, the way it sounds and the kinds of words and sentences it uses to communicate to the reader. Qualities of style contribute to the **tone** of a piece of writing, which refers to the mood or attitude that the reader *hears* in the words. Behind the silent words on a page, we are able to hear a voice, not necessarily the real voice of the flesh-and-blood writer, whom we may not know, but that of a possible or apparent speaker of the words. If we judge a writer to be condescending or patronizing, angry or deeply moved, open-minded or intolerant, sincere or hypocritical, we do so in part because the writer *sounds* that way.

If style communicates the writer's attitude to the reader, then a consideration of attitude might be a useful place to begin thinking about stylistic choices. Attitude is a combination of the writer's feelings toward the subject, toward the intended audience, and toward the writer's self. These feelings change from situation to situation, and even from time to time as the writer works on a composition. The purpose of this discussion is to give you some basis for thinking about how the stylistic choices you make reflect your attitudes.

The first consideration is that the self reflected in your writing is not necessarily the same self that you reflect in other situations. Even in different pieces of writing, depending on their purpose, you construct an image of yourself that may be different. The aspects of our personalities that we present to others at different times reflect the circumstances within which we act and the purposes behind our actions. There are times when it is appropriate for us to emphasize one aspect of ourselves while making certain to deemphasize other aspects. We do this not because we are dishonest, but because we are adaptable. In writing, this means that we choose how we wish to appear to our reader, based on who the reader is and what we wish our writing to accomplish. I may come across as an entirely different sort of person when I write a letter to my parents, to my former professor, or to my senator. I may seem like an angry person if I am writing to complain about something, a tolerant person if I am writing to defend someone, a serious-minded person if I am writing to express my concern over an injustice, or a clown if I am writing to get people to see something in a comical light. All of these are aspects of my true self, but I may choose from them to fit my purpose and my reader.

How well you are able to find the right self for your writing depends on how well you judge the situation, how clearly you understand your own purposes, how you view the subject, and how you wish the reader to view it. As you think about the ideas you wish to present to the reader and the reasons you wish to offer in support of those ideas, you are engaged in defining all of those attitudes at once, and you will already have done most of the work of adapting the right style. It is not necessary to do all the thinking first, and then to make all of the decisions about how to present yourself, because by doing the thinking you will have already been working on this presentation. You have been adjusting your attitude to fit the subject simply by giving it your best thinking in the first place.

All of us have probably encountered writing that we thought was somehow flawed in its tone and have judged it accordingly. Whether we accepted the ideas in spite of this or not, we could characterize our response to the writer's way of presenting himself or herself to us by using adjectives that otherwise would apply to personality: This writer is childish, we might say, or self-indulgent or selfish or dishonest or conceited or petty or condescending or closed-minded. All such adjectives, when applied to writing, reflect our judgment of the writer's attitude toward the subject, toward us, or toward himself or herself. Thus, the writer's tone is determined by how well those attitudes are shaped in the writing and kept in harmony with one another. Let's take a closer look at those attitudes and see how they may work for or against a writer's purpose.

When we are led to characterize a writer's style by using adjectives such as *pedantic, lifeless, monotonous,* or even *trivial,* we are probably responding to our feeling that the writer has taken the subject more seriously than it deserves, by neglecting to consider the needs of the reader who must be helped to understand it.

Here, for instance, is an example of writing that is serious about its subject but contains inappropriate stylistic choices:

> *It is often contended that the citizens who protested this nation's involvement in the conflict in Vietnam during the anti-Vietnam demonstrations of the 1960s did so out of an abiding sense of patriotism for the country. Indeed, it is so often said by those who have not thoroughly analyzed the conflict that to suggest otherwise is to make one vulnerable to the charge that one believes in the slogan "My Country Right or Wrong." It is the case, however, that one can come to the inevitable conclusion that the protesters acted out of treasonous motives, in sufficient numbers of cases to warrant a skeptical attitude toward the protest movement in general, without becoming guilty oneself of any rashly suspect form of blind patriotic fervor. . . .*

What about this writing gives us the impression that the writer has neglected to consider the needs of the reader? It is enough, perhaps, to hear the writer's sneering tone and to conclude that he has no respect for the opinions of any reader who does not already agree with his stance. This blindness to other points of view emerges as disrespect; any reader who might entertain another opinion has been labeled as someone who has "not thoroughly analyzed the conflict." His attitude of superiority makes the prose sound pompous. His contempt for the audience is evident also in the kind of appeal he makes in his reasoning; he asserts his own invulnerability to emotional stereotyping while engaging in the same tactic himself. He calls others names while attempting to defend himself against name-calling used against his own position.

The style of the paragraph contributes to this impression. Notice that the writer has tried to stay aloof from the discussion by making the prose impersonal. The paragraph contains three long sentences, each of which starts with the vague "it is" construction. The structures of these sentences make them unnecessarily difficult to read. The first one contains wordy repetitions ("who protested this nation's involvement in the conflict in Vietnam during the anti-Vietnam demonstrations of the 1960s," "patriotism for the country"). The second one has an awkward word order, forcing the reader to have to reconstruct its meaning after reaching the conclusion. The third is interrupted by a distracting subordinate clause, one that makes a new point worth a sentence of its own. Notice too that the writer's diction is inflated. He uses *citizens* because it seems to sound more high-toned than *people*, and it may seem to the writer that he is being scornfully ironic to call them *citizens* rather than *protesters*. Likewise, the words *involvement* and *conflict* are chosen to make the role of the United States sound innocent; they are euphemisms. Some of the language is loaded; the writer uses *inevitable* and *treasonous* in ways that implicitly threaten the reader who might not accept them. The phrase *rashly suspect* is simply a clumsy oratorical flourish that makes no sense, and *blind patriotic fervor* is a bumbled cliché.

The subject matter of this paragraph is not so unfamiliar or complex that it can't be communicated plainly and inoffensively. There are subjects, however, that may seem to call for writing that the reader will find difficult, simply because they are complex or unfamiliar. If you have a specialized knowledge that your reader is assumed to lack, your writing may contain concepts or vocabulary that make the reader's task difficult. If the ideas you are trying to communicate are especially complicated, it won't help to translate them into baby talk just to satisfy the reader's need for simplicity. You must use your best judgment about the appropriateness of stylistic choices; it is as easy to insult the reader's intelligence by condescending as it is by obfuscating simple concepts.

Style, in this sense, is like logic: Its clarity and effectiveness depend not only on what is said but also on what assumptions about the reader are appealed to in the saying. Stylistic choices, like logical connections, are often neither good nor bad in an absolute sense, but only in their appropriateness to the knowledge shared by the reader and the writer. What appears obscure to one reader is clear to another. It is your task to adjust the style, as well as the reasoning, to the audience. The writer who tries to sound intelligent or educated by adding stylistic flourishes—complex sentences and inflated diction—will not fool the careful reader. But the writer whose style makes appropriate assumptions about the reader's knowledge and reflects a shared understanding and respect for the subject will have earned the reader's goodwill.

Writers who believe that they can improve their image by inflating their diction sometimes turn to a thesaurus in search of synonyms. This misuse of an otherwise useful resource generally results in stylistic problems. The writer who tries to substitute a high-falutin' word for a simple one, consulting the thesaurus for a better-sounding word, risks two undesirable effects. The first is the possibility of misusing a word that sounds better but that doesn't quite mean what the writer wishes the word to say. If a word is not part of a writer's working vocabulary, if he or she never would have thought of it without looking in a thesaurus, then chances are the writer doesn't really understand what the word means. It is better to let the meaning choose the word for you than to let some unfamiliar word alter your meaning. The second potential effect is that the writer's tone will become pompous as a result of putting long or fancy words in place of simple, direct ones. When Mark Twain said, "I never use *metropolis* when I can get the same price for *city*," he was exaggerating. *Metropolis* has some appropriate uses, or it wouldn't be in the language. But *city* will do in most situations where *metropolis* would be phony.

Writers may pay too much attention to the reader and too little to the subject, producing styles that are inappropriate because they suggest an attitude of someone who would rather conform to the reader's tastes than tell the truth. If a writer's tone sounds condescending or patronizing, it is because the style is out of control somehow; the balance between respect for the subject, respect for the reader, and respect for the self has somehow been lost. Here is an extreme example of this sort of imbalance:

> *In this essay, I will try to persuade you that college athletic programs benefit all students. As a fellow student at this college, you are aware of this controversy, so I need not explain to you why it is important. You have heard that the college pays too much attention to sports, and perhaps you agree that the college could pay more attention to your education if sports programs were eliminated or cut back. As I discuss this issue, I will begin by describing the sports programs and their relation to academics, and then I will list the benefits that you receive as a student from the existence of these programs. I will also attempt to refute whatever objections you may have to my reasoning, as I argue that athletics is indeed a benefit to you, whether you realize it or not.*

All this talk addressed to the reader is unnecessary. It seems to imply, although inadvertently, that the writer thinks the reader is unable to understand the writer's purpose without this hand-holding. The writer also makes assumptions about the reader's beliefs that may or may not be shared with actual readers, and the essay further insults the reader's intelligence, therefore, by pretending that the writing is addressed only to those readers who need the writer's superior guidance. Even though there is nothing wrong with refuting potential objections in a persuasive essay, this writer gives the reader no credit for having any objections that are valid.

The paragraph actually says very little. It announces its stance and refers to a controversy. The first three sentences contain information that could be communicated quite efficiently in a single sentence introducing the issue. Then the last two sentences explain what the essay will proceed to do. These are also unnecessary; if the essay is well organized, there is no reason to provide the reader with these advance clues to what will come later. Sentences of this sort often find their way into writing, unnecessarily.

> *I am now going to take up the second part of my topic. . . .*
>
> *At this point, let us look at the related question of . . .*
>
> *I will now begin the discussion of my reasons. . . .*

Such road signs are seldom necessary, but writers often include them out of a sense that the reader needs help. Such overt transitional markers bring unnecessary attention to the structure and distract the reader's attention from the content. If you construct a clear transition from a given discussion to a related question, showing what the relation is, there should be no need to say, "At this point, let us look at the related question of . . ." It will go without saying. Too many such phrases, meant to help the reader through the structure, can seem like condescension. They should be used sparingly. (Sparingly does not mean never. Do you think I have overused such phrases in this book?)

You may have encountered a writer who seems to care more about pleasing the reader than about telling the truth. A writer's failure to write from a point of view that does justice to the writer's thoughts on an issue, can result in a desire to entertain that overwhelms any desire to find good reasons. Thus, the writing can take the form of an elaborate bluff. This is likely to be the case if we detect in the writer's style some attempt to use language to draw attention away from the subject and to the style itself. Here's an example from an essay on evolution:

> What's all the trouble about anyway? If our grand-daddies and grand-mommies got created in one big bang (no pun intended), or if they crawled out of the water, shook off their feathers and said, "where's the exit of this zoo?", it really can't make much difference to us. We all have to get born, whether the chicken came first or the egg. But, you know, some people are never satisfied with not knowing something, so they feel like they have to invent an answer or bust. So the scientists, who could be trying to cure cancer, put their big brains to work theorizing about "evil-lution," while the glory brigade sing hallelujah to a creator who didn't have to make cancer in the first place.

This clever style has some interesting and original turns of phrase, and even some sophisticated uses of sentence structure (such as the parallel clauses about cancer in the last sentence). But are we amused, as the writer clearly intends that we should be? Maybe, but also puzzled. What's the point of this glib talk? We would like to see a spark of wit in the things we read rather than an unremitting glumness. But wit can be purposeful or it can be a way of thumbing one's nose at ideas in order to avoid having to think about them. That's the impression I get from this writer, who clowns at the expense of confronting the questions the writing raises.

The issue of whether to use humor, like other stylistic questions, cannot be answered with a rule. The only rule is this: It depends. It would be as mistaken to take everything more seriously than it deserves as it would be to take nothing seriously enough. A balance, some kind of golden mean, is the best answer, and it is found when the writer is conscious of having a choice. How do I want to sound in this essay? What attitude do I want to reflect, given my stance and my readers' attitudes? What kind of style do my subject and my audience deserve? These considerations do not guarantee that the style will be appropriate in every case, but without them a writer may fall back on convenient habit, sheer clumsiness, or bluff.

Style and Clear Thinking

It is important to pay attention to style in order to be sure that your writing conveys an attitude that is appropriate to the reasoning. There is another reason that paying attention to style is important. We not only write in words and sentences, but think in them as well. The thoughts we think can be affected by any habits that we may have in the use of words. This is not a reason to use any particular style in a particular piece of writing. It is a reason to remain conscious of the possibility of being controlled by stylistic habits.

The potential effect of stylistic habits on mental habits is discussed in a famous essay by George Orwell, the British author whose novels include *Animal Farm* and *Nineteen Eighty-Four*. As you know if you have read these novels, Orwell was keenly interested in *groupthink*, or the control of how and what people think by totalitarian regimes. He showed how language can be a powerful tool to suppress freedom of thought, open-mindedness, and independent judgment. The control of language by the state, he believed, was the same as the power to control thinking. Similarly, he believed that control of language by the individual was the same as freedom of thought, and that consciousness of style could, therefore, help the individual remain free of the unwarranted power of others' uncritical ideas.

Orwell's argument, in his essay "Politics and the English Language" (which may be found beginning on page 246) goes something like this: It is easy for people to imitate stylistic habits that become conventional in the language they hear all around them. Some of these habits have their origins in uses of language that are deceptive, such as the euphemisms, half-truths, or misleading expressions that may be found in political writing, advertising, or journalism. Some may be caused by simple neglect: Sloppy and inaccurate thinking has given rise to sloppy and inaccurate expressions. Whatever the origin of such habits, they can in turn become the cause of poor thinking. The English language, Orwell wrote, "becomes ugly and inaccurate because our thoughts are foolish, but the slovenliness of our language makes it easier for us to have foolish thoughts." Thus, failure to pay attention to style can produce unclear thinking, without our being aware of it. But, Orwell believed, "if one gets rid of these habits one can think more clearly."

Thus, although Orwell believed that language can have an insidious effect on our thinking, we can prevent this effect by taking the trouble to choose our manner of expression carefully. In what is to me the most powerful part of his essay, Orwell put it this way:

> A scrupulous writer, in every sentence that he writes, will ask himself at least four questions, thus: What am I trying to say? What words will express it? What image or idiom will make it clearer? Is the image fresh enough to have an effect? And he will probably ask himself two more: Can I put it more shortly? Have I said anything that is avoidably ugly? But you are not obliged to go to all this trouble. You can shirk it by simply throwing your mind open and letting the ready-made phrases come crowding in. They will construct your sentences for you—even think your thoughts for you, to a certain extent—and at need they will perform the important service of partially concealing your meaning even from yourself.

It is that closing irony that makes this passage most effective, I think. Orwell has reminded us that life would be simpler if we did not have to think for ourselves, and we are often ready to give up freedom of thought for the comfort of conformity. But the price we pay for this comfort is self-deception.

Orwell supported his argument with many examples drawn from contemporary writing. It is amazing how many of his examples continue to be found in popular language habits of today. Language, like other fashions, has fads and trends, some of which last longer than others. If you read Orwell's essay, you will be able to think of many expressions in fashion today that could be added to his list of examples. Based on his examples, Orwell devised six general rules of style, which he said could be relied on "when instinct fails." His rules are:

1. Never use a metaphor, simile or other figure of speech which you are used to seeing in print.
2. Never use a long word when a short one will do.
3. If it is possible to cut a word out, always cut it out.
4. Never use the passive when you can use the active.
5. Never use a foreign phrase, a scientific word or a jargon word if you can think of an everyday English equivalent.
6. Break any of these rules sooner than say anything outright barbarous.

Orwell's rule number six is another reminder that when it comes to style there are no real "rules," in the sense of laws that cannot be broken. Style serves a purpose. The purpose must determine the validity of the rule. It depends.

As a writer, you could probably not keep these rules in mind all of the time while you are composing. Worrying too much about rules can distract you from your ideas. The point at which you ought to think about such rules consciously is during revision. Rules, as Orwell said, are at our service when instinct fails. Applying them thoughtfully, as a means of revising, can help to make them instinctive.

Editing as Rethinking

Editing a rough draft is a process of looking at the words and sentences with the intention of making them express just what you mean and do just what you want them to do. Deliberately editing according to certain principles can also provide you with a source of critical distance. By looking for particular features, perhaps those that someone has made you aware of by offering you criticism, you can separate yourself somewhat from the flow of your thoughts and look at the writing *as writing*. But because the question of whether any specific editing change actually improves the essay will depend on the purpose of the writing and the context of the whole argument, editing in this way leads to rethinking the ideas.

Before we consider some editing techniques that may help you improve your writing, I want to say something about the difference between editing on paper and editing with a word processing program on a computer. On page 116 I have reproduced a piece of rough draft from an earlier section of this book that was written by Brad Hawley and that I then edited and retyped. It's not the particular editing decisions I made that I am illustrating by reproducing this page, but the messiness of the process. When I retyped the page, and entered it into my computer, this messiness disappeared, of course. Then I edited again, and on the computer screen it continued to look neat and clean, even though what I was doing was the same kind of editing that I had done with a pen on paper. Computers remove from our sight the actual editing changes we make. As we insert and delete on a computer no record is left behind such as there is when we edit on paper.

This is a great advantage of computers, but consider that it may also have some hidden risks. For one thing, when the computer erases the deleted words or phrases, we no longer have them in front of us to compare, and it may be harder to change our minds and return to the original phrasing (even though we can use the undelete command to bring back some deleted text). But more importantly, the very neatness of the writing we produce on a computer screen can sometimes delude us into thinking that we do not have to change anything: It looks like a typeset page. Parts of this book were delivered to the printer looking a bit like this illustration; what I submitted as editing changes to the text of the second edition was in the form of handwritten additions and deletions. So the neatness that you see on the page now is not the result of my editing but of the typesetter's cleaning up of my editing. The computer does not write and edit; it sets type. So don't be fooled by the neat appearance on the page; edit anyway and reread the result carefully.

For this course, you will Most often, read nonfiction argumentative essays and develop questions at issue in response to those essays. But how do we come up with questions at issue when reading a different kind of text? How do we understand an author's argument when it is presented through a fictional text? Asking this question assumes that fictional works—short stories, novels, plays, poems, and films—actually do convey arguments. Remember that even though you are writing academic essays to make your arguments, all writing is an act of communication, intended to have an effect on an audience. This means that all writing, even fiction, conveys a kind of argument.

The best way to understand the arguments made in fiction is to consider one of the main differences between essays and stories: While a non-fiction essays presents an argument that is given *directly* to the audience, fictional stories present plots with characters to whom we respond and through whom a complex argument is made *indirectly*. This indirection makes the arguments presented in fiction harder for us to respond to because we usually can't locate a directly stated thesis. We respond sympathetically or unsympathetically to characters rather than to reasons.

This difference between fiction and non-fiction will lead us to different kinds of questions at issue. These questions will be based on what Wayne C. Booth, a rhetorical critic, calls understanding and overstanding. Questions of *understanding* will get us to ask how an author presents his or her arguments through fiction. Such questions are questions of interpretation. Since we can't be said to agree or disagree with a plot, because it makes no claim,

This advice may sound strange to you because a word processor actually makes editing easier. Cutting and pasting, moving text, inserting words . . . all of these become easier on the computer. But the experience of many teachers suggests that most students do less editing when they edit on computers than when they edit on paper. And despite the ease of editing on a computer, many teachers have found that students who edit on computers make more mistakes than those who edit on paper. Because of the finished appearance of words on a computer screen, perhaps we simply feel less responsibility to reread our writing or to look carefully for mistakes. Do we think the computer is doing this for us? It can't.

So be cautious of giving your responsibilities as a writer away to the computer. If you use a spell-check program, for instance, remember that it won't guarantee that you will use words correctly. Spell checks do not know the difference between words like *their, they're,* and *there,* for example; and if you make the mistake of using one of these instead of the correct one, the computer will not fix it for you. A spell check or even a grammar check can't tell you whether a word you have used is the *right* word in the *right* place. You know more about grammar than your computer's grammar check does, and if you don't read your writing carefully but simply feel that putting it through such a program is enough, strange mistakes will enter your writing that you would not have put there.

So in learning to apply the editing techniques in this chapter, perhaps it would be a good idea to start out doing most of your editing on paper and then entering those changes into the text on the computer. This will make it easier to learn to edit well, and when you have become a proficient editor of your own prose, you will be able to use the computer's advantages more purposefully.

Now, let's take a closer look at each of Orwell's editing principles.

Using Figurative Language

Orwell's first "rule" refers to the use of figurative language: *Never use a metaphor, simile or other figure of speech which you are used to seeing in print.* Notice that Orwell is not telling us to avoid figurative language, but cautioning us against using it thoughtlessly. When certain figures of speech become overused, they lose their power to communicate and become clichés. Because such phrases are overused, they often cease to convey a precise idea and reflect instead the writer's disregard for precision.

A figure of speech is simply a means by which words are able to say one thing while communicating something else. From this fact comes the power of figurative language—its novelty and ability to suggest unique connections—but this is also the source of its potential imprecision. For example, the philosopher Aristotle took advantage of the suggestive power of language when he wrote, "Poverty is the parent of revolution." He assumed that his readers would know that he did not mean "parent" literally. He assumed that they would associate the relation between poverty and revolution with the relation between parent and child. If he could not assume these things, he would have risked being misunderstood. Because figurative language works by suggestion, one must control figurative language to get just the right effect from it.

When writers use figures of speech that have become clichés, this control is surrendered. Consider this passage:

> *The administration is grasping at straws in its policy toward Albania. We hear harsh words being spoken about ethnic cleansing on the one hand, and on the other we hear glowing praise of the Albanian government. Our waffling Congress should get its act together and tell the White House to get off its horse. The bottom line is whether we are going to support any government that condones the moral bloodbath taking place in the name of economic necessity.*

The only clear idea being communicated here is that the writer wishes the Congress to impel the administration to condemn ethnic cleansing practices. The overuse of figures of speech makes the meaning harder to find than necessary. *Straws* and *waffles* clash in meaning, *house* and *horse* in sound. Some of the phrases are simply not clear. This writer blurts out commonplace sentiments without giving them much thought—an impression that does not depend on whether the reader agrees with the stance.

Figures of speech and clichés are not always easy to find, because some "dead" metaphors seem to have become literal. You probably identified the following as clichés:

> *grasping at straws*
> *waffling Congress*
> *get its act together*
> *get off its horse*
> *moral bloodbath*

But other figurative phrases are more subtle:

> *harsh words*
> *glowing praise*
> *on the one hand . . . on the other hand*
> *White House*
> *bottom line*
> *in the name of*

These phrases have become so common that we can easily forget they are metaphors. Whether a metaphor communicates the writer's meaning precisely is a question that must be asked of all such phrases, no matter how literal they may sound. This is why a careful assessment of one's own metaphors as Orwell prescribed is important.

Figurative language nearly always works by means of comparison. A simile ("He worked on that project like a fiend") is a direct comparison. A metaphor ("He sweat blood to get it done") is an implied comparison. Figurative language thus gets its power from its ability to relate one realm of experience to another. Figurative speech is so common that readers usually understand it without hesitation. In the Declaration of Independence, Thomas Jefferson wrote, "When, in the course of human events, it becomes necessary for one people to dissolve the political bands which have connected them to another. . . ." As we read those words, we associate qualities that we understand *dissolve* and *bands* to have in their literal sense with the new context in which Jefferson used them. Bands do not literally connect people, nor was Jefferson calling for bands to be literally dissolved. But because we know that to dissolve something is to dilute its power, and that bands can inhibit freedom, we are not confused by his meaning. We understand it all the more powerfully because it is communicated in well-chosen figures.

Forgetting that figurative language draws on one aspect of experience in order to describe another can lead to losing control of its use. As in the example from Jefferson, there must be an appropriate connection between the kinds of experiences being associated. Examples of experiences inappropriately connected may be found today in the popular application of metaphors deriving from computers. For instance, consider these phrases:

> *I will provide my input to our discussion of Plato's concept of beauty.*
> *Abusive parents have difficulty interfacing with their children.*

The metaphors here seem inappropriate to the subject matter because there is no reason to compare the experiences under discussion to associations that we have with computers. *Input* was originally technical jargon for entering data into machines, but it has now become a common metaphor for thoughts, opinions, or ideas. Similarly, *interface* is jargon for the capacity of computers to combine functions, but it is often used to refer to human relations as well—such as *talking* or *understanding*. As these terms lose their metaphoric power through overuse, it becomes easier to apply them to experiences for which they are inappropriate. The popular overuse of this kind of language to refer to human actions or problems (as well as other metaphors taken from business or military or education jargon, such as *bottom line, target of opportunity,* or *gifted*) can change the way we think about people or issues, if we do not remember that they are metaphors. You probably have your own favorite examples of metaphors that affect how people perceive reality when they are taken too literally.

It is not possible, and certainly not necessary, to write without ever using expressions that are commonplace. Avoiding all such phrases could produce a style that is sterile and officious, lacking a human voice. Figurative expressions give our speech color and liveliness, they suggest the personality of the writer, and they communicate special meanings. Orwell's rule cautions us against using worn-out and commonplace figures of speech, but it does not prevent us from using occasional figures that contribute to the effectiveness of the writing.

Inflated Diction

Orwell's second rule, *Never use a long word when a short one will do,* returns us to the caution against inflated diction. It is worth going into further. Don't assume that long words will make you sound more intelligent or that short ones will make you sound simple-minded. Let the meaning choose the right word and length will take care of itself. What Orwell is getting at is the habit common to many writers of substituting polysyllabic monstrosities (!) for the simple, direct terms of everyday English. As an editing technique, Orwell's rule would lead us to examine the long words we use, to see whether we have chosen them because they are right or simply because they are long.

The way some writers try to imitate a "learned" style, editing for precision can seem like translating from one variety of English to another. Here's an extreme case:

> *Utilizing civil disobedience methodologies pursuant to the conceptualizations of Thoreau facilitated the efficacious attainment of the primary objective of civil rights activists, namely the modification of statutory prohibitions deleterious toward racial minorities.*

Translated into plain English, this means:

> *Using civil disobedience according to the ideas of Thoreau made it easier for civil rights activists to reach their goal of changing laws harmful to racial minorities.*

Although the meaning is much the same, the effect on the reader is much different.

Notice that the goal of the editor of this sentence was not to get rid of all words over two syllables long. That would be silly. Rather, the goal was to get rid of long words for which perfectly good short ones exist. Thus, the phrase *civil disobedience* remained, because no shorter phrase could be substituted for it without changing the meaning. The same is true for *activists* and *minorities.* But because all of the other monstrosities found in the sentence have simple equivalents, they are easily replaced.

utilizing	=	*using*
pursuant to	=	*according to*
conceptualization	=	*idea*
facilitate	=	*make easy*
efficacious attainment	=	*reaching*
objective	=	*goal*
modification	=	*change*
statutory prohibitions	=	*laws*
deleterious	=	*harmful*

Some long words are perfectly appropriate in some contexts, but they are misused by writers who habitually prefer the puffed-up to the plain. Orwell blames politicians for overusing such words, which are parroted by others—those who can be fooled into thinking that *selective disinformation* means something other than "lying." Many long words cannot and should not be avoided. But the English vocabulary is so vast that many words have become popular whose only function is to bedevil those who wish to express themselves clearly. Remember that you aren't trying to achieve the fewest possible number of syllables. You are trying to avoid the ponderous effect of wordiness. This brings us to Orwell's next rule.

Cutting

If it is possible to cut a word out, always cut it out. Clumsy writers not only use longer words than necessary, they also crowd their writing with empty words and roundabout phrases. Empty words contribute no meaning to the sentence in which they occur. Roundabout phrases are those that substitute several words for one.

Almost any word can be an empty word if it contributes no additional meaning to a sentence. Here are some examples:

> *Her decision was painful in nature.*
> *I am majoring in the field of accounting.*
> *Despite various minor flaws, the essay shows a good reasoning process.*

Each of these sentences could be made more economical by cutting words that have no function, thus:

> *Her decision was painful.*
> *I am majoring in accounting.*
> *Despite minor flaws, the essay shows good reasoning.*

No reader would respond to these sentences by wondering, "Do you mean painful in *nature*?" or "Do you mean the *field* of accounting?" or "Do you mean a good reasoning *process*?" or "Are the flaws *various*?" These words contribute nothing essential. Yet they are all words that in other contexts might have a specific function:

> *By nature, people question authority.*
> *You have to choose one field for your major.*
> *Writing is a process, leading to a product.*
> *The same end can be reached by various means.*

The words that were not contributing meaning before are doing so here. Thus it isn't the word itself that is empty; it depends on the role it plays. The context of a sentence within the whole composition will determine if any words are superfluous. Editing for economy thus requires a writer to reexamine the meaning carefully and to ask what each word contributes to it.

Here's a passage in which the writer would face many such considerations as he or she edited for economy. I have exaggerated the wordiness on purpose to illustrate several different ways that language can be inflated.

> *The question to pose now is whether or not the acceptance of the basic concept of renewable energy resource production is justified at this time. Each and every kind of nonfossil fuel energy source, such as hydroelectric, nuclear, solar, and wind, etc., has recognized advantages over fossil fuels, but due to the fact that each also has unsolved problems attendant with its use, there is no consensus of opinion up to this point in time that the various benefits tend to outweigh the actual costs. Hydroelectric power resources make use of abundantly available supplies of water, but nevertheless there is opposition against their use from many who view the protection of lakes and streams from negative effects as a higher priority than meeting the energy needs of this nation. The reason why nuclear power is a controversial issue is that the extent to which nuclear waste materials will have lasting effects on the surrounding environment cannot be determined at the present time. Notwithstanding the fact that wind power is a feasible approach technologically, it is not practical from the standpoint of cost-effectiveness. Solar power is dependent on the climate situation to a large degree, and in consequence its maximum possible potential may be viewed as restricted to certain regions of the country. But yet it is the one other alternative that does not have drawbacks sufficient enough to prevent us from directing our efforts toward its further development on a widespread scale.*

Get out the blue pencil. Let's start cutting words. (In the following discussion, be prepared to refer to this passage, because I will make lists of words from it, out of context.) This gassy writer has used more than twice the number of words necessary. Does anybody really write this badly? Maybe not, but many writers slip into one or another kind of wordiness. Some of the gas results from the kind of empty words we have already discussed. These phrases add no meaning to the passage, in context:

to pose   (What other kinds of questions are there?)

basic   (The word is just noise.)

the concept of   (More noise.)

attendant   (Can problems ever not be attendant?)

various   (Sheer humbug.)

situation   (More noise.)

Getting rid of those is a start, but the writing still overflows with other kinds of waste. It is polluted by many other phrases that are simply redundant.

now . . . at this time

whether or not

each and every

such as . . . , etc.

unsolved problems

consensus of opinion

this point in time

but nevertheless

opposition against

reason why

controversial issue

surrounding environment

possible potential

but yet

other alternative

sufficient enough

further development

Eliminate half the words and they say the same thing.

Another kind of redundancy persists in the passage (not *continues to persist*). It results from including words that refer to concepts already clear from the context, as in these cases:

resource production   (*Production* is understood in context.)

energy source   (In context, *source* is redundant.)

recognized advantages   (If they were unrecognized, would we be describing them?)

problems . . . with its use   (More empty words.)

up to this point   (Implied by the use of the present tense.)

tend to outweigh   (Either they do or they don't.)

available   (How could they be abundant but not available?)

protection . . . from negative effects   (Who protects anything from positive effects?)

the energy needs of this nation   (We weren't thinking of any other nation.)

nuclear waste materials   (What else could the wastes be if not materials?)

at the present time   (We weren't thinking of any other time.)

feasible . . . approach   (Just wind.)

practical . . . cost-effectiveness   (Cost is practical by definition.)

maximium . . . potential   (A useless modifier.)

regions of the country   (Could it be regions of anything else?)

Practice the art of not saying the obvious by eliminating such repetitions. The paragraph is shrinking before our very eyes.

The passage contains yet another kind of wordiness. Many of its phrases consist of strings of words that can be replaced by one word that means the same thing. These stringy roundabout expressions should be translated into their economical equivalents:

due to the fact that	=	*because* or *since*
not withstanding the fact that	=	*although*
from the standpoint of	=	*in*
to a large degree	=	*largely*
in consequence	=	*so*
may be viewed as	=	*may be (or is)*
directing our efforts toward	=	*trying*
on a widespread scale	=	*widely*

With these changes, the passage is really shaping up. It may even be starting to sound human.

But before we finish with it, we still have to attack one last source of wordiness, the extended noun phrases that hide verbs. One way in which writers unknowingly add extra words is to transform verbs into nouns by attaching suffixes and auxiliary words to them, as in these examples from the paragraph:

the acceptance of	=	*accept*
make use of	=	*use*
there is opposition to	=	*(someone) opposes*
the protection of	=	*protect*
is dependent on	=	*depends on*
directing our attention toward its development	=	*trying to develop*

When you edit your writing for economy, then, look for verbs hidden inside noun phrases. The offending nouns often contain these suffixes:

-ive	(*is indicative of* instead of *indicates*)
-sion	(*made a decision* instead of *decided*)
-tion	(*gave consideration to* instead of *considered*)
-ment	(*made an improvement* instead of *improved*)
-ance	(*has the appearance of* instead of *appears*)
-al	(*made an arrival* instead of *arrived*)

Sometimes no suffix is needed to turn a verb into a noun, although it does require adding words, as in

do harm to	instead of	*harm*
is in need of	instead of	*needs*
effect a change in	instead of	*change*

None of these phrases by itself will make your writing clumsy, and there may be times when any such phrase is more appropriate than its shorter equivalent. But the habit of substituting noun phrases for verbs will result in wordiness if it is not kept under control.

It may seem that editing for economy is fairly mechanical: Remove empty words, cut redundancy, transform hidden verbs. These are good principles, but they do not automatically result in a neat, economically worded product without further editing. Applying the blue pencil to our long passage of overwritten prose might result in some sentences that are still in need of polishing. The result of cutting—or of any revision—can be quite messy, as in the illustration below. Editing like this is not intended for your readers' eyes. A rough draft is like a sketchbook, a record of your thoughts-in-process.

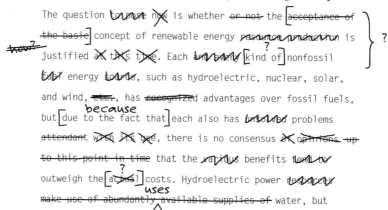

Having edited the passage for each kind of wordiness, we may still have to touch up the prose. When you cut words from a sentence, you will often have to rephrase some parts of the sentence to make it sound right. Now that we have cut out the verbal fat and put the sentences back together, here is the result:

The question is whether using renewable energy resources is justified. Each alternative to fossil fuels has advantages, but since each also has problems there is no consensus that the benefits outweigh the costs. Hydroelectric power uses abundant supplies of water, but many oppose it who view protecting lakes and streams as a higher priority than more energy, Nuclear power is controversial because the extent of lasting effects on the environment from nuclear waste cannot be determined. Although wind power is feasible technologically, it is not cost-effective. Solar power depends largely on climate, so its potential is restricted regionally. Yet it is the one alternative that does not have drawbacks sufficient to prevent us from developing it further.

The edited version of the paragraph could probably be reduced still further, although not much would be accomplished by cutting alone at this point. It now has 117 words, compared with the 243 of the original version. That's a "flab factor" of 52 percent.

The Passive Voice

Orwell's next rule is *never use the passive when you can use the active.* Some writers overuse the passive voice out of habit, and the result is confusion. The passive voice can result in unclear statements or in deceptive ones. A simple example shows how it works. Here's a sentence in the active voice:

The chicken crossed the road.

In this sentence the **agent** of the action is the chicken; that's what's doing whatever the verb indicates is happening. The **object** of the action is the road. In the passive voice, the agent and the object change places, thus:

The road was crossed by the chicken.

These two sentences describe the same action, but the change from active to passive changes the emphasis, from the chicken to the road. Both sentences are clear, although the second one is wordier. What makes the passive voice potentially unclear is that it permits a writer to ignore the agent, as in:

The road was crossed.

This is a grammatical sentence, whereas if we tried to get rid of the agent while keeping the verb in the active voice we would not have a complete sentence: ". . . crossed the road." This is what makes the passive risky, or convenient, depending on how you look at it: It permits you to get rid of the chicken! Actions take place in the passive, but nobody *does* them.

The need for higher standards is established.

It is believed that the strike should be canceled.

The new theory is regarded as practical, but it has not yet been tried.

Because they eliminate the agent, these sentences also hide information. The reader is left to wonder what that information is: "Is established" by whom? "Is believed" by whom? "Should be canceled" by whom? "Is regarded" by whom? "Hasn't been tried" by whom? When writers habitually use the passive voice, they seem to be hiding something. In fact, the passive voice has gotten its bad reputation because it is often used when people do have something to hide: "A decision was made to cut your budget," an administrator might say, so that he or she can avoid having to admit that he or she decided it. The deliberate use of the passive to deceive is probably rare, but unintended deceptions happen frequently when writers habitually use passive verbs and fail to ask whether the excluded information is relevant. In editing, you should first identify the passive verbs and then ask whether they exclude necessary information.

Jargons

A long discussion of Orwell's next rule would repeat much of what I covered earlier. It too concerns diction: *Never use a foreign phrase, a scientific word or a jargon word if you can think of an everyday English equivalent.* Jargon words and scientific words belong to the specialized vocabulary shared by a specific group. If you are writing for an audience that cannot be expected to share such terms, avoid them. If a jargon term or a scientific term is more convenient because it is precise and eliminates the need to repeat a string of plainer, explanatory words, use it, but not without being sure that your audience will understand it. If your motive for using jargon or scientific language is to impress the reader with your knowledge or to make your ideas sound more important than they really are, forget it.

The same might be said for foreign expressions, if their meaning would be obscure to the intended audience, unless there is some particular reason for using another language. If you were writing an essay about the way in which American tourists use foreign idioms, for instance, you could hardly do the subject justice without giving examples in the foreign languages. Or, if you were arguing that a translation of a poem sacrificed emotional intensity for literal meaning, you would want to use examples to clarify and support your thesis. In such cases, you would have to depend on your knowledge of the audience to decide what examples to use and whether to provide translations. Reasons to include foreign expressions depend on the writer's purpose. Why, for instance, does Gloria Anzaldúa use Spanish passages in her essay (beginning on page 274), and why are there foreign phrases and passages in the legal writings of Warren and Brandeis (beginning on page 288)? These writers not only have particular purposes but also need to make particular demands on their readers to fulfill them. If you are unreasonable in your expectation that a reader will know the meaning of a foreign expression, or need that expression to understand your point, then that expression may be functioning, like some jargon, to bluff rather than to communicate.

Rules Are Not Laws

Orwell's final rule is the least specific and the most interesting. *Break any of these rules sooner than say anything outright barbarous.* What Orwell is saying, perhaps, is that rules can take you only so far, and if you rely on them slavishly, they might result in making your writing worse instead of better. Rules are for convenience, but they cannot replace good judgment. Applying editing rules can help you gain control over your writing. To be in control of your writing means that *you* decide how to phrase what *you* have to say; it is not control to let rules decide for you. But you earn the right to break rules when you know your options and have good reasons for choosing one way instead of another.

What does Orwell mean by *barbarous*? I'm not sure I know. I think he chose the word to make us think about what it means to be educated and civil, or whatever we think of as the dialectical opposite of *barbarous*. Although the word is usually applied to behavior in general, it has special connotations when it is applied to language. To write barbarously is to write without care, without respect for the reader or the subject. It is to mimic the prevailing style of others without thinking. But, ironically, to write in an "educated" way can often mean the same thing, when the writer uses big words or padding or passive verbs to bluff and bluster and impress rather than to speak honestly and clearly. The educated writer may be the most barbarous of all, if he or she has learned how to imitate official-sounding prose without at the same time learning to think more responsibly. Once again, ideas come first. The educated writer should be one for whom reasoning well is the most important goal. Editing well is a responsibility that follows from this goal and that helps the writer achieve it.

Proofreading

Revision generally occurs in the rough draft stage, when a piece of writing is meant to be recopied or reprinted. The final draft is the actual manuscript that a writer submits. The reader of this version assumes that the writer intends no further changes. Proofreading refers to the limited kind of revising that a writer does to a final printed or typed draft. Proofreading appears to the reader as last-minute changes that the writer has made, usually to correct typographical or spelling or grammatical errors, or to make minor stylistic changes overlooked in earlier drafts.

Careful proofreading is a sign that the writer has said exactly what he or she intended to say. If it matters to a writer that his or her ideas are communicated, the burden of making all parts of the writing work—from the reasoning and structure to the style and finally to the correctness of mechanics and grammar—is assumed by the writer. Proofreading is the final check that what the reader actually sees is what the writer intends.

It is during the proofreading stage that writers must think about aspects of grammar that may not have occurred to them earlier. Most of the time, grammatical errors will be caught and corrected during revision, so the following advice applies to revision and to proofreading. If there is any aspect of grammar that you are uncertain about, take the trouble to look it up or ask someone who knows the answer, like your teacher. You may make some mistakes in English usage that you do not know are mistakes—and you shouldn't be afraid to make them because you should hope to learn from having them pointed out to you. But at this point in your education, you probably know those areas of grammar that give you trouble. When in doubt, find out. Not knowing when to use *who* and *whom*, for instance, is not a sign of stupidity or of moral negligence, but such a mistake may distract your reader from your ideas. You can avoid such errors and learn the grammatical principle involved by consulting a good handbook. The conscientious writer will keep such a reference handy to consult when any question of grammar arises.

Proofreading consists of neat, legible corrections added to the final draft. Your reader should not be distracted by such corrections. Too many of them might mean that you should consider recopying, but it is better to include all necessary corrections than to give the reader the impression that you did not see errors or did not care whether they existed. The example at the bottom of this page shows part of a manuscript that has been carefully proofread and corrected. Notice that most of the changes are minor. A stylistic change here and there does not detract from the writer's credibility; it suggests that the writer is still thinking. Notice that some of the errors corrected on the illustration would be caught by a computer program, but others would not.

Be sure that you understand any particular kinds of proofreading marks that your teacher may prefer or require, because there are many ways of indicating such changes. A good handbook will describe specific proofreading conventions. The main objective of careful proofreading is to make sure that the final manuscript says exactly what you want it to say.

Teachers appreciate careful proofreading because it tells them exactly what the student understands about his or her own writing. A writing teacher is justified in thinking that any error you leave in your writing is the result of your ignorance of some aspect of English usage, and the teacher will therefore mark your errors for you in order to teach you. If you allow errors to go uncorrected in your writing when you do understand the correct way, you are not getting credit for what you know and you may be putting an unnecessary obstacle between your reader and your meaning.

The film attempted to explore the question of what is "normal" behavior in our society by having the main characters reverse roles and putting them in situations where their otherwise "abnormal" attributes make them more able to cope. Tom, the radical dropout, does not suffer the anxietes of his fellow workers because he does not take the business world all that seriously. And Sarah, who is equally fanatic in her desire to be upwardly mobile, is never persuaded that the revolution is just, but she makes it more efficient with her businesslike approach to organizing people. As light farce, the film leaves too many issues unexplored, however, and this reviewer missed the depth of questioning found in films like One Flew Over the Cuckoo's Nest or King of Hearts. Compared to these, this film suffers from myopia.

Questions for Thought, Discussion, and Writing

1. Analyze the style of a piece of argumentative writing that you think is effectively written. What stylistic choices seem to be present in order to make the sentences more readable? What choices seem to be present in order to make the writer sound more reasonable, credible, honest, sincere? What choices may hinder the writer's credibility?

2. Analyze a piece of your own writing in this same way.

3. After looking carefully for features that characterize the texture of your prose, make a list of any stylistic *habits* that you find in it.

4. Read George Orwell's "Politics and the English Language," and discuss these questions:
   a. Orwell admits that he has violated his own rules in his essay. Can you find some examples? Why does Orwell do so, and what does this tell you about the nature of language and rules for its use?
   b. Find examples from present-day political language that illustrate Orwell's principles, and say how you think their use has affected political thinking.
   c. Look carefully at an example of your own previous writing to find usages of which Orwell would disapprove. How might you change them? Do the same kind of analysis of the writing of a friend, a political columnist, or other writer.

5. A literary critic once said that "Every change in style is a change in meaning." Do you agree with this claim? Why or why not?

6. In your outside reading, locate several examples of figurative language used effectively and ineffectively. What reasons do you have for judging the examples in these ways?

7. Find examples of metaphors common in speech and writing that have the power to affect how people perceive reality. What gives them this power?

8. Find a piece of writing that you completed some time ago for a different class. Then:
   a. Locate and list all the metaphors. Do they work? Would you want to eliminate them? Why?
   b. Edit the writing by looking carefully at the diction, cutting unnecessary words, changing passive verbs to active ones in appropriate cases, changing the length and shape of your sentences, and trying to find effective, honest transitional phrases where they might be needed.

9. Once you have completed a rough draft of an essay for class, revise it according to principles discussed in this chapter. Try first to get someone to read it to you aloud. Listen carefully. By hearing it read, what do you learn?

10. After you receive an essay back from your teacher, analyze the comments according to the advice in this chapter. Reread your essay. What do the comments *teach* you as you think about applying them?

11. Along with the essay by George Orwell discussed in this chapter are the other essays grouped with it in Section 3 that also deal with the issue of the relationship between language and our thinking or the way in which we perceive the world. Do you think that the writers of the other essays view this relationship in the same way that Orwell does or do you think they view it differently? What are the differences and similarities among all of these essays? Based on these arguments, how do you think language is formed by culture and culture by language?

8

Implications for Research

Much of the writing that you will do in college requires some kind of research. Because some students sometimes produce writing that looks like research, but really isn't, we should consider for a moment what the term means in a college setting. Research is inquiry into the unknown. It is the pursuit of answers to questions that are yet unanswered. Research takes different forms, of course, but all research derives from a basic desire: to find out what is true.

Given these definitions, you can see why I said that the writing of college students sometimes resembles research but is, in fact, something else. The standard term paper—sometimes called a research paper—might not involve any genuine research at all, if, for instance, the writer only repeats information found in sources to confirm a conclusion that was never in doubt. Merely going to the library or using the Internet to compile information is not research; it is more like reporting on the research of others. Thus, a research paper is misnamed if the writer only repeats what others have asserted, without in some way testing that knowledge or using it to solve a problem. Yet, the term paper often turns out to be just such an exercise, in which greater importance is placed on the bulk of gathered information and the formalities of footnotes and bibliographies than on the search for answers.

A long essay, with correctly documented footnotes from many bibliographic sources, is a research paper only if it results from the writer's having sought and found an answer to a question. Research writing is the process of arguing that answer in such a way that the knowledge the writer has discovered can be shared with others. Research is like learning: It proceeds from not knowing to knowing. Research writing is like argumentation: It shows why answers should be accepted.

Research is not a process that begins with complete uncertainty and ends with complete certainty; it is, therefore, not possible to become "fully" informed first and then to decide what to believe. There are always gaps in one's knowledge—even if one reaches the point, after years of research and study, of becoming an expert. One learns by doing research that there is always something more to know before absolute certainty is possible. Thus, the research writer must always argue for his or her discoveries on the basis of the best information available. The research writer, in other words, must know how to argue well and responsibly without having "all" the answers. The researcher, as a writer of argumentation, must seek clarification and belief within the limits of what it is possible to know. As a writer of argumentative essays, you should be learning to measure conclusions against the quality, not the quantity, of the available reasons. This is exactly what a good researcher also needs to know how to do.

In the sections that follow, I will develop some of the implications for research, as I have just defined it, of some of the key concepts of this book.

Critical Reading and Research

As a student—and as a voter, a consumer, a person who must decide things—you will often need to find out more than you already know about some subject before committing yourself to a conclusion or a course of action. Critical reading is necessary in order to know what to make of the knowledge that you discover when you look into some subject, but it will also help you to decide what needs looking into. When, in your further reading, you try to judge the conclusions you find against the adequacy of the reasons given for them, you will be able to isolate the particular areas in which your knowledge needs to be increased. By reading critically, you may find that you need not read further in one area, such as anesthesia, but do need to know more about some other, such as sodium pentothal.

In formal research, you will be responsible for finding information to explain a phenomenon and evidence for arguing a reasonable conclusion about it. In informal research—the kind we do whenever we have unanswered questions, even if no writing will result from it—you will want to assure yourself that your ideas or actions are founded on reasons that you understand and trust. The goal of either kind of research is confidence in what you know. Critical reading will guide you in gaining that confidence, even though, as we saw in Chapter 2, that confidence is not easy to come by.

Because of its convenience, the Internet has increasingly become a place to start when one is looking for information as part of a research project. One can access a wealth of information on the Internet from the comfort of one's own room or from nearly anywhere using a modem. However, if you look for information on the Internet exclusively, without adding to what you know the ideas and information potentially available in a research library, you are probably limiting your inquiry too narrowly. And, given the nature of the Internet, you need to consider some of its limitations as well as its strengths.

As in the case of using any limited research source, you must be aware that simply reporting information or repeating arguments that you find on the

Internet is not genuine research but merely gathering the ideas and information of others. *Research,* as I have defined it above, is "inquiry into the unknown." To answer questions, and repeat the obvious or download some source, isn't inquiry in this sense. When you perform research on the Internet, despite the air of authority computers impart to information because of their speed of access and the sometimes seductive forms in which that information is graphically displayed, you are still responsible for being a critical reader, an independent evaluator of ideas and information. You will find that the questions for critical reading from Chapter 2 will help you evaluate Internet sites in the same way they are meant to help you evaluate the printed texts you encounter in books, newspapers, or magazines.

There is, though, a significant difference between information presented on most Internet sites and certain kinds of printed information. Printed texts, before they are published and located in libraries or bookstores, especially if they are written by experts in their field and published as scholarly research, go through a rigorous process of evaluation by other experts in the field. This process cannot guard against all errors of unsound reasoning and may require much time before the information is available in print. Yet because of that peer review process, printed texts generally have been reviewed for accuracy and soundness in a way that most Internet sites have not.

The nature of the Internet is to enable anyone with a little knowledge of Web site design and an Internet connection to set up a Web site and put anything on it that that person wishes. In most cases, there is no peer review of that process at all. So information found there is more likely to be dated, incomplete, prejudicially opinionated (as opposed to reasoned), or just plain wrong. Because it is so easy to put up a Web page, what is found there may not have the thoroughness or carefully researched quality that is likely to be found, say, in a good scholarly book or reference guide on the subject. Also Internet Web sites often emphasize graphic design over content, and many of the sites that are constructed thoughtlessly let the graphic design determine the nature and quality of the information rather than the other way around.

Therefore, as a responsible researcher, you will need to be cautious when researching on the Internet, and if you are seriously investigating a subject, follow up with some time in a research library, such as the one at your college. The following questions can help you toward becoming a more critical Internet reader: Who is the author? Is he or she taking responsibility for the information? Is he or she connected with an organization that can be trusted to be unbiased in its reporting of information? Does the author provide a bibliography or other resource materials that allow you to check on the accuracy of the information cited? Is the argument developed as thoroughly as it would be in a printed medium? Is the information developed for that site or simply downloaded from another? Is it timely? Are there political, or commercial, motives that might make you suspicious of the site's rigor or thoroughness? How has the graphic design of the site been used—as an aid to understanding the information or as a substitute for or mask for information?

Of course the Internet is also a wonderful resource for many kinds of visual or reference texts, and it can link us to others in ways nothing else can. It provides, for instance, the ability to put us in direct, almost instantaneous touch with researchers or experts. Taking advantage of these wonders is an important part of your education. But if you experience these benefits of the Internet without knowing about the many wonders of the library as well, your research will be incomplete. And you will be depriving yourself of the kinds and quality of resources and research texts to be found in libraries that are not available on the Web.

If you are interested in looking further into the issue of critical evaluation of Internet sites, you might want to take a look at a World Wide Web site called Evaluating Internet Information at milton.mse.jhu.edu.8001/research/education/net.html. Now, does it seem ironic to you that in my cautioning you to be critical of Internet research, I would direct you to the Internet for more information? Indeed. So, be sure to evaluate this site using the same criteria.

Asking Questions for Research

It may have seemed from Chapter 4 that coming up with a reasonable thesis is a matter of thinking only about what you already know, that it does not require you to become well informed before jumping off into speculation. Not so. Coming up with a reasonable thesis is *primarily* a matter of thinking hard about what you know. You will not find your own thesis by going to the library or surfing the Net in search of what to think. But in the process of thinking about potential theses, you will encounter gaps in your knowledge of a subject, and if these gaps prevent you from thinking about that subject further because you do not know something that is vital to your understanding, then you should attempt to fill those gaps. There is a difference between rash speculation and honest speculation. If you are unsure of something that is crucial to your position, or if you are assuming that some part of your idea is true because you "heard it somewhere" or because "my sister told me," then you are being rash. An honest commitment to an idea should be based on your confidence that the knowledge that idea seems to assert is real knowledge.

The lesson here is simple. You must think hard about your ideas; there's no way around that, except to be irresponsible. But you might, by thinking hard, discover that you need to look something up, to find out or to verify the knowledge you want to claim. If that is the case, then finding out becomes your further responsibility.

Formulating a research question can be an aid to conducting such an inquiry. It should enable you to define the unknowns, to determine the boundaries of the inquiry, and to keep the inquiry focused as you seek to become better informed. Of course, the question starts out as a tentative formulation, subject to change. The more you discover and the more thought you give to the possible answers, the clearer you may become about the kind of question that you wish to answer. Research is seldom so straightforward that no side trips, dead ends, detours, or unexpected changes of plan happen along the road to answers. The process of becoming informed seldom follows a predictable route.

Having formulated a research question, you might ask yourself something like, "What do I need to know to answer this question?" At this point you might sketch out a plan, listing some of the specific areas you need to know more about. Any question can be broken down into constituent parts, even if the categories are temporary or turn out later to be irrelevant. You may not yet know what all of the categories are—research is, after all, exploring the unknown. Yet you are never starting out without some knowledge to begin with, because you had to understand something already in order to perceive the significance of the question you have decided to explore. Trust that knowledge and sketch out some possibilities, based on the question you have formulated.

The available resources of libraries are so vast that it is, of course, necessary to know how each library is organized and what kinds of catalogs and indexes exist to give researchers access to its holdings. If you have not become familiar with the resources of a research library, you can ask the reference staff for their advice. All good libraries have educational material available to students who wish to acquaint themselves with the basic functions of the library. Descriptions of different kinds of reference materials (subject or author/title indexes for books, indexes to periodicals, bibliographies, abstracts of research, and more) can also be found in a good college writing handbook. Rather than discuss these here, I assume you are able to look them up if you need to. Often, the best way to discover what kinds of resources the library has available in your own areas of interest is to get in there with your questions and begin to follow leads wherever they take you. It isn't efficient, of course, just to plunge in without a good idea of where to look for the information you seek. But it is often adventurous and fun to explore somewhat as a means of becoming familiar with the library at the same time that you seek to inform yourself about your subject. A researcher, like a detective, has to be watchful for unexpected clues. The library is full of these, and you should be prepared to investigate any that might take you into important discoveries.

Research in the library has one crucial limitation. Only by knowing what kind of question you are researching, and what unknowns define the inquiry, can you know whether this limitation will apply to any particular research project you might undertake. This limitation is probably best described by distinguishing secondary research from primary research. Secondary research consists of locating and using the research that other people have already conducted and written about. One way of going about answering research questions is to read the writing of other researchers who have investigated the same or related questions. Primary research consists of investigating any phenomenon on one's own by working directly with the phenomenon rather than reading about other people's work with it. Secondary research is ordinarily conducted in the library, because that is where one usually goes to find out what others have written. Primary research is ordinarily conducted outside the library.

The distinction between primary and secondary research applies to all fields of inquiry. Science provides the most obvious examples. A biologist, for instance, may be interested in discovering how a particular species of plant reacts to changes in light. There are many things about this question that she might learn in the library. To answer it, she would have to know as much about the plant as possible and about how other species of plants react to similar changes, information that can be found in the published research of other biologists. She would also want to know whether anyone has already discovered the answer to her question or to questions that bear on it. But having informed herself in this way, the researcher would have to move from the library to the laboratory to complete the study by conducting experiments with plants and light sources. The secondary research provides preparation for the primary research. Depending on the kind of question under investigation, primary research takes place in the laboratory or in the field or simply in the privacy of one's thoughts. An anthropologist investigating what kinds of traditions accompany marriage in urban subcultures may learn a lot by reading, but at some point he would want to go out and collect some primary information by talking to people and observing the phenomena firsthand. A sociologist studying the attitudes of teenagers toward alcohol abuse can learn much by reading in the library, but she would also have to question teenagers to find her answers. A scholar studying the possible influence of impressionist painting on the literary style of Gertrude Stein would learn much by finding sources in the library, but her primary research would consist of careful observations about the paintings and the writing. The way in which primary research is conducted varies from discipline to discipline, depending on the kinds of questions being asked, but all research moves from the secondary collecting and assessment of others' ideas to the primary study of the phenomenon under study. Primary research *extends* secondary research. Without both, no research would be complete.

Finally, remember that the researcher enters the process of becoming informed without knowing where that process may lead. The research question, like the thesis of an argumentative essay, may change as the researcher discovers more information or complexities and continues to think about them. Further questions may arise. Answers may have to remain tentative. But just as the writer of an argumentative essay has to decide when a line of reasoning is adequate, a researcher must decide when a question can be answered reasonably. In either case, there is nothing wrong with admitting that the answer is only as good as the quality of the evidence that supports it, so that the possibility of further inquiry remains open.

Research and Reasons

Reasons, like conclusions, are assertions and therefore subject to verification if they rely on information that the writer is not absolutely confident about. In that case, everything I just said about the possible need to inform yourself before making rash statements in your thesis applies to the claims you decide to use as reasons. Your reasoning does not depend solely on the validity of your logic. It depends equally on the dependability of your information. But you know by now that simply looking up information is not sufficient. How do you know whether to trust what you find? Let's look at how some of the considerations in Chapter 5 might help to answer this question. As you read, for instance, consider the *kind of appeal* that the writer is making. Does this give you more or less confidence in the source? As you read, isolate the enthymemes and reconstruct the assumptions that you are expected to accept as self-evident. What does this say about the writer's view of his or her reader? How does this affect your understanding of the subject?

Rather than try to offer a dependable procedure for knowing when a source is right or wrong, let me describe the worst kind of uncritical research and see what it tells us about our responsibilities as evaluators of reasoning. I have seen student term papers in which many sources were cited to support the writer's idea, but in each case those sources consisted exclusively of the conclusions of studies that agree with the writer. In other words, the writer's thesis is argued by constructing a list of authorities all saying the same thing, as if such a list alone proved the point. This catalog of authorities does not constitute an argument, however, because the *reasons* that these sources give for their conclusions are not explored. Such a writer has located many sources and found their conclusions, but he or she has not tried to assess those conclusions according to the process by which they were derived. The resulting "research paper" does not discriminate between conclusions derived by adequate means and conclusions derived by inadequate ones. As an argument, it is weak. As research, it is useless.

Clearly, then, anyone conducting serious research has the responsibility of doing more than skimming through sources to find conclusions. Once you have found a source that seems relevant, you must know not only what its conclusions are but also how those conclusions have been derived. In other words, you must consider the arguments that have been presented in support of those conclusions and assess the conclusions accordingly.

What does it claim?

By what process have the conclusions been derived? What reasons are presented? What qualifiers?

On what assumptions do the reasons depend?

How adequate is the logic?

Your answers to these questions are just as important to your research as the conclusions themselves. Your own presentation of the results of your research must demonstrate that your inquiry has included such questions. Your reader, after all, can be assumed to be capable of asking them about your own conclusions.

It is also the researcher's responsibility to have located and considered studies that do not support whatever potential conclusion he or she may intend to reach. Research questions are open-ended, but researchers often work from a hypothesis, whether it is defined early in the study or late. Whenever answers begin to emerge, it is essential to know which reasons may contradict those answers as well as which reasons support them. This way of looking at arguments, whether others' or one's own, is called **falsification.**

The process of falsifying ideas is an important mental exercise, involving seriously trying to answer questions like:

What if this idea is wrong?

What kinds of reasons could be used to argue against it?

What would have to be true for those reasons to be valid?

What assumptions are available to support those reasons?

To be able to consider such questions seriously, a researcher must have the mental agility to shift points of view. (We all probably increase our mental agility simply by trying to answer such questions.) It helps to see the weakness in a given line of reasoning to know how a different conclusion might be argued. To learn this requires that we be able to imagine how someone who holds a different view might defend it. No harm is done if by this means we come to question our ideas, or even to change our minds.

Structuring Research

Every researcher is also a communicator. Because the progress of research goes from formulating a question and becoming informed to drawing and testing conclusions, these same elements constitute the essence of what the researcher must communicate. These, of course, are the elements of an argumentative essay. Formulating a thesis, developing a principal line of reasoning, structuring the reasoning into major parts of the composition, revising the argument, generating a structure, and drafting the essay do not change for the researcher. The research paper adds to these responsibilities certain others that follow from having used secondary sources and conducted primary research of some kind.

The researcher, in the process of gathering information and discovering reasons to support a hypothesis, has amassed much information and tested its relevance and validity. Not everything that the inquiry has turned up will necessarily be relevant, and the writer may eventually use only a portion of the actual information he or she has discovered. The writer should include whatever is necessary and sufficient to lead to a conclusion, as well as whatever may need to be said to refute the arguments of others or suggest limitations on one's own. To do this requires planning, along the lines discussed in Chapter 6. The writer can perceive the necessary structure of the essay by analyzing the parts of the whole argument, which can be summarized in an enthymeme. It is important to remember here that the order in which the research findings appear in the essay will not necessarily be the same as the order in which the researcher discovered them. The structure of the final essay is not, usually, a narrative of what happened to the researcher during the inquiry. The structure of the final argument is made up of ideas discovered during research, in whatever logical order binds those ideas into a whole, developing argument.

The structure of research writing in some disciplines is determined in part by conventional formats. It may or may not be necessary for you to follow them in writing for college courses, because the formats generally derive from the conventions of publication in different fields. Thus, an academic journal of research in psychology may specify that papers submitted for publication have a certain form. Articles in the social sciences often follow the conventional divisions of scientific reports, with all the material organized under headings, such as:

Problem and hypothesis

Review of relevant literature

Experiment design

Results

Analysis

Conclusion and discussion

The specific headings differ from discipline to discipline, and even from publication to publication, so you should not try to reproduce a standard format of this kind unless you are fulfilling an assignment that specifically calls for one, or writing for a publication that does. If your audience expects to find your research organized in such a way, then your use of a conventional format will make their reading easier. If not, you should be guided only by the ideas you present. Do not confuse structure with format. You are no less responsible for structuring your ideas *within* each of these conventional sections, if you use them.

As a research writer you have a special obligation to provide whatever the reader needs to know to assess the validity of your findings. Remember that you are interested in finding the best possible reasons for drawing a conclusion, not in bullying the reader into believing some idea that you haven't adequately supported. This means that you should consider including a description of the methods that you have used in your study and any limitations imposed by those methods. In some cases, this may mean a description of an experiment, a survey, or some other form of primary research, together with a description of the sorts of conclusions that such methods are not able to support. Or it may mean that you should inform the reader about any prior assumptions or perspectives that have guided your inquiry. If you have doubts about any of your sources, you can say so. If you think there are weaknesses in your conclusions, qualify them accordingly. If you have discovered reasons against your case (by reading sources that disagree or by falsifying your conclusions), present them fairly and let the reader assess them as you have done. Be sure that your reason for leaving anything out is that it isn't relevant or necessary, not that you wish to hide anything.

Honest research, like honest argumentative writing, is intended to put the whole case forward, as you see it, so that the reader's understanding and agreement are *earned.*

Questions for Thought, Discussion, and Writing

1. What have been your experiences as a researcher before this point in your education? Did the research you conducted fit the definition of genuine research I presented at the beginning of this chapter? Under what circumstances did it fit that definition or not fit it? If you have a copy of a research paper you wrote for another class, consider these questions in regard to that paper:
   a. Did you begin with an open mind, or was your conclusion already established before you began to look for sources?
   b. Did you read your sources critically or just look for conclusions in them that supported your own ideas?
   c. Did you evaluate the credibility of your sources?
   d. Did you look for sources of opinion that were different from your conclusions, and did you incorporate them into your argument?
   e. Did you engage in primary as well as secondary research?
   f. Independent of the grade you may have gotten for the paper, how do your answers to these questions affect your assessment of the quality of that writing now?

2. As you read many of the essays included in this book, you will notice that I have usually provided brief notes about the authors. These incomplete notes are only intended to provide some context for your reading of the essays. You will also notice that I have not included notes or references to unfamiliar words or names used by these authors in their essays. If you think the notes do not tell you all that you want to know about the author, or if you encounter words or names in the essays that are unfamiliar to you, formulate a research plan that will result in giving you the information you need. As you look up the information, consider these questions:
   a. What *kind* of resource best provides the *kind* of information I need?
   b. How much information is enough for my purposes?
   c. How is my understanding of the essay improved by this information?
   d. What further questions does the information raise?

3. As you do the preceding exercise, or as you look up information for another purpose, deliberately seek the same information in several different library and Internet sources. Compare the results by asking these questions:
   a. Which resource is more likely to provide accurate, thorough, or sufficient information?
   b. How do different kinds of library and Internet resources differ in terms of their potential usefulness for research?
   c. How do the library and Internet resources differ in the way information is presented?

4. As you formulate a thesis in the form of an enthymeme for an argumentative essay, construct a series of research questions that need to be answered before you can make the argument responsibly. Create a research strategy that will begin your search for answers. As you conduct that research, consider how what you discover may change the argument you have drafted. Deliberately search for credible arguments that come to different conclusions from your own, and consider how your own argument needs to be written in order to acknowledge or to do justice to those opposing arguments you have found.

5. What is the difference between research that is ethical and research that is unethical? How do you know?

Readings for Analysis, Discussion, and Written Response

Issues about the Limits of Civil Authority

Crito

Plato

Plato (c. 428–348 B.C.) lived in Athens, Greece. Most of his writing is in the form of dialogues between the philosopher Socrates and other Athenian citizens. Socrates was Plato's teacher, whose trial and martyrdom Plato dramatized in three dialogues: "The Apology," "Crito," and "Phaedo." Socrates himself left behind no writings.

Socrates: Here already, Crito? Surely it is still early?

Crito: Indeed it is.

Socrates: About what time?

Crito: Just before dawn.

Socrates: I wonder that the warder paid any attention to you.

Crito: He is used to me now, Socrates, because I come here so often; besides, he is under some small obligation to me.

Socrates: Have you only just come, or have you been here for long?

Crito: Fairly long.

Socrates: Then why didn't you wake me at once, instead of sitting by my bed so quietly?

Crito: I wouldn't dream of such a thing, Socrates. I only wish I were not so sleepless and depressed myself. I have been wondering at you, because I saw how comfortably you were sleeping; and I deliberately didn't wake you because I wanted you to go on being as comfortable as you could. I have often felt before in the course of my life how fortunate you are in your disposition, but I feel it more than ever now in your present misfortune when I see how easily and placidly you put up with it.

Socrates: Well, really, Crito, it would be hardly suitable for a man of my age to resent having to die.

Crito: Other people just as old as you are get involved in these misfortunes, Socrates, but their age doesn't keep them from resenting it when they find themselves in your position.

Socrates: Quite true. But tell me, why have you come so early?

Crito: Because I bring bad news, Socrates; not so bad from your point of view, I suppose, but it will be very hard to bear for me and your other friends, and I think that I shall find it hardest of all.

Socrates: Why, what is this news? Has the boat come in from Delos—the boat which ends my reprieve when it arrives?

Crito: It hasn't actually come in yet, but I expect that it will be here today, judging from the report of some people who have just arrived from Sunium and left it there. It's quite clear from their account that it will be here today; and so by tomorrow, Socrates, you will have to—to end your life.

Socrates: Well, Crito, I hope that it may be for the best; if the gods will it so, so be it. All the same, I don't think it will arrive today.

Crito: What makes you think that?

Socrates: I will try to explain. I think I am right in saying that I have to die on the day after the boat arrives?

Crito: That's what the authorities say, at any rate.

Socrates: Then I don't think it will arrive on this day that is just beginning, but on the day after. I am going by a dream that I had in the night, only a little while ago. It looks as though you were right not to wake me up.

Crito: Why, what was the dream about?

Socrates: I thought I saw a gloriously beautiful woman dressed in white robes, who came up to me and addressed me in these words: "Socrates, to the pleasant land of Phthia on the third day thou shalt come."

Crito: Your dream makes no sense, Socrates.

Socrates: To my mind, Crito, it is perfectly clear.

Crito: Too clear, apparently. But look here, Socrates, it is still not too late to take my advice and escape. Your death means a double calamity for me. I shall not only lose a friend whom I can never possibly replace, but besides a great many people who don't know you and me very well will be sure to think that I let you down, because I could have saved you if I had been willing to spend the money; and what could be more contemptible than to get a name for thinking more of money than of your friends? Most people will never believe that it was you who refused to leave this place although we tried our hardest to persuade you.

Socrates: But my dear Crito, why should we pay so much attention to what "most people" think? The really reasonable people, who have more claim to be considered, will believe that the facts are exactly as they are.

Crito: You can see for yourself, Socrates, that one has to think of popular opinion as well. Your present position is quite enough to show that the capacity of ordinary people for causing trouble is not confined to petty annoyances, but has hardly any limits if you once get a bad name with them.

Socrates: I only wish that ordinary people *had* unlimited capacity for doing harm; then they might have an unlimited power for doing good; which would be a splendid thing, if it were so. Actually they have neither. They cannot make a man wise or stupid; they simply act at random.

Crito: Have it that way if you like; but tell me this, Socrates. I hope that you aren't worrying about the possible effects on me and the rest of your friends, and thinking that if you escape we shall have trouble with informers for having helped you to get away, and have to forfeit all our property or pay an enormous fine, or even incur some further punishment? If any idea like that is troubling you, you can dismiss it altogether. We are quite entitled to run that risk in saving you, and even worse, if necessary. Take my advice, and be reasonable.

Socrates: All that you say is very much in my mind, Crito, and a great deal more besides.

Crito: Very well, then, don't let it distress you. I know some people who are willing to rescue you from here and get you out of the country for quite a moderate sum. And then surely you realize how cheap these informers are to buy off; we shan't need much money to settle them; and I think you've got enough of my money for yourself already. And then even supposing that in your anxiety for my safety you feel that you oughtn't to spend my money, there are these foreign gentlemen staying in Athens who are quite willing to spend theirs. One of them, Simmias of Thebes, has actually brought the money with him for this very purpose; and Cebes and a number of others are quite ready to do the same. So as I say, you mustn't let any fears on these grounds make you slacken your efforts to escape; and you mustn't feel any misgivings about what you said at your trial, that you wouldn't know what to do with yourself if you left this country. Wherever you go, there are plenty of places where you will find a welcome; and if you choose to go to Thessaly, I have friends there who will make much of you and give you complete protection, so that no one in Thessaly can interfere with you.

Besides, Socrates, I don't even feel that it is right for you to try to do what you are doing, throwing away your life when you might save it. You are doing your best to treat yourself in exactly the same way as your enemies would, or rather did, when they wanted to ruin you. What is more, it seems to me that you are letting your sons down too. You have it in your power to finish their bringing up and education, and instead of that you are proposing to go off and desert them, and so far as you are concerned they will have to take their chance. And what sort of chance are they likely to get? The sort of thing that usually happens to orphans when they lose their parents. Either one ought not to have children at all, or one ought to see their upbringing and education through to the end. It strikes me that you are taking the line of least resistance, whereas you ought to make the choice of a good man and a brave one, considering that you profess to have made goodness your object all through life. Really, I am ashamed, both on your account and on ours your friends'; it will look as though we had played something like a coward's part all through this affair of yours. First, there was the way you came into court when it was quite unnecessary—that was the first act; then there was the conduct of the defense—that was the second; and finally, to complete the farce, we get this situation, which makes it appear that we have let you slip out of our hands through some lack of courage and enterprise on our part, because we didn't save you, and you didn't save yourself, when it would have been quite possible and practicable, if we had been any use at all.

There, Socrates; if you aren't careful, besides the suffering there will be all this disgrace for you and us to bear. Come, make up your mind. Really it's too late for that now; you ought to have it made up already. There is no alternative; the whole thing must be carried through during this coming night. If we lose any more time, it can't be done, it will be too late. I appeal to you, Socrates, on every ground; take my advice and please don't be unreasonable!

Socrates: My dear Crito, I appreciate your warm feelings very much—that is, assuming that they have some justification; if not, the stronger they are, the harder they will be to deal with. Very well, then; we must consider whether we ought to follow your advice or not. You know that this is not a new idea of mine; it has always been my nature never to accept advice from any of my friends unless reflection shows that it is the best course that reason offers. I cannot abandon the principles which I used to hold in the past simply because this accident has happened to me; they seem to me to be much as they were, and I respect and regard the same principles now as before. So unless we can find better principles on this occasion, you can be quite sure that I shall not agree with you; not even if the power of the people conjures up fresh hordes of bogies to terrify our childish minds, by subjecting us to chains and executions and confiscations of our property.

Well, then, how can we consider the question most reasonably? Suppose that we begin by reverting to this view which you hold about people's opinions. Was it always right to argue that some opinions should be taken seriously but not others? Or was it always wrong? Perhaps it was right before the question of my death arose, but now we can see clearly that it was a mistaken persistence in a point of view which was really irresponsible nonsense. I should like very much to inquire into this problem, Crito, with your help, and to see whether the argument will appear in any different light to me now that I am in this position, or whether it will remain the same; and whether we shall dismiss it or accept it.

Serious thinkers, I believe, have always held some such view as the one which I mentioned just now: that some of the opinions which people entertain should be respected, and others should not. Now I ask you, Crito, don't you think that this is a sound principle?—You are safe from the prospect of dying tomorrow, in all human probability; and you are not likely to have your judgment upset by this impending calamity. Consider, then; don't you think that this is a sound enough principle, that one should not regard all the opinions that people hold, but only some and not others? What do you say? Isn't that a fair statement?

Crito: Yes, it is.

Socrates: In other words, one should regard the good ones and not the bad?

Crito: Yes.

Socrates: The opinions of the wise being good, and the opinions of the foolish bad?

Crito: Naturally.

Socrates: To pass on, then: What do you think of the sort of illustration that I used to employ? When a man is in training, and taking it seriously, does he pay attention to all praise and criticism and opinion indiscriminately, or only when it comes from the one qualified person, the actual doctor or trainer?

Crito: Only when it comes from the one qualified person.

Socrates: Then he should be afraid of the criticism and welcome the praise of the one qualified person, but not those of the general public.

Crito: Obviously.

Socrates: So he ought to regulate his actions and exercises and eating and drinking by the judgment of his instructor, who has expert knowledge, rather than by the opinions of the rest of the public.

Crito: Yes, that is so.

Socrates: Very well. Now if he disobeys the one man and disregards his opinion and commendations, and pays attention to the advice of the many who have no expert knowledge, surely he will suffer some bad effect?

Crito: Certainly.

Socrates: And what is this bad effect? Where is it produced?—I mean, in what part of the disobedient person?

Crito: His body, obviously; that is what suffers.

Socrates: Very good. Well now, tell me, Crito—we don't want to go through all the examples one by one—does this apply as a general rule, and above all to the sort of actions which we are trying to decide about: just and unjust, honorable and dishonorable, good and bad? Ought we to be guided and intimidated by the opinion of the many or by that of the one—assuming that there is someone with expert knowledge? Is it true that we ought to respect and fear this person more than all the rest put together; and that if we do not follow his guidance we shall spoil and mutilate that part of us which, as we used to say, is improved by right conduct and destroyed by wrong? Or is this all nonsense?

Crito: No, I think it is true, Socrates.

Socrates: Then consider the next step. There is a part of us which is improved by healthy actions and ruined by unhealthy ones. If we spoil it by taking the advice of nonexperts, will life be worth living when this part is once ruined? The part I mean is the body; do you accept this?

Crito: Yes.

Socrates: Well, is life worth living with a body which is worn out and ruined by health?

Crito: Certainly not.

Socrates: What about the part of us which is mutilated by wrong actions and benefited by right ones? Is life worth living with this part ruined? Or do we believe that this part of us, whatever it may be, in which right and wrong operate, is of less importance than the body?

Crito: Certainly not.

Socrates: It is really more precious?

Crito: Much more.

Socrates: In that case, my dear fellow, what we ought to consider is not so much what people in general will say about us but how we stand with the expert in right and wrong, the one authority, who represents the actual truth. So in the first place your proposition is not correct when you say that we should consider popular opinion in questions of what is right and honorable and good, or the opposite. Of course one might object, "All the same, the people have the power to put us to death."

Crito: No doubt about that! Quite true, Socrates; it is a possible objection.

Socrates: But so far as I can see, my dear fellow, the argument which we have just been through is quite unaffected by it. At the same time I should like you to consider whether we are still satisfied on this point: that the really important thing is not to live, but to live well.

Crito: Why, yes.

Socrates: And that to live well means the same thing as to live honorably or rightly?

Crito: Yes.

Socrates: Then in the light of this agreement we must consider whether or not it is right for me to try to get away without an official discharge. If it turns out to be right, we must make the attempt; if not, we must let it drop. As for the considerations you raise about expense and reputation and bringing up children, I am afraid, Crito, that they represent the reflections of the ordinary public, who put people to death, and would bring them back to life if they could, with equal indifference to reason. Our real duty, I fancy, since the argument leads that way, is to consider one question only, the one which we raised just now: Shall we be acting rightly in paying money and showing gratitude to these people who are going to rescue me, and in escaping or arranging the escape ourselves, or shall we really be acting wrongly in doing all this? If it becomes clear that such conduct is wrong, I cannot help thinking that the question whether we are sure to die, or to suffer any other ill effect for that matter, if we stand our ground and take no action, ought not to weigh with us at all in comparison with the risk of doing what is wrong.

Crito: I agree with what you say, Socrates; but I wish you would consider what we ought to *do.*

Socrates: Let us look at it together, my dear fellow; and if you can challenge any of my arguments, do so and I will listen to you; but if you can't, be a good fellow and stop telling me over and over again that I ought to leave this place without official permission. I am very anxious to obtain your approval before I adopt the course which I have in mind; I don't want to act against your convictions. Now give your attention to the starting point of this inquiry—I hope that you will be satisfied with my way of stating it—and try to answer my questions to the best of your judgment.

Crito: Well, I will try.

Socrates: Do we say that one must never willingly do wrong, or does it depend upon circumstance? Is it true, as we have often agreed before, that there is no sense in which wrongdoing is good or honorable? Or have we jettisoned all our former convictions in these last few days? Can you and I at our age, Crito, have spent all these years in serious discussions without realizing that we were no better than a pair of children? Surely the truth is just what we have always said. Whatever the popular view is, and whether the alternative is pleasanter than the present one or even harder to bear, the fact remains that to do wrong is in every sense bad and dishonorable for the person who does it. Is that our view, or not?

Crito: Yes, it is.

Socrates: Then in no circumstances must one do wrong.

Crito: No.

Socrates: In that case one must not even do wrong when one is wronged, which most people regard as the natural course.

Crito: Apparently not.

Socrates: Tell me another thing, Crito: Ought one to do injuries or not?

Crito: Surely not, Socrates.

Socrates: And tell me: Is it right to do an injury in retaliation, as most people believe, or not?

Crito: No, never.

Socrates: Because, I suppose, there is no difference between injuring people and wronging them.

Crito: Exactly.

Socrates: So one ought not to return a wrong or an injury to any person, whatever the provocation is. Now be careful, Crito, that in making these single admissions you do not end by admitting something contrary to your real beliefs. I know that there are and always will be few people who think like this; and consequently between those who do think so and those who do not there can be no agreement on principle; they must always feel contempt when they observe one another's decisions. I want even you to consider very carefully whether you share my views and agree with me, and whether we can proceed with our discussion from the established hypothesis that it is never right to do a wrong or return a wrong or defend one's self against injury by retaliation; or whether you dissociate yourself from any share in this view as a basis for discussion. I have held it for a long time, and still hold it; but if you have formed any other opinion, say so and tell me what it is. If, on the other hand, you stand by what we have said, listen to my next point.

Crito: Yes, I stand by it and agree with you. Go on.

Socrates: Well, here is my next point, or rather question. Ought one to fulfill all one's agreements, provided that they are right, or break them?

Crito: One ought to fulfill them.

Socrates: Then consider the logical consequence. If we leave this place without first persuading the State to let us go, are we or are we not doing an injury, and doing it in a quarter where it is least justifiable? Are we or are we not abiding by our just agreements?

Crito: I can't answer your question, Socrates; I am not clear in my mind.

Socrates: Look at it in this way. Suppose that while we were preparing to run away from here (or however one should describe it) the Laws and Constitution of Athens were to come and confront us and ask this question: "Now, Socrates, what are you proposing to do? Can you deny that by this act which you are contemplating you intend, so far as you have the power, to destroy us, the Laws, and the whole State as well? Do you imagine that a city can continue to exist and not be turned upside down, if the legal judgments which are pronounced in it have no force but are nullified and destroyed by private persons?"—how shall we answer this question, Crito, and others of the same kind? There is much that could be said, especially by a professional advocate, to protest against the invalidation of this law which enacts that judgments once pronounced shall be binding. Shall we say "Yes, I do intend to destroy the laws, because the State wronged me by passing a faulty judgment at my trial"? Is this to be our answer, or what?

Crito: What you have just said, by all means, Socrates.

Socrates: Then what supposing the Laws say, "Was there provision for this in the agreement between you and us, Socrates? Or did you undertake to abide by whatever judgments the State pronounced?" If we expressed surprise at such language, they would probably say: "Never mind our language, Socrates, but answer our questions; after all, you are accustomed to the method of question and answer. Come now, what charge do you bring against us and the State, that you are trying to destroy us? Did we not give you life in the first place? Was it not through us that your father married your mother and begot you? Tell us, have you any complaint against those of us Laws that deal with marriage?" "No, none," I should say. "Well, have you any against the laws which deal with children's upbringing and education, such as you had yourself? Are you not grateful to those of us Laws which were instituted for this end, for requiring your father to give you a cultural and physical education?" "Yes," I should say. "Very good. Then since you have been born and brought up and educated, can you deny, in the first place, that you were our child and servant, both you and your ancestors? And if this is so, do you imagine that what is right for us is equally right for you, and that whatever we try to do to you, you are justified in retaliating? You did not have equality of rights with your father, or your employer (supposing that you had had one), to enable you to retaliate; you were not allowed to answer back when you were scolded or to hit back when you were beaten, or to do a great many other things of the same kind. Do you expect to have such license against your country and its laws that if we try to put you to death in the belief that it is right to do so, you on your part will try your hardest to destroy your country and us its Laws in return? And will you, the true devotee of goodness, claim that you are justified in doing so? Are you so wise as to have forgotten that compared with your mother and father and all the rest of your ancestors your country is something far more precious, more venerable, more sacred, and held in greater honor both among gods and among all reasonable men? Do you not realize that you are even more bound to respect and placate the anger of your country than your father's anger? That if you cannot persuade your country you must do whatever it orders, and patiently submit to any punishment that it imposes, whether it be flogging or imprisonment? And if it leads you out to war, to be wounded or killed, you must comply, and it is right that you should do so; you must not give way or retreat or abandon your position. Both in war and in the law courts and everywhere else you must do whatever your city and your country commands, or else persuade it in accordance with universal justice; but violence is a sin even against your parents, and it is a far greater sin against your country"—What shall we say to this, Crito?— that what the Laws say is true, or not?

Crito: Yes, I think so.

Socrates: "Consider, then, Socrates," the Laws would probably continue, "whether it is also true for us to say that what you are now trying to do to us is not right. Although we have brought you into the world and reared you and educated you, and given you and all your fellow citizens a share in all the good things at our disposal, nevertheless by the very fact of granting our permission we openly proclaim this principle: that any Athenian, on attaining to manhood and seeing for himself the political organization of the State and us its Laws, is permitted, if he is not satisfied with us, to take his property and go away wherever he likes. If any of you chooses to go to one of our colonies, supposing that he should not be satisfied with us and the State, or to emigrate to any other country, not one of us Laws hinders or prevents him from going away wherever he likes, without any loss of property. On the other hand, if any one of you stands his ground when he can see how we administer justice and the rest of our public organization, we hold that by so doing he has in fact undertaken to do anything that we tell him; and we maintain that anyone who disobeys is guilty of doing wrong on three separate counts: first because we are his parents, and secondly because we are his guardians; and thirdly because, after promising obedience, he is neither obeying us nor persuading us to change our decision if we are at fault in any way; and although all our orders are in the form of proposals, not of savage commands, and we give him the choice of either persuading us or doing what we say, he is actually doing neither. These are the charges, Socrates, to which we say that you will be liable if you do what you are contemplating; and you will not be the least culpable of your fellow countrymen, but one of the most guilty." If I said "Why do you say that?" they would no doubt pounce upon me with perfect justice and point out that there are very few people in Athens who have entered into this agreement with them as explicitly as I have. They would say "Socrates, we have substantial evidence that you are satisfied with us and with the State. You would not have been so exceptionally reluctant to cross the borders of your country if you had not been exceptionally attached to it. You have never left the city to attend a festival or for any other purpose, except on some military expedition; you have never traveled abroad as other people do, and you have never felt the impulse to acquaint yourself with another country or constitution; you have been content with us and with our city. You have definitely chosen us, and undertaken to observe us in all your activities as a citizen; and as the crowning proof that you are satisfied with our city, you have begotten children in it. Furthermore, even at the time of your trial you could have proposed the penalty of banishment, if you had chosen to do so; that is, you could have done then with the sanction of the State what you are now trying to do without it. But whereas at that time you made a noble show of indifference if you had to die, and in fact preferred death, as you said, to banishment, now you show no respect for your earlier professions, and no regard for us, the Laws, whom you are trying to destroy; you are behaving like the lowest type of menial, trying to run away in spite of the contracts and undertakings by which you agreed to live as a member of our State. Now first answer this question: Are we or are we not speaking the truth when we say that you have undertaken, in deed if not in word, to live your life as a citizen in obedience to us?" What are we to say to that, Crito? Are we not bound to admit it?

Crito: We cannot help it, Socrates.

Socrates: "It is a fact, then," they would say, "that you are breaking covenants and undertakings made with us, although you made them under no compulsion or misunderstanding, and were not compelled to decide in a limited time; you had seventy years in which you could have left the country, if you were not satisfied with us or felt that the agreements were unfair. You did not choose Sparta or Crete—your favorite models of good government—or any other Greek or foreign state; you could not have absented yourself from the city less if you had been lame or blind or decrepit in some other way. It is quite obvious that you stand by yourself above all other Athenians in your affection for this city and for us its Laws;—who would care for a city without laws? And now, after all this, are you not going to stand by your agreement? Yes, you are, Socrates, if you will take our advice; and then you will at least escape being laughed at for leaving the city.

"We invite you to consider what good you will do to yourself or your friends if you commit this breach of faith and stain your conscience. It is fairly obvious that the risk of being banished and either losing their citizenship or having their property confiscated will extend to your friends as well. As for yourself, if you go to one of the neighboring states, such as Thebes or Megara, which are both well governed, you will enter them as an enemy to their constitution and all good patriots will eye you with suspicion as a destroyer of law and order. Incidentally you will confirm the opinion of the jurors who tried you that they gave a correct verdict; a destroyer of laws might very well be supposed to have a destructive influence upon young and foolish human beings. Do you intend, then, to avoid well governed states and the higher forms of human society? And if you do, will life be worth living? Or will you approach these people and have the impudence to converse with them? What arguments will you use, Socrates? The same which you used here, that goodness and integrity, institutions and laws, are the most precious possessions of mankind? Do you not think that Socrates and everything about him will appear in a disreputable light? You certainly ought to think so. But perhaps you will retire from this part of the world and go to Crito's friends in Thessaly? That is the home of indiscipline and laxity, and no doubt they would enjoy hearing the amusing story of how you managed to run away from prison by arraying yourself in some costume or putting on a shepherd's smock or some other conventional runaway's disguise, and altering your personal appearance. And will no one comment on the fact that an old man of your age, probably with only a short time left to live, should dare to cling so greedily to life, at the price of violating the most stringent laws? Perhaps not, if you avoid irritating anyone. Otherwise, Socrates, you will hear a good many humiliating comments. So you will live as the toady and slave of all the populace, literally 'roistering in Thessaly,' as though you had left this country for Thessaly to attend a banquet there; and where will your discussions about goodness and uprightness be then, we should like to know? But of course you want to live for your children's sake, so that you may be able to bring them up and educate them. Indeed! by first taking them off to Thessaly and making foreigners of them, so that they may have that additional enjoyment? Or if that is not your intention, supposing that they are brought up here with you still alive, will they be better cared for and educated without you, because of course your friends will look after them? Will they look after your children if you go away to Thessaly, and not if you go away to the next world? Surely if those who profess to be your friends are worth anything, you must believe that they would care for them.

"No, Socrates; be advised by us your guardians, and do not think more of your children or of your life or of anything else than you think of what is right; so that when you enter the next world you may have all this to plead in your defense before the authorities there. It seems clear that if you do this thing, neither you nor any of your friends will be the better for it or be more upright or have a cleaner conscience here in this world, nor will it be better for you when you reach the next. As it is, you will leave this place, when you do, as the victim of a wrong done not by us, the Laws, but by your fellow men. But if you leave in that dishonorable way, returning wrong for wrong and evil for evil, breaking your agreements and covenants with us, and injuring those whom you least ought to injure—yourself, your friends, your country, and us—then you will have to face our anger in your lifetime, and in that place beyond when the laws of the other world know that you have tried, so far as you could, to destroy even us their brothers, they will not receive you with a kindly welcome. Do not take Crito's advice, but follow ours."

That, my dear friend Crito, I do assure you, is what I seem to hear them saying, just as a mystic seems to hear the strains of music; and the sound of their arguments rings so loudly in my head that I cannot hear the other side. I warn you that, as my opinion stands at present, it will be useless to urge a different view. However, if you think that you will do any good by it, say what you like.

Crito: No, Socrates, I have nothing to say.

Socrates: Then give it up, Crito, and let us follow this course, since God points out the way.

Resistance to Civil Government

Henry David Thoreau

Henry David Thoreau (1817–1862) was an American naturalist and philosopher. His most famous book, Walden *(1854), is based on journals he kept when he lived alone in the woods for two years. This essay, written in 1859, influenced the thinking of Mahatma Gandhi and Martin Luther King, Jr.*

I heartily accept the motto,—"That government is best which governs least;" and I should like to see it acted up to more rapidly and systematically. Carried out, it finally amounts to this, which also I believe,—"That government is best which governs not at all;" and when men are prepared for it, that will be the kind of government which they will have. Government is at best but an expedient; but most governments are usually, and all governments are sometimes, inexpedient. The objections which have been brought against a standing army, and they are many and weighty, and deserve to prevail, may also at last be brought against a standing government. The standing army is only an arm of the standing government. The government itself, which is only the mode which the people have chosen to execute their will, is equally liable to be abused and perverted before the people can act through it. Witness the present Mexican war, the work of comparatively a few individuals using the standing government as their tool; for, in the outset, the people would not have consented to this measure.

This American government,—what is it but a tradition, though a recent one, endeavoring to transmit itself unimpaired to posterity, but each instant losing some of its integrity? It has not the vitality and force of a single living man; for a single man can bend it to his will. It is a sort of wooden gun to the people themselves. But it is not the less necessary for this; for the people must have some complicated machinery or other, and hear its din, to satisfy that idea of government which they have. Governments show thus how successfully men can be imposed on, even impose on themselves, for their own advantage. It is excellent, we must all allow. Yet this government never of itself furthered any enterprise, but by the alacrity with which it got out of its way. *It* does not keep the country free. *It* does not settle the West. *It* does not educate. The character inherent in the American people has done all that has been accomplished; and it would have done somewhat more, if the government had not sometimes got in its way. For government is an expedient by which men would fain succeed in letting one another alone; and, as has been said, when it is most expedient, the governed are most let alone by it. Trade and commerce, if they were not made of India-rubber, would never manage to bounce over the obstacles which legislators are continually putting in their way; and, if one were to judge these men wholly by the effects of their actions and not partly by their intentions, they would deserve to be classed and punished with those mischievous persons who put obstructions on the railroads.

But, to speak practically and as a citizen, unlike those who call themselves no-government men, I ask for, not at once no government, but *at once* a better government. Let every man make known what kind of government would command his respect, and that will be one step toward obtaining it.

After all, the practical reason why, when the power is once in the hands of people, a majority are permitted, and for a long period continue, to rule is not because they are most likely to be in the right, nor because this seems fairest to the minority, but because they are physically the strongest. But a government in which the majority rule in all cases cannot be based on justice, even as far as men understand it. Can there not be a government in which majorities do not virtually decide right and wrong, but conscience?—in which majorities decide only those questions to which the rule of expediency is applicable? Must the citizen ever for a moment, or in the least degree, resign his conscience to the legislator? Why has every man a conscience, then? I think that we should be men first, and subjects afterward. It is not desirable to cultivate a respect for the law, so much as for the right. The only obligation which I have a right to assume is to do at any time what I think right. It is truly enough said, that a corporation has no conscience; but a corporation of conscientious men is a corporation *with* a conscience. Law never made men a whit more just; and, by means of their respect for it, even the well-disposed are daily made the agents of injustice. A common and natural result of an undue respect for law is, that you may see a file of soldiers, colonel, captain, corporal, privates, powder-monkeys, and all, marching in admirable order over hill and dale to the wars, against their wills, ay, against their common sense and consciences, which makes it very steep marching indeed, and produces a palpitation of the heart. They have no doubt that it is a damnable business in which they are concerned; they are all peaceably inclined. Now, what are they? Men at all? or small movable forts and magazines, at the service of some unscrupulous man in power? Visit the Navy-Yard, and behold a marine, such a man as an American government can make, or such as it can make a man with its black arts,—a mere shadow and reminiscence of humanity, a man laid out alive and standing, and already, as one may say, buried under arms with funeral accompaniments, though it may be,—

> "Not a drum was heard, not a funeral note,
>   As his corse to the rampart we hurried;
> Not a soldier discharged his farewell shot
>   O'er the grave where our hero we buried."

The mass of men serve the state thus, not as men mainly, but as machines, with their bodies. They are the standing army, and the militia, jailers, constables, posse comitatus, etc. In most cases there is not free exercise whatever of the judgment or of the moral sense; but they put themselves on a level with wood and earth and stones; and wooden men can perhaps be manufactured that will serve the purpose as well. Such command no more respect than men of straw or a lump of dirt. They have the same sort of worth only as horses and dogs. Yet such as these even are commonly esteemed good citizens. Others—as most legislators, politicians, lawyers, ministers, and office-holders—serve the state chiefly with their heads; and, as they rarely make any moral distinctions, they are as likely to serve the Devil, without *intending* it, as God. A very few, as heroes, patriots, martyrs, reformers in the great sense, and *men,* serve the state with their consciences also, and so necessarily resist it for the most part; and they are commonly treated as enemies by it. A wise man will only be useful as a man, and will not submit to be "clay," and "stop a hole to keep the wind away," but leave that office to his dust at least:—

"I am too high-born to be propertied,
To be a secondary at control,
Or useful serving-man and instrument
To any sovereign state throughout the world."

He who gives himself entirely to his fellow-men appears to them useless and selfish; but he who gives himself partially to them is pronounced a benefactor and philanthropist.

How does it become a man to behave toward this American government to-day? I answer, that he cannot without disgrace be associated with it. I cannot for an instant recognize that political organization as *my* government which is the *slave's* government also.

All men recognize the right of revolution; that is, the right to refuse allegiance to, and to resist, the government, when its tyranny or its inefficiency are great and unendurable. But almost all say that such is not the case now. But such was the case, they think, in the Revolution of '75. If one were to tell me that this was a bad government because it taxed certain foreign commodities brought to its ports, it is most probable that I should not make an ado about it, for I can do without them. All machines have their friction; and possibly this does enough good to counterbalance the evil. At any rate, it is a great evil to make a stir about it. But when the friction comes to have its machine, and oppression and robbery are organized, I say, let us not have such a machine any longer. In other words, when a sixth of the population of a nation which has undertaken to be the refuge of liberty are slaves, and a whole country is unjustly overrun and conquered by a foreign army, and subjected to military law, I think that it is not too soon for honest men to rebel and revolutionize. What makes this duty the more urgent is the fact that the country so overrun is not our own, but ours is the invading army.

Paley, a common authority with many on moral questions, in his chapter on the "Duty of Submission to Civil Government," resolves all civil obligation into expediency; and he proceeds to say, "that so long as the interest of the whole society requires it, that is. so long as the established government cannot be resisted or changed without public inconveniency, it is the will of God that the established government be obeyed, and no longer. . . . This principle being admitted, the justice of every particular case of resistance is reduced to a computation of the quantity of the danger and grievance on the one side, and of the probability and expense of redressing it on the other." Of this, he says, every man shall judge for himself. But Paley appears never to have contemplated those cases to which the rule of expediency does not apply, in which a people, as well as an individual, must do justice, cost what it may. If I have unjustly wrested a plank from a drowning man, I must restore it to him though I drown myself. This, according to Paley, would be inconvenient. But he that would save his life, in such a case, shall lose it. This people must cease to hold slaves, and to make war on Mexico, though it cost them their existence as a people.

In their practice, nations agree with Paley; but does any one think that Massachusetts does exactly what is right at the present crisis?

"A drab of state, a cloth-o'-silver slut,
To have her train borne up, and her soul trail in the dirt."

Practically speaking, the opponents to a reform in Massachusetts are not a hundred thousand politicians at the South, but a hundred thousand merchants and farmers here, who are more interested in commerce and agriculture than they are in humanity, and are not prepared to do justice to the slave and to Mexico, *cost what it may.* I quarrel not with far-off foes, but with those who, near at home, cooperate with, and do the bidding of, those far away, and without whom the latter would be harmless. We are accustomed to say, that the mass of men are unprepared; but improvement is slow, because the few are not materially wiser or better than the many. It is not so important that many should be as good as you, as that there be some absolute goodness somewhere; for that will leaven the whole lump. There are thousands who are *in opinion* opposed to slavery and to the war, who yet in effect do nothing to put an end to them; who, esteeming themselves children of Washington and Franklin, sit down with their hands in their pockets, and say that they know not what to do, and do nothing; who even postpone the question of freedom to the question of free-trade, and quietly read the prices-current along with the latest advices from Mexico, after dinner, and, it may be, fall asleep over them both. What is the price-current of an honest man and patriot to-day? They hesitate, and they regret, and sometimes they petition; but they do nothing in earnest and with effect. They will wait, well disposed, for others to remedy the evil, that they may no longer have it to regret. At most, they give only a cheap vote, and a feeble countenance and Godspeed, to the right, as it goes by then. There are nine hundred and ninety-nine patrons of virtue to one virtuous man. But it is easier to deal with the real possessor of a thing than with the temporary guardian of it.

All voting is a sort of gaming, like checkers or backgammon, with a slight moral tinge to it, a playing with right and wrong, with moral questions; and betting naturally accompanies it. The character of the voters is not staked. I cast my vote, perchance, as I think right; but I am not vitally concerned that that right should prevail. I am willing to leave it to the majority. Its obligation, therefore, never exceeds that of expediency. Even voting *for the right* is *doing* nothing for it. It is only expressing to men feebly your desire that it should prevail. A wise man will not leave the right to the mercy of chance, nor wish it to prevail through the power of the majority. There is but little virtue in the action of masses of men. When the majority shall at length vote for the abolition of slavery, it will be because they are indifferent to slavery, or because there is but little slavery left to be abolished by their vote. *They* will then be the only slaves. Only *his* vote can hasten the abolition of slavery who asserts his own freedom by his vote.

I hear of a convention to be held at Baltimore, or elsewhere, for the selection of a candidate for the Presidency, made up chiefly of editors, and men who are politicians by profession; but I think, what is it to any independent, intelligent, and respectable man what decision they may come to? Shall we not have the advantage of his wisdom and honesty, nevertheless? Can we not count upon some independent votes? Are there not many individuals in the country who do not attend conventions? But no: I find that the respectable man, so called, has immediately drifted from his position, and despairs of his country, when his country has more reason to despair of him. He forthwith adopts one of the candidates thus selected as the only *available* one, thus proving that he is himself *available* for any purposes of the demagogue. His vote is of no more worth than that of any unprincipled foreigner or hireling native, who may have been bought. O for a man who is a *man,* and, as my neighbor says, has a bone in his back which you cannot pass your hand through! Our statistics are at fault: the population has been returned too large. How many *men* are there to a square thousand miles in this country? Hardly one. Does not America offer any inducement for men to settle here? The American has dwindled into an Odd Fellow,—one who may be known by the development of his organ of gregariousness, and a manifest lack of intellect and cheerful self-reliance; whose first and chief concern, on coming into the world, is to see that the Almshouses are in good repair; and, before yet he has lawfully donned the virile garb, to collect a fund for the support of the widows and orphans that may be; who, in short, ventures to live only by the aid of the Mutual Insurance company, which has promised to bury him decently.

It is not a man's duty, as a matter of course, to devote himself to the eradication of any, even the most enormous wrong; he may still properly have other concerns to engage him; but it is his duty, at least, to wash his hands of it, and, if he gives it no thought longer, not to give it practically his support. If I devote myself to other pursuits and contemplations, I must first see, at least, that I do not pursue them sitting upon another man's shoulders. I must get off him first, that he may pursue his contemplations too. See what gross inconsistency is tolerated. I have heard some of my townsmen say, "I should like to have them order me out to help put down an insurrection of the slaves, or to march to Mexico;—see if I would go;" and yet these very men have each, directly by their allegiance, and so indirectly, at least, by their money, furnished a substitute. The soldier is applauded who refuses to serve in an unjust war by those who do not refuse to sustain the unjust government which makes the war; is applauded by those whose own act and authority he disregards and sets at naught; as if the state were penitent to that degree that it hired one to scourge it while it sinned, but not to that degree that it left off sinning for a moment. Thus, under the name of Order and Civil Government, we are all made at last to pay homage to and support our own meanness. After the first blush of sin comes its indifference; and from immoral it becomes, as it were, *un*moral and not quite unnecessary to that life which we have made.

The broadest and most prevalent error requires the most disinterested virtue to sustain it. The slight reproach to which the virtue of patriotism is commonly liable, the noble are most likely to incur. Those who, while they disapprove of the character and measures of a government, yield to it their allegiance and support are undoubtedly its most conscientious supporters, and so frequently the most serious obstacles to reform. Some are petitioning the state to dissolve the Union, to disregard the requisitions of the President. Why do they not dissolve it themselves,—the union between themselves and the state,—and refuse to pay their quota into its treasury? Do not they stand in the same relation to the state that the state does to the Union? And have not the same reasons prevented the state from resisting the Union which have prevented them from resisting the state?

How can a man be satisfied to entertain an opinion merely, and enjoy *it*? Is there any enjoyment in it, if his opinion is that he is aggrieved? If you are cheated out of a single dollar by your neighbor, you do not rest satisfied with knowing that you are cheated, or with saying that you are cheated, or even with petitioning him to pay you your due; but you take effectual steps at once to obtain the full amount, and see that you are never cheated again. Action from principle, the perception and the performance of right, changes things and relations; it is essentially revolutionary, and does not consist wholly with anything which was. It not only divides states and churches, it divides families; ay, it divides the *individual,* separating the diabolical in him from the divine.

Unjust laws exist: shall we be content to obey them, or shall we endeavor to amend them, and obey them until we have succeeded, or shall we transgress them at once? Men generally, under such a government as this, think that they ought to wait until they have persuaded the majority to alter them. They think that, if they should resist, the remedy would be worse than the evil. But it is the fault of the government itself that the remedy *is* worse than the evil. *It* makes it worse. Why is it not more apt to anticipate and provide for reform? Why does it not cherish its wise minority? Why does it cry and resist before it is hurt? Why does it not encourage its citizens to be on the alert to point out its faults, and *do* better than it would have them? Why does it always crucify Christ, and excommunicate Copernicus and Luther, and pronounce Washington and Franklin rebels?

One would think, that a deliberate and practical denial of its authority was the only offense never contemplated by government; else, why has it not assigned its definite, its suitable and proportionate penalty? If a man who has no property refuses but once to earn nine shillings for the state, he is put in prison for a period unlimited by any law that I know, and determined only by the discretion of those who placed him there; but if he should steal ninety times nine shillings from the state, he is soon permitted to go at large again.

If the injustice is part of the necessary friction of the machine of government, let it go, let it go: perchance it will wear smooth,—certainly the machine will wear out. If the injustice has a spring, or a pulley, or a rope, or a crank, exclusively for itself, then perhaps you may consider whether the remedy will not be worse than the evil; but if it is of such a nature that it requires you to be the agent of injustice to another, then, I say, break the law. Let your life be a counter friction to stop the machine. What I have to do is to see, at any rate, that I do not lend myself to the wrong which I condemn.

As for adopting the ways which the state has provided for remedying the evil, I know not of such ways. They take too much time, and a man's life will be gone. I have other affairs to attend to. I came into this world, not chiefly to make this a good place to live in, but to live in it, be it good or bad. A man has not everything to do, but something; and because he cannot do *everything,* it is not necessary that he should do *something* wrong. It is not my business to be petitioning the Governor or the Legislature any more than it is theirs to petition me; and if they should not hear my petition, what should I do then? But in this case the state has provided no way: its very Constitution is the evil. This may seem to be harsh and stubborn and unconciliatory; but it is to treat with the utmost kindness and consideration the only spirit that can appreciate or deserves it. So is all change for the better, like birth and death, which convulse the body.

I do not hesitate to say, that those who call themselves Abolitionists should at once effectually withdraw their support, both in person and property, from the government of Massachusetts, and not wait till they constitute a majority of one, before they suffer the right to prevail through them. I think that it is enough if they have God on their side, without waiting for that other one. Moreover, any man more right than his neighbors constitutes a majority of one already.

I meet this American government, or its representative, the state government, directly, and face to face, once a year—no more—in the person of its taxgatherer; this is the only mode in which a man situated as I am necessarily meets it; and it then says distinctly, Recognize me; and the simplest, the most effectual, and, in the present posture of affairs, the indispensablest mode of treating with it on this head, of expressing your little satisfaction with and love for it, is to deny it then. My civil neighbor, the tax-gatherer, is the very man I have to deal with,—for it is, after all, with men and not with parchment that I quarrel,—and he has voluntarily chosen to be an agent of the government. How shall he ever know well what he is and does as an officer of the government, or as a man, until he is obliged to consider whether he shall treat me, his neighbor, for whom he has respect, as a neighbor and well-disposed man, or as a maniac and disturber of the peace, and see if he can get over this obstruction to his neighborliness without a ruder and more impetuous thought or speech corresponding with his action. I know this well, that if one thousand, if one hundred, if ten men whom I could name,—if ten *honest* men only,—ay, if *one* HONEST man, in this State of Massachusetts, *ceasing to hold slaves,* were actually to withdraw from this copartnership, and be locked up in the county jail therefor, it would be the abolition of slavery in America. For it matters not how small the beginning may seem to be: what is once well done is done forever. But we love better to talk about it: that we say is our mission. Reform keeps many scores of newspapers in its service, but not one man. If my esteemed neighbor, the State's ambassador, who will devote his days to the settlement of the question of human rights in the Council Chamber, instead of being threatened with the prisons of Carolina, were to sit down the prisoner of Massachusetts, that State which is so anxious to foist the sin of slavery upon her sister,—though at present she can discover only an act of inhospitality to be the ground of a quarrel with her,—the Legislature would not wholly waive the subject the following winter.

Under a government which imprisons any unjustly, the true place for a just man is also a prison. The proper place to-day, the only place which Massachusetts has provided for her freer and less desponding spirits, is in her prisons, to be put out and locked out of the State by her own act, as they have already put themselves out by their principles. It is there that the fugitive slave, and the Mexican prisoner on parole, and the Indian come to plead the wrongs of his race should find them; on that separate, but more free and honorable ground, where the State places those who are not *with* her, but *against* her,—the only house in a slave State in which a free man can abide with honor. If any think that their influence would be lost there, and their voices no longer afflict the ear of the State, that they would not be as an enemy within its walls, they do not know by how much truth is stronger than error, nor how much more eloquently and effectively he can combat injustice who has experienced a little in his own person. Cast your whole vote, not a strip of paper merely, but your whole influence. A minority is powerless while it conforms to the majority; it is not even a minority then; but it is irresistible when it clogs by its whole weight. If the alternative is to keep all just men in prison, or give up war and slavery, the State will not hesitate which to choose. If a thousand men were not to pay their tax-bills this year that would not be a violent and bloody measure, as it would be to pay them, and enable the State to commit violence and shed innocent blood. This is, in fact, the definition of a peaceable revolution, if any such is possible. If the tax-gatherer, or any other public officer, asks me, as one has done, "But what shall I do?" my answer is, "If you really wish to do anything, resign your office." When the subject has refused allegiance, and the officer has resigned his office, then the revolution is accomplished. But even suppose blood should flow. Is there not a sort of blood shed when the conscience is wounded? Through this wound a man's real manhood and immortality flow out, and he bleeds to an everlasting death. I see this blood flowing now.

I have contemplated the imprisonment of the offender, rather than the seizure of his goods,—though both will serve the same purpose,—because they who assert the purest right, and consequently are most dangerous to a corrupt State, commonly have not spent much time in accumulating property. To such the State renders comparatively small service, and a slight tax is wont to appear exorbitant, particularly if they are obliged to earn it by special labor with their hands. If there were one who lived wholly without the use of money, the State itself would hesitate to demand it of him. But the rich man—not to make any invidious comparison—is always sold to the institution which makes him rich. Absolutely speaking, the more money, the less virtue; for money comes between a man and his objects, and obtains them for him; and it was certainly no great virtue to obtain it. It puts to rest many questions which he would otherwise be taxed to answer; while the only new question which it puts is the hard but superfluous one, how to spend it. Thus his moral ground is taken from under his feet. The opportunities of living are diminished in proportion as what are called the "means" are increased. The best thing a man can do for his culture when he is rich is to endeavor to carry out those schemes which he entertained when he was poor. Christ answered the Herodians according to their condition. "Show me the tribute-money," said he;—and one took a penny out of his pocket;—if you use money which has the image of Caesar on it, and which he has made current and valuable, that is, *if you are men of the State,* and gladly enjoy the advantages of Caesar's government, then pay him back some of his own when he demands it. "Render therefore to Caesar that which is Caesar's, and to God those things which are God's,"—leaving them no wiser than before as to which was which; for they did not wish to know.

When I converse with the freest of my neighbors, I perceive that, whatever they may say about the magnitude and seriousness of the question, and their regard for the public tranquillity, the long and the short of the matter is, that they cannot spare the protection of the existing government, and they dread the consequences to their property and families of disobedience to it. For my own part, I should not like to think that I ever rely on the protection of the State. But, if I deny the authority of the State when it presents its tax-bill, it will soon take and waste all my property, and so harass me and my children without end. This is hard. This makes it impossible for a man to live honestly, and at the same time comfortably, in outward respects. It will not be worth the while to accumulate property; that would be sure to go again. You must hire or squat somewhere, and raise but a small crop, and eat that soon. You must live within yourself, and depend upon yourself always tucked up and ready for a start, and not have many affairs. A man may grow rich in Turkey even, if he will be in all respects a good subject of the Turkish government. Confucius said: "If a state is governed by the principles of reason, poverty and misery are subjects of shame; if a state is not governed by the principles of reason, riches and honors are the subjects of shame." No: until I want the protection of Massachusetts to be extended to me in some distant Southern port, where my liberty is endangered, or until I am bent solely on building up an estate at home by peaceful enterprise, I can afford to refuse allegiance to Massachusetts, and her right to my property and life. It costs me less in every sense to incur the penalty of disobedience to the State than it would to obey. I should feel as if I were worth less in that case.

Some years ago, the State met me in behalf of the Church, and commanded me to pay a certain sum toward the support of a clergyman whose preaching my father attended, but never I myself. "Pay," it said, "or be locked up in the jail." I declined to pay. But, unfortunately, another man saw fit to pay it. I did not see why the schoolmaster should be taxed to support the priest, and not the priest the schoolmaster; for I was not the State's schoolmaster, but I supported myself by voluntary subscription. I did not see why the lyceum should not present its tax-bill, and have the State to back its demand, as well as the Church. However, at the request of the selectmen, I condescended to make some such statement as this in writing:—"Know all men by these presents, that I, Henry Thoreau, do not wish to be regarded as a member of any incorporated society which I have not joined." This I gave to the town clerk; and he has it. The State, having thus learned that I did not wish to be regarded as a member of that church, has never made a like demand on me since; though it said that it must adhere to its original presumption that time. If I had known how to name them, I should then have signed off in detail from all the societies which I never signed on to; but I did not know where to find a complete list.

I have paid no poll-tax for six years. I was put into a jail once on this account, for one night; and, as I stood considering the walls of solid stone, two or three feet thick, the door of wood and iron, a foot thick, and the iron grating which strained the light, I could not help being struck with the foolishness of that institution which treated me as if I were mere flesh and blood and bones, to be locked up. I wondered that it should have concluded at length that this was the best use it could put me to, and had never thought to avail itself of my services in some way. I saw that, if there was a wall of stone between me and my townsmen, there was a still more difficult one to climb or break through before they could get to be as free as I was. I did not for a moment feel confined, and the walls seemed a great waste of stone and mortar. I felt as if I alone of all my townsmen had paid my tax. They plainly did not know how to treat me, but behaved like persons who are underbred. In every threat and in every compliment there was a blunder; for they thought that my chief desire was to stand the other side of that stone wall. I could not but smile to see how industriously they locked the door on my meditations, which followed them out again without let or hindrance, and *they* were really all that was dangerous. As they could not reach me, they had resolved to punish my body; just as boys, if they cannot come at some person against whom they have a spite, will abuse his dog. I saw that the State was half-witted, that it was timid as a lone woman with her silver spoons, and that it did not know its friends from its foes, and I lost all my remaining respect for it, and pitied it.

Thus the State never intentionally confronts a man's sense, intellectual or moral, but only his body, his senses. It is not armed with superior wit or honesty, but with superior physical strength. I was not been to be forced. I will breathe after my own fashion. Let us see who is the strongest. What force has a multitude? They only can force me who obey a higher law than I. They force me to become like themselves. I do not hear of *men* being *forced* to live this way or that by masses of men. What sort of life were that to live? When I meet a government which says to me, "Your money or your life," why should I be in haste to give it my money? It may be in a great strait, and not know what to do: I cannot help that. It must help itself; do as I do. It is not worth the while to snivel about it. I am not responsible for the successful working of the machinery of society. I am not the son of the engineer. I perceive that, when an acorn and a chestnut fall side by side, the one does not remain inert to make way for the other, but both obey their own laws, and spring and grow and flourish as best they can, till one, perchance, overshadows and destroys the other. If a plant cannot live according to its nature, it dies; and so a man.

The night in prison was novel and interesting enough. The prisoners in their shirt-sleeves were enjoying a chat and the evening air in the doorway, when I entered. But the jailer said, "Come, boys, it is time to lock up;" and so they dispersed, and I heard the sound of their steps returning into the hollow apartments. My room-mate was introduced to me by the jailer as "a first-rate fellow and a clever man." When the door was locked, he showed me where to hang my hat, and how he managed matters there. The rooms were whitewashed once a month; and this one, at least, was the whitest, most simply furnished, and probably the neatest apartment in the town. He naturally wanted to know where I came from, and what brought me there; and, when I had told him, I asked him in my turn how he came there, presuming him to be an honest man, of course; and, as the world goes, I believe he was. "Why," said he, "they accuse me of burning a barn; but I never did it." As near as I could discover, he had probably gone to bed in a barn when drunk, and smoked his pipe there; and so a barn was burnt. He had the reputation of being a clever man, had been there some three months waiting for his trial to come on, and would have to wait as much longer; but he was quite domesticated and contented, since he got his board for nothing, and thought that he was well treated.

He occupied one window, and I the other; and I saw that if one stayed there long, his principal business would be to look out the window. I had soon read all the tracts that were left there, and examined where former prisoners had broken out, and where a grate had been sawed off, and heard the history of the various occupants of that room; for I found that even here there was a history and a gossip which never circulated beyond the walls of the jail. Probably this is the only house in the town where verses are composed, which are afterward printed in a circular form, but not published. I was shown quite a long list of verses which were composed by some young men who had been detected in an attempt to escape, who avenged themselves by singing them.

I pumped my fellow-prisoner as dry as I could, for fear I should never see him again; but at length he showed me which was my bed, and left me to blow out the lamp.

It was like traveling into a far country, such as I had never expected to behold, to lie there for one night. It seemed to me that I never had heard the town-clock strike before, nor the evening sounds of the village; for we slept with the windows open, which were inside the grating. It was to see my native village in the light of the Middle Ages, and our Concord was turned into a Rhine stream, and visions of knights and castles passed before me. They were the voices of old burghers that I heard in the streets. I was an involuntary spectator and auditor of whatever was done and said in the kitchen of the adjacent village-inn,—a wholly new and rare experience to me. It was a closer view of my native town. I was fairly inside of it. I never had seen its institutions before. This is one of its peculiar institutions; for it is a shire town. I began to comprehend what its inhabitants were about.

In the morning, our breakfasts were put through the hole in the door, in small oblong-square tin pans, made to fit, and holding a pint of chocolate, with brown bread, and an iron spoon. When they called for the vessels again, I was green enough to return what bread I had left; but my comrade seized it, and said that I should lay that up for lunch or dinner. Soon after he was let out to work at haying in a neighboring field, whither he went every day, and would not be back till noon; so he bade me goodday, saying that he doubted if he should see me again.

When I came out of prison,—for some one interfered, and paid that tax,—I did not perceive that great changes had taken place on the common, such as he observed who went in a youth and emerged a tottering and gray-headed man; and yet a change had to my eyes come over the scene,—the town, and State, and country,—greater than any that mere time could effect. I saw yet more distinctly the State in which I lived. I saw to what extent the people among whom I lived could be trusted as good neighbors and friends; that their friendship was for summer weather only; that they did not greatly propose to do right; that they were a distinct race from me by their prejudices and superstitions, as the Chinamen and Malays are; that in their sacrifices to humanity they ran no risks, not even to their property; that after all they were not so noble but they treated the thief as he had treated them, and hoped, by a certain outward observance and a few prayers, and by walking in a particular straight though useless path from time to time, to save their souls. This may be to judge my neighbors harshly; for I believe that many of them are not aware that they have such an institution as the jail in their village.

It was formerly the custom in our village, when a poor debtor came out of jail, for his acquaintances to salute him, looking through their fingers, which were crossed to represent the grating of a jail window, "How do ye do?" My neighbors did not thus salute me, but first looked at me, and then at one another, as if I had returned from a long journey. I was put into jail as I was going to the shoemaker's to get a shoe which was mended. When I was let out the next morning, I proceeded to finish my errand, and, having put on my mended shoe, joined a huckleberry party, who were impatient to put themselves under my conduct; and in half an hour,—for the horse was soon tackled,—was in the midst of a huckleberry field, on one of our highest hills, two miles off, and then the State was nowhere to be seen.

This is the whole history of "My Prisons."

I have never declined paying the highway tax, because I am as desirous of being a good neighbor as I am of being a bad subject; and as for supporting schools, I am doing my part to educate my fellow-country men now. It is for no particular item in the tax-bill that I refuse to pay it. I simply wish to refuse allegiance to the State, to withdraw and stand aloof from it effectually. I do not care to trace the course of my dollar, if I could, till it buys a man or a musket to shoot one with,—the dollar is innocent,—but I am concerned to trace the effects of my allegiance. In fact, I quietly declare war with the State, after my fashion, though I will still make what use and get what advantage of her I can, as is usual in such cases.

If others pay the tax which is demanded of me, from a sympathy with the State, they do but what they have already done in their own case, or rather they abet injustice to a greater extent than the State requires. If they pay the tax from a mistaken interest in the individual taxed, to save his property, or prevent his going to jail, it is because they have not considered wisely how far they let their private feelings interfere with the public good.

This, then, is my position at present. But one cannot be too much on his guard in such a case, lest his action be biased by obstinacy or an undue regard for the opinions of men. Let him see that he does only what belongs to himself and to the hour.

I think sometimes, Why, this people mean well, they are only ignorant; they would do better if they knew how; why give your neighbors this pain to treat you as they are not inclined to? But I think again, this is no reason why I should do as they do, or permit others to suffer much greater pain of a different kind. Again, I sometimes say to myself, When many millions of men, without heat, without ill will, without personal feeling of any kind, demand of you a few shillings only, without the possibility, such is their constitution, of retracting or altering their present demand, and without the possibility, on your side, of appeal to any other millions, why expose yourself to this overwhelming brute force? You do not resist cold and hunger, the winds and the waves, thus obstinately; you quietly submit to a thousand similar necessities. You do not put your head into the fire. But just in proportion as I regard this as not wholly a brute force, but partly a human force, and consider that I have relations to those millions as to so many millions of men, and not of mere brute or inanimate things, I see that appeal is possible, first and instantaneously, from them to the Maker of them, and, secondly, from them to themselves. But if I put my head deliberately into the fire, there is no appeal to fire or to the Maker of fire, and I have only myself to blame. If I could convince myself that I have any right to be satisfied with men as they are, and to treat them accordingly, and not according, in some respects, to my requisitions and expectations of what they and I ought to be, then, like a good Mussulman and fatalist, I should endeavor to be satisfied with things as they are, and say it is the will of God. And, above all, there is this difference between resisting this and a purely brute or natural force, that I can resist this with some effect; but I cannot expect, like Orpheus, to change the nature of the rocks and trees and beasts.

I do not wish to quarrel with any man or nation. I do not wish to split hairs, to make fine distinctions, or set myself up as better than my neighbors. I seek rather, I may say, even an excuse for conforming to the laws of the land. I am but too ready to conform to them. Indeed, I have reason to suspect myself on this head; and each year, as the tax-gatherer comes round, I find myself disposed to review the acts and position of the general and State governments, and the spirit of the people, to discover a pretext for conformity.

> "We must affect our country as our parents,
> And if at any time we alienate
> Our love or industry from doing it honor,
> We must respect effects and teach the soul
> Matter of conscience and religion,
> And not desire of rule or benefit."

I believe that the State will soon be able to take all my work of this sort out of my hands, and then I shall be no better a patriot than my fellow-countrymen. Seen from a lower point of view, the Constitution, with all its faults, is very good; the law and the courts are very respectable; even this State and this American government are, in many respects, very admirable, and rare things, to be thankful for, such as a great many have described them; but seen from a point of view a little higher, they are what I have described them; seen from a higher still, and the highest, who shall say what they are, or that they are worth looking at or thinking of at all?

However, the government does not concern me much, and I shall bestow the fewest possible thoughts on it. It is not many moments that I live under a government, even in this world. If a man is thought-free, fancy-free, imagination-free, that which *is not* never for a long time appearing *to be* to him, unwise rulers or reformers cannot fatally interrupt him.

I know that most men think differently from myself, but those whose lives are by profession devoted to the study of these or kindred subjects content me as little as any. Statesmen and legislators, standing so completely within the institution, never distinctly and nakedly behold it. They speak of moving society, but have no resting-place without it. They may be men of a certain experience and discrimination, and have no doubt invented ingenious and even useful systems, for which we sincerely thank them; but all their wit and usefulness lie within certain not very wide limits. They are wont to forget that the world is not governed by policy and expediency. Webster never goes behind government, and so cannot speak with authority about it. His words are wisdom to those legislators who contemplate no essential reform in the existing government; but for thinkers, and those who legislate for all time, he never once glances at the subject. I know of those whose serene and wise speculations on this theme would soon reveal the limits of his mind's range and hospitality. Yet, compared with the cheap professions of most reformers, and the still cheaper wisdom and eloquence of politicians in general, his are almost the only sensible and valuable words, and we thank Heaven for him. Comparatively, he is always strong, original, and, above all, practical. Still, his quality is not wisdom, but prudence. The lawyer's truth is not Truth, but consistency or a consistent expediency. Truth is always in harmony with herself, and is not concerned chiefly to reveal the justice that may consist with wrong-doing. He well deserves to be called, as he has been called, the Defender of the Constitution. There are really no blows to be given by him but defensive ones. He is not a leader, but a follower. His leaders are the men of '87. "I have never made an effort," he says, "and never propose to make an effort; I have never countenanced an effort, and never mean to countenance an effort, to disturb the arrangement as originally made, by which the various States came into the Union." Still thinking of the sanction which the Constitution gives to slavery, he says, "Because it was a part of the original compact,—let it stand." Notwithstanding his special acuteness and ability, he is unable to take a fact out of its merely political relations, and behold it as it lies absolutely to be disposed of by the intellect,—what, for instance, it behooves a man to do here in America to-day with regard to slavery,—but ventures, or is driven, to make some such desperate answer as the following, while professing to speak absolutely, and as a private man,—from which what new and singular code of social duties might be inferred? "The manner," says he, "in which the governments of those States where slavery exists are to regulate it is for their own consideration, under their responsibility to their constituents, to the general laws of propriety, humanity, and justice, and to God. Associations formed elsewhere, springing from a feeling of humanity, or any other cause, have nothing whatever to do with it. They have never received any encouragement from me, and they never will."

They who know of no purer sources of truth, who have traced up its stream no higher, stand, and wisely stand, by the Bible and the Constitution, and drink at it there with reverence and humility; but they who behold where it comes trickling into this lake or that pool, gird up their loins once more, and continue their pilgrimage toward its fountain-head.

No man with a genius for legislation has appeared in America. They are rare in the history of the world. There are orators, politicians, and eloquent men, by the thousand; but the speaker has not yet opened his mouth to speak who is capable of settling the much-vexed questions of the day. We love eloquence for its own sake, and not for any truth which it may utter, or any heroism it may inspire. Our legislators have not yet learned the comparative value of free-trade and of freedom, of union, and of rectitude, to a nation. They have no genius or talent for comparatively humble questions of taxation and finance, commerce and manufactures and agriculture. If we were left solely to the wordy wit of legislators in Congress for our guidance, uncorrected by the seasonable experience and the effectual complaints of the people, America would not long retain her rank among the nations. For eighteen hundred years, though perchance I have no right to say it, the New Testament has been written; yet where is the legislator who has wisdom and practical talent enough to avail himself of the light which it sheds on the science of legislation?

The authority of government, even such as I am willing to submit to,—for I will cheerfully obey those who know and can do better than I, and in many things even those who neither know nor can do so well,—is still an impure one: to be strictly just, it must have the sanction and consent of the governed. It can have no pure right over my person and property but what I concede to it. The progress from an absolute to a limited monarchy, from a limited monarchy to a democracy, is a progress toward a true respect for the individual. Even the Chinese philosopher was wise enough to regard the individual as the basis of the empire. Is a democracy, such as we know it, the last improvement possible in government? Is it not possible to take a step further towards recognizing and organizing the rights of man? There will never be a really free and enlightened State until the State comes to recognize the individual as a higher and independent power, from which all its own power and authority are derived, and treats him accordingly. I please myself with imagining a State at last which can afford to be just to all men, and to treat the individual with respect as a neighbor; which even would not think it inconsistent with its own repose if a few were to live aloof from it, not meddling with it, nor embraced by it, who fulfilled all the duties of neighbors and fellowmen. A State which bore this kind of fruit, and suffered it to drop off as fast as it ripened, would prepare the way for a still more perfect and glorious State, which also I have imagined, but not yet anywhere seen.

A Call for Unity

Eight Birmingham Clergy

This letter appeared in a Birmingham, Alabama, newspaper in 1963 during civil rights demonstrations protesting legal segregation.

April 12, 1963

We the undersigned clergymen are among those who, in January, issued "An Appeal for Law and Order and Common Sense," in dealing with racial problems in Alabama. We expressed understanding that honest convictions in racial matters could properly be pursued in the courts, but urged that decisions of those courts should in the meantime be peacefully obeyed.

Since that time there had been some evidence of increased forebearance and a willingness to face facts. Responsible citizens have undertaken to work on various problems which cause racial friction and unrest. In Birmingham, recent public events have given indication that we all have opportunity for a new constructive and realistic approach to racial problems.

However, we are now confronted by a series of demonstrations by some of our Negro citizens, directed and led in part by outsiders. We recognize the natural impatience of people who feel that their hopes are slow in being realized. But we are convinced that these demonstrations are unwise and untimely.

We agree rather with certain local Negro leadership which has called for honest and open negotiation of racial issues in our area. And we believe this kind of facing of issues can best be accomplished by citizens of our own metropolitan area, white and Negro, meeting with their knowledge and experience of the local situation. All of us need to face that responsibility and find proper channels for its accomplishment.

Just as we formerly pointed out that "hatred and violence have no sanction in our religious and political traditions," we also point out that such actions as incite to hatred and violence, however technically peaceful those actions may be, have not contributed to the resolution of our local problems. We do not believe that these days of new hope are days when extreme measures are justified in Birmingham.

We commend the community as a whole, and the local news media and law enforcement officials in particular, on the calm manner in which these demonstrations have been handled. We urge the public to continue to show restraint should the demonstrations continue, and the law enforcement officials to remain calm and continue to protect our city from violence.

We further strongly urge our own Negro community to withdraw support from these demonstrations, and to unite locally in working peacefully for a better Birmingham. When rights are consistently denied, a cause should be pressed in the courts and in negotiations among local leaders, and not in the streets. We appeal to both our white and Negro citizenry to observe the principles of law and order and common sense.

C.C.J. Carpenter, D.D., L.L.D.,
    Bishop of Alabama
Joseph A. Durick, D.D.,
        Auxiliary Bishop,
        Diocese of Mobile-Birmingham
Rabbi Milton L. Grafman, Temple
        Emanu-El, Birmingham, Alabama
Bishop Paul Hardin, Bishop of the
        Alabama–West Florida Conference
        of the Methodist Church

Bishop Nolan B. Harmon, Bishop of
        the North Alabama Conference
        of the Methodist Church
George M. Murray, D.D., L.L.D.,
        Bishop Coadjutor, Episcopal
        Diocese of Alabama
Edward V. Ramage, Moderator,
        Synod of the Alabama Presby-
        terian Church in the United States
Earl Stallings, Pastor, First Baptist
        Church, Birmingham, Alabama

Letter from Birmingham Jail

Martin Luther King, Jr.

The Reverend Martin Luther King, Jr. (1929–1968) won the Nobel Prize for Peace in 1964 for his leadership in the civil rights movement. He was assassinated in 1968.

April 16, 1963

My Dear Fellow Clergyman:

While confined here in the Birmingham city jail, I came across your recent statement calling my present activities "unwise and untimely."[1] Seldom do I pause to answer criticism of my work and ideas. If I sought to answer all the criticisms that cross my desk, my secretaries would have little time for anything other than such correspondence in the course of the day, and I would have no time for constructive work. But since I feel that you are men of genuine good will and that your criticisms are sincerely set forth, I want to try to answer your statement in what I hope will be patient and reasonable terms.

I think I should indicate why I am here in Birmingham, since you have been influenced by the view which argues against "outsiders coming in." I have the honor of serving as president of the Southern Christian Leadership Conference, an organization operating in every southern state, with headquarters in Atlanta, Georgia. We have some eighty-five affiliated organizations across the South, and one of them is the Alabama Christian Movement for Human Rights. Frequently we share staff, educational, and financial resources with our affiliates. Several months ago the affiliate here in Birmingham asked us to be on call to engage in a nonviolent direct action program if such were deemed necessary. We readily consented, and when the hour came we lived up to our promise. So I, along with several members of my staff, am here because I was invited here. I am here because I have organizational ties here.

But more basically, I am in Birmingham because injustice is here. Just as the prophets of the eighth century B.C. left their villages and carried their "thus saith the Lord" far beyond the boundaries of their home towns, and just as the Apostle Paul left his village of Tarsus and carried the gospel of Jesus Christ to the far corners of the Greco-Roman world, so am I compelled to carry the gospel of freedom

[1]This response to a published statement by eight fellow clergymen from Alabama (Bishop C.C.J. Carpenter, Bishop Joseph A. Durick, Rabbi Milton L. Grafman, Bishop Paul Hardin, Bishop Nolan B. Harmon, the Reverend George M. Murray, the Reverend Edward V. Ramage, and the Reverend Earl Stallings) was composed under somewhat constricting circumstances. Begun on the margins of the newspaper in which the statement appeared while I was in jail, the letter was continued on scraps of writing paper supplied by a friendly Negro trusty, and concluded on a pad my attorneys were eventually permitted to leave me. Although the text remains in substance unaltered, I have indulged in the author's prerogative of polishing it for publication. [King's note.]

beyond my own home town. Like Paul, I must constantly respond to the Macedonian call for aid.

Moreover, I am cognizant of the interrelatedness of all communities and states. I cannot sit idly by in Atlanta and not be concerned about what happens in Birmingham. Injustice anywhere is a threat to justice everywhere. We are caught in an inescapable network of mutuality; tied in a single garment of destiny. Whatever affects one directly, affects all indirectly. Never again can we afford to live with the narrow, provincial "outside agitator" idea. Anyone who lives inside the United States can never be considered an outsider anywhere within its bounds.

You deplore the demonstrations taking place in Birmingham. But your statement, I am sorry to say, fails to express a similar concern for the conditions that brought about the demonstrations. I am sure that none of you would want to rest content with the superficial kind of social analysis that deals merely with effects and does not grapple with underlying causes. It is unfortunate that demonstrations are taking place in Birmingham, but it is even more unfortunate that the city's white power structure left the Negro community with no alternative.

In any nonviolent campaign there are four basic steps: collection of the facts to determine whether injustices exist; negotiation; self-purification; and direct action. We have gone through all these steps in Birmingham. There can be no gainsaying the fact that racial injustice engulfs this community. Birmingham is probably the most thoroughly segregated city in the United States. Its ugly record of brutality is widely known. Negroes have experienced grossly unjust treatment in the courts. There have been more unsolved bombings of Negro homes and churches in Birmingham than in any other city in the nation. These are the hard, brutal facts of the case. On the basis of these conditions, Negro leaders sought to negotiate with the city fathers. But the latter consistently refused to engage in good-faith negotiation.

Then, last September, came the opportunity to talk with leaders of Birmingham's economic community. In the course of the negotiations, certain promises were made by the merchants—for example, to remove the stores' humiliating racial signs. On the basis of these promises, the Reverend Fred Shuttlesworth and the leaders of the Alabama Christian Movement for Human Rights agreed to a moratorium on all demonstrations. As the weeks and months went by, we realized that we were the victims of a broken promise. A few signs, briefly removed, returned; the others remained.

As in so many past experiences, our hopes had been blasted, and the shadow of deep disappointment settled upon us. We had no alternative except to prepare for direct action, whereby we would present our very bodies as a means of laying our case before the conscience of the local and the national community. Mindful of the difficulties involved, we decided to undertake a process of self-purification. We began a series of workshops on nonviolence, and we repeatedly asked ourselves: "Are you able to accept blows without retaliating?" "Are you able to endure the ordeal of jail?" We decided to schedule our direct-action program for the Easter season, realizing that except for Christmas, this is the main shopping period of the year. Knowing that a strong economic-withdrawal program would be the by-product of direct action, we felt that this would be the best time to bring pressure to bear on the merchants for the needed change.

Then it occurred to us that Birmingham's mayoralty election was coming up in March, and we speedily decided to postpone action until after election day. When we discovered that the Commissioner of Public Safety, Eugene "Bull" Connor, had piled up enough votes to be in the run-off, we decided again to postpone action until the day after the run-off so that the demonstrations could not be used to cloud the issues. Like many others, we waited to see Mr. Connor defeated, and to this end we endured postponement after postponement. Having aided in this community need, we felt that our direct-action program could be delayed no longer.

You may well ask: "Why direct action? Why sit-ins, marches, and so forth? Isn't negotiation a better path?" You are quite right in calling for negotiation. Indeed, this is the very purpose of direct action. Nonviolent direct action seeks to create such a crisis and foster such a tension that a community which has constantly refused to negotiate is forced to confront the issue. It seeks so to dramatize the issue that it can no longer be ignored. My citing the creation of tension as part of the work of the nonviolent-resister may sound rather shocking. But I must confess that I am not afraid of the word "tension." I have earnestly opposed violent tension, but there is a type of constructive, nonviolent tension which is necessary for growth. Just as Socrates felt that it was necessary to create a tension in the mind so that individuals could rise from the bondage of myths and half-truths to the unfettered realm of creative analysis and objective appraisal, so must we see the need for nonviolent gadflies to create the kind of tension in society that will help men rise from the dark depths of prejudice and racism to the majestic heights of understanding and brotherhood.

The purpose of our direct-action program is to create a situation so crisis-packed that it will inevitably open the door to negotiation. I therefore concur with you in your call for negotiation. Too long has our beloved Southland been bogged down in a tragic effort to live in monologue rather than dialogue.

One of the basic points in your statement is that the action that I and my associates have taken in Birmingham is untimely. Some have asked: "Why didn't you give the new city administration time to act?" The only answer that I can give to this query is that the new Birmingham administration must be prodded about as much as the outgoing one, before it will act. We are sadly mistaken if we feel that the election of Albert Boutwell as mayor will bring the millennium to Birmingham. While Mr. Boutwell is a much more gentle person than Mr. Connor, they are both segregationists, dedicated to maintenance of the status quo. I have hope that Mr. Boutwell will be reasonable enough to see the futility of massive resistance to desegregation. But he will not see this without pressure from devotees of civil rights. My friends, I must say to you that we have not made a single gain in civil rights without determined legal and nonviolent pressure.

Lamentably, it is an historical fact that privileged groups seldom give up their privileges voluntarily. Individuals may see the moral light and voluntarily give up their unjust posture; but as Reinhold Niebuhr has reminded us, groups tend to be more immoral than individuals.

We know through painful experience that freedom is never voluntarily given by the oppressor; it must be demanded by the oppressed. Frankly, I have yet to engage in a direct-action campaign that was "well timed" in the view of those who have not suffered unduly from the disease of segregation. For years now I have heard the word "Wait!" It rings in the ear of every Negro with piercing familiarity. This "Wait" has almost always meant "Never." We must come to see, with one of our distinguished jurists, that "justice too long delayed is justice denied."

We have waited for more than 340 years for our constitutional and God-given rights. The nations of Asia and Africa are moving with jetlike speed toward gaining political independence, but we still creep at horse-and-buggy pace toward gaining a cup of coffee at a lunch counter. Perhaps it is easy for those who have never felt the stinging darts of segregation to say, "Wait." But when you have seen vicious mobs lynch your mothers and fathers at will and drown your sisters and brothers at whim; when you have seen hate-filled policemen curse, kick, and even kill your black brothers and sisters; when you see the vast majority of your twenty million Negro brothers smothering in an airtight cage of poverty in the midst of an affluent society; when you suddenly find your tongue twisted and your speech stammering as you seek to explain to your 6-year-old daughter why she can't go to the public amusement park that has just been advertised on television, and see tears welling up in her eyes when she is told that Funtown is closed to colored children, and see ominous clouds of inferiority beginning to form in her little mental sky, and see her beginning to distort her personality by developing an unconscious bitterness toward white people; when you have to concoct an answer for a 5-year-old son who is asking: "Daddy, why do white people treat colored people so mean?"; when you take a cross-country drive and find it necessary to sleep night after night in the uncomfortable corners of your automobile because no motel will accept you; when you are humiliated day in and day out by nagging signs reading "white" and "colored"; when your first name becomes "nigger," your middle name becomes "boy" (however old you are) and your last name becomes "John," and your wife and mother are never given the respected title "Mrs."; when you are harried by day and haunted by night by the fact that you are a Negro, living constantly at tiptoe stance, never quite knowing what to expect next, and are plagued with inner fears and outer resentments; when you are forever fighting a degenerating sense of "nobodiness"—then you will understand why we find it difficult to wait. There comes a time when the cup of endurance runs over, and men are no longer willing to be plunged into the abyss of despair. I hope, sirs, you can understand our legitimate and unavoidable impatience.

You express a great deal of anxiety over our willingness to break laws. This is certainly a legitimate concern. Since we so diligently urge people to obey the Supreme Court's decision of 1954 outlawing segregation in the public schools, at first glance it may seem rather paradoxical for us consciously to break laws. One may well ask: "How can you advocate breaking some laws and obeying others?" The answer lies in the fact that there are two types of laws: just and unjust. I would be the first to advocate obeying just laws. One has not only a legal but a moral responsibility to obey just laws. Conversely, one has a moral responsibility to disobey unjust laws. I would agree with St. Augustine that "an unjust law is no law at all."

Now, what is the difference between the two? How does one determine whether a law is just or unjust? A just law is a man-made code that squares with the moral law or the law of God. An unjust law is a code that is out of harmony with the moral law. To put it in the terms of St. Thomas Aquinas: An unjust law is a human law that is not rooted in eternal law and natural law. Any law that uplifts human personality is just. Any law that degrades human personality is unjust. All segregation statutes are unjust because segregation distorts the soul and damages the personality. It gives the segregator a false sense of superiority and the segregated a false sense of inferiority. Segregation, to use the terminology of the Jewish philosopher Martin Buber, substitutes an "I-it" relationship for an "I-thou" relationship and ends up relegating persons to the status of things. Hence segregation is not only politically, economically, and sociologically unsound, it is morally wrong and sinful. Paul Tillich has said that sin is separation. Is not segregation an existential expression of man's tragic separation, his awful estrangement, his terrible sinfulness? Thus it is that I can urge men to obey the 1954 decision of the Supreme Court, for it is morally right; and I can urge them to disobey segregation ordinances, for they are morally wrong.

Let us consider a more concrete example of just and unjust laws. An unjust law is a code that a numerical or power majority group compels a minority group to obey but does not make binding on itself. This is *difference* made legal. By the same token, a just law is a code that a majority compels a minority to follow and that it is willing to follow itself. This is *sameness* made legal.

Let me give another explanation. A law is unjust if it is inflicted on a minority that, as a result of being denied the right to vote, had no part in enacting or devising the law. Who can say that the legislature of Alabama which set up that state's segregation laws was democratically elected? Throughout Alabama all sorts of devious methods are used to prevent Negroes from becoming registered voters, and there are some counties in which, even though Negroes constitute a majority of the population, not a single Negro is registered. Can any law enacted under such circumstances be considered democratically structured?

Sometimes a law is just on its face and unjust in its application. For instance, I have been arrested on a charge of parading without a permit. Now, there is nothing wrong in having an ordinance which requires a permit for a parade. But such an ordinance becomes unjust when it is used to maintain segregation and to deny citizens the First Amendment privilege of peaceful assembly and protest.

I hope you are able to see the distinction I am trying to point out. In no sense do I advocate evading or defying the law, as would the rabid segregationist. That would lead to anarchy. One who breaks an unjust law must do so openly, lovingly, and with a willingness to accept the penalty. I submit that an individual who breaks a law that conscience tells him is unjust, and who willingly accepts the penalty of imprisonment in order to arouse the conscience of the community over its injustice, is in reality expressing the highest respect for law.

Of course, there is nothing new about this kind of civil disobedience. It was evidenced sublimely in the refusal of Shadrach, Meshach, and Abednego to obey the laws of Nebuchadnezzar, on the ground that a higher moral law was at stake. It was practiced superbly by the early Christians, who were willing to face hungry lions and the excruciating pain of chopping blocks rather than submit to certain unjust laws of the Roman Empire. To a degree, academic freedom is a reality today because Socrates practiced civil disobedience. In our own nation, the Boston Tea Party represented a massive act of civil disobedience.

We should never forget that everything Adolf Hitler did in Germany was "legal" and everything the Hungarian freedom fighters did in Hungary was "illegal." It was "illegal" to aid and comfort a Jew in Hitler's Germany. Even so, I am sure that, had I lived in Germany at the time, I would have aided and comforted my Jewish brothers. If today I lived in a Communist country where certain principles dear to the Christian faith are suppressed, I would openly advocate disobeying that country's antireligious laws.

I must make two honest confessions to you, my Christian and Jewish brothers. First, I must confess that over the past few years I have been gravely disappointed with the white moderate. I have almost reached the regrettable conclusion that the Negro's great stumbling block in his stride toward freedom is not the White Citizen's Counciler or the Ku Klux Klanner, but the white moderate, who is more devoted to "order" than to justice; who prefers a negative peace which is the absence of tension to a positive peace which is the presence of justice; who constantly says: "I agree with you in the goal you seek, but I cannot agree with your methods or direct action"; who paternalistically believes he can set the timetable for another man's freedom; who lives by a mythical concept of time and who constantly advises the Negro to wait for a "more convenient season." Shallow understanding from people of good will is more frustrating than absolute misunderstanding from people of ill will. Lukewarm acceptance is much more bewildering than outright rejection.

I had hoped that the white moderate would understand that law and order exist for the purpose of establishing justice and that when they fail in this purpose they become the dangerously structured dams that block the flow of social progress. I had hoped that the white moderate would understand that the present tension in the South is a necessary phase of the transition from an obnoxious negative peace, in which the Negro passively accepted his unjust plight, to a substantive and positive peace, in which all men will respect the dignity and worth of human personality. Actually, we who engage in nonviolent direct action are not the creators of tension. We merely bring to the surface the hidden tension that is already alive. We bring it out in the open, where it can be seen and dealt with. Like a boil that can never be cured so long as it is covered up but must be opened with all its ugliness to the natural medicines of air and light, injustice must be exposed, with all the tension its exposure creates, to the light of human conscience and the air of national opinion before it can be cured.

In your statement you assert that our actions, even though peaceful, must be condemned because they precipitate violence. But is this a logical assertion? Isn't this like condemning a robbed man because his possession of money precipitated the evil act of robbery? Isn't this like condemning Socrates because his unswerving commitment to truth and his philosophical inquiries precipitated the act by the misguided populace in which they made him drink hemlock? Isn't this like condemning Jesus because his unique God-consciousness and never-ceasing devotion to God's will precipitated the evil act of crucifixion? We must come to see that, as the federal courts have consistently affirmed, it is wrong to urge an individual to cease his efforts to gain his basic constitutional rights because the quest may precipitate violence. Society must protect the robbed and punish the robber.

I had also hoped that the white moderate would reject the myth concerning time in relation to the struggle for freedom. I have just received a letter from a white brother in Texas. He writes: "All Christians know that the colored people will receive equal rights eventually, but it is possible that you are in too great a religious hurry. It has taken Christianity almost two thousand years to accomplish what it has. The teachings of Christ take time to come to earth." Such an attitude stems from a tragic misconception of time, from the strangely irrational notion that there is something in the very flow of time that will inevitably cure all ills. Actually, time itself is neutral; it can be used either destructively or constructively. More and more I feel that the people of ill will have used time much more effectively than have the people of good will. We will have to repent in this generation not merely for the hateful words and actions of the bad people but for the appalling silence of the good people. Human progress never rolls in on wheels of inevitability; it comes through the tireless efforts of men willing to be co-workers with God, and without this hard work, time itself becomes an ally of the forces of social stagnation. We must use time creatively, in the knowledge that the time is always ripe to do right. Now is the time to make real the promise of democracy and transform our pending national elegy into a creative psalm of brotherhood. Now is the time to lift our national policy from the quicksand of racial injustice to the solid rock of human dignity.

You speak of our activity in Birmingham as extreme. At first I was rather disappointed that fellow clergymen would see my nonviolent efforts as those of an extremist. I began thinking about the fact that I stand in the middle of two opposing forces in the Negro community. One is a force of complacency, made up in part of Negroes who, as a result of long years of oppression, are so drained of self-respect and a sense of "somebodiness" that they have adjusted to segregation; and in part of a few middle-class Negroes who, because of a degree of academic and economic security and because in some ways they profit by segregation, have become insensitive to the problems of the masses.

The other force is one of bitterness and hatred, and it comes perilously close to advocating violence. It is expressed in the various black nationalist groups that are springing up across the nation, the largest and best-known being Elijah Muhammad's Muslim movement. Nourished by the Negro's frustration over the continued existence of racial discrimination, this movement is made up of people who have lost faith in America, who have absolutely repudiated Christianity, and who have concluded that the white man is an incorrigible "devil."

I have tried to stand between these two forces, saying that we need emulate neither the "do-nothingism" of the complacent nor the hatred and despair of the black nationalist. For there is the more excellent way of love and nonviolent protest. I am grateful to God that, through the influence of the Negro church, the way of nonviolence became an integral part of our struggle.

If this philosophy had not emerged, by now many streets of the South should, I am convinced, be flowing with blood. And I am further convinced that if our white brothers dismiss as "rabble-rousers" and "outside agitators" those of us who employ nonviolent direct action, and if they refuse to support our non-violent efforts, millions of Negroes will, out of frustration and despair, seek solace and security in black-nationalist ideologies—a development that would inevitably lead to a frightening racial nightmare.

Oppressed people cannot remain oppressed forever. The yearning for freedom eventually manifests itself, and that is what has happened to the American Negro. Something within has reminded him of his birthright of freedom, and something without has reminded him that it can be gained. Consciously or unconsciously, he has been caught up by the *Zeitgeist,* and with his black brothers of Africa and his brown and yellow brothers of Asia, South America, and the Caribbean, the United States Negro is moving with a sense of great urgency toward the promised land of racial justice. If one recognizes this vital urge that has engulfed the Negro community, one should readily understand why public demonstrations are taking place. The Negro has many pent-up resentments and latent frustrations, and he must release them. So let him march; let him make prayer pilgrimages to the city hall; let him go on freedom rides—and try to understand why he must do so. If his repressed emotions are not released in non-violent ways, they will seek expression through violence; this is not a threat but a fact of history. So I have not said to my people: "Get rid of your discontent." Rather, I have tried to say that this normal and healthy discontent can be channeled into the creative outlet of nonviolent direct action. And now this approach is being termed extremist.

But though I was initially disappointed at being categorized as an extremist, as I continued to think about the matter I gradually gained a measure of satisfaction from the label. Was not Jesus an extremist for love: "Love your enemies, bless them that curse you, do good to them that hate you, and pray for them which despitefully use you, and persecute you." Was not Amos an extremist for justice: "Let justice roll down like waters and righteousness like an ever-flowing stream." Was not Paul an extremist for the Christian gospel: "I bear in my body the marks of the

Lord Jesus." Was not Martin Luther an extremist: "Here I stand; I cannot do otherwise, so help me God." And John Bunyan: "I will stay in jail to the end of my days before I make a butchery of my conscience." And Abraham Lincoln: "This nation cannot survive half slave and half free." And Thomas Jefferson: "We hold these truths to be self-evident, that all men are created equal. . . ." So the question is not whether we all be extremists, but what kind of extremists we will be. Will we be extremists for hate or for love? Will we be extremists for the preservation of injustice or for the extension of justice? In that dramatic scene on Calvary's hill three men were crucified. We must never forget that all three were crucified for the same crime—the crime of extremism. Two were extremists for immorality, and thus fell below their environment. The other, Jesus Christ, was an extremist for love, truth, and goodness, and thereby rose above his environment. Perhaps the South, the nation, and the world are in dire need of creative extremists.

I had hoped that the white moderate would see this need. Perhaps I was too optimistic; perhaps I expected too much. I suppose I should have realized that few members of the oppressor race can understand the deep groans and passionate yearnings of the oppressed race, and still fewer have the vision to see that injustice must be rooted out by strong, persistent, and determined action. I am thankful, however, that some of our white brothers in the South have grasped the meaning of this social revolution and committed themselves to it. They are still all too few in quantity, but they are big in quality. Some—such as Ralph McGill, Lillian Smith, Harry Golden, James McBride Dabbs, Ann Braden, and Sarah Patton Boyle—have written about our struggle in eloquent and prophetic terms. Others have marched with us down nameless streets of the South. They have languished in filthy, roach-infested jails, suffering the abuse and brutality of policemen who view them as "dirty nigger-lovers." Unlike so many of their moderate brothers and sisters, they have recognized the urgency of the moment and sensed the need for powerful "action" antidotes to combat the disease of segregation.

Let me take note of my other major disappointment. I have been so greatly disappointed with the white church and its leadership. Of course, there are some notable exceptions. I am not unmindful of the fact that each of you has taken some significant stands on this issue. I commend you, Reverend Stallings, for your Christian stand on this past Sunday, in welcoming Negroes to your worship service on a nonsegregated basis. I commend the Catholic leaders of this state for integrating Spring Hill College several years ago.

But despite these notable exceptions, I must honestly reiterate that I have been disappointed with the church. I do not say this as one of those negative critics who can always find something wrong with the church. I say this as a minister of the gospel, who loves the church; who was nurtured in its bosom; who has been sustained by its spiritual blessings and who will remain true to it as long as the cord of life shall lengthen.

When I was suddenly catapulted into the leadership of the bus protest in Montgomery, Alabama, a few years ago, I felt we would be supported by the white church. I felt that the white ministers, priests, and rabbis of the South would be among our strongest allies. Instead, some have been outright opponents, refusing to understand the freedom movement and misrepresenting its leaders; all too many others have been more cautious than courageous and have remained silent behind the anesthetizing security of stained-glass windows.

In spite of my shattered dreams, I came to Birmingham with the hope that the white religious leadership of this community would see the justice of our cause and, with deep moral concern, would serve as the channel through which our just grievances could reach the power structure. I had hoped that each of you would understand. But again I have been disappointed.

I have heard numerous southern religious leaders admonish their worshipers to comply with a desegregation decision because it is the law, but I have longed to hear white ministers declare: "Follow this decree because integration is morally right and because the Negro is your brother," In the midst of blatant injustices inflicted upon the Negro, I have watched white churchmen stand on the sideline and mouth pious irrelevancies and sanctimonious trivialities. In the midst of a mighty struggle to rid our nation of racial and economic injustice, I have heard many ministers say: "Those are social issues, with which the gospel has no real concern." And I have watched many churches commit themselves to a completely otherworldly religion which makes a strange, unbiblical distinction between body and soul, between the sacred and the secular.

I have traveled the length and breadth of Alabama, Mississippi, and all the other southern states. On sweltering summer days and crisp autumn mornings I have looked at the South's beautiful churches with their lofty spires pointing heavenward. I have beheld the impressive outlines of her massive religious-education buildings. Over and over I have found myself saying: "What kind of people worship here? Who is their God? Where were their voices when the lips of Governor Barnett dripped with words of interposition and nullification? Where were they when Governor Wallace gave a clarion call for defiance and hatred? Where were their voices of support when bruised and weary Negro men and women decided to rise from the dark dungeons of complacency to the bright hills of creative protest?"

Yes, these questions are still in my mind. In deep disappointment I have wept over the laxity of the church. But be assured that my tears have been tears of love. There can be no deep disappointment where there is not deep love. Yes, I love the church. How could I do otherwise? I am in the rather unique position of being the son, the grandson, and the great-grandson of preachers. Yes, I see the church as the body of Christ. But, Oh! How we have blemished and scarred that body through social neglect and through fear of being nonconformists.

There was a time when the church was very powerful—in the time when the early Christians rejoiced at being deemed worthy to suffer for what they believed. In those days the church was not merely a thermometer that recorded the ideas and principles of popular opinion; it was a thermostat that transformed the mores of society. Whenever the early Christians entered a town, the people in power became disturbed and immediately sought to convict the Christians for being "disturbers of the peace" and "outside agitators." But the Christians pressed on, in the conviction that they were "a colony of heaven," called to obey God rather than man. Small in number, they were big in commitment. They were too God-intoxicated to be "astronomically intimidated." By their effort and example they brought an end to such ancient evils as infanticide and gladiatorial contests.

Things are different now. So often the contemporary church is a weak, ineffectual voice with an uncertain sound. So often it is an archdefender of the status quo. Far from being disturbed by the presence of the church, the power structure of the average community is consoled by the church's silent—and often even vocal—sanction of things as they are.

But the judgment of God is upon the church as never before. If today's church does not recapture the sacrificial spirit of the early church, it will lose its authenticity, forfeit the loyalty of millions, and be dismissed as an irrelevant social club with no meaning for the twentieth century. Every day I meet young people whose disappointment with the church has turned into outright disgust.

Perhaps I have once again been too optimistic. Is organized religion too inextricably bound to the status quo to save our nation and the world? Perhaps I must turn my faith to the inner spiritual church, the church within the church, as the true *ekklesia* and the hope of the world. But again I am thankful to God that some noble souls from the ranks of organized religion have broken loose from the paralyzing chains of conformity and joined us as active partners in the struggle for freedom. They have left their secure congregations and walked the streets of Albany, Georgia, with us. They have gone down the highways of the South on tortuous rides for freedom. Yes, they have gone to jail with us. Some have been dismissed from their churches, have lost the support of their bishops and fellow ministers. But they have acted in the faith that right defeated is stronger than evil triumphant. Their witness has been the spiritual salt that has preserved the true meaning of the gospel in these troubled times. They have carved a tunnel of hope through the dark mountain of disappointment.

I hope the church as a whole will meet the challenge of this decisive hour. But even if the church does not come to the aid of justice, I have no despair about the future. I have no fear about the outcome of our struggle in Birmingham, even if our motives are at present misunderstood. We will reach the goal of freedom in Birmingham and all over the nation, because the goal of America is freedom. Abused and scorned though we may be, our destiny is tied up with America's destiny. Before the pilgrims landed at Plymouth, we were here. Before the pen of Jefferson etched the majestic words of the Declaration of Independence across the pages of history, we were here. For more than two centuries our forebears labored in this country without wages; they made cotton king; they built the homes of their masters while suffering gross injustice and shameful humiliation—and yet out of a bottomless vitality they continue to thrive and develop. If the inexpressible cruelties of slavery could not stop us, the opposition we now face will surely fail. We will win our freedom because the sacred heritage of our nation and the eternal will of God are embodied in our echoing demands.

Before closing I feel impelled to mention one other point in your statement that has troubled me profoundly. You warmly commended the Birmingham police force for keeping "order" and "preventing violence." I doubt that you would have so warmly commended the police force if you had seen its dogs sinking their teeth into unarmed, nonviolent Negroes. I doubt that you would so quickly commend the policemen if you were to observe their ugly and inhumane treatment of Negroes here in the city jail; if you were to watch them push and curse old Negro women and young Negro girls; if you were to see them slap and kick old Negro men and young boys; if you were to observe them, as they did on two occasions, refuse to give us food because we wanted to sing our grace together. I cannot join you in your praise of the Birmingham police department.

It is true that the police have exercised a degree of discipline in handling the demonstrators. In this sense they have conducted themselves rather "nonviolently" in public. But for what purpose? To preserve the evil system of segregation. Over the past few years I have consistently preached that nonviolence demands that the means we use must be as pure as the ends we seek. I have tried to make clear that it is wrong to use immoral means to attain moral ends. But now I must affirm that it is just as wrong, or perhaps even more so, to use moral means to preserve immoral ends. Perhaps Mr. Connor and his policemen have been rather nonviolent in public, as was Chief Pritchett in Albany, Georgia, but they used the moral means of nonviolence to maintain the immoral end of racial injustice. As T. S. Eliot has said: "The last temptation is the greatest treason: To do the right deed for the wrong reason."

I wish you had commended the Negro sit-inners and demonstrators of Birmingham for their sublime courage, their willingness to suffer, and their amazing discipline in the midst of great provocation. One day the South will recognize its real heroes. They will be the James Merediths, with the noble sense of purpose that enables them to face jeering and hostile mobs, and with the agonizing loneliness that characterizes the life of the pioneer. They will be old, oppressed, battered Negro women, symbolized in a 72-year-old woman in Montgomery, Alabama, who rose up with a sense of dignity and with her people decided not to ride segregated buses, and who responded with ungrammatical profundity to one who inquired about her weariness: "My feets is tired, but my soul is at rest." They will be the young high school and college students, the young ministers of the gospel and a host of their elders, courageously and nonviolently sitting in at lunch counters and willingly going to jail for conscience' sake. One day the South will know that when these disinherited children of God sat down at lunch counters, they were in reality standing up for what is best in the American dream and for the most sacred values in our Judaeo-Christian heritage, thereby bringing our nation back to those great wells of democracy which were dug deep by the founding fathers in their formulation of the Constitution and the Declaration of Independence.

Never before have I written so long a letter. I'm afraid it is much too long to take your precious time. I can assure you that it would have been much shorter if I had been writing from a comfortable desk, but what else can one do when he is alone in a narrow jail cell, other than write long letters, think long thoughts, and pray long prayers?

If I have said anything in this letter that overstates the truth and indicates an unreasonable impatience, I beg you to forgive me. If I have said anything that understates the truth and indicates my having a patience that allows me to settle for anything less than brotherhood, I beg God to forgive me.

I hope this letter finds you strong in the faith. I also hope that circumstances will soon make it possible for me to meet each of you, not as an integrationist or a civil-rights leader but as a fellow clergyman and a Christian brother. Let us all hope that the dark clouds of racial prejudice will soon pass away and the deep fog of misunderstanding will be lifted from our fear-drenched communities, and in some not too distant tomorrow the radiant stars of love and brotherhood will shine over our great nation with all their scintillating beauty.

Yours for the cause of Peace and Brotherhood,
Martin Luther King, Jr.

The Feminization of Earth First!

Judi Bari

Judi Bari (1949–1997) was an environmental activist. She protested the logging of old-growth redwood forests in California and survived a car bombing in 1990, which is still unsolved. This essay first appeared in Ms. *magazine.*

It is impossible to live in the redwood region without being profoundly affected by the massive destruction of this once-magnificent ecosystem. Miles and miles of clearcuts cover our bleeding hillsides. Ancient forests are being strip-logged to pay off corporate junk bonds. Log trucks fill our roads, heading to the sawmills with loads ranging from 1,000-year-old redwoods, one tree trunk filling an entire logging truck, to six-inch-diameter baby trees that are chipped for pulp.

So it is not surprising that I, a lifelong activist, would become an environmentalist. What is surprising is that I, a feminist, single mother, and blue-collar worker, would end up in Earth First!, a "no compromise" direct action group with the reputation of being beer-drinking ecodudes. Little did I know that combining the feminist elements of collectivism and nonviolence with the spunk and outrageousness of Earth First! would spark a mass movement. And little did I know that I would pay for our success by being bombed and nearly killed, and subjected to a campaign of hatred and misogyny.

I was attracted to Earth First! because its activists were the only people willing to put their bodies in front of the bulldozers and chain saws to save the trees.

They were also funny and irreverent, and they played music. But it was the philosophy of Earth First! that ultimately won me over. This philosophy, known as biocentrism or deep ecology, states that the Earth is not just here for human consumption. All species have a right to exist for their own sake, and humans must learn to live in balance with the needs of nature instead of trying to mold nature to fit the needs of humans.

I see no contradiction between deep ecology and ecofeminism, but Earth First! was founded by five men, and its principal spokespeople have all been male. As in all such groups, there have always been competent women doing the real work behind the scenes. But they have been virtually invisible behind the public Earth First! persona of "big man goes into big wilderness to save big trees." I certainly objected to this. Yet despite the image, the structure of Earth First! was decentralized and nonhierarchical, so we could develop any way we wanted in our local northern California group.

In many ways the northwest timber country resembles Appalachia more than California. It is sparsely populated and set in mountainous terrain. Some of the more isolated communities are located hours away from the nearest sheriff, and have become virtually lawless areas, with a wild West mentality. The economy is dominated by a few large timber corporations. Louisiana-Pacific, Georgia-Pacific, and Maxxam are the most powerful, and in our impoverished rural communities local government, police, schools, and others all bow to the economic blackmail of King Timber. The town of Scotia, one of the last actual company towns in the U.S., is owned and operated by Maxxam, and you are not allowed to rent a house in Scotia unless you work for the company.

For years the strategy of Earth First!, under male leadership, had been based on individual acts of daring. "Nomadic action groups" of maybe ten people would travel to remote areas and bury themselves in logging roads, chain themselves to heavy equipment, or sit in trees. There were certainly brave and principled women who engaged in these actions. But by and large, most of the people who had the freedom for that kind of travel and risk-taking were men.

I have nothing against individual acts of daring. But the flaw in this strategy is the failure to engage in long-term community-based organizing. There is no way that a few isolated individuals, no matter how brave, can bring about the massive social change necessary to save the planet. So we began to organize with local people, planning our logging blockades around local issues. And we began to build alliances with progressive timber workers based on our common interests against the big corporations. As our success grew, more women and more people with families and roots in the community began calling themselves Earth First!ers in our area.

But as our exposure and influence grew, so did the use of violence against us. At one demonstration a 50-year-old nonviolent woman was punched so hard her nose was broken. In another incident, my car was rammed Karen Silkwood–style by the same logging truck that we had blockaded less than 24 hours earlier. In both these cases, as in other instances of violence against us, local police refused even to investigate our assailants.

Earth First! had never initiated any violence. But I felt we needed a much more explicit nonviolence code in the face of an increasingly volatile situation on the front lines. So, drawing on the lessons of the civil rights movement, we put out a nationwide call for Freedom Riders for the Forest to come to northern California and engage in nonviolent mass actions to stop the slaughter of the redwoods. We called the campaign Redwood Summer and, as it became clear that we were successfully drawing national interest, the level of repression escalated again.

I began to receive a series of increasingly frightening death threats, obviously written on behalf of Big Timber. The most frightening was a photo of me with a rifle scope and cross hairs superimposed on my face and a yellow ribbon (the timber industry's symbol) attached. My complaints to the local police and to the county board of supervisors were ignored. Finally, on May 24,1990, as I was driving through Oakland on a concert tour to promote Redwood Summer, a bomb exploded under my car seat. I remember my thoughts as it ripped through me. I thought, this is what men do to each other in wars.

The bomb was meant to kill me, and it nearly did. It shattered my pelvis and left me crippled for life. My organizing companion, Darryl Cherney, who was riding with me in the car, was slightly injured. Then, adding to the outrage, police and the FBI moved in immediately and arrested Darryl and me, saying that it was our bomb and we were knowingly carrying it. For eight weeks they slandered us in the press, attempting to portray us as violent and to discredit Redwood Summer, until they finally admitted there was no evidence against us.

There were indications in advance that the attack on me was specifically misogynist. One of the death threats described Earth First!ers as "whores, lesbians, and members of NOW." But soon after the bombing a letter was received that left no doubt. It was signed "The Lord's Avenger," and it took credit for the bombing. It described the bomb in exact detail and explained in chilling prose why the Lord's Avenger wanted me dead.

It was not just my "paganism" and defense of the forest that outraged him. The Lord's Avenger also recalled an abortion clinic defense I had led years ago, and quoted Timothy 2:11: "Let the woman learn in silence with all subjection. But I suffer not a woman to teach, nor to usurp authority over the man, but to be in silence."

Meanwhile, out in the forest, Redwood Summer went on without me. Before the bombing I was one of very few women leaders in Earth First! But after the bombing it was the women who rose to take my place. Redwood Summer was the feminization of Earth First!, with three quarters of the leadership made up of women. Our past actions had drawn no more than 150 participants. But 3,000 people came to Redwood Summer, blocking logging operations and marching through timber towns in demonstrations reminiscent of civil rights protests against the Klan in the South. Despite incredible provocation, and despite the grave violence done to me, Earth First! maintained our nonviolence throughout the summer.

Being the first women-led action, Redwood Summer has never gotten the respect it deserves from the old guard of Earth First! nationally. But it has profoundly affected the redwood region. The 2,000-year-old trees of Headwaters Forest, identified, named, and made an issue of by Earth First!, are now being preserved largely due to our actions. And the movement here, recently renamed Ecotopia Earth First!, is probably the only truly gender-balanced group I have ever worked in.

I recently attended a workshop in Tennessee on violence and harassment in the environmental movement. As the 32 people from all over the country shared their stories, I was struck by the fact that the most serious acts of violence had all been done to women. This is no surprise because it is the hatred of the feminine, which is the hatred of life, that has contributed to the destruction of the planet. And it is the strength of women that can restore the balance we need to survive.

Civil Disobedience: Destroyer of Democracy

Lewis H. Van Dusen, Jr.

Lewis H. Van Dusen, Jr. is a distinguished lawyer who has served as president of the Pennsylvania Bar Association and as chair of the American Bar Association's Standing Committee on Ethics and Professional Responsibility. This essay appeared in The ABA Journal: The Lawyer's Magazine, *published by the American Bar Association, in 1969.*

As Charles E. Wyzanski, Chief Judge of the United States District Court in Boston, wrote in the February 1968, *Atlantic:* "Disobedience is a long step from dissent. Civil disobedience involves a deliberate and punishable breach of legal duty." Protesters might prefer a different definition. They would rather say that civil disobedience is the peaceful resistance of conscience.

The philosophy of civil disobedience was not developed in our American democracy, but in the very first democracy of Athens. It was expressed by the poet Sophocles and the philosopher Socrates. In Sophocle's tragedy, Antigone chose to obey her conscience and violate the state edict against providing burial for her brother, who had been decreed a traitor. When the dictator Creon found out that Antigone had buried her fallen brother, he confronted her and reminded her that there was a mandatory death penalty for this deliberate disobedience of the state law. Antigone nobly replied, "Nor did I think your orders were so strong that you, a mortal man, could overrun the gods' unwritten and unfailing laws."

Conscience motivated Antigone. She was not testing the validity of the law in the hope that eventually she would be sustained. Appealing to the judgment of the community, she explained her action to the chorus. She was not secret and surreptitious—the interment of her brother was open and public. She was not violent; she did not trespass on another citizen's rights. And finally, she accepted without resistance the death sentence—the penalty for violation. By voluntarily accepting the law's sanctions, she was not a revolutionary denying the authority of the state. Antigone's behavior exemplifies the classic case of civil disobedience.

Socrates believed that reason could dictate a conscientious disobedience of state law, but he also believed that he had to accept the legal sanctions of the state. In Plato's *Crito,* Socrates from his hanging basket accepted the death penalty for his teaching of religion to youths contrary to state laws.

The sage of Walden, Henry David Thoreau, took this philosophy of nonviolence and developed it into a strategy for solving society's injustices. First enunciating it in protest against the Mexican War, he then turned it to use against slavery. For refusing to pay taxes that would help pay the enforcers of the fugitive slave law, he went to prison. In Thoreau's words, "If the alternative is to keep all just men in prison or to give up slavery, the state will not hesitate which to choose."

Sixty years later, Gandhi took Thoreau's civil disobedience as his strategy to wrest Indian independence from England. The famous salt march against a British imperial tax is his best-known example of protest.

But the conscientious law breaking of Socrates, Gandhi, and Thoreau is to be distinguished from the conscientious law testing of Martin Luther King, Jr., who was not a civil disobedient. The civil disobedient withholds taxes or violates state laws knowing he is legally wrong, but believing he is morally right. While he wrapped himself in the mantle of Gandhi and Thoreau, Dr. King led his followers in violation of state laws he believed were contrary to the Federal Constitution. But since Supreme Court decisions in the end generally upheld his many actions, he should not be considered a true civil disobedient.

The civil disobedience of Antigone is like that of the pacifist who withholds paying the percentage of his taxes that goes to the Defense Department, or the Quaker who travels against State Department regulations to Hanoi to distribute medical supplies, or the Vietnam war protester who tears up his draft card. This civil disobedient has been nonviolent in his defiance of the law; he has been unfurtive in his violation; he has been submissive to the penalties of the law. He has neither evaded the law nor interfered with another's rights. He has been neither a rioter nor a revolutionary. The thrust of his cause has not been the might of coercion but the martyrdom of conscience.

Was the Boston Tea Party Civil Disobedience?

Those who justify violence and radical action as being in the tradition of our Revolution show a misunderstanding of the philosophy of democracy.

James Farmer, former head of the Congress of Racial Equality, in defense of the mass action confrontation method, has told of a famous organized demonstration that took place in opposition to political and economic discrimination. The protestors beat back and scattered the law enforcers and then proceeded to loot and destroy private property. Mr. Farmer then said he was talking about the Boston Tea Party and implied that violence as a method for redress of grievances was an American tradition and a legacy of our revolutionary heritage. While it is true that there is no more sacred document than our Declaration of Independence, Jefferson's "inherent right of rebellion" was predicated on the tyrannical denial of democratic means. If there is no popular assembly to provide an adjustment of ills, and if there is no court system to dispose of injustices, then there is, indeed, a right to rebel.

The seventeenth century's John Locke, the philosophical father of the Declaration of Independence, wrote in his *Second Treatise on Civil Government:* "Wherever law ends, tyranny begins . . . and the people are absolved from any further obedience. Governments are dissolved from within when the legislative [chamber] is altered. When the government [becomes] . . . arbitrary disposers of lives, liberties and fortunes of the people, such revolutions happen. . . ."

But there are some sophisticated proponents of the revolutionary redress of grievances who say that the test of the need for radical action is not the unavailability of democratic institutions but the ineffectuality of those institutions to remove blatant social inequalities. If social injustice exists, they say, concerted disobedience is required against the constituted government, whether it be totalitarian or democratic in structure.

Of course, only the most bigoted chauvinist would claim that America is without some glaring faults. But there has never been a utopian society on earth and there never will be unless human nature is remade. Since inequities will mar even the best-framed democracies, the injustice rationale would allow a free right of civil resistance to be available always as a shortcut alternative to the democratic way of petition, debate and assembly. The lesson of history is that civil insurgency spawns far more injustices than it removes. The Jeffersons, Washingtons, and Adamses resisted tyranny with the aim of promoting the procedures of democracy. They would never have resisted a democratic government with the risk of promoting the techniques of tyranny.

Legitimate Pressures and Illegitimate Results

There are many civil rights leaders who show impatience with the process of democracy. They rely on the sit-ins, boycott or mass picketing to gain speedier solutions to the problems that face every citizen. But we must realize that the legitimate pressures that won concessions in the past can easily escalate into the illegitimate power plays that might extort demands in the future. The victories of these civil rights leaders must not shake our confidence in the democratic procedures, as the pressures of demonstration are desirable only if they take place within the limits allowed by law. Civil rights gains should continue to be won by the persuasion of Congress and other legislative bodies and by the decision of courts. Any illegal entreaty for the rights of some can be an injury to the rights of others, for mass demonstrations often trigger violence.

Those who advocate taking the law into their own hands should reflect that when they are disobeying what they consider to be an immoral law, they are deciding on a possibly immoral course. Their answer is that the process for democratic relief is too slow, that only mass confrontation can bring immediate action, and that any injuries are the inevitable cost of the pursuit of justice. Their answer is, simply put, that the end justifies the means. It is this justification of any form of demonstration as a form of dissent that threatens to destroy a society built on the rule of law.

Our Bill of Rights guarantees wide opportunities to use mass meetings, public parades, and organized demonstrations to stimulate sentiment, to dramatize issues, and to cause change. The Washington freedom march of 1963 was such a call for action. But the rights of free expression cannot be mere force cloaked in the garb of free speech. As the courts have decreed in labor cases, free assembly does not mean mass picketing or sit-down strikes. These rights are subject to limitations of time and place so as to secure the rights of others. When militant students storm a college president's office to achieve demands, when certain groups plan rush-hour car stalling to protest discrimination in employment, these are not dissent, but a denial of rights to others. Neither is it the lawful use of mass protest, but rather the unlawful use of mob power.

Justice Black, one of the foremost advocates and defenders of the right of protest and dissent, has said:

> . . . Experience demonstrates that it is not a far step from what to many seems to be the earnest, honest, patriotic, kind-spirited multitude of today, to the fanatical, threatening, lawless mob of tomorrow. And the crowds that press in the streets for noble goals today can be supplanted tomorrow by street mobs pressuring the courts for precisely opposite ends.[1]

Society must censure those demonstrators who would trespass on the public peace, as it must condemn those rioters whose pillage would destroy the public peace. But more ambivalent is society's posture toward the civil disobedient. Unlike the rioter, the true civil disobedient commits no violence. Unlike the mob demonstrator, he commits no trespass on others' rights. The civil disobedient, while deliberately violating a law, shows an oblique respect for the law by voluntarily submitting to its sanctions. He neither resists arrest nor evades punishment. Thus, he breaches the law but not the peace.

But civil disobedience, whatever the ethical rationalization, is still an assault on our democratic society, an affront to our legal order and an attack on our constitutional government. To indulge civil disobedience is to invite anarchy, and the permissive arbitrariness of anarchy is hardly less tolerable than the repressive arbitrariness of tyranny. Too often the license of liberty is followed by the loss of liberty, because into the desert of anarchy comes the man on horseback, a Mussolini or a Hitler.

Violations of Law Subvert Democracy

Law violations, even for ends recognized as laudable, are not only assaults on the rule of law, but subversions of the democratic process. The disobedient act of conscience does not ennoble democracy; it erodes it.

First, it courts violence, and even the most careful and limited use of non-violent acts of disobedience may help sow the dragon-teeth of civil riot. Civil disobedience is the progenitor of disorder, and disorder is the sire of violence.

Second, the concept of civil disobedience does not invite principles of general applicability. If the children of light are morally privileged to resist particular laws on grounds of conscience, so are the children of darkness. Former Deputy Attorney General Burke Marshall said: "If the decision to break the law really turned on individual conscience, it is hard to see in law how [the civil rights leader] is better off than former Governor Ross Barnett of Mississippi who also believed deeply in his cause and was willing to go to jail."[2]

Third, even the most noble act of civil disobedience assaults the rule of law. Although limited as to method, motive and objective, it has the effect of inducing others to engage in different forms of law breaking characterized by methods unsanctioned and condemned by classic theories of law violation. Unfortunately, the most patent lesson of civil disobedience is not so much nonviolence of action as defiance of authority.

Finally, the greatest danger in condoning civil disobedience as a permissible strategy for hastening change is that it undermines our democratic processes. To adopt the techniques of civil disobedience is to assume that representative government does not work. To resist the decisions of courts and the laws of elected assemblies is to say that democracy has failed.

There is no man who is above the law, and there is no man who has a right to break the law. Civil disobedience is not above the law, but against the law. When the civil disobedient disobeys one law, he invariably subverts all law. When the civil disobedient says that he is above the law he is saying that democracy is beneath him. His disobedience shows a distrust for the democratic system. He is merely saying that since democracy does not work, why should he help make it work. Thoreau expressed well the civil disobedient's disdain for democracy:

> As for adopting the ways which the state has provided for remedying the evil, I know not of such ways. They take too much time and a man's life will be gone. I have other affairs to attend to. I came into this world not chiefly to make this a good place to live in, but to live in it, be it good or bad.[3]

Thoreau's position is not only morally irresponsible but politically reprehensible. When citizens in a democracy are called on to make a profession of faith, the civil disobedients offer only a confession of failure. Tragically, when civil disobedients for lack of faith abstain from democratic involvement, they help attain their own gloomy prediction. They help create the social and political basis for their own despair. By foreseeing failure, they help forge it. If citizens rely on antidemocratic means of protest, they will help bring about the undemocratic result of an authoritarian or anarchic state.

How far demonstrations properly can be employed to produce political and social change is a pressing question, particularly in view of the provocations accompanying the National Democratic Convention in Chicago last August and the reaction of the police to them. A line must be drawn by the judiciary between the demands of those who seek absolute order, which can lead only to a dictatorship, and those who seek absolute freedom, which can lead only to anarchy. The line, wherever it is drawn by our courts, should be respected on the college campus, on the streets, and elsewhere.

Undue provocation will inevitably result in overreaction, human emotions being what they are. Violence will follow. This cycle undermines the very democracy it is designed to preserve. The lesson of the past is that democracies will fall if violence, including the intentional provocations that will lead to violence, replaces democratic procedures, as in Athens, Rome, and the Weimar Republic. This lesson must be constantly explained by the legal profession.

We should heed the words of William James:

> Democracy is still upon its trial. The civic genius of our people is its only bulwark and . . . neither battleships nor public libraries nor great newspapers nor booming stocks: neither mechanical invention nor political adroitness, nor churches nor universities nor civil service examinations can save us from degeneration if the inner mystery be lost.
>
> That mystery, at once the secret and the glory of our English-speaking race, consists of nothing but two habits. . . . [O]ne of them is the habit of trained and disciplined good temper towards the opposite party when it fairly wins its innings. The other is that of fierce and merciless resentment toward every man or set of men who break the public peace.[4]

Notes

1. In *Cox v. Louisiana*, 379 U.S. 536, 575, 584 (1965).
2. "The Protest Movement and the Law," *Virginia Legal Review* 51 (1965), 785.
3. Thoreau, "Civil Disobedience" (see page 637).
4. James, *Pragmatism* (1907), pp. 127–28.

Señor Payroll

William E. Barrett

William E. Barrett (1900–1986) was a prolific author of novels and short stories whose work, including the book Lilies of the Field *(1962), often addressed issues of religious faith and social justice. This story appeared in* Southwest Review *in 1943.*

Larry and I were Junior Engineers in the gas plant, which means that we were clerks. Anything that could be classified as paper work came to the flat double desk across which we faced each other. The Main Office downtown sent us a bewildering array of orders and rules that were to be put into effect.

Junior Engineers were beneath the notice of everyone except the Mexican laborers at the plant. To them we were the visible form of a distant, unknowable paymaster. We were Señor Payroll.

Those Mexicans were great workmen; the aristocrats among them were the stokers, big men who worked Herculean eight-hour shifts in the fierce heat of the retorts. They scooped coal with huge shovels and hurled it with uncanny aim at tiny doors. The coal streamed out from the shovels like black water from a high-pressure nozzle, and never missed the narrow opening. The stokers worked stripped to the waist, and there was pride and dignity in them. Few men could do such work, and they were the few.

The Company paid its men only twice a month, on the fifth and on the twentieth. To a Mexican, this was absurd. What man with money will make it last fifteen days? If he hoarded money beyond the spending of three days, he was a miser—and when, Señor, did the blood of Spain flow in the veins of misers? Hence, it was the custom for our stokers to appear every third or fourth day to draw the money due to them.

There was a certain elasticity in the Company rules, and Larry and I sent the necessary forms to the Main Office and received an "advance" against a man's pay check. Then, one day, Downtown favored us with a memorandum:

"There have been too many abuses of the advance-against-wages privilege. Hereafter, no advance against wages will be made to any employee except in a case of genuine emergency."

We had no sooner posted the notice when in came stoker Juan Garcia. He asked for an advance. I pointed to the notice. He spelled it through slowly, then said, "What does this mean, this 'genuine emergency'?"

I explained to him patiently that the Company was kind and sympathetic, but that it was a great nuisance to have to pay wages every few days. If someone was ill or if money was urgently needed for some other good reason, then the Company would make an exception to the rule.

Juan Garcia turned his hat over and over slowly in his big hands. "I do not get my money?"

"Next payday, Juan. On the twentieth."

He went out silently and I felt a little ashamed of myself. I looked across the desk at Larry. He avoided my eyes.

In the next hour two other stokers came in, looked at the notice, had it explained and walked solemnly out; then no more came. What we did not know was that Juan Garcia, Pete Mendoza, and Francisco Gonzalez had spread the word, and that every Mexican in the plant was explaining the order to every other Mexican. "To get money now, the wife must be sick. There must be medicine for the baby."

The next morning Juan Garcia's wife was practically dying, Pete Mendoza's mother would hardly last the day, there was a veritable epidemic among children, and, just for variety, there was one sick father. We always suspected that the old man was really sick; no Mexican would otherwise have thought of him. At any rate, nobody paid Larry and me to examine private lives; we made out our forms with an added line describing the "genuine emergency." Our people got paid.

That went on for a week. Then came a new order, curt and to the point; "Hereafter, employees will be paid ONLY on the fifth and the twentieth of the month. No exceptions will be made except in the cases of employees leaving the service of the Company."

The notice went up on the board, and we explained its significance gravely. "No, Juan Garcia, we cannot advance your wages. It is too bad about your wife and your cousins and your aunts, but there is a new rule."

Juan Garcia went out and thought it over. He thought out loud with Mendoza and Gonzales and Ayala, then, in the morning, he was back. "I am quitting this company for different job. You pay me now?"

We argued that it was a good company and that it loved its employees like children, but in the end we paid off, because Juan Garcia quit. And so did Gonzalez, Mendoza, Obregon, Ayala and Ortez, the best stokers, men who could not be replaced.

Larry and I looked at each other; we knew what was coming in about three days. One of our duties was to sit on the hiring line early each morning, engaging transient workers for the handy gangs. Any man was accepted who could walk up and ask for a job without falling down. Never before had we been called upon to hire such skilled virtuosos as stokers for handy-gang work, but we were called upon to hire them now.

The day foreman was wringing his hands and asking the Almighty if he was personally supposed to shovel this condemned coal, while there in a stolid, patient line were skilled men—Garcia, Mendoza, and others—waiting to be hired. We hired them, of course. There was nothing else to do.

Every day we had a line of resigning stokers, and another line of stokers seeking work. Our paper work became very complicated. At the Main Office they were jumping up and down. The procession of forms showing Juan Garcia's resigning and being hired over and over again was too much for them. Sometimes Downtown had Garcia on the payroll twice at the same time when someone down there was slow in entering a resignation. Our phone rang early and often.

Tolerantly and patiently we explained: "There's nothing we can do if a man wants to quit, and if there are stokers available when the plant needs stokers, we hire them."

Out of chaos, Downtown issued another order. I read it and whistled. Larry looked at it and said, "It is going to be very quiet around here."

The order read: "Hereafter, no employee who resigns may be rehired within a period of 30 days."

Juan Garcia was due for another resignation, and when he came in we showed him the order and explained that standing in line the next day would do him no good if he resigned today. "Thirty days is a long time, Juan."

It was a grave matter and he took time to reflect on it. So did Gonzalez, Mendoza, Ayala and Ortez. Ultimately, however, they were all back—and all resigned.

We did our best to dissuade them and we were sad about the parting. This time it was for keeps and they shook hands with us solemnly. It was very nice knowing us. Larry and I looked at each other when they were gone and we both knew that neither of us had been pulling for Downtown to win this duel. It was a blue day.

In the morning, however, they were all back in line. With the utmost gravity, Juan Garcia informed me that he was a stoker looking for a job.

"No dice, Juan," I said. "Come back in thirty days. I warned you."

His eyes looked straight into mine without a flicker. "There is some mistake, Señor," he said. "I am Manuel Hernandez. I work as the stoker in Pueblo, in Santa Fe, in many places."

I stared back at him, remembering the sick wife and the babies without medicine, the mother-in-law in the hospital, the many resignations and the rehirings. I knew that there was a gas plant in Pueblo, and that there wasn't any in Santa Fe; but who was I to argue with a man about his own name? A stoker is a stoker.

So I hired him. I hired Gonzalez, too, who swore that his name was Carrera, and Ayala, who had shamelessly become Smith.

Three days later the resigning started.

Within a week our payroll read like a history of Latin America. Everyone was on it: Lopez and Obregon, Villa, Diaz, Batista, Gomez, and even San Martín and Bolívar. Finally Larry and I, growing weary of staring at familiar faces and writing unfamiliar names, went to the Superintendent and told him the whole story. He tried not to grin, and said, "Damned nonsense!"

The next day the orders were taken down. We called our most prominent stokers into the office and pointed to the board. No rules any more.

"The next time we hire you hombres," Larry said grimly, "come in under the names you like best, because that's the way you are going to stay on the books."

They looked at us and they looked at the board; then for the first time in the long duel, their teeth flashed white. "Si, Señores," they said.

And so it was.

Issues about the Content of Education

On the Uses of a Liberal Education
As Lite Entertainment
for Bored College Students

Mark Edmundson

Mark Edmundson is a professor of English at the University of Virginia. He is also the author of a book about the gothic in contemporary culture entitled Nightmare of Mainstreet, *published by Harvard University Press. This essay appeared in* Harper's Magazine *in September 1997. The essay generated a range of responses from readers, published in the "Letters" section of subsequent issues of the magazine.*

Today is evaluation day in my Freud class, and everything has changed. The class meets twice a week, late in the afternoon, and the clientele, about fifty undergraduates, tends to drag in and slump, looking disconsolate and a little lost, waiting for a jump start. To get the discussion moving, they usually require a joke, an anecdote, an off-the-wall question—When you were a kid, were your Halloween getups ego costumes, id costumes, or superego costumes? That sort of thing. But today, as soon as I flourish the forms, a buzz rises in the room. Today they write their assessments of the course, their assessments of *me,* and they are without a doubt wide-awake. "What is your evaluation of the instructor?" asks question number eight, entreating them to circle a number between five (excellent) and one (poor, poor). Whatever interpretive subtlety they've acquired during the term is now out the window. Edmundson: one to five, stand and shoot.

And they do. As I retreat through the door—I never stay around for this phase of the ritual—I look over my shoulder and see them toiling away like the devil's auditors. They're pitched into high writing gear, even the ones who struggle to squeeze out their journal entries word by word, stoked on a procedure they have by now supremely mastered. They're playing the informed consumer, letting the provider know where he's come through and where he's not quite up to snuff.

But why am I so distressed, bolting like a refugee out of my own classroom, where I usually hold easy sway? Chances are the evaluations will be much like what they've been in the past—they'll be just fine. It's likely that I'll be commended for being "interesting" (and I am commended, many times over), that I'll be cited for my relaxed and tolerant ways (that happens, too), that my sense of humor and capacity to connect the arcana of the subject matter with current culture will come in for some praise (yup). I've been hassled this term, finishing a manuscript, and so haven't given their journals the attention I should have, and for that I'm called—quite civilly, though—to account. Overall, I get off pretty well.

Yet I have to admit that I do not much like the image of myself that emerges from these forms, the image of knowledgeable, humorous detachment and bland tolerance. I do not like the forms themselves, with their number ratings, reminiscent of the sheets circulated after the TV pilot has just played to its sample audience in Burbank. Most of all I dislike the attitude of calm consumer expertise that pervades the responses. I'm disturbed by the serene belief that my function—and, more important, Freud's, or Shakespeare's, or Blake's—is to divert, entertain, and interest. Observes one respondent, not at all unrepresentative: "Edmundson has done a fantastic job of presenting this difficult, important & controversial material in an enjoyable and approachable way."

Thanks but no thanks. I don't teach to amuse, to divert, or even, for that matter, to be merely interesting. When someone says she "enjoyed" the course—and that word crops up again and again in my evaluations—somewhere at the edge of my immediate complacency I feel encroaching self-dislike. That is not at all what I had in mind. The off-the-wall questions and the sidebar jokes are meant as lead-ins to stronger stuff—in the case of the Freud course, to a complexly tragic view of life. But the affability and the one-liners often seem to be all that land with the students; their journals and evaluations leave me little doubt.

I want some of them to say that they've been changed by the course. I want them to measure themselves against what they've read. It's said that some time ago a Columbia University instructor used to issue a harsh two-part question. One: What book did you most dislike in the course? Two: What intellectual or characterological flaws in you does that dislike point to? The hand that framed that question was surely heavy. But at least it compels one to see intellectual work as a confrontation between two people, student and author, where the stakes matter. Those Columbia students were being asked to relate the quality of an *encounter*, not rate the action as though it had unfolded on the big screen.

Why are my students describing the Oedipus complex and the death drive as being interesting and enjoyable to contemplate? And why am I coming across as an urbane, mildly ironic, endlessly affable guide to this intellectual territory, operating without intensity, generous, funny, and loose?

Because that's what works. On evaluation day, I reap the rewards of my partial compliance with the culture of my students and, too, with the culture of the university as it now operates. It's a culture that's gotten little exploration. Current critics tend to think that liberal-arts education is in crisis because universities have been invaded by professors with peculiar ideas: deconstruction, Lacanianism, feminism, queer theory. They believe that genius and tradition are out and that P.C., multiculturalism, and identity politics are in because of an invasion by tribes of tenured radicals, the late millennial equivalents of the Visigoth hordes that cracked Rome's walls.

But mulling over my evaluations and then trying to take a hard, extended look at campus life both here at the University of Virginia and around the country eventually led me to some different conclusions. To me, liberal-arts education is as ineffective as it is now not chiefly because there are a lot of strange theories in the air. (Used well, those theories *can* be illuminating.) Rather, it's that university culture, like American culture writ large, is, to put it crudely, ever more devoted to consumption and entertainment, to the using and using up of goods and images. For someone growing up in America now, there are few available alternatives to the cool consumer worldview. My students didn't ask for that view, much less create it, but they bring a consumer weltanschauung to school, where it exerts a powerful, and largely unacknowledged, influence. If we want to understand current universities, with their multiple woes, we might try leaving the realms of expert debate and fine ideas and turning to the classrooms and campuses, where a new kind of weather is gathering.

From time to time I bump into a colleague in the corridor and we have what I've come to think of as a Joon Lee fest. Joon Lee is one of the best students I've taught. He's endlessly curious, has read a small library's worth, seen every movie, and knows all about showbiz and entertainment. For a class of mine he wrote an essay using Nietzsche's Apollo and Dionysus to analyze the pop group The Supremes. A trite, cultural-studies bonbon? Not at all. He said striking things about conceptions of race in America and about how they shape our ideas of beauty. When I talk with one of his other teachers, we run on about the general splendors of his work and presence. But what inevitably follows a JL fest is a mournful reprise about the divide that separates him and a few other remarkable students from their contemporaries. It's not that some aren't nearly as bright—in terms of intellectual ability, my students are all that I could ask for. Instead, it's that Joon Lee has decided to follow his interests and let them make him into a singular and rather eccentric man; in his charming way, he doesn't mind being at odds with most anyone.

It's his capacity for enthusiasm that sets Joon apart from what I've come to think of as the reigning generational style. Whether the students are sorority/fraternity types, grunge aficionados, piercer/tattooers, black or white, rich or middle class (alas, I teach almost no students from truly poor backgrounds), they are, nearly across the board, very, very self-contained. On good days they display a light, appealing glow; on bad days, shuffling disgruntlement. But there's little fire, little passion to be found.

This point came home to me a few weeks ago when I was wandering across the university grounds. There, beneath a classically cast portico, were two students, male and female, having a rip-roaring argument. They were incensed, bellowing at each other, headstrong, confident, and wild. It struck me how rarely I see this kind of full-out feeling in students anymore. Strong emotional display is forbidden. When conflicts arise, it's generally understood that one of the parties will say something sarcastically propitiating ("whatever" often does it) and slouch away.

How did my students reach this peculiar state in which all passion seems to be spent? I think that many of them have imbibed their sense of self from consumer culture in general and from the tube in particular. They're the progeny of 100 cable channels and omnipresent Blockbuster outlets. TV, Marshall McLuhan famously said, is a cool medium. Those who play best on it are low-key and nonassertive; they blend in. Enthusiasm, à la Joon Lee, quickly looks absurd. The form of character that's most appealing on TV is calmly self-interested though never greedy, attuned to the conventions, and ironic. Judicious timing is preferred to sudden self-assertion. The TV medium is inhospitable to inspiration, improvisation, failures, slipups. All must run perfectly.

Naturally, a cool youth culture is a marketing bonanza for producers of the right products, who do all they can to enlarge that culture and keep it grinding. The Internet, TV, and magazines now teem with what I call persona ads, ads for Nikes and Reeboks and Jeeps and Blazers that don't so much endorse the capacities of the product per se as show you what sort of person you will be once you've acquired it. The Jeep ad that features hip, outdoorsy kids whipping a Frisbee from mountaintop to mountaintop isn't so much about what Jeeps can do as it is about the kind of people who own them. Buy a Jeep and be one with them. The ad is of little consequence in itself, but expand its message exponentially and you have the central thrust of current consumer culture—buy in order to be.

Most of my students seem desperate to blend in, to look right, not to make a spectacle of themselves. (Do I have to tell you that those two students having the argument under the portico turned out to be acting in a role-playing game?) The specter of the uncool creates a subtle tyranny. It's apparently an easy standard to subscribe to, this Letterman-like, Tarantino-like cool, but once committed to it, you discover that matters are rather different. You're inhibited, except on ordained occasions, from showing emotion, stifled from trying to achieve anything original. You're made to feel that even the slightest departure from the reigning code will get you genially ostracized. This is a culture tensely committed to a laid-back norm.

Am I coming off like something of a crank here? Maybe. Oscar Wilde, who is almost never wrong, suggested that it is perilous to promiscuously contradict people who are much younger than yourself. Point taken. But one of the lessons that consumer hype tries to insinuate is that we must never rebel against the new, never even question it. If it's new—a new need, a new product, a new show, a new style, a new generation—it must be good. So maybe, even at the risk of winning the withered, brown laurels of crankdom, it pays to resist newness-worship and cast a colder eye.

Praise for my students? I have some of that too. What my students are, at their best, is decent. They are potent believers in equality. They help out at the soup kitchen and volunteer to tutor poor kids to get a stripe on their résumés, sure. But they also want other people to have a fair shot. And in their commitment to fairness they are discerning; there you see them at their intellectual best. If I were on trial and innocent, I'd want them on the jury.

What they will not generally do, though, is indict the current system. They won't talk about how the exigencies of capitalism lead to a reserve army of the unemployed and nearly inevitable misery. That would be getting too loud, too brash. For the pervading view is the cool consumer perspective, where passion and strong admiration are forbidden. "To stand in awe of nothing, Numicus, is perhaps the one and only thing that can make a man happy and keep him so," says Horace in the *Epistles,* and I fear that his lines ought to hang as a motto over the university in this era of high consumer capitalism.

It's easy to mount one's high horse and blame the students for this state of affairs. But they didn't create the present culture of consumption. (It was largely my own generation, that of the Sixties, that let the counterculture search for pleasure devolve into a quest for commodities.) And they weren't the ones responsible, when they were six and seven and eight years old, for unplugging the TV set from time to time or for hauling off and kicking a hole through it. It's my generation of parents who sheltered these students, kept them away from the hard knocks of everyday life, making them cautious and overfragile, who demanded that their teachers, from grade school on, flatter them endlessly so that the kids are shocked if their college profs don't reflexively suck up to them.

Of course, the current generational style isn't simply derived from culture and environment. It's also about dollars. Students worry that taking too many chances with their educations will sabotage their future prospects. They're aware of the fact that a drop that looks more and more like one wall of the Grand Canyon separates the top economic tenth from the rest of the population. There's a sentiment currently abroad that if you step aside for a moment, to write, to travel, to fall too hard in love, you might lose position permanently. We may be on a conveyor belt, but it's worse down there on the filth-strewn floor. So don't sound off, don't blow your chance.

But wait. I teach at the famously conservative University of Virginia. Can I extend my view from Charlottesville to encompass the whole country, a whole generation of college students? I can only say that I hear comparable stories about classroom life from colleagues everywhere in America. When I visit other schools to lecture, I see a similar scene unfolding. There are, of course, terrific students everywhere. And they're all the better for the way they've had to strive against the existing conformity. At some of the small liberal-arts colleges, the tradition of strong engagement persists. But overall, the students strike me as being sweet and sad, hovering in a nearly suspended animation.

Too often now the pedagogical challenge is to make a lot from a little. Teaching Wordsworth's "Tintern Abbey," you ask for comments. No one responds. So you call on Stephen. Stephen: "The sound, this poem really flows." You: "Stephen seems interested in the music of the poem. We might extend his comment to ask if the poem's music coheres with its argument. Are they consistent? Or is there an emotional pain submerged here that's contrary to the poem's appealing melody?" All right, it's not usually that bad. But close. One friend describes it as rebound teaching: they proffer a weightless comment, you hit it back for all you're worth, then it comes dribbling out again. Occasionally a professor will try to explain away this intellectual timidity by describing the students as perpetrators of postmodern irony, a highly sophisticated mode. Everything's a slick counterfeit, a simulacrum, so by no means should any phenomenon be taken seriously. But the students don't have the urbane, Oscar Wilde–type demeanor that should go with this view. Oscar was cheerful, funny, confident, strange. (Wilde, mortally ill, living in a Paris flophouse: "My wallpaper and I are fighting a duel to the death. One or the other of us has to go.") This generation's style is considerate, easy to please, and a touch depressed.

Granted, you might say, the kids come to school immersed in a consumer mentality—they're good Americans, after all—but then the university and the professors do everything in their power to fight that dreary mind-set in the interest of higher ideals, right? So it should be. But let us look at what is actually coming to pass.

Over the past few years, the physical layout of my university has been changing. To put it a little indecorously, the place is looking more and more like a retirement spread for the young. Our funds go to construction, into new dorms, into renovating the student union. We have a new aquatics center and ever-improving gyms, stocked with StairMasters and Nautilus machines. Engraved on the wall in the gleaming aquatics building is a line by our founder, Thomas Jefferson, declaring that everyone ought to get about two hours' exercise a day. Clearly even the author of the Declaration of Independence endorses the turning of his university into a sports-and-fitness emporium.

But such improvements shouldn't be surprising. Universities need to attract the best (that is, the smartest *and* the richest) students in order to survive in an ever more competitive market. Schools want kids whose parents can pay the full freight, not the ones who need scholarships or want to bargain down the tuition costs. If the marketing surveys say that the kids require sports centers, then, trustees willing, they shall have them. In fact, as I began looking around, I came to see that more and more of what's going on in the university is customer driven. The consumer pressures that beset me on evaluation day are only a part of an overall trend.

From the start, the contemporary university's relationship with students has a solicitous, nearly servile tone. As soon as someone enters his junior year in high school, and especially if he's living in a prosperous zip code, the informational material—the advertising—comes flooding in. Pictures, testimonials, videocassettes, and CD ROMs (some bidden, some not) arrive at the door from colleges across the country, all trying to capture the student and his tuition cash. The freshman-to-be sees photos of well-appointed dorm rooms; of elaborate phys-ed facilities; of fine dining rooms; of expertly kept sports fields; of orchestras and drama troupes; of students working alone (no overbearing grown-ups in range), peering with high seriousness into computers and microscopes; or of students arrayed outdoors in attractive conversational garlands.

Occasionally—but only occasionally, for we usually photograph rather badly; in appearance we tend at best to be styleless—there's a professor teaching a class. (The college catalogues I received, by my request only, in the late Sixties were austere affairs full of professors' credentials and course descriptions; it was clear on whose terms the enterprise was going to unfold.) A college financial officer recently put matters to me in concise, if slightly melodramatic, terms: "Colleges don't have admissions offices anymore, they have marketing departments." Is it surprising that someone who has been approached with photos and tapes, bells and whistles, might come in thinking that the Freud and Shakespeare she had signed up to study were also going to be agreeable treats?

How did we reach this point? In part the answer is a matter of demographics and (surprise) of money. Aided by the G.I. bill, the college-going population in America dramatically increased after the Second World War. Then came the baby boomers, and to accommodate them, schools continued to grow. Universities expand easily enough, but with tenure locking faculty in for lifetime jobs, and with the general reluctance of administrators to eliminate their own slots, it's not easy for a university to contract. So after the baby boomers had passed through—like a fat meal digested by a boa constrictor—the colleges turned to energetic promotional strategies to fill the empty chairs. And suddenly college became a buyer's market. What students and their parents wanted had to be taken more and more into account. That usually meant creating more comfortable, less challenging environments, places where almost no one failed, everything was enjoyable, and everyone was nice.

Just as universities must compete with one another for students, so must the individual departments. At a time of rank economic anxiety, the English and history majors have to contend for students against the more success-insuring branches, such as the sciences and the commerce school. In 1968, more than 21 percent of all the bachelor's degrees conferred in America were in the humanities; by 1993, that number had fallen to about 13 percent. The humanities now must struggle to attract students, many of whose parents devoutly wish they would study something else.

One of the ways we've tried to stay attractive is by loosening up. We grade much more softly than our colleagues in science. In English, we don't give many Ds, or Cs for that matter. (The rigors of Chem 101 create almost as many English majors per year as do the splendors of Shakespeare.) A professor at Stanford recently explained grade inflation in the humanities by observing that the undergraduates were getting smarter every year; the higher grades simply recorded how much better they were than their predecessors. Sure.

Along with softening the grades, many humanities departments have relaxed major requirements. There are some good reasons for introducing more choice into curricula and requiring fewer standard courses. But the move, like many others in the university now, jibes with a tendency to serve—and not challenge—the students. Students can also float in and out of classes during the first two weeks of each term without making any commitment. The common name for this time span—shopping period—speaks volumes about the consumer mentality that's now in play. Usually, too, the kids can drop courses up until the last month with only an innocuous "W" on their transcripts. Does a course look too challenging? No problem. Take it pass-fail. A happy consumer is, by definition, one with multiple options, one who can always have what he wants. And since a course is something the students and their parents have bought and paid for, why can't they do with it pretty much as they please?

A sure result of the university's widening elective leeway is to give students more power over their teachers. Those who don't like you can simply avoid you. If the clientele dislikes you en masse, you can be left without students, period. My first term teaching I walked into my introduction to poetry course and found it inhabited by one student, the gloriously named Bambi Lynn Dean. Bambi and I chatted amiably awhile, but for all that she and the pleasure of her name could offer, I was fast on the way to meltdown. It was all a mistake, luckily, a problem with the scheduling book. Everyone was waiting for me next door. But in a dozen years of teaching I haven't forgotten that feeling of being ignominiously marooned. For it happens to others, and not always because of scheduling glitches. I've seen older colleagues go through hot embarrassment at not having enough students sign up for their courses: they graded too hard, demanded too much, had beliefs too far out of keeping with the existing disposition. It takes only a few such instances to draw other members of the professoriat further into line.

And if what's called tenure reform—which generally just means the abolition of tenure—is broadly enacted, professors will be yet more vulnerable to the whims of their customer-students. Teach what pulls the kids in, or walk. What about entire departments that don't deliver? If the kids say no to Latin and Greek, is it time to dissolve classics? Such questions are being entertained more and more seriously by university administrators.

How does one prosper with the present clientele? Many of the most successful professors now are the ones who have "decentered" their classrooms. There's a new emphasis on group projects and on computer-generated exchanges among the students. What they seem to want most is to talk to one another. A classroom now is frequently an "environment," a place highly conducive to the exchange of existing ideas, the students' ideas. Listening to one another, students sometimes change their opinions. But what they generally can't do is acquire a new vocabulary, a new perspective, that will cast issues in a fresh light.

🖉 The Socratic method—the animated, sometimes impolite give-and-take between student and teacher—seems too jagged for current sensibilities. Students frequently come to my office to tell me how intimidated they feel in class; the thought of being embarrassed in front of the group fills them with dread. I remember a student telling me how humiliating it was to be corrected by the teacher, by me. So I asked the logical question: "Should I let a major factual error go by so as to save discomfort?" The student—a good student, smart and earnest—said that was a tough question. He'd need to think about it.

Disturbing? Sure. But I wonder, are we really getting students ready for Socratic exchange with professors when we push them off into vast lecture rooms, two and three hundred to a class, sometimes face them with only grad students until their third year, and signal in our myriad professorial ways that we often have much better things to do than sit in our offices and talk with them? How bad will the student-faculty ratios have to become, how teeming the lecture courses, before we hear students righteously complaining, as they did thirty years ago, about the impersonality of their schools, about their decline into knowledge factories? "This is a firm," said Mario Savio at Berkeley during the Free Speech protests of the Sixties, "and if the Board of Regents are the board of directors, . . . then . . . the faculty are a bunch of employees and we're the raw material. But we're a bunch of raw material that don't mean . . . to be made into any product."

Teachers who really do confront students, who provide significant challenges to what they believe, *can* be very successful, granted. But sometimes such professors generate more than a little trouble for themselves. A controversial teacher can send students hurrying to the deans and the counselors, claiming to have been offended. ("Offensive" is the preferred term of repugnance today, just as "enjoyable" is the summit of praise.) Colleges have brought in hordes of counselors and deans to make sure that everything is smooth, serene, unflustered, that everyone has a good time. To the counselor, to the dean, and to the university legal squad, that which is normal, healthy, and prudent is best.

An air of caution and deference is everywhere. When my students come to talk with me in my office, they often exhibit a Franciscan humility. "Do you have a moment?" "I know you're busy. I won't take up much of your time." Their presences tend to be very light; they almost never change the temperature of the room. The dress is nondescript: clothes are in earth tones; shoes are practical—cross-trainers, hiking boots, work shoes, Dr. Martens, with now and then a stylish pair of raised-sole boots on one of the young women. Many, male and female both, peep from beneath the bills of monogrammed baseball caps. Quite a few wear sports, or even corporate, logos, sometimes on one piece of clothing but occasionally (and disconcertingly) on more. The walk is slow; speech is careful, sweet, a bit weary, and without strong inflection. (After the first lively week of the term, most seem far in debt to sleep.) They are almost unfailingly polite. They don't want to offend me; I could hurt them, savage their grades.

Naturally, there are exceptions, kids I chat animatedly with, who offer a joke, or go on about this or that new CD (almost never a book, no). But most of the traffic is genially sleepwalking. I have to admit that I'm a touch wary, too. I tend to hold back. An unguarded remark, a joke that's taken to be off-color, or simply an uncomprehended comment can lead to difficulties. I keep it literal. They scare me a little, these kind and melancholy students, who themselves seem rather frightened of their own lives.

Before they arrive, we ply the students with luscious ads, guaranteeing them a cross between summer camp and lotusland. When they get here, flattery and nonstop entertainment are available, if that's what they want. And when they leave? How do we send our students out into the world? More and more, our administrators call the booking agents and line up one or another celebrity to usher the graduates into the millennium. This past spring, Kermit the Frog won himself an honorary degree at Southampton College on Long Island; Bruce Willis and Yogi

Berra took credentials away at Montclair State; Arnold Schwarzenegger scored at the University of Wisconsin–Superior. At Wellesley, Oprah Winfrey gave the commencement address. (*Wellesley*—one of the most rigorous academic colleges in the nation.) At the University of Vermont, Whoopi Goldberg laid down the word. But why should a worthy administrator contract the likes of Susan Sontag, Christopher Hitchens, or Robert Hughes—someone who might actually say something, something disturbing, something "offensive"—when he can get what the parents and kids apparently want and what the newspapers will softly commend—more lite entertainment, more TV?

Is it a surprise, then, that this generation of students—steeped in consumer culture before going off to school, treated as potent customers by the university well before their date of arrival, then pandered to from day one until the morning of the final kiss-off from Kermit or one of his kin—are inclined to see the books they read as a string of entertainments to be placidly enjoyed or languidly cast down? Given the way universities are now administered (which is more and more to say, given the way that they are currently marketed), is it a shock that the kids don't come to school hot to learn, unable to bear their own ignorance? For some measure of self-dislike, or self-discontent—which is much different than simple depression—seems to me to be a prerequisite for getting an education that matters. My students, alas, usually lack the confidence to acknowledge what would be their most precious asset for learning: their ignorance.

Not long ago, I asked my Freud class a question that, however hoary, never fails to solicit intriguing responses: Who are your heroes? Whom do you admire? After one remarkable answer, featuring T. S. Eliot as hero, a series of generic replies rolled in, one gray wave after the next: my father, my best friend, a doctor who lives in our town, my high school history teacher. Virtually all the heroes were people my students had known personally, people who had done something local, specific, and practical, and had done it for them. They were good people, unselfish people, these heroes, but most of all they were people who had delivered the goods.

My students' answers didn't exhibit any philosophical resistance to the idea of greatness. It's not that they had been primed by their professors with complex arguments to combat genius. For the truth is that these students don't need debunking theories. Long before college, skepticism became their habitual mode. They are the progeny of Bart Simpson and David Letterman, and the hyper-cool ethos of the box. It's inane to say that theorizing professors have created them, as many conservative critics like to do. Rather, they have substantially created a university environment in which facile skepticism can thrive without being substantially contested.

Skeptical approaches have *potential* value. If you have no all-encompassing religious faith, no faith in historical destiny, the future of the West, or anything comparably grand, you need to acquire your vision of the world somewhere. If it's from literature, then the various visions literature offers have to be inquired into skeptically. Surely it matters that women are denigrated in Milton and in Pope, that some novelistic voices assume an overbearing godlike authority, that the poor are, in this or that writer, inevitably cast as clowns. You can't buy all of literature wholesale if it's going to help draw your patterns of belief.

But demystifying theories are now overused, applied mechanically. It's all logocentrism, patriarchy, ideology. And in this the student environment—laid-back, skeptical, knowing—is, I believe, central. Full-out debunking is what plays with this clientele. Some have been doing it nearly as long as, if more crudely than, their deconstructionist teachers. In the context of the contemporary university, and cool consumer culture, a useful intellectual skepticism has become exaggerated into a fundamentalist caricature of itself. The teachers have buckled to their students' views.

At its best, multiculturalism can be attractive as well-deployed theory. What could be more valuable than encountering the best work of far-flung cultures and becoming a citizen of the world? But in the current consumer environment, where flattery plays so well, the urge to encounter the other can devolve into the urge to find others who embody and celebrate the right ethnic origins. So we put aside the African novelist Chinua Achebe's abrasive, troubling *Things Fall Apart* and gravitate toward hymns on Africa, cradle of all civilizations.

What about the phenomenon called political correctness? Raising the standard of civility and tolerance in the university has been—who can deny it?—a very good thing. Yet this admirable impulse has expanded to the point where one is enjoined to speak well—and only well—of women, blacks, gays, the disabled, in fact of virtually everyone. And we can owe this expansion in many ways to the student culture. Students now do not wish to be criticized, not in any form. (The culture of consumption never criticizes them, at least not *overtly.*) In the current university, the movement for urbane tolerance has devolved into an imperative against critical reaction, turning much of the intellectual life into a dreary Sargasso Sea. At a certain point, professors stopped being usefully sensitive and became more like careful retailers who have it as a cardinal point of doctrine never to piss the customers off.

To some professors, the solution lies in the movement called cultural studies. What students need, they believe, is to form a critical perspective on pop culture. It's a fine idea, no doubt. Students should be able to run a critical commentary against the stream of consumer stimulations in which they're immersed. But cultural-studies programs rarely work, because no matter what you propose by way of analysis, things tend to bolt downhill toward an uncritical discussion of students' tastes, into what they like and don't like. If you want to do a Frankfurt School–style analysis of *Braveheart,* you can be pretty sure that by mid-class Adorno and Horkheimer will be consigned to the junk heap of history and you'll be collectively weighing the charms of Mel Gibson. One sometimes wonders if cultural studies hasn't prospered because, under the guise of serious intellectual analysis, it gives the customers what they most want—easy pleasure, more TV. Cultural studies becomes nothing better than what its detractors claim it is—Madonna studies—when students kick loose from the critical perspective and groove to the product, and that, in my experience teaching film and pop culture, happens plenty.

On the issue of genius, as on multiculturalism and political correctness, we professors of the humanities have, I think, also failed to press back against our students' consumer tastes. Here we tend to nurse a pair of—to put it charitably—disparate views. In one mode, we're inclined to a programmatic debunking criticism. We call the concept of genius into question. But in our professional lives per se, we aren't usually disposed against the idea of distinguished achievement. We argue animatedly about the caliber of potential colleagues. We support a star system, in which some professors are far better paid, teach less, and under better conditions than the rest. In our own profession, we are creating a system that is the mirror image of the one we're dismantling in the curriculum. Ask a professor what she thinks of the work of Stephen Greenblatt, a leading critic of Shakespeare, and you'll hear it for an hour. Ask her what her views are on Shakespeare's genius and she's likely to begin questioning the term along with the whole "discourse of evaluation." This dual sensibility may be intellectually incoherent. But in its awareness of what plays with students, it's conducive to good classroom evaluations and, in its awareness of where and how the professional bread is buttered, to self-advancement as well.

My overall point is this: It's not that a left-wing professorial coup has taken over the university. It's that at American universities, left-liberal politics have collided with the ethos of consumerism. The consumer ethos is winning.

Then how do those who at least occasionally promote genius and high literary ideals look to current students? How do we appear, those of us who take teaching to be something of a performance art and who imagine that if you give yourself over completely to your subject you'll be rewarded with insight beyond what you individually command?

I'm reminded of an old piece of newsreel footage I saw once. The speaker (perhaps it was Lenin, maybe Trotsky) was haranguing a large crowd. He was expostulating, arm waving, carrying on. Whether it was flawed technology or the man himself, I'm not sure, but the orator looked like an intricate mechanical device that had sprung into fast-forward. To my students, who mistrust enthusiasm in every form, that's me when I start riffing about Freud or Blake. But more and more, as my evaluations showed, I've been replacing enthusiasm and intellectual animation with stand-up routines, keeping it all at arm's length, praising under the cover of irony.

It's too bad that the idea of genius has been denigrated so far, because it actually offers a live alternative to the demoralizing culture of hip in which most of my students are mired. By embracing the works and lives of extraordinary people, you can adapt new ideals to revise those that came courtesy of your parents, your neighborhood, your clan—or the tube. The aim of a good liberal-arts education was once, to adapt an observation by the scholar Walter Jackson Bate, to see that "we need not be the passive victims of what we deterministically call 'circumstances' (social, cultural, or reductively psychological-personal), but that by linking ourselves through what Keats calls an 'immortal free-masonry' with the great we can become freer—freer to be ourselves, to be what we most want and value."

But genius isn't just a personal standard; genius can also have political effect. To me, one of the best things about democratic thinking is the conviction that genius can spring up anywhere. Walt Whitman is born into the working class and thirty-six years later we have a poetic image of America that gives a passionate dimension to the legalistic brilliance of the Constitution. A democracy needs to constantly develop, and to do so it requires the most powerful visionary minds to interpret the present and to propose possible shapes for the future. By continuing to notice and praise genius, we create a culture in which the kind of poetic gamble that Whitman made—a gamble in which failure would have entailed rank humiliation, depression, maybe suicide—still takes place. By rebelling against established ways of seeing and saying things, genius helps us to apprehend how malleable the present is and how promising and fraught with danger is the future. If we teachers do not endorse genius and self-overcoming, can we be surprised when our students find their ideal images in TV's latest persona ads?

A world uninterested in genius is a despondent place, whose sad denizens drift from coffee bar to Prozac dispensary, unfired by ideals, by the glowing image of the self that one might become. As Northrop Frye says in a beautiful and now dramatically unfashionable sentence, "The artist who uses the same energy and genius that Homer and Isaiah had will find that he not only lives in the same palace of art as Homer and Isaiah, but lives in it at the same time." We ought not to deny the existence of such a place simply because we, or those we care for, find the demands it makes intimidating, the rent too high.

What happens if we keep trudging along this bleak course? What happens if our most intelligent students never learn to strive to overcome what they are? What if genius, and the imitation of genius, become silly, outmoded ideas? What you're likely to get are more and more one-dimensional men and women. These will be people who live for easy pleasures, for comfort and prosperity, who think of money first, then second, and third, who hug the status quo; people who believe in God as a sort of insurance policy (cover your bets); people who are never surprised. They will be people so pleased with themselves (when they're not in despair at the general pointlessness of their lives) that they cannot imagine humanity could do better. They'll think it their highest duty to clone themselves as frequently as possible. They'll claim to be happy, and they'll live a long time.

It is probably time now to offer a spate of inspiring solutions. Here ought to come a list of reforms, with due notations about a core curriculum and various requirements. What the traditionalists who offer such solutions miss is that no matter what our current students are given to read, many of them will simply translate it into melodrama, with flat characters and predictable morals. (The unabated capitalist culture that conservative critics so often endorse has put students in a position to do little else.) One can't simply wave a curricular wand and reverse acculturation.

Perhaps it would be a good idea to try firing the counselors and sending half the deans back into their classrooms, dismantling the football team and making the stadium into a playground for local kids, emptying the fraternities, and boarding up the student-activities office. Such measures would convey the message that American colleges are not northern outposts of Club Med. A willingness on the part of the faculty to defy student conviction and affront them occasionally—to be usefully offensive—also might not be a bad thing. We professors talk a lot about subversion, which generally means subverting the views of people who never hear us talk or read our work. But to subvert the views of our students, our customers, that would be something else again.

Ultimately, though, it is up to individuals—and individual students in particular—to make their own way against the current sludgy tide. There's still the library, still the museum, there's still the occasional teacher who lives to find things greater than herself to admire. There are still fellow students who have not been cowed. Universities are inefficient, cluttered, archaic places, with many unguarded corners where one can open a book or gaze out onto the larger world and construe it freely. Those who do as much, trusting themselves against the weight of current opinion, will have contributed something to bringing this sad dispensation to an end. As for myself, I'm canning my low-key one-liners; when the kids' TV-based tastes come to the fore, I'll aim and shoot. And when it's time to praise genius, I'll try to do it in the right style, full-out, with faith that finer artistic spirits (maybe not Homer and Isaiah quite, but close, close), still alive somewhere in the ether, will help me out when my invention flags, the students doze, or the dean mutters into the phone. I'm getting back to a more exuberant style; I'll be expostulating and arm waving straight into the millennium, yes I will.

Revising Our College Education: Participation Is the Key

Mindy Dodge

Mindy Dodge wrote this essay when she was a student in Writing 121 at the University of Oregon.

In the essay, "On the Uses of a Liberal Education," Mark Edmundson argues that American universities are no longer places where students look for a challenging and enriching education. According to Edmundson, university culture has been overtaken by consumerism and now the entertainment value of instructors and their courses is what reigns supreme. Although this image of an entire population seems rather harsh (especially to those of us who are currently students), there can be no doubt that over the years the profile of American college students has changed. Change of course is inevitable. Edmundson, however, describes the majority of today's students as either being apathetic or entirely missing the point of the material he teaches. He complains that there is no intellectual discourse among classmates and that these days they have to be spoon-fed answers to the questions he asks. Although I would like to argue that this is a false representation of today's college population, I have witnessed (and sometimes displayed) this behavior in most of my own classes during the past four years. Does this point to some inherent flaw in the current student population, or does it signal that today's teachers are missing the mark? Edmundson would argue that the fault lies with those who perpetuate popular consumer culture by following the crowd and not acting out as individuals, in any capacity. I agree with his conclusion that the responsibility for change rests with both parties. In order for college classrooms to once again become places for intellectual discourse and sounding boards for novel ideas, active and constructive participation by both students and professors is necessary.

What does this entail for students? Active participation inside the classroom is a start. Why do students, myself included, try at all costs to avoid being called upon when a teacher asks a question of the class? We refuse to make eye contact, look suddenly enthralled with the notes that we've just written, or (and this is my favorite diversion tactic) rifle through papers like we are searching for the answer. What are we so afraid of? Is it that we will give the wrong answer and be contradicted by the teacher and embarrassed in front of other students, or that we are just nervous about how our answers will be perceived and how others will judge us? Speaking from my own experience, I would say that often it is a combination of both. Obviously, no one likes to appear ignorant in front of others. However, the drive to fit in and be accepted by our peers is an incredibly strong one, one that I believe governs the majority of students' classroom behavior. In my own classes I notice that if I am interested in a particular topic, and I am the only one doing much talking, I will tend to modulate my behavior so that I will not appear overeager to others. Although this type of self-monitoring to avoid the negative judgment of peers is comfortable, hiding within the status quo is a complete waste of an education. By not presenting your view or asking intelligent questions during your classes, not only might you be missing out on valuable information that you never thought of before, you might be missing out on the opinions and viewpoints of others that arise from such discourse. Arming ourselves with the power to approach and analyze issues from all sides, learning how to make informed decisions, and thereby growing intellectually, is the purpose of college. None of this will occur, however, if we are satisfied just to sit through our classes witlessly accepting information as it is "spoon-fed" to us.

Students are not the only ones to blame for the climate in today's classrooms. Professors and teaching assistants set the tone for the way a class is run. Although this goes against Edmundson and his dislike for popular consumer culture, presentation is everything. Just as students must take an active role in processing and analyzing the information given them, teachers must first present the material in an interesting and effective way. By effective I mean that teachers need to demonstrate genuine interest in what they are teaching. Students are not going to be interested in or care about subject material that a professor cannot even find the will to muster excitement about, especially considering that it is supposed to be his or her area of expertise. In some of the classes I have taken, there have been professors who have acted like they would much rather be concentrating on their own research projects than be anywhere near the classroom. This kind of indifference toward the subject matter and teaching in general is almost always transmitted to the students. As a result, students show little concern for delving deeper into the subject material.

Presenting material in a way that is "enjoyable" for students and catches their attention does not have to mean selling out to consumerism as Edmundson suggests. Professors can present information in novel ways, that relate it to present-day issues. These are techniques that usually help me remember material because it makes it more *accessible*. After all, isn't this really the teacher's job? Also, what is wrong with instructors asking themselves the same questions before they teach that we do before we begin writing? "Who is the audience and is this an issue?" To me, a consumer culture (the one described by Edmundson) suggests one in which students, and my generation in general, are looking for the quick fix or the easy out. With this view, we are looking for information that is heavy on the entertainment but light on content. There is a distinction, however. Entertaining does not have to equal devoid-of-challenge. When I am presented with material in one of my classes that is challenging, yet also interesting and applicable, I actually do get excited. These experiences reinforce my joy of learning and make me remember why I am pursuing a higher education. I do not believe that I am alone in my opinion either. There are too many students out there who do incredibly well in their classes for me to believe that they do not derive some enjoyment from what they are learning.

In some ways this societal shift toward consumerism does not seem altogether terrible. Students are now allowed to take a more active role in what their education consists of (through course evaluations and the like), and why shouldn't they? With the skyrocketing costs of tuition and fees leaving many of us with thousands of dollars of debt as soon as we are handed our diplomas, haven't we earned the right to be picky?! I think it only fair that we be able to exercise some control over the money we spend.

Edmundson is correct when he asserts that consumerism has overtaken colleges and universities. These days universities are businesses aimed at attracting potential customers. Although this is a sad commentary on our society, it does not have to follow that the quality of our education is also for sale. It is the responsibility of both students and teachers to ensure that the classroom is a place conducive to intellectual discourse. The first step toward achieving this kind of challenging and motivational atmosphere is through participation by both students and teachers.

The Truth about "The Truth"

Laura Lewis

Laura Lewis, a University of Oregon student, wrote the following essay in response to Francis Bacon's "The Four Idols" (page 239).

Santa Claus does not exist. Mickey Mouse at Disneyland—some college student who is desperate for money. Tooth fairies are your parents. Your "best friend" stole your Barbie. Your parents are getting a divorce. Grandpa Steve has a new *boy*friend. Your wife of ten years is having an affair. These are all truths that may occur in one's life, and because we are humans—creatures of customs and familiarity—they will be difficult to swallow. An *instilled* idea is easy to grow accustomed to because it is always what we've seen and learned to be comfortable with; the idea has been instilled in us through various forms of observation and experience. One the other hand, a *new* notion is hard to accept, and we will always pass through a phase of denial before (if ever) we accept it.

Being told to believe something that you have not had time to warm up to will cause some amount of shock. Think, for example, of the way a fish from the pet shop must be "floated." When you purchase a fish, you need to leave it in the bag of water in the tank for half an hour to make sure the change in temperature is not too severe and will not cause the fish to go into shock and die. I'm not saying that being told the truth about something trivial will send a human into convulsions, but hearing that your favorite teacher from elementary school has lung cancer will generate a response something like "You're joking" or "No way." There, in the natural reaction, lies the tendency to deny or disbelieve those ideas to which you are accustomed. Unfortunately, there is really no way to "float" the truth. When you decide to get married to your boyfriend, you can't just hint to your parents that you really like white wedding cake with raspberry filling. It's just something you have to come out and say. Although they may be excited and happy about the engagement, they will probably go through an "I can't believe it" phase.

Granted, sometimes one will not practically care about an issue at hand, so his or her reaction will not be as great as someone who has thought or felt strongly about that issue for a long time. The latter of the cases is what, for our purposes, we will examine. When an issue carries with it some degree of importance to an individual, and one is told and realizes the opposite is true, he or she will have a paramount time adjusting to the reality. This is where complications come into play. It is easy to see that being told something different from what you believed will cause you to be upset. The reason we have trouble with accepting the truth is because, as human creatures eager to be pleased, we really do not care about the truth. The truth, no matter how negative, positive, important, or unimportant, must be entertaining or have the ability to make us happy or we don't want to hear it. The most important thing to note is that we would rather, in most cases, hear something that makes us feel good or comfortable. Rather than hearing the truth about Grandpa Steve moving on from Grandma Esther to men, we want to hear how much he misses Grandma and wishes she was still with us.

One of the oldest sayings in the book applies here: "What we don't know won't hurt us." The main thing to acknowledge is that while things we believe may not be true in many cases, they fit perfectly with the need to spare ourselves from the fish-in-the-fishbowl syndrome. It would not hurt us much as young children if we never found out about Grandpa and his friend Bob. It would not hurt us much to hear that our teacher moved to Minnesota, instead of Rolling Hills Cemetery. The truth in many cases may be a necessary evil, something that has to come out in order to ensure the mental or physical safety of an individual (for example, a cheating spouse). But that in no way disproves the rule that we, as individuals or as a society, *don't* want to know the truth, the whole truth, and nothing but the truth about many issues.

From personal experience, my most concrete example of not wanting to hear the truth is this: I wholeheartedly believed, until the moment my mother told me otherwise, that Santa Claus existed. When she told me the truth, I felt horrible. I did not want the myth to be gone. I did not want the magic to be taken away. But unfortunately, we all have to grow up and realize that we were being naive. This is the problem: naivete. Because we wish to be smart and intelligent, we never want to feel as though we've been naive enough to be misled, or believed something that we realize was impossible once we knew the truth.

We have recognized the problems associated with humans and the truth. We do not want to know the truth because the adjustment is too great and may be too painful. We do not want to know the truth because it might make us uncomfortable. We do not want to know the truth because we will feel like we have been naive. The fact is, we would rather just be content, naive, and unaware in our own little world of "truths."

What Does a Woman Need to Know?

Adrienne Rich

Adrienne Rich, a distinguished American poet, received the National Book Award for Poetry in 1974. She declined the award for herself but accepted it "on behalf of all women." This essay first appeared in Women and the Power to Change.

I have been very much moved that you, the class of 1979, chose me for your commencement speaker. It is important to me to be here, in part because Smith is one of the original colleges for women, but also because she has chosen to continue identifying herself as a women's college. We are at a point in history where this fact has enormous potential, even if that potential is as yet unrealized. The possibilities for the future education of women that haunt these buildings and grounds are enormous, when we think of what an independent women's college might be: a college dedicated both to teaching women what women need to know and, by the same token, to changing the landscape of knowledge itself. The germ of those possibilities lies symbolically in The Sophia Smith Collection, an archive much in need of expansion and increase, but which by its very existence makes the statement that women's lives and work are valued here and that our foresisters, buried and diminished in male-centered scholarship, are a living presence, necessary and precious to us.

Suppose we were to ask ourselves simply: What does a woman need to know to become a self-conscious, self-defining human being? Doesn't she need a knowledge of her own history, of her much-politicized female body, of the creative genius of women of the past—the skills and crafts and techniques and visions possessed by women in other times and cultures, and how they have been rendered anonymous, censored, interrupted, devalued? Doesn't she, as one of that majority who are still denied equal rights as citizens, enslaved as sexual prey, unpaid or underpaid as workers, withheld from her own power—doesn't she need an analysis of her condition, a knowledge of the women thinkers of the past who have reflected on it, a knowledge, too, of women's world-wide individual rebellions and organized movements against economic and social injustice, and how these have been fragmented and silenced?

Doesn't she need to know how seemingly natural states of being, like heterosexuality, like motherhood, have been enforced and institutionalized to deprive her of power? Without such education, women have lived and continue to live in ignorance of our collective context, vulnerable to the projections of men's fantasies about us as they appear in art, in literature, in the sciences, in the media, in the so-called humanistic studies. I suggest that not anatomy, but enforced ignorance, has been a crucial key to our powerlessness.

There is—and I say this with sorrow—there is no women's college today which is providing young women with the education they need for survival as whole persons in a world which denies women wholeness—that knowledge which, in the words of Coleridge, "returns again as power." The existence of Women's Studies courses offers at least some kind of life line. But even Women's Studies can amount simply to compensatory history; too often they fail to challenge the intellectual and political structures that must be challenged if women as a group are ever to come into collective, nonexclusionary freedom. The belief that established science and scholarship—which have so relentlessly excluded women from their making—are "objective" and "value-free" and that feminist studies are "unscholarly," "biased," and "ideological" dies hard. Yet the fact is that all science, and all scholarship, and all art are ideological; there is no neutrality in culture. And the ideology of the education you have just spent four years acquiring in a women's college has been largely, if not entirely, the ideology of white male supremacy, a construct of male subjectivity. The silences, the empty spaces, the language itself, with its excision of the female, the methods of discourse tell us as much as the content, once we learn to watch for what is left out, to listen for the unspoken, to study the patterns of established science and scholarship with an outsider's eye. One of the dangers of a privileged education for women is that we may lose the eye of the outsider and come to believe that those patterns hold for humanity, for the universal, and that they include us.

And so I want to talk today about privilege and about tokenism and about power. Everything I can say to you on this subject comes hard-won, from the lips of a woman privileged by class and skin color, a father's favorite daughter, educated at Radcliffe, which was then casually referred to as the Harvard "Annex." Much of the first four decades of my life was spent in a continuous tension between the world the Fathers taught me to see, and had rewarded me for seeing, and the flashes of insight that came through the eye of the outsider. Gradually those flashes of insight, which at times could seem like brushes with madness, began to demand that I struggle to connect them with each other, to insist that I take them seriously. It was only when I could finally affirm the outsider's eye as the source of a legitimate and coherent vision, that I began to be able to do the work I truly wanted to do, live the kind of life I truly wanted to live, instead of carrying out the assignments I had been given as a privileged woman and a token.

For women, all privilege is relative. Some of you were not born with class or skin-color privilege; but you all have the privilege of education, even if it is an education which has largely denied you knowledge of yourselves as women. You have, to begin with, the privilege of literacy; and it is well for us to remember that, in an age of increasing illiteracy, 60 percent of the world's illiterates are women. Between 1960 and 1970, the number of illiterate men in the world rose by 8 million, while the number of illiterate women rose by 40 million.[1] And the number of illiterate women is increasing. Beyond literacy, you have the privilege of training and tools which can allow you to go beyond the content of your education and re-educate yourselves—to debrief yourselves, we might call it, of the false messages of your education in this culture, the messages telling you that women have not really cared about power or learning or creative opportunities because of a psychobiological need to serve men and produce children; that only a few atypical women have been exceptions to this rule; the messages telling you that woman's experience is neither normative nor central to human experience. You have the training and the tools to do independent research, to evaluate data, to criticize, and to express in language and visual forms what you discover. This is a privilege, yes, but only if you do not give up in exchange for it the deep knowledge of the

[1]United Nations, Department of International Economics and Social Affairs, Statistical Office, *1977 Compendium of Social Statistics* (New York: United Nations, 1980).

unprivileged, the knowledge that, as a woman, you have historically been viewed and still are viewed as existing, not in your own right, but in the service of men. And only if you refuse to give up your capacity to think as a woman, even though in the graduate schools and professions to which many of you will be going you will be praised and rewarded for "thinking like a man."

The word *power* is highly charged for women. It has been long associated for us with the use of force, with rape, with the stockpiling of weapons, with the ruthless accrual of wealth and the hoarding of resources, with the power that acts only in its own interest, despising and exploiting the powerless—including women and children. The effects of this kind of power are all around us, even literally in the water we drink and the air we breathe, in the form of carcinogens and radioactive wastes. But for a long time now, feminists have been talking about redefining power, about that meaning of power which returns to the root—*posse, potere, pouvoir:* to be able, to have the potential, to possess and use one's energy of creation—*transforming power.* An early objection to feminism—in both the nineteenth and twentieth centuries—was that it would make women behave like men—ruthlessly, exploitatively, oppressively. In fact, radical feminism looks to a transformation of human relationships and structures in which power, instead of a thing to be hoarded by a few, would be released to and from within the many, shared in the form of knowledge, expertise, decision making, access to tools, as well as in the basic forms of food and shelter and health care and literacy. Feminists—and many nonfeminists—are, and rightly so, still concerned with what power would mean in such a society, and with the relative differences in power among and between women here and now.

Which brings me to a third meaning of power where women are concerned: the false power which masculine society offers to a few women, on condition that they use it to maintain things as they are, and that they essentially "think like men." This is the meaning of female tokenism: that power withheld from the vast majority of women is offered to a few, so that it appears that any "truly qualified" woman can gain access to leadership, recognition, and reward; hence, that justice based on merit actually prevails. The token woman is encouraged to see herself as different from most other women, as exceptionally talented and deserving, and to separate herself from the wider female condition; and she is perceived by "ordinary" women as separate also, perhaps even as stronger than themselves.

Because you are, within the limits of all women's ultimate outsiderhood, a privileged group of women, it is extremely important for your future sanity that you understand the way tokenism functions. Its most immediate contradiction is that, while it seems to offer the individual token woman a means to realize her creativity, to influence the course of events, it also, by exacting of her certain kinds of behavior and style, acts to blur her outsider's eye, which could be her real source of power and vision. Losing her outsider's vision, she loses the insight which both binds her to other women and affirms her in herself. Tokenism essentially demands that the token deny her identification with women as a group, especially with women less privileged than she: if she is a lesbian, that she deny her relationships with individual women; that she perpetuate rules and structures and criteria and methodologies which have functioned to exclude women; that she renounce or leave undeveloped the critical perspective of her female consciousness. Women unlike herself—poor women, women of color, waitresses, secretaries, housewives in the supermarket, prostitutes, old women—become invisible to her; they may represent too acutely what she has escaped or wished to flee.

President Conway tells me that ever-increasing numbers of you are going on from Smith to medical and law schools. The news, on the face of it, is good: that, thanks to the feminist struggle of the past decade, more doors into these two powerful professions are open to women. I would like to believe that any profession would be better for having more women practicing it, and that any woman practicing law or medicine would use her knowledge and skill to work to transform the realm of health care and the interpretations of the law, to make them responsive to the needs of all those—women, people of color, children, the aged, the dispossessed—for whom they function today as repressive controls. I would like to believe this. but it will not happen even if 50 percent of the members of these professions are women, unless those women refuse to be made into token insiders, unless they zealously preserve the outsider's view and the outsider's consciousness.

For no woman is really an insider in the institutions fathered by masculine consciousness. When we allow ourselves to believe we are, we lose touch with parts of ourselves defined as unacceptable by that consciousness; with the vital toughness and visionary strength of the angry grandmothers, the shamanesses, the fierce marketwomen of the Ibo Women's War, the marriage-resisting women silkworkers of prerevolutionary China, the millions of widows, midwives, and women healers tortured and burned as witches for three centuries in Europe, the Beguines of the twelfth century, who formed independent women's orders outside the domination of the Church, the women of the Paris Commune who marched on Versailles, the uneducated housewives of the Women's Cooperative Guild in England who memorized poetry over the washtub and organized against their oppression as mothers, the women thinkers discredited as "strident," "shrill," "crazy," or "deviant" whose courage to be heretical, to speak their truths, we so badly need to draw upon in our own lives. I believe that every woman's soul is haunted by the spirits of earlier women who fought for their unmet needs and those of their children and their tribes and their peoples, who refused to accept the prescriptions of a male church and state, who took risks and resisted, as women today—like Inez Garcia, Yvonne Wanrow, Joan Little, Cassandra Peten—are fighting their rapists and batterers. Those spirits dwell in us, trying to speak to us. But we can choose to be deaf, and tokenism, the myth of the "special" woman, the unmothered Athena sprung from her father's brow, can deafen us to their voices.

In this decade now ending, as more women are entering the professions (though still suffering sexual harassment in the workplace, though still, if they have children, carrying two full-time jobs, though still vastly outnumbered by men in upper-level and decision-making jobs), we need most profoundly to re-member that early insight of the feminist movements as it evolved in the late sixties: *that no woman is liberated until we all are liberated.* The media flood us with messages to the contrary, telling us that we live in an era when "alternate life styles" are freely accepted, when "marriage contracts" and "the new inti-macy" are revolutionizing heterosexual relationships, that shared parenting and the "new fatherhood" will change the world. And we live in a society leeched upon by the "personal growth" and "human potential" industry, by the delusion that individual self-fulfillment can be found in thirteen weeks or a weekend, that the alienation and injustice experience by women, by Black and Third World people, by the poor, in a world ruled by white males, in a society which fails to meet the most basic needs and which is slowly poisoning itself, can be mitigated or dispersed by Transcendental Meditation. Perhaps the most succinct expres-sion of this message I have seen is the appearance of a magazine for women called *Self.* The insistence of the feminist movement, that each woman's self-hood is precious, that the feminine ethic of self-denial and self-sacrifice must give way to a true woman identification, which would affirm our connectedness with all women, is perverted into a commercially profitable and politically de-bilitating narcissism. It is important for each of you, toward whom many of these messages are especially directed, to discriminate clearly between "liberated life style" and feminist struggle, and to make a conscious choice.

It's a cliché of commencement speeches that the speaker ends with a per-oration telling the new graduates that however badly past generations have be-haved, their generation must save the world. I would rather say to you, women of the class of 1979: Try to be worthy of your foresisters, learn from your history, look for inspiration to your ancestresses. If this history has been poorly taught to you, if you do not know it, then use your educational privilege to learn it. Learn how some women of privilege have compromised the greater liberation of women, how others have risked their privileges to further it; learn how brilliant and successful women have failed to create a more just and caring society, pre-cisely because they have tried to do so on terms that the powerful men around them would accept and tolerate. Learn to be worthy of the women of every class, culture, and historical age who did otherwise, who spoke boldly when women were jeered and physically harassed for speaking in public, who—like Anne Hutchinson, Mary Wollstonecraft, the Grimké sisters, Abby Kelley, Ida B. Wells-Barnett, Susan B. Anthony, Lillian Smith, Fannie Lou Hamer—broke taboos, who resisted slavery—their own and other people's. To become a token woman—whether you win the Nobel prize or merely get tenure at the cost of denying your sisters—is to become something less than a man indeed, since men are loyal at least to their own world view, their laws of brotherhood and male self-interest. I am not suggesting that you imitate male loyalties; with the philosopher Mary Daly, I believe that the bonding of women must be utterly different and for an utterly different end: not the misering of resources and power, but the release, in each other, of the yet unexplored resources and transformative power of women, so long despised, confined, and wasted. Get all the knowledge and skill you can in whatever professions you enter; but remember that most of your education must be self-education, in learning the things women need to know and in calling up the voices we need to hear within ourselves.

At Miss Porter's, Girls Are Taking On a Winning (Gasp!) Attitude

Anna Seaton Huntington

Anna Seaton Huntington is a journalist whose credits include a 1997 book about the first women's sailing team to compete for the America's Cup. This article appeared in the New York Times *in 1998.*

Farmington, Conn.—Bridgid Godbout entered Miss Porter's School four years ago, knowing she would get a good education at an institution with a history of instructing the nation's young female elite that stretches back before the Civil War. Godbout also knew she was going to lose a lot of lacrosse and soccer games. The all-girls preparatory school nestled in this bucolic community counts Jacqueline Bouvier Kennedy Onassis and Laura Rockefeller among its alumnae and has long held to a tradition of emphasizing courteous recreation and participation rather than winning on its athletic fields.

"There was this attitude of: 'Oh, we're Miss Porter's. If we lose, that's O.K. And if we lose to a good team by not that much, then that's kind of a win,' " Godbout said. Godbout, a senior from West Hartford, Connecticut, had played on winning lacrosse and soccer teams in middle school at the coeducational Loomis Chaffee School in Connecticut. "When the upper-school teams at Loomis went to play Miss Porter's, it was like a joke," she said. "When I came here, I didn't want people to think that about me."

Fortunately for Godbout, her enrollment at Miss Porter's coincided with a decision by the new head of school, M. Burch Tracy Ford, to build a strong, competitive program for its 15 interscholastic sports. Now Godbout is on her way to Villanova, where she will play lacrosse next year. She is one of nearly a dozen senior athletes recruited by Division I colleges this year, a new phenomenon at Miss Porter's.

That one of the oldest girls' schools in this country is pushing to shed its image of white gloves and cotillions in favor of softball mitts and basketball games reflects a broader change in the culture of girls and women's sports from a focus on politeness to competitiveness, and may signal a fundamental change in what it means to educate a girl in this country. "There is still a tremendous amount of ambivalence about girls being competitive in our society," Ford, head of Miss Porter's for the last five years, said. "But I think for girls to really be successful, in their personal lives, in a business or political context, or any other venue, they have to learn from boys and men about exercising their strength and power, and sports are a perfect vehicle for teaching that."

In her campaign to transform the athletics ethos at Miss Porter's, a boarding and day school of 280 students with basic tuition of $16,750, Ford has run into some resistance among coaches and faculty who do not appreciate the new emphasis or some methods used to push girls to win. It is a discussion that is going on at a national level, where women's sports are growing bigger and becoming more visible. Most recently, the University of Connecticut senior Nyke-sha Sales found herself at the center of a national polemic when she injured an Achilles' tendon and her coach, Geno Auriemma, arranged for her to take an uncontested shot during the team's last regular-season game in order to secure the school's scoring record.

That set off a debate about whether the coach was right to offer his athlete the free shot, and whether women's sports would be better off maintaining a kinder, gentler standard than men's sports traditionally have had. The sentiment that women's sports should focus on moderation and the good of the whole instead of competition has deep roots. One of the earliest and most regarded proponents of women's sports, Lucille (Gym) Hill, got her start at Wellesley College in 1882, home of the country's first women's collegiate rowing program begun in 1875. With a disdain for what she considered the evils of men's athletics, particularly the emphasis on a few talented athletes rather than the whole team, Hill taught her students to row for grace and form, not speed. A scoring system based partly on technical merit determined the results of Wellesley crew races until 1964, when the team responded to a challenge by the M.I.T. crew and finally raced to see who could cross the finish line first.

A similar awakening to competition has occurred at Miss Porter's, where the sprawling campus is dotted with grand old oak and maple trees and its 30 buildings include the white clapboard farmhouse that housed the original school in 1842. Winning has not been a part of Miss Porter's historic fabric, however. The school had fared so poorly in sports that in the late 1980s it dropped its brief membership in the Founders League because of its perennial finish at the bottom of the standing. But last season, in a move that was emblematic of Ford's attitude, the second-year athletic director, Kathy Noble, put Miss Porter's back in the league, one of the most competitive in New England.

As Noble knows well, the new approach hasn't been embraced by everyone. "In an initial meeting with a key administrator, I was told: 'But Kathy, we are a girls' school. That's not how we do things,' " Noble said. "When I said, 'I don't know what you mean by that,' I was told: 'We don't want to be that competitive, that headstrong. It's O.K. to play games, but to go that extra mile with preseason practices and two-hour-long practices six days a week just isn't right for girls.' "

Indeed, the assistant head of school, Paul Druzinsky, said, "Even though everyone here intends to be very pro-girl, there is still a sense that there are some things girls should not do, things they need to be protected from." Much of the controversy has been directed at the school's rowing program, which Ford started in her second year with the help of her husband, Brian Ford, and another teacher/coach, Brad Choyt, and which is presently on track to repeat last year's victory at the prestigious New England Championships.

Brian Ford, a highly successful coach of girls' crew at Nobles and Greenough in Massachusetts before he came to Miss Porter's, said he doesn't coach the girls any differently than he does the football team at nearby Westminster School, where he also teaches English. "Rowing may have preppy cachet, but it's a hard-nosed sport and you can't be soft," he said.

But Ford knows his style is not universally accepted, and as evidence of that, he related a conversation Choyt had with another teacher. "A faculty member at the lunch table recently told Brad: 'You'd get more out of the girls if you didn't yell at them. That's just not appropriate for girls.' There seems to be some residual fear that by turning the girls into winners, we are going to rob them of their femininity."

Noble has confronted similar objections. "It's an accusation I hear over and over again: 'All she wants to do is win,' " said Noble, who spent 18 years coaching in coed schools before coming to Miss Porter's, where she also coaches the field hockey and lacrosse teams. In her first year as field hockey coach, the team finished 8-5-2, its best record in 20 years. The lacrosse team is currently 7-1.

Among those who are uneasy with the school's direction is John Hale, who coaches badminton and squash, and has taught at Miss Porter's for 14 years. "I think women have more ambivalence about competition than men do," Hale said. "I'm not sure that's bad. Competition can bring out the best in us, but also the worst. I think we should take seriously that ambivalence because I think there are real problems with the level of hostility and violence in men's sports."

Other coaches said they liken teaching girls to embrace competition to teaching them to get over a fear of calculus. The assistant tennis coach, Stef Dwyer, was shocked during a doubles match last year to hear one of her players ask the girls on the other side of the net, midvolley, if they would be coming to a dance. "I tell them that we're not worrying more about whether she likes you than whether you're going to win," Dwyer said. "You have to teach them to do what they need to do to win or they will be at a serious disadvantage in their professional lives."

The varsity and junior varsity tennis teams have had winning records this season and have beaten teams recently considered unconquerable by Miss Porter's. The students at Miss Porter's seem pleased with the new direction, if blissfully unaware of any controversy. "The soccer coach tells us we had a great practice when we all know we didn't," said Erin DeGostin, who plans to play soccer at Rhodes College in Tennessee next year. "We don't take him seriously. But Miss Noble takes us seriously, and so we take her seriously. Even when we're dominating, she tells us to go out there and play like it's 0-0."

"It's the best feeling ever," said Merrielle MacLeod, a senior who turned down a scholarship to row at Boston University in favor of Dartmouth. "We are beating schools that have never been beaten in the history of this school."

INTERNET FORUM ON JOCK CULTURE

The following essay by sports columnist and novelist Robert Lipsyte appeared on the *New York Times'* Internet "Web Forum Sports," an interactive discussion site. Following the essay are on-line responses to it posted to the site.

The Jock Culture
Time to Debate the Questions

Robert Lipsyte

Yelling, "Sports, sports, don't you get it, everything in Glen Ridge is sports," a teen-age Jeremiah runs through a forgettable television movie Monday night with an inescapable message: love it, hate it or try to ignore it, jock culture haunts our national daydreams.

It may be as seemingly benign as renaming a New York highway after Joe DiMaggio, who last played here almost 50 years ago and afterward contributed little to the life of the city. It may be as threatening and damaging as Little League parents, the corruption of higher education by "revenue-producing" intercollegiate sports or the patterns of violence by individual athletes and by teams.

In recent weeks, in the frantic attempts to box and examine the high school massacre in Littleton, Colorado, jockcult became a hot topic again. The teen-age killers were quoted as shouting: "All jocks stand up. We're going to kill every one of you." To some, this marked the two former Little Leaguers as bitter athletic failures, which is probably not accurate. (Alternately, a hero of the massacre, Dave Sanders, who saved lives at the sacrifice of his own, has tended to be characterized by his after-school job as a girls' sports coach rather than his full-time job as a business teacher.)

Some commentators saw in the murders–suicides the ultimate pathological response of outsiders to a world from which they had been excluded. Within these theories were other assumptions: that jockhood was a golden goal, or at least an expression of mainstream values, and that perhaps the athletes had brought this upon themselves with their postures of entitlement and their drive to domination inside and outside the white lines.

The worship of high school athletes is hardly a new story and certainly never surprising. Why wouldn't you idolize—or resent—peers who are bigger, better and more confident at the time of life when it seems to matter most, adolescence. Furthermore, the school and the community often afford athletes special privileges, including relief from many rules.

This, of course, goes beyond high school. The greatest defensive football player of the century, the troubled Lawrence Taylor, caused havoc in the hallways of his high school and college and then went on to up the ante on the streets as a pro or, more recently, as a jock out of water. Felony arrests among pro and college athletes may or may not be rising, but better reporting makes it clear that many of them cannot turn off their aggressive behavior at the buzzer.

Meanwhile, the nice jocks, the ones we assume never trashed bars, raped dates or even made fun of fat boys—Michael Jordan, Wayne Gretzky, John Elway— were justifiably eulogized at retirement. In this time of fading family and community rituals, when major sports events have become our national campfires, who wants to cheer for clay feet?

Local campfires tend to afford more warmth, which is why the Glen Ridge rape story of 1989 was such a sensation. High school football players were accused of sexually molesting a mildly retarded female classmate while teammates watched. Glen Ridge, New Jersey, was seen as a bland, self-satisfied, mainly white Protestant suburb. Picture-book America. The football team was not particularly good, but the young athletes were regarded as the pride and extension of the community. Covering the story at the time, I was surprised at the fury of some residents toward the news media for "bothering" them, the annoyance of others that for so long we had bought into the myth of the Glen Ridges as exempt from class, race and gender problems. As with Littleton, Glen Ridge became a long-lasting symbol, somewhat unfairly, of the American dream come apart at the seams.

In his fine, absorbing 1997 book, *Our Boys,* Bernard Lefkowitz raised the level of discourse. He suggested that as individuals, the pack of Glen Ridge football players and wrestlers were not as confident as they seemed. He wrote: "A compelling argument can be made that the hyper-masculine style they were asked to assume by parents and brothers and sports enthusiasts was a heavy burden for a kid to carry through adolescence."

Lefkowitz added: "The swagger they affected—the jock swagger—was a handy way to camouflage their doubts."

It would be a long time, if ever, before the nerds, blacks, greasers, geeks, burnouts and non-"Jockette" girls that the "Ridgers" terrorized would figure that out.

The book has been made into a flat, disappointing movie that airs tomorrow night on ABC. But it will hopefully reinvigorate explorations of sports' role in American society. And by focusing on Glen Ridge and Littleton, where most of the athletes were white, it may be possible to discuss some of the bio-anthropological theories of violence.

In their 1996 book, *Demonic Males: Apes and the Origins of Human Violence,* Richard Wrangham and Dale Peterson trace patterns of imperialistic behavior in male gorilla and chimpanzee groups that are recapitulated in prestate warrior societies and urban gangs.

They write: "The psychology engaged may be hardly different from that expressed in predominantly male team sports—American football and hockey, for example. Demonic males gather in small, self-perpetuating, self-aggrandizing bands.

"What matters is the opportunity to engage in the vast and compelling drama of belonging to the gang, identifying the enemy, going on the patrol, participating in the attack."

And we, of course, are caught up in that compelling, relentlessly promoted drama. The noted Rutgers anthropologist Lionel Tiger offers his own jeremiad. In his new book, *The Decline of Males* (Golden Books), he writes: "Television sport is to male personal achievement as videocassette pornography is to love."

Tiger, best known for his exploration of male bonding in his famous *Men in Groups,* has taken a controversial tack in his current work. He asserts that the power given to women through effective contraception has made men feel "obsolete and out of control." Men have turned to drugs, porn and obsessive sports fandom which "may reveal a turbulent male preoccupation with competition and physical assertiveness that is no longer available to ordinary men."

Some of these issues deserve national forums, although such airings-out seem less and less likely as media conglomerates invest in sports programming that promotes athletes as soap opera stars, if not icons. Their excuse—the fans want it!—is true. A mildly critical look at Joe DiMaggio here several weeks ago brought a flood of negative mail, some of it abusive. The angriest were those who felt that sympathy toward a supposedly treacherous ingrate like Darryl Strawberry was somehow an oil spill on the Clipper's memory.

All the more reason to press on. In future columns, perhaps with the help of forward-thinking psychiatrists, psychologists, anthropologists, sociologists, historians, philosophers and, yes, even fans, we will try to open our own jockcult forum.

Some early, first-draft questions:

What is the role of sports beyond health and entertainment, as moral crucible, as national campfire?

Is there a thread of pathology among certain athletes that fuels their achievement? Do the psycho-scouts know and look for it?

Is the emotional neediness of some fans a pathology, and, if so, is it satisfied or exacerbated by their fandom?

How has the national struggle with matters of race, class and gender been affected by sports?

Has the media's promotion of violent, abusive sports heroes affected our definitions of masculinity?

Will female athletes change the game, or be changed?

Your thoughts are welcomed. Requested.

Responses to Lipsyte's "The Jock Culture"

jg1937—10:37 A.M. May 14, 1999 EST (#94 of 100)

Somehow, important things have been stripped from American conversation for fear of reprisal, and we are left to politically-correct tripe, namely, sports. Americans' communications are reduced to mind-numbing trivia which can be seen any way one wishes. We're like the plebes watching the gladiators while critical issues are ignored.

orchid17—11:30 A.M. May 14, 1999 EST (#95 of 100)

Amiante—While we are so eager to challenge our kids physically with sports, we neglect challenging their minds with academics. Somehow to Americans it is logical that kids should put time and effort into perfecting a jump shot, yet if we should dare suggest they learn something of world history, philosophy, or art it's unfair because "it's just too hard" or "not useful in the real world." Oops, forgot that fortune 500 companies are looking for recruits who can dribble a ball.

amiante—11:49 A.M. May 14, 1999 EST (#96 of 100)

Orchid, it's not kids that put sports and especially football at the complete center of high school education. It's our politics that does it. You have to ask yourself exactly WHO dictates that football and jock culture be so central? Who benefits? And yeah, you can pretty much look at any high school and figure out who is going to be successful twenty years down the road and who's not. The nerds are in the first category and the jocks are in the second. In other words, the schools, that should be reminding kids how important success in school is for career success in life, are instead encouraging and idolizing life choices that lead to failure. I think it's because of the same interests that basically want the school system, high schools and universities, to serve as farms for the production of professional athletes. The vast majority who never have a career in professional sports and who never get an education either are simply the "collateral damage" of this system.

dickmorr—12:11 P.M. May 14, 1999 EST (#97 of 100)

Frankly I am tired with the jock mentality. I was the little guy at the toughest high school in United States—Flint Northern. While we won Class A championships in football, track, wrestling, baseball the year I graduated, the academic levels of the jocks was horrible. The only way I survived the jocks was to do their homework. Most of them could not write their own names. My lifelong locker partner who was a jock, ended up going to prison three times and finally was shot and killed by the mafia—for drug related payoffs. Additionally, many of the jocks impregnated many of the girls in the area, and left them without taking responsibility. And, as we see what some of the big name jocks have done in recent years—like OJ killing his wife and a waiter and then having a jury ignore evidence that would convict any other American—I am sick to death about any sport. I refuse to even watch professional football, basketball, baseball because the players are pampered and overpaid. I would rather play golf, ride my mountain bike, and ski, rather than watch a bunch of overpaid jocks. By the way, I was one of the best cross country runners ever in the state—so I was a jock also. I am also sick to death over the way the college fans behave at games. Look at the irresponsible burning by the Michigan State students over their few victories in basketball and football. The President of Michigan State ought to be fired for permitting those students for acting like idiots.

The jocks are not all bad, but the bad ones are destroying the world's impression of all the others. The good jocks need to get rid of their own bad kinds.

America is getting a very bad image because of people that lack character, values, integrity, morals, etc. Look at our sleazy President—and I voted for the jerk. I will never again vote for any Democrat because the Democrats in Congress, like the OJ jury, gave a criminal a free pass. That kind of behavior must be fought by all of our votes.

amiante—12:24 P.M. May 14, 1999 EST (#98 of 100)

What do you think would be the fate of a high school principal who said, "OK, this school is about academics. No more sports as in no football, no cheerleaders, no band (we'll have an orchestra instead), no homecoming queens, and kings, etc."? How long do you think it would be before s/he got fired?

Even though I bet such a school would be radically better.

urbanshock1—12:57 P.M. May 14, 1999 EST (#99 of 100)

I am stunned that less than one month after the worst school shooting in our nation's history, the Senate has decided to make it easier for felons, fugitives and other prohibited purchasers to buy guns. —Janet Reno

Sports doesn't necessarily lead to a life of failure. The emphasis should be on sports for sports sake, not sports as a career. Playing sports can teach a kid confidence in herself or himself, and can teach teamwork, a very important skill for success in life.

shuar1—01:17 P.M. May 14, 1999 EST(#100 of 100)

The jock culture and the related cult of worship of all kinds of celebrities in the entertainment and sports areas are reflections of American anti-intellectualism (long-established and well-documented) and American laziness, that is the American inclination to be a spectator rather than a participant. This takes on a really ugly cast when you have spectator parents foaming at the mouth over the sports performance of their little league aged boys. At an age when boys should be having Tom Sawyer types of experiences with their buddies without parental pressure, those poor kids have to endure the sickness of their frustrated parents screaming at them to perform, No wonder some of these kids end up being sadistic themselves.

The New Tribalism

David Frohnmayer

*David Frohnmayer is the president of the University of Oregon. This essay was writ-
ten to be delivered orally, as a public speech.*

I hear an ancient noise rising in Oregon. To my ears, it is a raucous, ragged sound.
I hear it when I watch parts of the local TV news, when I read about some of the
new initiative petitions in the newspaper, when I open a piece of junk mail urg-
ing me to contribute to an "anti-something" campaign. It sounds like a hundred
drummers with different drums, each beating their own rhythm. It sounds like the
cacophony of a hundred tribes, each speaking its own tongue. It sounds like a
hundred calls to battle. It is the emergence of what I call the New Tribalism. What
is the New Tribalism? It is the growth of a politics based upon narrow concerns,
rooted in the exploitation of divisions of class, cash, gender, region, religion, eth-
nicity, morality and ideology—a give-no-quarter and take-no-prisoners activism
that demands satisfaction and accepts no compromise. It is a raw permissiveness
that escalates rhetorical excess sometimes even to physical violence. And it is an
environment where our political system of limited government is asked to take
on social and religious disputes that the system cannot possibly resolve.

In Oregon we see it in arguments over timber issues and the control of federal and private lands, in the white-hot rhetoric of racial supremacists, in arguments about gay rights and property taxes, and controversies over immigration
and affirmative action. It manifests itself in sound-bite attacks and talk-show
manifestos, in personal smears and incendiary language. The result of this vitu-
peration and negativity can be disastrous for our political system.

Two University of Oregon professors have studied "attack ads" and found
the effect of one candidate going negative on the other was to turn off all voters.
Instead of voting for the attacking candidate, many of his supporters decided not
to vote at all. Terms like "fascist" and "wimp," "extremist" and "FemiNazi" have
become commonplace not only on radio and TV talk shows, but increasingly in
our legislative halls. One United States Senator, leaving the chamber after a recent budget debate, was reported to declare, "I'd like to take an Uzi in there and
spray the place." It is no wonder we hear jokes like the story of the candidate
who spoke for an hour, then asked, "Are there any more questions?" " Yes," came
a voice from the back. "Who else is running?"

This erosion of civility in public discourse is only a surface manifestation of
the New Tribalism. Below it are the tribes themselves, small groups of like-
minded people who zealously support narrowly focused political issues. As a former attorney general and one-time candidate for governor of Oregon, I have
seen this New Tribalism expressed as an atmosphere of hatred, of raw emotion,
of people asking not whether you are going to be fair, but "are you with us all the

way"—not with us 95 percent, but with us 100 percent on our own special issues. I should add here that I don't mean to attack the motives of the many citizen groups whose focus on single issues arises from legitimate concerns about social justice. In some ways, single-issue activism is noble in its purity. It is not the volunteers' sense of underlying outrage about issues that I believe is wrong, but the unreflective superiority and intolerance that this outrage often can spawn—a moral righteousness that puts down good faith differences as unworthy of debate. Once it becomes impossible to talk to the other side, to find points of agreement and compromise, the stage is set for social disintegration.

How have we gotten here? How has our public dialogue become debased to hot-button sound-bites designed to inflame emotions, not increase understanding? How has political correctness on single issues become more important than moving forward together as a society? How has this politics of division, this tribal politics, now become so powerful?

There is no one answer. But there are many contributing factors. First among them is surely economic dislocation. We are in the midst of enormous economic changes on a global level, and that change is occurring at an unprecedented pace. By one estimate, the world between 1985 and 1987 experienced more technological change than in the entire 140 years of the Industrial Revolution. With that pace comes a horrifying incapacity of many people to adapt. Indeed, many once-secure people at firms as established as IBM, ATT, and Sears know now that they may be the subjects of massive layoffs as once impregnable giants now "downsize," "rightsize" or capsize. Several Oregon pollsters not long ago came to an identical conclusion about the effects of these trends on people in our state. To a person, they reported that they had never seen such insecurity—personal, financial and political—at any time in modern history.

And we know from a reading of history that economic insecurity breeds psychic insecurity and political extremism. It fosters disconnection with social institutions. That sense of disconnection has been deepened by other factors, including the disappearance of the Cold War. We are now, for the first time in a half-century, bereft of a sinister outside force to unite us. The paradox here is that something in human nature demands an enemy, an "other" against whom we can fight a common fight. Without one outside our nation, we seem to look for enemies at home.

Religious fundamentalism, I believe, plays a role. Perhaps my perspective is colored by my experience with the Rajneesh commune in central Oregon when I was attorney general. But it is my unyielding conclusion that religious zeal corrupts government and government corrupts religion, if the two are not kept separate and distinct with the kind of wisdom that the establishment clause of our First Amendment has commanded in American history. I choose my words carefully here, because I know how vital strongly held religious beliefs are on a personal basis, as a way of guiding families and finding strength. But I say again that the attempt to create a heavenly city on earth often is accompanied by an urge to exterminate the nonbelievers. That is a price that we cannot pay here in a nation devoted to ensuring the rights of all, especially in a society marked by such rich religious pluralism.

Having said that, let me quickly add that another reason for the rise of the New Tribalism comes directly from a long emphasis on individual rights and the rights of small groups. We have seen several decades of self-assertiveness on the parts of groups that have demanded much-needed change and the counter-reactions of those who believe their own values are threatened by these changes. As I'll mention later, this trend may be on the wane. But for now, the tone of "We need to get ours" to the exclusion of all else has been well established in our society.

New advances in communications technology are also helping fuel the New Tribalism. It is now possible, with great certainty, minor expense and the assistance of computer technology, to find demographic subgroups, whole communities not otherwise identified by geography or census tract, and to target mailings and messages to them. The common thread is not a local community, but a zealous commitment to a particular narrow cause. These cyber-communities can generate enormous amounts of energy and money for single-issue politics. The media, the arts and entertainment also play a part.

Do not take my comments as bashing these enterprises, because indeed I am devoted to them. But there are at least three ways current trends in the media further destabilize our political environment.

- First, media of all stripes tend to cover the fringes and extremes. There's an old saying in journalism, "If it bleeds, it leads." Conflict sells better than process. Perhaps it has ever been thus, but the pack certainly is fueled by the audio-visual media, because the written press must be more extreme and sensational simply to compete. Sensationalism has spilled over into the afternoon talk shows, with their rosters of professional victims. Will we see left-handed cross-dressers become the next set of tribal victims?

- Second, the media desensitizes us to violence. Think of the unending litany of murder, rape, and casual beatings that we see every day. We all know the depressing statistic that by the age of 18 the average teenager will have seen 200,000 televised acts of violence, including 40,000 killings. I am one of those convinced that there is a causal link between this flood of images and a grotesque desensitization that makes violence in real life more common. It makes the extravagant into the norm, and makes extreme action—without the experience of offsetting psychic pain—seem acceptable, even routine!

- Finally, the New Tribalism is fueled by the fragmentation of the media. We can now simply hear what we want to hear, rather than listen thoughtfully to the main chords of common discourse. With 100 channels of cable TV and hundreds of thousands of different information sites on the Internet, we are now free to simply reinforce our own ignorance, our own biases. We are losing the common pool of information that might force us to face ideas with which we disagree.

There is an old adage that "you can always tell a Harvard Man, but you can't tell him very much." Well, that is now writ large as we seek out specialized news and talk shows that fit our own preconceptions and fuel our own biases.

Another major reason for the rise of the New Tribalism comes from pressures on the family. If families do not thrive, tribes provide a crude substitute. Pressure on the modern family unit is intense, both economically and socially. An enormous number of kids in our society feel unwanted, and they act it. Most hate crimes—expressions of Tribal Politics in its crudest form—are committed by children under the age of 21.

Another reason is more obscure, because it's hard to talk with precision about a "national character" or ethos. But I think of a Christmas season when someone gave me a tie, a relic from the '80s, that said in bold letters, "Dear Santa, I Want It All." That, in fact, is the motto emblazoned on the banners of the New Tribalism. It is not enough to get part of what you want, or even most of what you want— it's getting it all that counts. If you draw up an initiative, you and four or five of your friends and fellow believers can ask for it all, no compromise, no give-and-take, no counterarguments. Just put it all out there for an up-or-down vote, "give me mine and leave the thinking or questioning people out." Finally, the New Tribalism thrives because there are those who profit from it. There is money in promoting these single issue causes, sometimes big money, for those in this society who have no stake in consensus. Indeed the perpetuation of conflict and divisiveness is both their meal ticket and their egotistical pathway to power.

It is much easier to describe this phenomenon than it is to suggest prescriptions to help us get beyond this "us versus them" politics. But it is absolutely vital that we try. Let me offer a few thoughts about how we might start.

First, we must distrust the language of moral righteousness employed by those who ask for our support, our votes, our money. Distrust those who bathe in the purity of their motives. Judge people not by their passion for one cause, but by their capacity to calculate the consequences, long and short term, of their actions in its pursuit.

A second approach is to find our common ground. Happily, my friends, we have it. In Oregon, a group with which I am involved sponsored a large-scale survey of the attitudes of our citizens. We asked Oregonians what they really treasured, to identify their core beliefs. The results were, to me, enormously reassuring. Foremost was the feeling that we live where we live because we want to. We have an allegiance to our land, a sense of place. The feeling of home, of an emotional tie to a landscape that you love, is a powerful one—and one that can serve as the basis for a larger sense of shared community and unity. Second, when asked where they wanted to put their energy, almost 90 percent responded not about their jobs or careers, but said they most valued "spending time with family and my loved ones." There is an enormous sense of caring about the family unit, whether defined traditionally or nontraditionally. This, too, can serve as a basis for shared values and shared understanding.

Now we need to expand that feeling—just a little—from our families to our schools and neighborhoods. We need to turn our schools into communities of learning, places where students come not only to learn facts, but to learn about shared responsibility, common goals, the importance of compromise in the pursuit of objectives. On a societal basis, we need the twentieth century equivalent of barn raisings. We need to reach out to our neighbors in community celebrations, community service projects, and community self-help, everything from Neighborhood Watch programs to Habitat for Humanity. We need to cool the overheated political discourse that dominates our media.

- We must refuse to accept simple slogans in place of thoughtful analysis;
- We must demand of our local media coverage of meaning and context of issues in addition to simple events;
- We must talk to our friends and neighbors conscientiously about the consequences of sudden and extreme action in the service of an inflammatory single issue;
- And we must let no single-issue demagogue dominate our thinking.

Our shared belief in community education plays a vital role here. We must demand these things not only of ourselves, but must also help our communities to reach a new level of understanding.

Finally, and perhaps with too much hope, let me suggest that perhaps the New Tribalism will cure itself. Arthur Schlesinger wrote a book several years ago called *Cycles in American History.* He identified a pendulum swinging back and forth in American history between social attitudes that could be regarded as selfish, grasping, and highly individualistic, and those in which community values became ascendant. A number of observers, myself among them, detect the cycle swinging back toward community as opposed to the individual.

I am particularly fond of one period of our history, the American Revolution. A couple set an example during that time. Their names were John and Abigail Adams. Contrary to the myths of some of the old storybooks we used to read, only a third of the colonists were on the side of the American Revolution, a third were officially "neutral," and a third sympathized with the Tories. One time when John was away at the front, Abigail wrote to him asking, "What shall we tell our neighbors? Why is it that we do what we do, laboring to create a new society?" And he wrote back a wonderful letter in which he said this: "You tell them that I study war, so that our children can study business, law, commerce and invention, so that their children can study art, poetry and music."

Among the many wonderful things that letter conveys is an enormous sense of trusteeship, of personal responsibility, not merely for the here and now, but for building a better society that you will never see, because that is the birthright of your children's children. This is the American spirit. We possessed it before, and I think it is possible to have it again. The New Tribalism does not have to be our destiny.

The American Dream

Beverly Ajie

Beverly Ajie wrote this essay when she was a student in Writing 121 at the University of Oregon. The Orwell essay it refers to can be found on page 246.

The American Dream. It's why most of us are here pursuing an education. It's why so many of our parents work at jobs they don't like. It's why millions of people have immigrated to this country with such high hopes and settled for minimum wage or less. But what IS IT? In his essay "Politics and the English Language," Orwell discussed prepackaged phrases and words that have no meaning, or several that are contradictory. He argued the cyclical ability of thought to corrupt language and language to corrupt thought. "But an effect can become a cause, reinforcing the original cause and producing the same effect in an intensified form, and so on indefinitely." I cannot think of two words that better illustrate his point.

American: a native or inhabitant of North America or the USA.
Dream: a series of *images* one sees while sleeping; *ideal,* hope or aspiration; state of mind without proper perception, *fantasy.*

To my surprise I did find the phrase *American Dream* in the dictionary with the following definition:

The *traditional* ideals of the *American people* such as *democracy, equality,* and *material prosperity.* (emphasis added)

The presence of this phrase in the dictionary illustrates what an integral part of our culture it is, but the words defining it are as vague and open to interpretation as the phrase itself. They are political jargon, words that evoke a programmed response from us; they think for us.

Thought Corrupts Language: The Nature of the Dream

Today the American Dream is primarily focused on material prosperity, even at the expense of the other two ideals. When we hear those words we think of having a big house, two cars in the garage, and a dog in the yard. We think of being financially secure, which of course varies according to your preferred standard of living, with a little (or a lot of) money to spare. However, our thought has corrupted this phrase in much more serious ways. In addition to goals of wealth, we have incorporated a personal aspect in the form of lifestyle related goals, which being often rooted in beliefs about morality, are more expressions of social values than goals. For example in that dream house described earlier we can also not help picturing a man, woman and two children living there each playing their appropriate role according to *tradition*. We picture the man being the primary breadwinner and the woman, a dutiful housewife and primary caregiver. These may not be values that we intentionally associate or even believe in, but they are implicit in the notion of the American Dream as we have constructed it.

The American Dream, then, is no longer a political aspiration (democracy, equality, etc.), but a measure of an individual's achievement financially and socially. This is problematic because the basic premise of the American Dream has always been that it is available to everyone and anyone. Our motto is that hard work pays off, that it is the "key to success," also known as the American Dream. We believe, or at least we are told, that if you work hard enough and long enough you can accomplish anything. However, in the attempt to assign meaning to those words/ideals that had none we created a version of the American Dream that is elitist and exclusionary because by its own definition not everyone is able to attain it.

As it stands, the majority of our society will never live the American Dream no matter how much they try or believe. Whether it's due to economic status or race or lifestyle, many of us will never lead the ideal life embodied in this phrase. If the obstacle is material prosperity, there is hope. Occasionally those who are not born into wealth gain access to the resources and opportunities, like education, that are necessary to achieve it. But this is more often an exception to rule than a common occurrence. Why? Our ever-increasing focus on material prosperity is relative, which means that those at the top are pursuing their own version of the American Dream and acquiring more and more material prosperity. The result is that one percent of the population controls ninety-nine percent of the nation's wealth so that the gap and the difficulty the rest of us must overcome is large enough to be nearly impossible. If, however, the obstacle is one of race or lifestyle the task is even more difficult. Though this is becoming less of an issue, it is still true that minorities are at a disadvantage at least in terms of material prosperity. Consider a gay/lesbian couple, or just a woman who does not desire children: as long as the ideal life includes having a "traditional" family, they are automatically excluded from the goal. This is further complicated by the fact that America is no longer a cohesive unit, if it ever was. Today our culture entertains a wide variety of social, political, religious, and personal beliefs, and yet we hold and pursue as a goal a standard that is not representative and not inclusive of the majority of those beliefs. As it has been constructed, then, the American Dream is a contradiction in conception.

Language Corrupts Thought

As much as we have corrupted the well-intended, though vague, original ideals behind the American Dream in the past, they corrupt our thoughts and actions today. The ideal has been so well "imprinted on our psyche" that we struggle toward it without questioning what it is. One generation after the next quietly toils away, and dutifully pays their taxes to the country that guarantees them success if they "really want it." But the nature of the American Dream is such that our very belief in and pursuit of it distracts us from and sometimes perpetuates the social and political injustices that prevent us from achieving what we want.

I'm not a conspiracy theorist myself, but Orwell might say that the idea of the American Dream has done for us what Big Brother did for the people in the novel *1984*. Like "think-speak," it is language that prevents us from deciding what we really want and what stands in our way. I see this happening in the following two ways.

The importance placed on and ambiguity of "material prosperity" together create a situation where we, our thoughts, are occupied with the quest for some far-off promise of happiness, in the form of wealth. The catch is that there is always more to be acquired, so that we are not satisfied with just having food on the table and a place to live once we have it. The grass always looks greener in someone else's yard so no matter what we achieve, so we continue striving. If we are not careful we can go through school, get a job, start a family, and work in the rest of our lives without making a conscious decision to do so. We assume only that it is what we are supposed to do—after all it is the American Dream, right? Not that this is a bad life, just a bad reason to pursue it.

Our belief in the American Dream distracts us in another way. If we hold true the very principle behind it, its availability to everyone, and at the same time limit access to it, by definition, we create an impossible situation. The blame is placed on the the individual. If one is struggling to achieve those ideals it is only because they are not working hard enough. We often hear and say things like, "if he wanted it badly enough . . ." or "if she would just try harder . . ." The same logic compels us to believe that people who do not want it, or cannot have it, are just lazy and leading a deprived life. Thus we are pitted against one another instead of coming together to reform the ideals which are exclusionary, and the system that does not support equally all of its subjects.

Thoreau said that men who served the state with their conscience served it best. If we blindly pursue the American Dream and all it entails without question we are not serving the state in this way but instead "as machines mainly, with our bodies," providing not much more than the resource of labor. And without "a free exercise whatever of the judgment or of the moral sense" (Thoreau).

So the cycle is complete. Be it race or sexuality or class we judge people on their ability and willingness to live out the American Dream, the traditional, ideal lifestyle. And by excluding some people from the start we create a section of society to discriminate against, which in turn intensifies the difficulty they face in achieving it (if they desire), or just being accepted by society (if they don't).

We forget in our haste to achieve that which is both cleverly defined and undefined, making it virtually unattainable, to pay attention to those things which actually hold us back like discrimination, poor education, lack of jobs, or any number of things that can only be changed if we stop long enough to realize that our goals and ideals are no longer inclusive of all of America. That it is time for a social and political change and a makeover of the American Dream.

Luckily for us this is not some great oppressive force, but rather a self-imposed and self-perpetuating cycle. We continue to think the way we do about the American Dream not because we believe it especially, but because it is habit, tradition. "The point is that the process is reversible" (Orwell). If we modify our definition, the language associated with the American Dream, our thought will likely follow. "Modern English . . . is full of bad habits which spread by imitation. . . . If one gets rid of these habits one can think more clearly, and to think more clearly is a necessary first step towards political regeneration" (Orwell).

Issues about Language and Human Community

The Four Idols

Francis Bacon

English philosopher and parliamentarian Sir Francis Bacon (1561–1626) was one of the innovators of the essay form. This argument is part of a longer work, Novum Organum *(1620), which, together with his* The Advancement of Learning *(1605), exerted a powerful influence on the development of scientific methods of inquiry.*

The idols and false notions which are now in possession of the human understanding, and have taken deep root therein, not only so beset men's minds that truth can hardly find entrance, but even after entrance obtained, they will again in the very instauration of the sciences meet and trouble us, unless men being forewarned of the danger fortify themselves as far as may be against their assaults.

There are four classes of idols which beset men's minds. To these for distinction's sake I have assigned names—calling the first class *Idols of the Tribe;* the second, *Idols of the Cave;* the third, *Idols of the Marketplace;* the fourth, *Idols of the Theater.*

The formation of ideas and axioms by true induction is no doubt the proper remedy to be applied for the keeping off and clearing away of idols. To point them out, however, is of great use; for the doctrine of idols is to the interpretation of nature what the doctrine of the refutation of sophisms is to common logic.

The *Idols of the Tribe* have their foundation in human nature itself, and in the tribe or race of men. For it is a false assertion that the sense of man is the measure of things. On the contrary, all perceptions as well of the sense as of the mind are according to the measure of the individual and not according to the measure of the universe. And the human understanding is like a false mirror, which, receiving rays irregularly, distorts and discolors the nature of things by mingling its own nature with it.

The *Idols of the Cave* are the idols of the individual man. For everyone (besides the errors common to human nature in general) has a cave or den of his own, which refracts and discolors the light of nature; owing either to his own proper and peculiar nature; or to his education and conversation with others; or to the reading of books, and the authority of those whom he esteems and admires; or to the differences of impressions, accordingly as they take place in a mind preoccupied and predisposed or in a mind indifferent and settled; or the like. So that the spirit of man (according as it is meted out to different individuals) is in fact a thing variable and full of perturbation, and governed as it were by chance. Whence it was well observed by Heraclitus that men look for sciences in their own lesser worlds, and not in the greater or common world.

There are also idols formed by the intercourse and association of men with each other, which I call *Idols of the Marketplace,* on account of the commerce and consort of men there. For it is by discourse that men associate; and words are imposed according to the apprehension of the vulgar. And therefore the ill and unfit choice of words wonderfully obstructs the understanding. Nor do the definitions or explanations wherewith in some things learned men are wont to guard and defend themselves, by any means set the matter right. But words plainly force and overrule the understanding, and throw all into confusion and lead men away into numberless empty controversies and idle fancies.

Lastly, there are idols which have immigrated into men's minds from the various dogmas of philosophies, and also from wrong laws of demonstration. These I call *Idols of the Theater;* because in my judgment all the received systems are but so many stage-plays, representing worlds of their own creation after an unreal and scenic fashion. Nor is it only of the systems now in vogue, or only of the ancient sects and philosophies, that I speak; for many more plays of the same kind may yet be composed and in like artificial manner set forth; seeing that errors the most widely different have nevertheless causes for the most part alike. Neither again do I mean this only of entire systems, but also of many principles and axioms in science, which by tradition, credulity, and negligence, have come to be received.

But of these several kinds of idols I must speak more largely and exactly, that the understanding may be duly cautioned.

The human understanding is of its own nature prone to suppose the existence of more order and regularity in the world than it finds. And though there be many things in nature which are singular and unmatched, yet it devises for them parallels and conjugates and relatives which do not exist. Hence the fiction that all celestial bodies move in perfect circles; spirals and dragons being (except in name) utterly rejected. Hence too the element of fire with its orb is brought in, to make up the square with the other three which the sense perceives. Hence also the ratio of density of the so-called elements is arbitrarily fixed at ten to one. And so on of other dreams. And these fancies affect not dogmas only, but simple notions also.

The human understanding when it has once adopted an opinion (either as being the received opinion or as being agreeable to itself) draws all things else to support and agree with it. And though there be a greater number and weight of instances to be found on the other side, yet these it either neglects and despises, or else by some distinction sets aside and rejects; in order that by this great and pernicious predetermination the authority of its former conclusions may remain inviolate. And therefore it was a good answer that was made by one who when they showed him hanging in a temple a picture of those who had paid their vows as having escaped shipwreck, and would have him say whether he did not now acknowledge the power of the gods—"Ay," asked he again, "but where are they painted that were drowned after their vows?" And such is the way of all superstition, whether in astrology, dreams, omens, divine judgments, or the like; wherein men having a delight in such vanities, mark the events where they are fulfilled, but where they fail, though this happen much oftener, neglect and pass them by. But with far more subtlety does this mischief insinuate itself into philosophy and the sciences; in which the first conclusion colors and brings into conformity with itself all that come after, though far sounder and better. Besides, independently of that delight and vanity which I have described, it is the peculiar and perpetual error of the human intellect to be more moved and excited by affirmatives than by negatives; whereas it ought properly to hold itself indifferently disposed towards both alike. Indeed, in the establishment of any true axiom, the negative instance is the more forcible of the two.

The human understanding is moved by those things most which strike and enter the mind simultaneously and suddenly, and so fill the imagination; and then it feigns and supposes all other things to be somehow, though it cannot see how, similar to those few things by which it is surrounded. But for that going to and fro to remote and heterogeneous instances, by which axioms are tried as in the fire, the intellect is altogether slow and unfit, unless it be forced thereto by severe laws and overruling authority.

The human understanding is unquiet; it cannot stop or rest, and still presses onward, but in vain. Therefore it is that we cannot conceive of any end or limit to the world, but always as of necessity it occurs to us that there is something beyond. Neither again can it be conceived how eternity has flowed down to the present day; for that distinction which is commonly received of infinity in time past and in time to come can by no means hold; for it would thence follow that one infinity is greater than another, and that infinity is wasting away and tending to become finite. The like subtlety arises touching the infinite divisibility of lines, from the same inability of thought to stop. But this inability interferes more mischievously in the discovery of causes: for although the most general principles in nature ought to be held merely positive, as they are discovered, and cannot with truth be referred to a cause; nevertheless, the human understanding being unable to rest still seeks something prior in the order of nature. And then it is that in struggling towards that which is further off, it falls back upon that which is more nigh at hand; namely, on final causes: which have relation clearly to the nature of man rather than to the nature of the universe, and from this source have strangely defiled philosophy. But he is no less an unskilled and shallow philosopher who seeks causes of that which is most general, than he who in things subordinate and subaltern omits to do so.

The human understanding is no dry light, but receives an infusion from the will and affections; whence proceed sciences which may be called "sciences as one would." For what a man had rather were true he more readily believes. Therefore he rejects difficult things from impatience of research; sober things, because they narrow hope; the deeper things of nature, from superstition; the light of experience, from arrogance and pride, lest his mind should seem to be occupied with things mean and transitory; things not commonly believed, out of deference to the opinion of the vulgar. Numberless in short are the ways, and sometimes imperceptible, in which the affections color and infect the understanding.

But by far the greatest hindrance and aberration of the human understanding proceeds from the dullness, incompetency, and deceptions of the senses; in that things which strike the sense outweigh things which do not immediately strike it, though they be more important. Hence it is that speculation commonly ceases where sight ceases; insomuch that of things invisible there is little or no observation. Hence all the working of the spirits enclosed in tangible bodies lies hid and unobserved of men. So also all the more subtle changes of form in the parts of coarser substances (which they commonly call alteration, though it is in truth local motion through exceedingly small spaces) is in like manner unobserved. And yet unless these two things just mentioned be searched out and brought to light, nothing great can be achieved in nature, as far as the production of works is concerned. So again the essential nature of our common air, and of all bodies less dense than air (which are very many) is almost unknown. For the sense by itself is a thing infirm and erring; neither can instruments for enlarging or sharpening the senses do much; but all the truer kind of interpretation of nature is effected by instances and experiments fit and apposite; wherein the sense decides touching the experiment only, and the experiment touching the point in nature and the thing itself.

The human understanding is of its own nature prone to abstractions and gives a substance and reality to things which are fleeting. But to resolve nature into abstractions is less to our purpose than to dissect her into parts; as did the school of Democritus, which went further into nature than the rest. Matter rather than forms should be the object of our attention, its configurations and changes of configuration, and simple action, and law of action or motion; for forms are figments of the human mind, unless you will call those laws of action forms.

Such then are the idols which I call *Idols of the Tribe;* and which take their rise either from the homogeneity of the substance of the human spirit, or from its preoccupation, or from its narrowness, or from its restless motion, or from an infusion of the affections, or from the incompetency of the senses, or from the mode of impression.

The *Idols of the Cave* take their rise in the peculiar constitution, mental or bodily, of each individual; and also in education, habit, and accident. Of this kind there is a great number and variety; but I will instance those the pointing out of which contains the most important caution, and which have most effect in disturbing the clearness of the understanding.

Men become attached to certain particular sciences and speculations, either because they fancy themselves the authors and inventors thereof, or because they have bestowed the greatest pains upon them and become most habituated to them. But men of this kind, if they betake themselves to philosophy and contemplations of a general character, distort and color them in obedience to their former fancies; a thing especially to be noticed in Aristotle, who made his natural philosophy a mere bondservant to his logic, thereby rendering it contentious and well nigh useless. The race of chemists again out of a few experiments of the furnace have built up a fantastic philosophy, framed with reference to a few things; and Gilbert also, after he had employed himself most laboriously in the study and observation of the loadstone, proceeded at once to construct an entire system in accordance with his favorite subject.

There is one principal and, as it were, radical distinction between different minds, in respect of philosophy and the sciences, which is this: that some minds are stronger and apter to mark the differences of things, others to mark their resemblances. The steady and acute mind can fix its contemplations and dwell and fasten on the subtlest distinctions: the lofty and discursive mind recognizes and puts together the finest and most general resemblances. Both kinds however easily err in excess, by catching the one at gradations, the other at shadows.

There are found some minds given to an extreme admiration of antiquity, others to an extreme love and appetite for novelty; but few so duly tempered that they can hold the mean, neither carping at what has been well laid down by the ancients, nor despising what is well introduced by the moderns. This however turns to the great injury of the sciences and philosophy; since these affectations of antiquity and novelty are the humors of partisans rather than judgments; and truth is to be sought for not in the felicity of any age, which is an unstable thing, but in the light of nature and experience, which is eternal. These factions therefore must be abjured, and care must be taken that the intellect be not hurried by them into assent.

Contemplations of nature and of bodies in their simple form break up and distract the understanding, while contemplations of nature and bodies in their composition and configuration overpower and dissolve the understanding: a distinction well seen in the school of Leucippus and Democritus as compared with the other philosophies. For that school is so busied with the particles that it hardly attends to the structure; while the others are so lost in admiration of the structure that they do not penetrate to the simplicity of nature. These kinds of contemplation should therefore be alternated and taken by turns; that so the understanding may be rendered at once penetrating and comprehensive, and the inconveniences above mentioned, with the idols which proceed from them, may be avoided.

Let such then be our provision and contemplative prudence for keeping off and dislodging the *Idols of the Cave,* which grow for the most part either out of the predominance of a favorite subject, or out of an excessive tendency to compare or to distinguish, or out of partiality for particular ages, or out of the largeness or minuteness of the objects contemplated. And generally let every student of nature take this as a rule—that whatever his mind seizes and dwells upon with peculiar satisfaction is to be held in suspicion, and that so much the more care is to be taken in dealing with such questions to keep the understanding even and clear.

But the *Idols of the Marketplace* are the most troublesome of all: idols which have crept into the understanding through the alliances of words and names. For men believe that their reason governs words; but it is also true that words react on the understanding; and this it is that has rendered philosophy and the sciences sophistical and inactive. Now words, being commonly framed and applied according to the capacity of the vulgar, follow those lines of division which are most obvious to the vulgar understanding. And whenever an understanding of greater acuteness or a more diligent observation would alter those lines to suit the true divisions of nature, words stand in the way and resist the change. Whence it comes to pass that the high and formal discussions of learned men end oftentimes in disputes about words and names; with which (according to the use and wisdom of the mathematicians) it would be more prudent to begin, and so by means of definitions reduce them to order. Yet even definitions cannot cure this evil in deal-ing with natural and material things; since the definitions themselves consist of words, and those words beget others: so that it is necessary to recur to individual instances, and those in due series and order; as I shall say presently when I come to the method and scheme for the formation of notions and axioms.

The idols imposed by words on the understanding are of two kinds. They are either names of things which do not exist (for as there are things left unnamed through lack of observation, so likewise are there names which result from fan-tastic suppositions and to which nothing in reality responds), or they are names of things which exist, but yet confused and ill-defined, and hastily and irregularly derived from realities. Of the former kind are Fortune, the Prime Mover, Plane-tary Orbits, Element of Fire, and like fictions which owe their origin to false and idle theories. And this class of idols is more easily expelled, because to get rid of them it is only necessary that all theories should be steadily rejected and dis-missed as obsolete.

But the other class, which springs out of a faulty and unskillful abstraction, is intricate and deeply rooted. Let us take for example such a word as *humid;* and see how far the several things which the word is used to signify agree with each other; and we shall find the word *humid* to be nothing else than a mark loosely and con-fusedly applied to denote a variety of actions which will not bear to be reduced to any constant meaning. For it both signifies that which easily spreads itself round any other body; and that which in itself is indeterminate and cannot solidize; and that which readily yields in every direction; and that which easily divides and scat-ters itself; and that which easily unites and collects itself; and that which readily flows and is put in motion; and that which readily clings to another body and wets it; and that which is easily reduced to a liquid, or being solid easily melts. Accord-ingly when you come to apply the word—if you take it in one sense, flame is hu-mid; if in another, air is not humid; if in another, fine dust is humid; if in another, glass is humid. So that it is easy to see that the notion is taken by abstraction only from water and common and ordinary liquids, without any due verification.

There are however in words certain degrees of distortion and error. One of the least faulty kinds is that of names of substances, especially of lowest species and well-deduced (for the notion of *chalk* and of *mud* is good, of *earth* bad); a more faulty kind is that of actions, as *to generate, to corrupt, to alter;* the most faulty is of qualities (except such as are the immediate objects of the sense), as *heavy, light, rare, dense,* and the like. Yet in all these cases some notions are of ne-cessity a little better than others, in proportion to the greater variety of subjects that fall within the range of the human sense.

But the *Idols of the Theater* are not innate, nor do they steal into the under-standing secretly, but are plainly impressed and received into the mind from the play-books of philosophical systems and the perverted rules of demonstration. To attempt refutations in this case would be merely inconsistent with what I have already said: for since we agree neither upon principles nor upon demonstra-tions, there is no place for argument. And this is so far well, inasmuch as it leaves the honor of the ancients untouched. For they are no wise disparaged—the question between them and me being only as to the way. For as the saying is, the lame man who keeps the right road outstrips the runner who takes a wrong one. Nay, it is obvious that when a man runs the wrong way, the more active and swift he is the further he will go astray.

But the course I propose for the discovery of sciences is such as leaves but little to the acuteness and strength of wits, but places all wits and understandings nearly on a level. For as in the drawing of a straight line or perfect circle, much depends on the steadiness and practice of the hand, if it be done by aim of hand only, but if with the aid of rule or compass, little or nothing; so is it exactly with my plan. But though particular confutations would be of no avail, yet touching the sects and general divisions of such systems I must say something; something also touching the external signs which show that they are unsound; and finally something touching the causes of such great infelicity and of such lasting and general agreement in error; that so the access to truth may be made less difficult, and the human understanding may the more willingly submit to its purgation and dismiss its idols.

Idols of the Theater, or of systems, are many, and there can be and perhaps will be yet many more. For were it not that now for many ages men's minds have been busied with religion and theology; and were it not that civil governments, especially monarchies, have been averse to such novelties, even in matters speculative; so that men labor therein to the peril and harming of their fortunes—not only unrewarded, but exposed also to contempt and envy; doubtless there would have arisen many other philosophical sects like to those which in great variety flourished once among the Greeks. For as on the phenomena of the heavens many hypotheses may be constructed, so likewise (and more also) many various dogmas may be set up and established on the phenomena of philosophy. And in the plays of this philosophical theater you may observe the same thing which is found in the theater of the poets, that stories invented for the stage are more compact and elegant, and more as one would wish them to be, than true stories out of history.

In general, however, there is taken for the material of philosophy either a great deal out of a few things, or a very little out of many things; so that on both sides philosophy is based on too narrow a foundation of experiment and natural history, and decides on the authority of too few cases. For the rational school of philosophers snatches from experience a variety of common instances, neither duly ascertained nor diligently examined and weighed, and leaves all the rest to meditation and agitation of wit.

There is also another class of philosophers, who having bestowed much diligent and careful labor on a few experiments, have thence made bold to educe and construct systems; wresting all other facts in a strange fashion to conformity therewith.

And there is yet a third class, consisting of those who out of faith and veneration mix their philosophy with theology and traditions; among whom the vanity of some has gone so far aside as to seek the origin of sciences among spirits and genii. So that this parent stock of errors—this false philosophy—is of three kinds; the sophistical, the empirical, and the superstitious. . . .

But the corruption of philosophy by superstition and an admixture of theology is far more widely spread, and does the greatest harm, whether to entire systems or to their parts. For the human understanding is obnoxious to the influence of the imagination no less than to the influence of common notions. For the contentious and sophistical kind of philosophy ensnares the understanding; but this kind, being fanciful and tumid and half poetical, misleads it more by flattery. For there is in man an ambition of the understanding, no less than of the will, especially in high and lofty spirits.

Of this kind we have among the Greeks a striking example in Pythagoras, though he united with it a coarser and more cumbrous superstition; another in Plato and his school, more dangerous and subtle. It shows itself likewise in parts of other philosophies, in the introduction of abstract forms and final causes and first causes, with the omission in most cases of causes intermediate, and the like. Upon this point the greatest caution should be used. For nothing is so mischievous as the apotheosis of error; and it is a very plague of the understanding for vanity to become the object of veneration. Yet in this vanity some of the moderns have with extreme levity indulged so far as to attempt to found a system of natural philosophy on the first chapter of Genesis, on the book of Job, and other parts of the sacred writings; seeking for the dead among the living: which also makes the inhibition and repression of it the more important, because from this unwholesome mixture of things human and divine there arises not only a fantastic philosophy but also an heretical religion. Very meet it is therefore that we be sober-minded, and give to faith that only which is faith's. . . .

So much concerning the several classes of Idols, and their equipage: all of which must be renounced and put away with a fixed and solemn determination, and the understanding thoroughly freed and cleansed; the entrance into the kingdom of man, founded on the sciences, being not much other than the entrance into the kingdom of heaven, whereinto none may enter except as a little child.

Politics and the English Language

George Orwell

British writer George Orwell (1903–1950) is most famous for his novels Animal Farm *(1946) and* Nineteen Eighty-Four *(1949), which satirized collectivist political regimes and promoted individual liberty. In the latter he coined the term* groupthink *to describe the process of totalitarian mind control.*

Most people who bother with the matter at all would admit that the English language is in a bad way, but it is generally assumed that we cannot by conscious action do anything about it. Our civilization is decadent and our language—so the argument runs—must inevitably share in the general collapse. It follows that any struggle against the abuse of language is a sentimental archaism, like preferring candles to electric light or hansom cabs to aeroplanes. Underneath this lies the half-conscious belief that language is a natural growth and not an instrument which we shape for our own purposes.

Now, it is clear that the decline of a language must ultimately have political and economic causes: it is not due simply to the bad influence of this or that individual writer. But an effect can become a cause, reinforcing the original cause and producing the same effect in an intensified form, and so on indefinitely. A man may take to drink because he feels himself to be a failure, and then fail all the more completely because he drinks. It is rather the same thing that is happening to the English language. It becomes ugly and inaccurate because our thoughts are foolish, but the slovenliness of our language makes it easier for us to have foolish thoughts. The point is that the process is reversible. Modern English, especially written English, is full of bad habits which spread by imitation and which can be avoided if one is willing to take the necessary trouble. If one gets rid of these habits one can think more clearly, and to think clearly is a necessary first step towards political regeneration: so that the fight against bad English is not frivolous and is not the exclusive concern of professional writers. I will come back to this presently, and I hope that by that time the meaning of what I have said here will have become clearer. Meanwhile, here are five specimens of the English language as it is now habitually written.

These five passages have not been picked out because they are especially bad—I could have quoted far worse if I had chosen—but because they illustrate various of the mental vices from which we now suffer. They are a little below the average, but are fairly representative samples. I number them so that I can refer back to them when necessary:

(1) I am not, indeed, sure whether it is not true to say that the Milton who once seemed not unlike a seventeenth-century Shelley had not become, out of an experience ever more bitter in each year, more alien [*sic*] to the founder of that Jesuit sect which nothing could induce him to tolerate.

Professor Harold Laski
(Essay in *Freedom of Expression*).

(2) Above all, we cannot play ducks and drakes with a native battery of idioms which prescribes such egregious collocations of vocables as the Basic *put up with* for *tolerate* or *put at a loss* for *bewilder.*

Professor Lancelot Hogben
(*Interglossa*).

(3) On the one side we have the free personality: by definition, it is not neurotic, for it has neither conflict nor dream. Its desires, such as they are, are transparent, for they are just what institutional approval keeps in the forefront of consciousness; another institutional pattern would alter their number and intensity; there is little in them that is natural, irreducible, or culturally dangerous. But *on the*

other side, the social bond itself is nothing but the mutual reflection of these self-secure integrities. Recall the definition of love. Is not this the very picture of a small academic? Where is there a place in this hall of mirrors for either personality or fraternity?

Essay on psychology in *Politics* (New York).

(4)   All the "best people" from the gentlemen's clubs, and all the frantic fascist captains, united in common hatred of Socialism and bestial horror of the rising tide of the mass revolutionary movement, have turned to acts of provocation, to foul incendiarism, to medieval legends of poisoned wells, to legalize their own destruction of proletarian organizations, and rouse the agitated petty-bourgeoisie to chauvinistic fervor on behalf of the fight against the revolutionary way out of the crisis.

Communist pamphlet.

(5)   If a new spirit *is* to be infused into this old country, there is one thorny and contentious reform which must be tackled, and that is the humanization and galvanization of the B.B.C. Timidity here will bespeak cancer and atrophy of the soul. The heart of Britain may be sound and of strong beat, for instance, but the British lion's roar at present is like that of Bottom in Shakespeare's *Midsummer Night's Dream*—as gentle as any sucking dove. A virile new Britain cannot continue indefinitely to be traduced in the eyes or rather ears, of the world by the effete languors of Langham Place, brazenly masquerading as "standard English." When the Voice of Britain is heard at nine o'clock, better far and infinitely less ludicrous to hear aitches honestly dropped than the present priggish, inflated, inhibited, school-ma'amish arch braying of blameless bashful mewing maidens!

Letter in *Tribune*.

Each of these passages has faults of its own, but, quite apart from avoidable ugliness, two qualities are common to all of them. The first is staleness of imagery: the other is lack of precision. The writer either has a meaning and cannot express it, or he inadvertently says something else, or he is almost indifferent as to whether his words mean anything or not. The mixture of vagueness and sheer incompetence is the most marked characteristic of modern English prose, and especially of any kind of political writing. As soon as certain topics are raised, the concrete melts into the abstract and no one seems to think of turns of speech that are not hackneyed: prose consists less and less of *words* chosen for the sake of their meaning, and more and more of *phrases* tacked together like the sections of a prefabricated hen-house. I list below, with notes and examples, various of the tricks by means of which the work of prose-construction is habitually dodged:

Dying Metaphors

A newly invented metaphor assists thought by evoking a visual image, while on the other hand a metaphor which is technically "dead" (e.g., *iron resolution*) has in effect reverted to being an ordinary word and can generally be used without loss of vividness. But in between these two classes there is a huge dump of worn-out metaphors which have lost all evocative power and are merely used because they save people the trouble of inventing phrases for themselves. Examples are: *Ring the changes on, take up the cudgels for, toe the line, ride roughshod over, stand shoulder to shoulder with, play into the hands of, no axe to grind, grist to the mill, fishing in troubled waters, on the order of the day, Achilles' heel, swan song, hotbed.* Many of these are used without knowledge of their meaning (what is a "rift," for instance?), and incompatible metaphors are frequently mixed, a sure sign that the writer is not interested in what he is saying. Some metaphors now current have been twisted out of their original meaning without those who use them even being aware of the fact. For example, *toe the line* is sometimes written *tow the line.* Another example is *the hammer and the anvil,* now always used with the implication that the anvil gets the worst of it. In real life it is always the anvil that breaks the hammer, never the other way about: a writer who stopped to think what he was saying would be aware of this, and would avoid perverting the original phrase.

Operators or Verbal False Limbs

These save the trouble of picking out appropriate verbs and nouns, and at the same time pad each sentence with extra syllables which give it an appearance of symmetry. Characteristic phrases are: *render inoperative, militate against, make contact with, be subjected to, give rise to, give grounds for, have the effect of, play a leading part (role) in, make itself felt, take effect, exhibit a tendency to, serve the purpose of, etc., etc.* The keynote is the elimination of simple verbs. Instead of being a single word, such as *break, stop, spoil, mend, kill,* a verb becomes a *phrase,* made up of a noun or adjective tacked on to some general-purpose verb such as *prove, serve, form, play, render.* In addition, the passive voice is wherever possible used in preference to the active, and noun constructions are used instead of gerunds (*by examination of* instead of *by examining*). The range of verbs is further cut down by means of the *-ize* and *de-* formation, and the banal statements are given an appearance of profundity by means of the *not un-* formation. Simple conjunctions and prepositions are replaced by such phrases as *with respect to, having regard to, the fact that, by dint of, in view of, in the interests of, on the hypothesis that;* and the ends of sentences are saved from anticlimax by such resounding commonplaces as *greatly to be desired, cannot be left out of account, a development to be expected in the near future, deserving of serious consideration, brought to a satisfactory conclusion,* and so on and so forth.

Pretentious Diction

Words like *phenomenon, element, individual* (as noun), *objective, categorical, effective, virtual, basic, primary, promote, constitute, exhibit, exploit, utilize, eliminate, liquidate,* are used to dress up simple statements and give an air of scientific impartiality to biased judgments. Adjectives like *epoch-making, epic, historic,*

unforgettable, triumphant, age-old, inevitable, inexorable, veritable, are used to dig-
nify the sordid processes of international politics, while writing that aims at glorifying war usually takes on an archaic color, its characteristic words being: *realm,
throne, chariot, mailed fist, trident, sword, shield, buckler, banner, jackboot, clarion.*
Foreign words and expressions such as *cul de sac, ancien régime, deus ex machina,
mutatis mutandis, status quo, gleichshaltung, weltanschauung,* are used to give an
air of culture and elegance. Except for the useful abbreviations *i.e., e.g.,* and *etc.,*
there is no real need for any of the hundreds of foreign phrases now current in
English. Bad writers, and especially scientific, political and sociological writers,
are nearly always haunted by the notion that Latin or Greek words are grander
than Saxon ones, and unnecessary words like *expedite, ameliorate, predict, extra-
neous, deracinated, clandestine, subaqueous* and hundreds of others constantly gain
ground from their Anglo-Saxon opposite numbers.[1] The jargon peculiar to Marx-
ist writing (*hyena, hangman, cannibal, petty bourgeois, these gentry, lackey, flunkey,
mad dog, White Guard,* etc.) consists largely of words and phrases translated from
Russian, German or French; but the normal way of coining a new word is to use
a Latin or Greek root with the appropriate affix and, where necessary, the *-ize* formation. It is often easier to make up words of this kind (*deregionalize, impermis-
sible, extramarital, nonfragmentatory* and so forth) than to think up the English
words that will cover one's meaning. The result, in general, is an increase in
slovenliness and vagueness.

Meaningless Words

In certain kinds of writing, particularly in art criticism and literary criticism, it is
normal to come across long passages which are almost completely lacking in
meaning.[2] Words like *romantic, plastic, values, human, dead, sentimental, natural,
vitality,* as used in art criticism, are strictly meaningless in the sense that they
not only do not point to any discoverable object, but are hardly ever expected to
do so by the reader. When one critic writes, "The outstanding feature of Mr. X's
work is its living quality," while another writes, "The immediately striking thing
about Mr. X's work is its peculiar deadness," the reader accepts this as a simple
difference of opinion. If words like *black* and *white* were involved, instead of the
jargon words *dead* and *living,* he would see at once that language was being used

[1]An interesting illustration of this is the way in which the English flower names which
were in use till very recently are being ousted by Greek ones, *snapdragon* becoming *antir-
rhinum, forget-me-not* becoming *myosotis,* etc. It is hard to see any practical reason for this
change of fashion: it is probably due to an instinctive turning-away from the more homely word
and a vague feeling that the Greek word is scientific.

[2]Example: "Comfort's catholicity of perception and image, strangely Whitmanesque in
range, almost the exact opposite in aesthetic compulsion, continues to evoke that trembling at-
mospheric accumulative hinting at a cruel, an inexorably serene timelessness. . . . Wrey Gardiner
scores by aiming at simple bull's-eyes with precision. Only they are not so simple, and through
this contented sadness runs more than the surface bitter-sweet of resignation." (*Poetry Quarterly*)

in an improper way. Many political words are similarly abused. The word *Fascism* has now no meaning except in so far as it signifies "something not desirable." The words *democracy, socialism, freedom, patriotic, realistic, justice,* have each of them several different meanings which cannot be reconciled with one another. In the case of a word like *democracy,* not only is there no agreed definition, but the attempt to make one is resisted from all sides. It is almost universally felt that when we call a country democratic we are praising it: consequently the defenders of every kind of regime claim that it is a democracy, and fear that they might have to stop using the word if it were tied down to any one meaning. Words of this kind are often used in a consciously dishonest way. That is, the person who uses them has his own private definition, but allows his hearer to think he means something quite different. Statements like *Marshal Pétain was a true patriot, The Soviet Press is the freest in the world, The Catholic Church is opposed to persecution,* are almost always made with intent to deceive. Other words used in variable meanings, in most cases more or less dishonestly, are: *class, totalitarian, science, progressive, reactionary, bourgeois, equality.*

Now that I have made this catalogue of swindles and perversions, let me give another example of the kind of writing that they lead to. This time it must of its nature be an imaginary one. I am going to translate a passage of good English into modern English of the worst sort. Here is a well-known verse from *Ecclesiastes:*

> I returned and saw under the sun, that the race is not to the swift, nor the battle to the strong, neither yet bread to the wise, nor yet riches to men of understanding, nor yet favor to men of skill; but time and chance happeneth to them all.

Here it is in modern English:

> Objective consideration of contemporary phenomena compels the conclusion that success or failure in competitive activities exhibits no tendency to be commensurate with innate capacity, but that a considerable element of the unpredictable must invariably be taken into account.

This is a parody, but not a very gross one. Exhibit (3), above, for instance, contains several patches of the same kind of English. It will be seen that I have not made a full translation. The beginning and ending of the sentence follow the original meaning fairly closely, but in the middle the concrete illustrations—race, battle, bread—dissolve into the vague phrase "success or failure in competitive activities." This had to be so, because no modern writer of the kind I am discussing—no one capable of using phrases like "objective consideration of contemporary phenomena"—would ever tabulate his thoughts in that precise and detailed way. The whole tendency of modern prose is away from concreteness. Now analyze these two sentences a little more closely. The first contains forty-nine words but only sixty syllables, and all its words are those of everyday life. The second contains thirty-eight words of ninety syllables: eighteen of its words are from Latin roots, and one from Greek. The first sentence contains six vivid images, and only one phrase ("time and chance") that could be called vague. The second contains not a single fresh, arresting phrase, and in spite of its ninety syllables it gives only a shortened version of the meaning contained in the first. Yet without a doubt it is the second kind of sentence that is gaining ground in modern English. I do not want to exaggerate. This kind of writing is not yet universal, and outcrops of simplicity will occur here and there in the worst-written page. Still, if you or I were told to write a few lines on the uncertainty of human fortunes, we should probably come much nearer to my imaginary sentence than to the one from *Ecclesiastes*.

As I have tried to show, modern writing at its worst does not consist in picking out words for the sake of their meaning and inventing images in order to make the meaning clearer. It consists in gumming together long strips of words which have already been set in order by someone else, and making the results presentable by sheer humbug. The attraction of this way of writing is that it is easy. It is easier—even quicker once you have the habit—to say *In my opinion it is a not unjustifiable assumption that* than to say *I think*. If you use ready-made phrases, you not only don't have to hunt about for words; you also don't have to bother with the rhythms of your sentences, since these phrases are generally so arranged as to be more or less euphonious. When you are composing in a hurry—when you are dictating to a stenographer, for instance, or making a public speech—it is natural to fall into a pretentious, Latinized style. Tags like *a consideration which we should do well to bear in mind* or *a conclusion to which all of us would readily assent* will save many a sentence from coming down with a bump. By using stale metaphors, similes and idioms, you save much mental effort, at the cost of leaving your meaning vague, not only for your reader but for yourself. This is the significance of mixed metaphors. The sole aim of a metaphor is to call up a visual image. When these images clash—as in *The Fascist octopus has sung its swan song, the jackboot is thrown into the melting pot*—it can be taken as certain that the writer is not seeing a mental image of the objects he is naming; in other words he is not really thinking. Look again at the examples I gave at the beginning of this essay. Professor Laski (1) uses five negatives in fifty-three words. One of these is superfluous, making nonsense of the whole passage, and in addition there is the slip *alien* for akin, making further nonsense, and several avoidable pieces of clumsiness which increase the general vagueness. Professor Hogben (2) plays ducks and drakes with a battery which is able to write prescriptions, and, while disapproving of the every-day phrase *put up with,* is unwilling to look *egregious* up in the dictionary and see what it means. (3) If one takes an uncharitable attitude towards it, is simply meaningless: probably one could work out its intended meaning by reading the whole of the article in which it occurs. In (4), the writer knows more or less what he wants to say, but an accumulation of stale phrases chokes him like tea leaves blocking a sink. In (5), words and meaning have almost parted company. People who write in this manner usually have a general emotional meaning—they dislike one thing and want to express solidarity with another—but they are not interested in the detail of what they are saying. A scrupulous writer, in every sentence that he writes, will ask himself at least four questions, thus: What am I trying to say? What words will express it? What image or idiom will make it clearer? Is this image fresh enough to have an effect? And he will probably ask himself two more: Could I put it more shortly? Have I said anything that is avoidably ugly? But you are not obliged to go to all this trouble. You can shirk it by simply throwing your mind open and letting the ready-made phrases come crowding in. They will construct your sentences for you—even think your thoughts for you, to a certain extent—and at need they will perform the important service of partially concealing your meaning even from yourself. It is at this point that the special connection between politics and the debasement of language becomes clear.

In our time it is broadly true that political writing is bad writing. Where it is not true, it will generally be found that the writer is some kind of rebel, expressing his private opinions and not a "party line." Orthodoxy, of whatever color, seems to demand a lifeless, imitative style. The political dialects to be found in pamphlets, leading articles, manifestos, White Papers and the speeches of under-secretaries do, of course, vary from party to party, but they are all alike in that one almost never finds in them a fresh, vivid, home-made turn of speech. When one watches some tired hack on the platform mechanically repeating the familiar phrases— *bestial atrocities, iron heel, bloodstained tyranny, free peoples of the world, stand shoulder to shoulder*—one often has a curious feeling that one is not watching a live human being but some kind of dummy; a feeling which suddenly becomes stronger at moments when the light catches the speaker's spectacles and turns them into blank discs which seem to have no eyes behind them. And this is not altogether fanciful. A speaker who uses that kind of phraseology has gone some distance towards turning himself into a machine. The appropriate noises are coming out of his larynx, but his brain is not involved as it would be if he were choosing his words for himself. If the speech he is making is one that he is accustomed to make over and over again, he may be almost unconscious of what he is saying, as one is when one utters the responses in church. And this reduced state of consciousness, if not indispensable, is at any rate favorable to political conformity.

In our time, political speech and writing are largely the defense of the indefensible. Things like the continuance of British rule in India, the Russian purges and deportations, the dropping of the atom bombs on Japan, can indeed be defended, but only by arguments which are too brutal for most people to face, and which do not square with the professed aims of political parties. Thus political language has to consist largely of euphemism, question-begging and sheer cloudy vagueness. Defenseless villages are bombarded from the air, the inhabitants driven out into the countryside, the cattle machine-gunned, the huts set on fire with incendiary bullets: this is called *pacification*. Millions of peasants are robbed of their farms and sent trudging along the roads with no more than they can carry: this is called *transfer of population* or *rectification of frontiers*. People are imprisoned for years without trial, or shot in the back of the neck or sent to die of scurvy in Arctic lumber camps: this is called *elimination of unreliable elements*. Such phraseology is needed if one wants to name things without calling up mental pictures of them. Consider for instance some comfortable English professor defending Russian totalitarianism. He cannot say outright, "I believe in killing off your opponents when you can get good results by doing so." Probably, therefore, he will say something like this:

> While freely conceding that the Soviet regime exhibits certain features which the humanitarian may be inclined to deplore, we must, I think, agree that a certain curtailment of the right to political opposition is an unavoidable concomitant of transitional periods, and that the rigors which the Russian people have been called upon to undergo have been amply justified in the sphere of concrete achievement.

The inflated style is itself a kind of euphemism. A mass of Latin words fall upon the facts like soft snow, blurring the outlines and covering up all the details. The great enemy of clear language is insincerity. When there is a gap between one's real and one's declared aims, one turns as it were instinctively to long words and exhausted idioms, like a cuttlefish squirting out ink. In our age there is no such thing as "keeping out of politics." All issues are political issues, and politics itself is a mass of lies, evasions, folly, hatred and schizophrenia. When the general atmosphere is bad, language must suffer. I should expect to find— this is a guess which I have not sufficient knowledge to verify—that the German, Russian and Italian languages have all deteriorated in the last ten or fifteen years, as a result of dictatorship.

But if thought corrupts language, language can also corrupt thought. A bad usage can spread by tradition and imitation, even among people who should and do know better. The debased language that I have been discussing is in some ways very convenient. Phrases like a *not unjustifiable assumption, leaves much to be desired, would serve no good purpose, a consideration which we should do well to bear in mind,* are a continuous temptation, a packet of aspirins always at one's elbow. Look back through this essay, and for certain you will find that I have again and again committed the very faults I am protesting against. By this morning's post I have received a pamphlet dealing with conditions in Germany. The author tells me that he "felt impelled" to write it. I open it at random, and here is almost the first sentence that I see: "(The Allies) have an opportunity not only of achieving a radical transformation of Germany's social and political structure in such a way as to avoid a nationalistic reaction in Germany itself, but at the same time of laying the foundations of a co-operative and unified Europe." You see, he "feels impelled" to write—feels, presumably, that he has something new to say—and yet his words, like cavalry horses answering the bugle, group themselves automatically into the familiar dreary pattern. This invasion of one's mind by ready-made phrases (*lay the foundations, achieve a radical transformation*) can only be prevented if one is constantly on guard against them, and every such phrase anaesthetizes a portion of one's brain.

I said earlier that the decadence of our language is probably curable. Those who deny this would argue, if they produced an argument at all, that language merely reflects existing social conditions, and that we cannot influence its development by any direct tinkering with words and constructions. So far as the general tone or spirit of a language goes, this may be true, but it is not true in detail. Silly words and expressions have often disappeared, not through any evolutionary process but owing to the conscious action of a minority. Two recent examples were *explore every avenue* and *leave no stone unturned,* which were killed by the jeers of a few journalists. There is a long list of flyblown metaphors which could similarly be got rid of if enough people would interest themselves in the job; and it should also be possible to laugh the *not un-* formation out of existence,[3] to reduce the amount of Latin and Greek in the average sentence, to drive out foreign phrases and strayed scientific words, and, in general, to make pretentiousness unfashionable. But all these are minor points. The defense of the English language implies more than this, and perhaps it is best to start by saying what it does *not* imply.

To begin with it has nothing to do with archaism, with the salvaging of obsolete words and turns of speech, or with the setting up of a "standard English" which must never be departed from. On the contrary, it is especially concerned with the scrapping of every word or idiom which has outworn its usefulness. It has nothing to do with correct grammar and syntax, which are of no importance so long as one makes one's meaning clear, or with the avoidance of Americanisms, or with having what is called a "good prose style." On the other hand it is not concerned with fake simplicity and the attempt to make written English colloquial. Nor does it even imply in every case preferring the Saxon word to the Latin one, though it does imply using the fewest and shortest words that will cover one's meaning. What is above all needed is to let the meaning choose the word, and not the other way about. In prose, the worst thing one can do with words is to surrender to them. When you think of a concrete object, you think wordlessly, and then, if you want to describe the thing you have been visualizing you probably hunt about till you find the exact words that seem to fit. When you think of something abstract you are more inclined to use words from the start, and unless you make a conscious effort to prevent it, the existing dialect will come rushing in and do the job for you, at the expense of blurring or even changing your meaning. Probably it is better to put off using words as long as possible and get one's meaning as clear as one can through pictures or sensations. Afterwards one can choose—not simply *accept*—the phrases that will best cover the meaning, and then switch round and decide what impression one's words are likely to make on another person. This last effort of the mind cuts out all stale or mixed images, all prefabricated phrases, needless repetitions, and humbug and vagueness generally. But one can often be in doubt about the effect of a word or phrase, and one needs rules that one can rely on when instinct fails. I think the following rules will cover most cases:

[3]One can cure oneself of the *not un-* formation by memorizing this sentence. *A not unblack dog was chasing a not unsmall rabbit across a not ungreen field.*

(i)   Never use a metaphor, simile or other figure of speech which you are used to seeing in print.

(ii)   Never use a long word where a short one will do.

(iii)   If it is possible to cut a word out, always cut it out.

(iv)   Never use the passive where you can use the active.

(v)   Never use a foreign phrase, a scientific word or a jargon word if you can think of an everyday English equivalent.

(vi)   Break any of these rules sooner than say anything outright barbarous.

These rules sound elementary and so they are, but they demand a deep change in attitude in anyone who has grown used to writing in the style now fashionable. One could keep all of them and still write bad English, but one could not write the kind of stuff that I quoted in those five specimens at the beginning of this article.

I have not here been considering the literary use of language, but merely language as an instrument for expressing and not for concealing or preventing thought. Stuart Chase and others have come near to claiming that all abstract words are meaningless, and have used this as a pretext for advocating a kind of political quietism. Since you don't know what Fascism is, how can you struggle against Fascism? One need not swallow such absurdities as this, but one ought to recognize that the present political chaos is connected with the decay of language, and that one can probably bring about some improvement by starting at the verbal end. If you simplify your English, you are freed from the worst follies of orthodoxy. You cannot speak any of the necessary dialects, and when you make a stupid remark its stupidity will be obvious, even to yourself. Political language—and with variations this is true of all political parties, from Conservatives to Anarchists—is designed to make lies sound truthful and murder respectable, and to give an appearance of solidity to pure wind. One cannot change this all in a moment, but one can at least change one's own habits, and from time to time one can even, if one jeers loudly enough, send some worn-out and useless phrase—some *jackboot, Achilles' heel, hotbed, melting pot, acid test, veritable inferno* or other lump of verbal refuse—into the dustbin where it belongs.

From Outside, In

Barbara Mellix

Barbara Mellix teaches writing at the University of Pittsburgh. This essay originally appeared in The Georgia Review *in 1987.*

Two years ago, when I started writing this paper, trying to bring order out of chaos, my ten-year-old daughter was suffering from an acute attack of boredom. She drifted in and out of the room complaining that she had nothing to do, no one to "be with" because none of her friends were at home. Patiently I explained that I was working on something special and needed peace and quiet, and I suggested that she paint, read, or work with her computer. None of these interested her. Finally, she pulled up a chair to my desk and watched me, now and then heaving long, loud sighs. After two or three minutes (nine or ten sighs), I lost my patience. "Looka here, Allie," I said, "you too old for this kinda carryin' on. I done told you this is important. You wronger than dirt to be in here haggin' me like this and you know it. Now git on outta here and leave me off before I put my foot all the way down."

I was at home, alone with my family, and my daughter understood that this way of speaking was appropriate in that context. She knew, as a matter of fact, that it was almost inevitable; when I get angry at home, I speak some of my finest, most cherished black English. Had I been speaking to my daughter in this manner in certain other environments, she would have been shocked and probably worried that I had taken leave of my sense of propriety.

Like my children, I grew up speaking what I considered two distinctly different languages—black English and standard English (or as I thought of them then, the ordinary everyday speech of "country" coloreds and "proper" English)—and in the process of acquiring these languages, I developed an understanding of when, where, and how to use them. But unlike my children, I grew up in a world that was primarily black. My friends, neighbors, minister, teachers—almost everybody I associated with every day—were black. And we spoke to one another in our own special language: *That sho is a pretty dress you got on. If she don' soon leave me off I'm gon tell her head a mess. I was so mad I could'a pissed a blue nail. He all the time trying to low-rate somebody. Ain't that just about the nastiest thing you ever set ears on?*

Then there were the "others," the "proper" blacks, transplanted relatives and one-time friends who came home from the city for weddings, funerals, and vacations. And the whites. To these we spoke standard English. "Ain't?" my mother would yell at me when I used the term in the presence of "others." "You *know* better than that." And I would hang my head in shame and say the "proper" word.

I remember one summer sitting in my grandmother's house in Greeleyville, South Carolina, when it was full of the chatter of city relatives who were home on vacation. My parents sat quietly, only now and then volunteering a comment or answering a question. My mother's face took on a strained expression when she spoke. I could see that she was being careful to say just the right words in just the right way. Her voice sounded thick, muffled. And when she finished speaking, she would lapse into silence, her proper smile on her face. My father was more articulate, more aggressive. He spoke quickly, his words sharp and clear. But he held his proud head higher, a signal that he, too, was uncomfortable. My sisters and brothers and I stared at our aunts, uncles, and cousins, speaking only when prompted. Even then, we hesitated, formed our sentences in our minds, then spoke softly, shyly.

My parents looked small and anxious during those occasions, and I waited impatiently for our leave-taking when we would mock our relatives the moment we were out of their hearing. "Reeely," we would say to one another, flexing our wrists and rolling our eyes, "how dooo you stan' this heat? Chile, it just too hy*ooo*mid for words." Our relatives had made us feel "country," and this was our way of regaining pride in ourselves while getting a little revenge in the bargain. The words bubbled in our throats and rolled across our tongues, a balming.

As a child I felt this same doubleness in uptown Greeleyville where the whites lived. "Ain't that a pretty dress you're wearing!" Toby, the town policeman, said to me one day when I was fifteen. "Thank you very much," I replied, my voice barely audible in my own ears. The words felt wrong in my mouth, rigid, foreign. It was not that I had never spoken that phrase before—it was common in black English, too—but I was extremely conscious that this was an occasion for proper English. I had taken out my English and put it on as I did my church clothes, and I felt as if I were wearing my Sunday best in the middle of the week. It did not matter that Toby had not spoken grammatically correct English. He was white and could speak as he wished. I had something to prove. Toby did not.

Speaking standard English to whites was our way of demonstrating that we knew their language and could use it. Speaking it to standard-English-speaking blacks was our way of showing them that we, as well as they, could "put on airs." But when we spoke standard English, we acknowledged (to ourselves and to others—but primarily to ourselves) that our customary way of speaking was inferior. We felt foolish, embarrassed, somehow diminished because we were ashamed to be our real selves. We were reserved, shy in the presence of those who owned and/or spoke *the* language.

My parents never set aside time to drill us in standard English. Their forms of instruction were less formal. When my father was feeling particularly expansive, he would regale us with tales of his exploits in the outside world. In almost flawless English, complete with dialogue and flavored with gestures and embellishment, he told us about his attempt to get a haircut at a white barbershop; his refusal to acknowledge one of the town merchants until the man addressed him as "Mister"; the time he refused to step off the sidewalk uptown to let some whites pass; his airplane trip to New York City (to visit a sick relative) during which the stewardesses and porters—recognizing that he was a "gentleman"—addressed him as "Sir." I did not realize then—nor, I think, did my father—that he was teaching us, among other things, standard English and the relationship between language and power.

My mother's approach was different. Often, when one of us said, "I'm gon wash off my feet," she would say, "And what will you walk on if you wash them off?" Everyone would laugh at the victim of my mother's "proper" mood. But it was different when one of us children was in a proper mood. "You think you are so superior," I said to my oldest sister one day when we were arguing and she was winning. "Superior!" my sister mocked. "You mean I am acting 'biggidy'?" My sisters and brothers sniggered, then joined in teasing me. Finally, my mother said,

"Leave your sister alone. There's nothing wrong with using proper English." There was a half-smile on her face. I had gotten "uppity," had "put on airs" for no good reason. I was at home, alone with the family, and I hadn't been prompted by one of my mother's proper moods. But there was also a proud light in my mother's eyes; her children were learning English very well.

Not until years later, as a college student, did I begin to understand our ambivalence toward English, our scorn of it, our need to master it, to own and be owned by it—an ambivalence that extended to the public-school classroom. In our school, where there were no whites, my teachers taught standard English but used black English to do it. When my grammar-school teachers wanted us to write, for example, they usually said something like, "I want y'all to write five sentences that make a statement. Anybody git done before the rest can color." It was probably almost those exact words that led me to write these sentences in 1953 when I was in the second grade:

> The white clouds are pretty.
> There are only 15 people in our room.
> We will go to gym.
> We have a new poster.
> We may go out doors.

Second grade came after "Little First" and "Big First," so by then I knew the implied rules that accompanied all writing assignments. Writing was an occasion for proper English. I was not to write in the way we spoke to one another: The white clouds pretty; There ain't but 15 people in our room; We going to gym; We got a new poster; We can go out in the yard. Rather I was to use the language of "other": clouds *are,* there *are,* we *will,* we *have,* we *may.*

My sentences were short, rigid, perfunctory like the letters my mother wrote to relatives:

> Dear Papa,
>
> How are you? How is Mattie? Fine I hope. We are fine. We will come to see you Sunday. Cousin Ned will give us a ride.
>
> Love,
> Daughter

The language was not ours. It was something from outside us, something we used for special occasions.

But my coloring on the other side of that second-grade paper is different. I drew three hearts and a sun. The sun has a smiling face that radiates and envelops everything it touches. And although the sun and its world are enclosed in a circle, the colors I used—red, blue, green, purple, orange, yellow, black—indicate that I was less restricted with drawing and coloring than I was with writing standard English. My valentines were not just red. My sun was not just a yellow ball in the sky.

By the time I reached the twelfth grade, speaking and writing standard English had taken on new importance. Each year, about half of the newly graduated seniors of our school moved to large cities—particularly in the North—to live with relatives and find work. Our English teacher constantly corrected our grammar: "Not 'ain't,' but 'isn't.' " We seldom wrote papers, and even those few were usually plot summaries of short stories. When our teacher returned the papers, she usually lectured on the importance of using standard English: "I *am*; you *are*; he, she, or it *is*," she would say, writing on the chalkboard as she spoke. "How you gon git a job talking about 'I is,' or 'I isn't' or 'I ain't'?"

In Pittsburgh, where I moved after graduation, I watched my aunt and uncle—who had always spoken standard English when in Greeleyville—switch from black English to standard English to a mixture of the two, according to where they were or who they were with. At home and with certain close relatives, friends, and neighbors, they spoke black English. With those less close, they spoke a mixture. In public and with strangers, they generally spoke standard English.

In time, I learned to speak standard English with ease and to switch smoothly from black to standard or a mixture, and back again. But no matter where I was, no matter what the situation or occasion, I continued to write as I had in school:

> Dear Mommie,
>
> How are you? How is everybody else? Fine I hope. I am fine. So are Aunt and Uncle. Tell everyone I said hello. I will write again soon.
>
> > Love,
> > Barbara

At work, at a health insurance company, I learned to write letters to customers. I studied form letters and letters written by co-workers, memorizing the phrases and the ways in which they were used. I dictated:

> Thank you for your letter of January 5. We have made the changes in your coverage you requested. Your new premium will be $150 every three months. We are pleased to have been of service to you.

In a sense, I was proud of the letters I wrote for the company: they were proof of my ability to survive in the city, the outside world—an indication of my growing mastery of English. But they also indicate that writing was still mechanical for me, something that didn't require much thought.

Reading also became a more significant part of my life during those early years in Pittsburgh. I had always liked reading, but now I devoted more and more of my spare time to it. I read romances, mysteries, popular novels. Looking back, I realize that the books I liked best were simple, unambiguous: good versus bad and right versus wrong with right rewarded and wrong punished, mysteries unraveled and all set right in the end. It was how I remembered life in Greeleyville.

Of course I was romanticizing. Life in Greeleyville had not been so very uncomplicated. Back there I had been—first as a child, then as a young woman with limited experience in the outside word—living in a relatively closed-in society. But there were implicit and explicit principles that guided our way of life and shaped our relationships with one another and the people outside—principles that a newcomer would find elusive and baffling. In Pittsburgh, I had matured, become more experienced: I had worked at three different jobs, associated with a wider range of people, married, had children. This new environment with different prescripts for living required that I speak standard English much of the time, and slowly, imperceptibly, I had ceased seeing a sharp distinction between myself and "others." Reading romances and mysteries, characterized by dichotomy, was a way of shying away from change, from the person I was becoming.

But that other part of me—that part which took great pride in my ability to hold a job writing business letters—was increasingly drawn to the new developments in my life and the attending possibilities, opportunities for even greater change. If I could write letters for a nationally known business, could I not also do something better, more challenging, more important? Could I not, perhaps, go to college and become a school teacher? For years, afraid and a little embarrassed, I did no more than imagine this different me, this possible me. But sixteen years after coming north, when my younger daughter entered kindergarten, I found myself unable—or unwilling—to resist the lure of possibility. I enrolled in my first college course: Basic Writing, at the University of Pittsburgh.

For the first time in my life, I was required to write extensively about myself. Using the most formal English at my command, I wrote these sentences near the beginning of the term:

> One of my duties as a homemaker is simply picking up after others. A day seldom passes that I don't search for a mislaid toy, book, or gym shoe, etc. I change the Ty-D-Bol, fight "ring around the collar," and keep our laundry smelling "April fresh." Occasionally, I settle arguments between my children and suggest things to do when they're bored. Taking telephone messages for my oldest daughter is my newest (and sometimes most aggravating) chore. Hanging the toilet paper roll is my most insignificant.

My concern was to use "appropriate" language, to sound as if I belonged in a college classroom. But I felt separate from the language—as if it did not and could not belong to me. I couldn't think and feel genuinely in that language, couldn't make it express what I thought and felt about being a housewife. A part of me resented, among other things, being judged by such things as the appearance of my family's laundry and toilet bowl, but in that language I could only imagine and write about a conventional housewife.

For the most part, the remainder of the term was a period of adjustment, a time of trying to find my bearings as a student in a college composition class, to learn to shut out my black English whenever I composed, and to prevent it from creeping into my formulations; a time for trying to grasp the language of the classroom and reproduce it in my prose; for trying to talk about myself in that language, reach others through it. Each experience of writing was like standing naked and revealing my imperfection, my "otherness." And each new assignment was another chance to make myself over in language, reshape myself, make myself "better" in my rapidly changing image of a student in a college composition class.

But writing became increasingly unmanageable as the term progressed, and by the end of the semester, my sentences sounded like this:

> My excitement was soon dampened, however, by what seemed like a small voice in the back of my head saying that I should be careful with my long awaited opportunity. I felt frustrated and this seemed to make it difficult to concentrate.

There is a poverty of language in these sentences. By this point, I knew that the clichéd language of my Housewife essay was unacceptable, and I generally recognized trite expressions. At the same time, I hadn't yet mastered the language of the classroom, hadn't yet come to see it as belonging to me. Most notable is the lifelessness of the prose, the apparent absence of a person behind the words. I wanted those sentences—and the rest of the essay—to convey the anguish of yearning to, at once, become something more and yet remain the same. I had the sensation of being split in two, part of me going into a future the other part didn't believe possible. As that person, the student writer at that moment, I was essentially mute. I could not—in the process of composing—use the language of the old me, yet I couldn't imagine myself in the language of "others."

I found this particularly discouraging because at midsemester I had been writing in a much different way. Note the language of this introduction to an essay I had written then, near the middle of the term:

> Pain is a constant companion to the people in "Footwork." Their jobs are physically damaging. Employers are insensitive to their feelings and in many cases add to their problems. The general public wounds them further by treating them with disgrace because of what they do for a living. Although the workers are as diverse as they are similar, there is a definite link between them. They suffer a great deal of abuse.

The voice here is stronger, more confident, appropriating terms like "physically damaging," "wounds them further," "insensitive," "diverse"—terms I couldn't have imagined using when writing about my own experience—and shaping them into sentences like "Although the workers are as diverse as they are similar, there is a definite link between them." And there is the sense of a personality behind the prose, someone who sympathizes with the workers. "The general public wounds them further by treating them with disgrace because of what they do for a living."

What caused these differences? I was, I believed, explaining other people's thoughts and feelings, and I was free to move about in the language of "others" so long as I was speaking *of* others. I was unaware that I was transforming into my best classroom language my own thoughts and feelings about people whose experiences and ways of speaking were in many ways similar to mine.

The following year, unable to turn back or to let go of what had become something of an obsession with language (and hoping to catch and hold the sense of control that had eluded me in Basic Writing), I enrolled in a research writing course. I spent most of the term learning how to prepare for and write a research paper. I chose sex education as my subject and spent hours in libraries, searching for information, reading, taking notes. Then (not without messiness and often-demoralizing frustration) I organized my information into categories, wrote a thesis statement, and composed my paper—a series of paraphrases and quotations spaced between carefully constructed transitions. The process and results felt artificial, but as I would later come to realize I was passing through a necessary stage. My sentences sounded like this:

> This reserve becomes understandable with examination of who the abusers are. In an overwhelming number of cases, they are people the victims know and trust. Family members, relatives, neighbors and close family friends commit seventy-five percent of all reported sex crimes against children, and parents, parent substitutes and relatives are the offenders in thirty to eighty percent of all reported cases.[12] While assault by strangers does occur, it is less common, and is usually a single episode.[13] But abuse by family members, relatives and acquaintances may continue for an extended period of time. In cases of incest, for example, children are abused repeatedly for an average of eight years.[14] In such cases, "the use of physical force is rarely necessary because of the child's trusting, dependent relationship with the offender. The child's cooperation is often facilitated by the adult's position of dominance, an offer of material goods, a threat of physical violence, or a misrepresentation of moral standards."

The completed paper gave me a sense of profound satisfaction, and I read it often after my professor returned it. I know now that what I was pleased with was the language I used and the professional voice it helped me maintain. "Use better words," my teacher had snapped at me one day after reading the notes I'd begun accumulating from my research, and slowly I began taking on the language of my sources. In my next set of notes, I used the word "vacillating"; my professor applauded. And by the time I composed the final draft, I felt at ease with terms like "overwhelming number of cases," "single episode," and "reserve," and I shaped them into sentences similar to those of my "expert" sources.

If I were writing the paper today, I would of course do some things differently. Rather than open with an anecdote—as my teacher suggested—I would begin simply with a quotation that caught my interest as I was researching my paper (and which I scribbled, without its source, in the margin of my notebook): "Truth does not do so much good in the world as the semblance of truth does evil." The quotation felt right because it captured what was for me the central idea of my essay—an idea that emerged gradually during the making of my paper—and expressed it in a way I would like to have said it. The anecdote, a hypothetical situation I invented to conform to the information in the paper, felt forced and insincere because it represented—to a great degree—my teacher's understanding of the essay, *her* idea of what in it was most significant. Improving upon my previous experiences with writing, I was beginning to think and feel in the language I used, to find my own voices in it, to sense that how one speaks influences how one means. But I was not yet secure enough, comfortable enough with the language to trust my intuition.

Now that I know that to seek knowledge, freedom, and autonomy means always to be in the concentrated process of becoming—always to be venturing into new territory, feeling one's way at first, then getting one's balance, negotiating, accommodating, discovering one's self in ways that previously defined "others"—I sometimes get tired. And I ask myself why I keep on participating in this highbrow form of violence, this slamming against perplexity. But there is no real futility in the question, no hint of that part of the old me who stood outside standard English, hugging to herself a disabling mistrust of a language she thought could not represent a person with her history and experience. Rather, the question represents a person who feels the consequence of her education, the weight of her possibilities as a teacher and writer and human being, a voice in society. And I would not change that person, would not give back the good burden that accompanies my growing expertise, my increasing power to shape myself in language and share that self with "others."

"To speak," says Frantz Fanon, "means to be in a position to use a certain syntax, to grasp the morphology of this or that language, but it means above all to assume a culture, to support the weight of a civilization."[1] To write means to do the same, but in a more profound sense. However, Fanon also says that to achieve mastery means to "get" in a position of power, to "grasp," to "assume." This, I have learned both as a student and subsequently as a teacher—can involve tremendous emotional and psychological conflict for those attempting to master academic discourse. Although as a beginning student writer I had a fairly good grasp of ordinary spoken English and was proficient at what Labov calls "code-switching" (and what John Baugh in *Black Street Speech* terms "style shifting"), when I came face to face with the demands of academic writing, I grew increasingly self-conscious, constantly aware of my status as a black and a speaker of one of the many black English vernaculars—a traditional outsider. For the first time, I experienced my sense of doubleness as something menacing, a built-in enemy. Whenever I turned inward for salvation, the balm so available during my childhood, I found instead this new fragmentation which spoke to me in many voices. It was the voice of my desire to prosper, but at the same time it spoke of what I had relinquished and could not regain: a safe way of being, a state of powerlessness which exempted me from responsibility for who I was and might be. And it accused me of betrayal, of turning away from blackness. To recover balance, I had to take on the language of the academy, the language of "others." And to do that, I had to learn to imagine myself a part of the culture of that language, and therefore someone free to manage that language, to take

[1]*Black Skin, White Masks* (1952; rpt. New York: Grove Press, 1967), pp. 17–18.

liberties with it. Writing and rewriting, practicing, experimenting, I came to comprehend more fully the generative power of language. I discovered—with the help of some especially sensitive teachers—that through writing one can continually bring new selves into being, each with new responsibilities and difficulties, but also with new possibilities. Remarkable power, indeed. I write and continually give birth to myself.

FORUM ON EBONICS

The following three essays, by Courtland Milloy, Patricia J. Williams, and Carolyn Temple Adger, were written in response to the public controversy created when in 1996 the Oakland California Unified School District issued a policy statement on language development that referred to Ebonics as "the language structures unique to African American students." The text of the policy is found in Chapter 2 on page 15, along with a newspaper article about the controversy found on page 14. To pursue this controversy further, you might want to consult an archive of print and Internet resources on the issue of Ebonics at the Center for Applied Linguistics Web site at www.cal.org/Ebonics.

Accent on Human Potential

Courtland Milloy

Courtland Milloy is a Metro columnist for the Washington Post.

How did we let Oakland beat us to the educational punch?

Here we are in Washington, the nation's capital, so-called world-class city, tied up in race knots over the operation of a single Afrocentric charter school. We are still trying to get school toilets fixed, rotary telephones replaced and leaky roofs repaired.

Meanwhile, our West Coast sister, better known as the home town of Black Panther Party co-founder Huey P. Newton, is talking "Ebonics."

The Oakland Unified School District in California voted last week to recognize that many of today's descendants of African slaves speak a distinct dialect that makes them eligible for bilingual education.

Ebonics, coined in 1973 by a black professor of psychology at Washington University, in St. Louis, is formed by combining the words ebony and phonics.

You laugh. Look at the phonetic characters in this phrase:

\J^uwic^oj^Elo

Notice that a vowel follows each consonant. Studies of West African languages, especially the Kwa group, from which many African Americans originate, reveal a similar pattern, an absence of consonant clusters.

"Did you eat your jello?" That's what the phonetic phrase says. Sort of like, "Jueatyojello?" I know people who talk like that. I talk like that. But I also happen to speak and write another language, too, called English.

Unfortunately, a lot of black people do not. They still talk in a way that linguists have found to be deeply rooted in the noun-classed languages of West Africa, which discounts, among other things, use of the conjugated verb "to be."

I be darn, they might say.

Oakland is saying to its black children that the way they talk does not make them stupid or inferior. After all of these years, the school system is preparing to give black children what their forefathers had been denied because of their slave status—the same help given to other immigrants in learning to use English to make better lives for themselves.

"If I was Hispanic and spoke no English, you would communicate with me in Spanish and help me make the transition to English," said Robert Williams, professor emeritus at Washington University, who invented the word *Ebonics*. "Why not use the same model to teach African American children to use the language system?"

I wish someone would talk to Julius W. Becton Jr. about implementing a similar program here. Becton is the new chief executive of D.C. schools. But he's too busy right now trying to figure out how many people on the school payroll are alive and how many are dead. Who knows how long it will take him to get around to what's happening in the classrooms?

That's where the action is.

In Oakland, they've had it with the miseducation of black children. They are tired of blacks being overrepresented in programs for students identified as "academically deficient." For instance, 71 percent of Oakland's 28,000 blacks are in special education classes, and 64 percent are kept back a grade because of poor achievement. Their average grade point, on a 4.0 system, is 1.8.

Does that sound familiar? It is happening wherever poor black people remain concentrated in these urban American bantustands.

The consequences have been a mind-boggling waste of human potential. Such loss and pain, spanning generations, inevitably radicalizes a people and creates revolutionaries like Mary A.T. Anigbo. She heard the cries and felt the pain. And she was moved to start the Marcus Garvey Public Charter School for the education of black boys in Washington.

After granting her a charter, the D.C. Board of Education was no help, ignoring what Anigbo was doing as if to wash its own hands of the failures that gave rise to the need for such a school in the first place. Our city simply cannot continue this cycle: creating radicals by ignoring the cries of the children and then indicting them for being radical.

We must change the system, and I don't mean just replacing a colonial home-rule government with a control board-run dictatorship. I mean establishing a super-literate democracy that cares for the least fortunate among us.

In Oakland, an elected school board heard the cries of its children. Contrary to some reports, Oakland does not intend to teach Ebonics. The children already know it. The idea is to help teachers better understand those students who are so easily written off as "uneducable" or "mentally retarded" simply because they do not score well on standardized language tests.

"What teachers need to know is that the language of these children adheres closely to the rules of grammar in the Niger-Congo region of Africa," said Ernie Smith, a former professor of linguistics who teaches medicine at Drew University. "We're talking about English words being laid on top of an African grammar structure. Similar things have happened to the language throughout the African diaspora, when French or Spanish words are imposed. The problem is that nobody has bothered to study the body of literature on African languages in the context of how African Americans speak."

I hope an understanding of Ebonics will put an end to criticism of blacks as having "lazy tongues," for starters, because of the way we pronounce some words ending with *d*s or *t*s. African rules of grammar governing the pronunciation of words ending in consonants have simply survived—largely because of the refusal of America to fully integrate her people.

So be it.

It is possible to teach English to all black children, without degrading them, in the spirit of Kujichaguila. That's Swahili for one of the seven principles of Kwanza. It means self-determination, but they already know that in Oakland.

The Hidden Meanings of "Black English"

Patricia J. Williams

Patricia J. Williams is a legal scholar and writer about race relations.

The melting pot is boiling over again, this time with a decision by the school board in Oakland, Calif., to reclassify "ebonics," or black vernacular, as a distinct language. The battle is a familiar one that has raged at least since the 1960's. The issues it raises are too often polarized in a simplistic debate about whether black American speech is "good" West African traditionalism or just "bad" English.

There are more complex questions to consider. Can the notion of a singular black vernacular (if that is what ebonics purports to be) account for the enormous variations in black, American speech, which range from true dialects, like Gullah, to a panoply of distinctly regional accents? Is so-called Received Standard American English what most Americans speak anyway? And, as a prickly Oxford-educated acquaintance of mine wonders, when could any part of the American vernacular be called English?

The consensus in the media seems to be that, since black vernacular is indeed not a language in the strict linguistic sense, the Oakland board is just wrong. That leads to more wrangling about whether the board is full of Afrocentric neo-nationalists or whether it's just another example of Teachers Refusing to Teach.

It is true that most black speech is clearly comprehensible as a variant of American English, albeit with grammatical and syntax patterns that are strongly influenced by West African language structures. The contorted battles over rap lyrics as political speech—however densely vernacular the language is—have not been about the failure of the larger society to understand the words as English.

At the same time, part of the battle over ebonics is premised on the assertion that black vernacular cannot be understood: that its continued use accounts for the high numbers of blacks in remedial education, and high black unemployment rates. So maybe the Oakland school board was right.

If it's Greek to nonspeakers, then go ahead and treat it like Greek. And if funds are available for bilingual education to help recent immigrants assimilate into the mainstream, then maybe this isn't strictly about linguistic history, but more about an investment in the future. So by all means hitch the aspirations of the Middle Passage right onto the forward-lurching wagons of the progressive immigrant myth.

Perhaps the real argument is not about whether ebonics is a language or not. Rather, the tension is revealed in the contradiction of black speech being simultaneously understood yet not understood. Why is it so overwhelmingly, even colorfully comprehensible in some contexts, particularly in sports and entertainment, yet deemed so utterly incapable of effective communication when it comes to finding a job as a construction worker?

Causing further confusion in this debate is the apparent treatment of illiteracy as if it were black speech. Black children are crowded into remedial education classes and are disadvantaged in finding jobs because too many of them have never been taught *any* variation of the printed word, whether phonics, ebonics or Esperanto. Some young children learn more of the alphabet on "Sesame Street" than they can in overtaxed and overcrowded inner city schools.

Moreover, the very conflation of illiteracy and the reasoned, rich and expressive complexity of most forms of black speech is based on a peculiarly freighted symbolism in the American lexicon. While accent prompts many levels of discrimination in the United States, there is no greater talisman of lower or underclass status, than *the* black accent (or any, really), no greater license to mock than with some imitation of black speech. Whether in The Dartmouth Review or "The Lion King," black English is the perpetual symbolic code for ignorance, evil and jest, the lingo of hep cats and hyenas.

Even solidly middle-class blacks with strings of higher degrees and perfect command of standard grammatical structure can face discrimination if their accents are deemed in any way identifiably "black."

Is it really any wonder that there is such an ambivalent response to mainstream standardized speech patterns among black children when the "standard" is so often imparted with such missionary conviction about eliminating "bad" linguistic acts? It's as if the very spontaneity of their speaking were an extension of the general lawlessness of black existence.

Is there not a way to teach the rules of what is called Received Standard American English without such generous side dishes of humiliation?

Would the recognition that there really are rules and structures in black English help us get past those smug assertions of nobler, higher linguistic conventions? Can we resist the evocative echo of Henry James's fear of random, chaotic utterances spewed from the dark recesses of the vulgate (read Irish) mouth? Can we resist the nostalgia for an unalloyed classicism that never was?

I understand the effort of the Oakland school board to legitimize ebonics as one of translation, which is a generally respected enterprise, rather than cultural uplift, which is inherently condescending. That said, one thing that troubles me about the Oakland proposal is the reported plan to teach the city's teachers not only the structure and history of ebonics but also how to speak it.

It's hard enough to sort out the values embedded in the aversion to black speech as a "bad" version of what is rather too exclusively called "white" English. Imagine having teachers who speak standard classroom English flailing about in some really bad version of a standardized black English. If they end up speaking ebonics as badly as teachers who learn a little "professional Spanish," I cringe to think of the consequences: pidgin versions of Talking to Tonto. Ugh. And I do mean ugh in the most classical sense.

There are enough standard-English speakers who just love to "talk black," who at the drop of a hat break out in "basketball"—now there's an official language— and who, encountering any black person, start "dude"-ing and "I be"-ing up a storm, high- and low-fiving to beat the band. This phenomenon is part minstrelry, part presumptuousness and, most complicated of all, part of the mainstream's assimilation of black speech patterns that, once incorporated, are promptly forgotten as such.

I worry a bit that this natural and overlapping fluidity of American vernacular and its regionalisms will be rendered all the more invisible by falsely turning teachers into linguistic anthropologists, adventurers in the "foreign" terrain of alien verbiage.

Finally, a great concern about the Oakland school board's action has been the rather transparent strategy of categorizing ebonics as a distinct language in order to gain access to extra financing for the education of bilingual students. It's a strategy lawyers know well: Consider, as law students must, the question of whether a lame horse dipped in tar and beaten with pillows qualifies as a bird—technically defined as a two-legged creature with feathers. Ah, literalism.

So it's predictable that at a time of badly dwindling resources, if there is a pot of money earmarked for teaching in any way that substantively communicates with students—well, call it communication, call it language, call it a rose if need be. Just go for it.

Cynical, some say; to others, it's a creative manifestation of the instinct for survival. I think the whole thing is sad. While the Oakland proposal is quite understandably the practical result of a bureaucracy trying to maneuver the limits and roadblocks of category imperfections in a categorically imperfect world, maybe part of what we are sidestepping in the fight about standardized speech practices is the ongoing abandonment of public schools, a de facto flight begun with the resistance to the promise of Brown v. Board of Education.

After all, if this controversy boils down to the old familiar ingredients of struggle for respect, resources, opportunity and jobs, then we are really faced with just one more clarion call for commitment to public education as standard. This in turn, depends on a more generous evaluation of the standards by which we judge each other's humanity.

Dialect Education
Not Only for Oakland

Carolyn Temple Adger

Carolyn Temple Adger is a research scholar with the Center for Applied Linguistics.

When has any language issue gotten such public attention as the Oakland (CA) school district's new policy on teaching standard English to Ebonics speakers? Perhaps one reason that the discussion has been so pervasive and so passionate is that people misunderstand the basic sociolinguistic issues that the school district is addressing. Underinformed about what dialects are, how they relate to each other, and what functions they fulfill, people have voiced views about language in society that cannot be scientifically justified. Ebonics, or African American Vernacular English (AAVE), has been erroneously called "slang," "broken English," "poor grammar," or "improper usage," instead of the full-fledged dialect that it is. This is not just another harmless case of the lay audience having less technical information than the scientist. It is a matter of perpetuating the myth that there is one correct English. When this myth goes unchallenged, it is difficult for schools to treat students' competence in a vernacular dialect as relevant to developing additional uses and varieties of language. It is even more difficult for schools to present language as an intriguing system for scientific investigation. Without those two ingredients, however, dialect instruction is unlikely to succeed any better than it has in the past.

The Myth

The "correct English myth" holds that there is one real English, standard English, and that deviations from it are impoverished and unworthy. Sometimes standard English is located geographically in the Midwestern United States. In point of fact, casual observation confirms research showing that standard English is not the same everywhere. Even within the United States, standard English in the Northeast is different in some respects from standard English in the Southwest. All linguistic systems—phonology, syntax, lexicon, pragmatics—show regional variation. What is standard English in Oakland contrasts with standard English in Tampa or in Detroit.

Certainly standard written English is not as variable as standard spoken English. The distinction between written and spoken English seems to have been overlooked in the Ebonics debate, perhaps because the correct English myth holds written standard English as the criterion against which speech may be judged. Actually, written standard English contrasts both with oral standard English used for informal purposes and with AAVE.

Not only is standard English not standard in the sense of being invariant from place to place, situation to situation, and oral medium to written medium; it also is not standard in the sense of representing an ideal against which to judge other dialects. Sociolinguistic studies show that all dialects have linguistic integrity. None is more regular than another. The features of AAVE that contrast with standard English varieties are patterned and predictable, not random deviations. In other words, AAVE is just as standardized as standard English—though it is not subject to prescription as is standard English.

What makes standard English standard is a matter of social attitudes and the political power of those who speak the standard dialect. People believe that standard English equals "good grammar," and this belief is knitted into our institutions. Because standard English speakers control education, commerce, government, and other powerful institutions, the standard dialect is firmly associated with public life.

This perception of standard English as the language of public life is taken as a rationale for enhancing students' standard English proficiency: Everyone needs it for access to educational and job opportunities. Here again, however, beliefs outweigh empirical knowledge. We know surprisingly few details concerning the actual occurrence of standard and vernacular dialects in public life, including school, and the costs and benefits associated with dialect choice (Adger, in press). This may help to explain why standard English instruction has not been more successful in the past. Students may in fact see numbers of vernacular dialect users who are quite successful in life. Vernacular dialect may actually be considered appropriate in some academic situations (Foster, 1995). If what educators tell students about appropriate conditions for dialects does not match what students observe, dialect education becomes esoteric and irrelevant. Standard English is associated in a general way with education and the middle class. However, learning it as a second dialect carries no guarantee of social mobility, and certain social risks may be involved in using it (Fordham, 1996). Taking on the linguistic trappings of another group, particularly a group that has been perceived as oppressive, can present a real social identity dilemma.

Dialect Education

In the face of accumulating information about social and geographic variation in spoken American English, the correct English myth still dominates many textbooks and classrooms. A more scientific and socially useful approach to language education would include detailed dialect study in the curriculum. However, one of the aspects of Oakland's position on Ebonics that seems so hard for many people to accept is the notion that attention to vernacular dialect has any place in schools, let alone that students' proficiency in it offers a valuable language learning resource. (Certainly the school board's view of the role that Ebonics should play in schools has not been clear.) Seen repeatedly in the media is the belief that AAVE is without value, that it should be remediated, and that vernacular features should be corrected even at home. But this is the traditional approach that has had such limited success. One study found that when teachers corrected students' dialect, students actually increased their production of vernacular features (Piestrup, 1973).

What is needed is research into effective ways of teaching standard English. Because vernacular and standard dialects of English share almost all of their linguistic resources, standard dialect instruction should pinpoint exactly where vernacular and standard structures differ. For example, standard *had gone* ("Teachers had gone into classrooms") contrasts with vernacular *had went* ("Teachers had went into classrooms") according to a pattern that regularizes the past participle; and standard *mine* ("I've got mine today") is vernacular *mines* ("I've got mines today"). Rather than subjecting vernacular speakers to the traditional mind-numbing and inefficient translation drills, teachers might situate mini-lessons according to the dialect learning needs that students demonstrate. If class members agree that standard English is appropriate for classroom interaction and for writing, these lessons could help students progress toward their language development goals. Dialect contrasts that become relevant in students' talk and writing could be posted on a bulletin board (Delpit, 1990), noted in dialogue journals, and entered into a class log or student portfolios as part of a class standard English learning project. This approach seems useful not only for English language arts classes beginning in upper elementary school and extending into college, but in other classes where students and teacher agree that standard English learning is a goal.

Here, students' implicit linguistic knowledge becomes the basis for increasing competence in the standard dialect. Even in the unlikely case that no class member could identify the contrasting standard equivalent for a vernacular structure, students would recognize that they are dealing with an alternative for what they already do linguistically. They would also learn a great deal about how language works. Students can be guided to see that dialects of English are arrayed along a continuum from the most standard to the most vernacular, and that all speakers continually shift within a range along that continuum as they align to shifting social situations.

Because dialect prejudice is rampant and widely accepted, efforts to teach another dialect need to be grounded in scientific consideration of sociolinguistic facts. Students need to look at some of the evidence that all dialects are regular so that they can begin to question the inaccurate characterizations of dialects that they have been exposed to. They also need to examine dialect appropriateness in social settings as demonstrated by language use, in order to be convinced that bidialectalism is valuable. Informal experiments with dialect awareness curricula developed by Walt Wolfram and his colleagues have shown that upper elementary and middle school students find the study of sociolinguistic phenomena fascinating (Wolfram, Schilling-Estes, & Hazen, 1996). Students are introduced to dialect attitudes through the video, *American Tongues* (Alvarez & Kolker, 1987). The students then analyze contrasting data sets of phonological features, such as "r-drop" ("car" vs. "cah") in some New England dialects, to discover how the pattern works—where the final "r" sound can be dropped and where it cannot. They work through data sets to discover the pattern for "a-prefixing" in some rural dialects ("He's a-going over to Mike's this afternoon") and the rule for "habitual be" in AAVE. Informal evaluation indicates that students come to recognize that dialect contrasts occur regularly, rather than haphazardly, and they become aware that dialect prejudice is not justifiable.

Conclusion

Dialect awareness is not just for vernacular dialect speakers learning standard English as an additional dialect. All students need language education that includes the facts about language variation if they are to engage sensibly in discussions about dialect differences such as that occasioned by events in Oakland, and to get along in a dialectally diverse world (Wolfram, 1990). The challenge is to develop curricula and materials for students and teachers and to shape educational policy that includes substantial dialect study in language education.

References

Adger, C. T. (in press). Register shifting with dialect resources in instructional discourse. In S. Hoyle & C. T. Adger (Eds.), *Language practices of older children*. New York: Oxford University Press.

Alvarez, L., & Kolker, A. (1987). *American tongues* [Video]. New York: Center for New American Media.

Delpit, L. (1990). Language diversity and learning. In S. Hynds & D. Rubin (Eds.), *Perspectives on talk and learning* (pp. 247–266). Urbana, IL: NCTE.

Fordham, S. (1996). *Blacked out: Dilemmas of race, identity, and success at Capital High.* Chicago: University of Chicago Press.

Foster, M. (1995). Talking that talk: The language of control, curriculum, and critique. *Linguistics and Education, 7* (2), 129–151.

Piestrup, A. M. (1973). Black dialect interference and accommodation of reading instruction in first grade (Monograph No. 4). Berkeley: University of California, Language and Behavior Research Lab.

Wolfram, W. (1990). Incorporating dialect study into the language arts class. *ERIC Digest.* Washington, DC: ERIC Clearinghouse on Languages and Linguistics.

Wolfram, W., Schilling-Estes, N., & Hazen, K. (1996). Dialects and the Ocracoke brogue. Eighth grade curriculum. Raleigh, NC: North Carolina Language and Life Project.

Resources

Wolfram, W., Christian, D., & Adger, C. (in press). *Dialects in schools and communities.* Mahwah, NJ: Erlbaum.

How to Tame a Wild Tongue

Gloria Anzaldúa

Gloria Anzaldúa is a prominent Chicana writer and cultural theorist. She has received an NEA Fiction Award and the 1991 Lesbian Rights Award. The following is excerpted from her book, Borderlands/La Frontera: The New Mestiza, *published in 1987.*

"We're going to have to control your tongue," the dentist says, pulling out all the metal from my mouth. Silver bits plop and tinkle into the basin. My mouth is a motherlode.

The dentist is cleaning out my roots. I get a whiff of the stench when I gasp. "I can't cap that tooth yet, you're still draining," he says.

"We're going to have to do something about your tongue," I hear the anger rising in his voice. My tongue keeps pushing out the wads of cotton, pushing back the drills, the long thin needles. "I've never seen anything as strong or as stubborn," he says. And I think, how do you tame a wild tongue, train it to be quiet, how do you bridle and saddle it? How do you make it lie down?

Who is to say that robbing a people of its language is less violent than war?

Ray Gwyn Smith[1]

---

[1] Ray Gwyn Smith, *Moorland Is Cold Country,* unpublished book.

I remember being caught speaking Spanish at recess—that was good for three licks on the knuckles with a sharp ruler. I remember being sent to the corner of the classroom for "talking back" to the Anglo teacher when all I was trying to do was tell her how to pronounce my name. "If you want to be American, speak 'American.' If you don't like it, go back to Mexico where you belong."

"I want you to speak English. *Pa' hallar buen trabajo tienes que saber hablar el inglés bien. Qué vale toda tu educación si todavía hablas inglés* con un 'accent,' " my mother would say, mortified that I spoke English like a Mexican. At Pan American University, I, and all Chicano students were required to take two speech classes. Their purpose: to get rid of our accents.

Attacks on one's form of expression with the intent to censor are a violation of the First Amendment. *El Anglo con cara de inocente nos arrancó la lengua.* Wild tongues can't be tamed, they can only be cut out.

Overcoming the Tradition of Silence

Ahogadas, escupimos el oscuro.
Peleando con nuestra propia sombra
el silencio nos sepulta.

En boca cerrada no entran moscas. "Flies don't enter a closed mouth" is a saying I kept hearing when I was a child. *Ser habladora* was to be a gossip and a liar, to talk too much. *Muchachitas bien criadas,* well-bred girls don't answer back. *Es una falta de respeto* to talk back to one's mother or father. I remember one of the sins I'd recite to the priest in the confession box the few times I went to confession: talking back to my mother, *hablar pa' 'tras, repelar. Hocicona, repelona, chismosa,* having a big mouth, questioning, carrying tales are all signs of being *mal criada.* In my culture they are all words that are derogatory if applied to women—I've never heard them applied to men.

The first time I heard two women, a Puerto Rican and a Cuban, say the word "*nosotras,*" I was shocked. I had not known the word existed. Chicanas use *nosotros* whether we're male or female. We are robbed of our female being by the masculine plural. Language is a male discourse.

And our tongues have become
dry   the wilderness has
dried out our tongues   and
we have forgotten speech.

Irena Klepfisz[2]

Even our own people, other Spanish speakers *nos quieren poner candados en la boca.* They would hold us back with their bag of *reglas de academia.*

---

[2]Irena Klepfisz, "*Di rayze aheym/*The Journey Home," in *The Tribe of Dina: A Jewish Women's Anthology,* eds. Melanie Kaye/Kantrowitz, and Irena Klepfisz (Montpelier, VT: Sinister Wisdom Books, 1986), p. 49.

Oyé como ladra: el lenguaje de la frontera

Quien tiene boca se equivoca.

Mexican saying

"*Pocho*, cultural traitor, you're speaking the oppressor's language by speaking English, you're ruining the Spanish language," I have been accused by various Latinos and Latinas. Chicano Spanish is considered by the purist and by most Latinos deficient, a mutilation of Spanish.

But Chicano Spanish is a border tongue which developed naturally. Change, *evolución, enriquecimiento de palabras nuevas por invención o adopción* have created variants of Chicano Spanish, *un nuevo lenguaje. Un lenguaje que corresponde a un modo de vivir.* Chicano Spanish is not incorrect, it is a living language.

For a people who are neither Spanish nor live in a country in which Spanish is the first language; for a people who live in a country in which English is the reigning tongue but who are not Anglo; for a people who cannot entirely identify with either standard (formal, Castillian) Spanish nor standard English, what recourse is left to them but to create their own language? A language which they can connect their identity to, one capable of communicating the realities and values true to themselves—a language with terms that are neither *español ni inglés,* but both. We speak a patois, a forked tongue, a variation of two languages.

Chicano Spanish sprang out of the Chicanos' need to identify ourselves as a distinct people. We needed a language with which we could communicate with ourselves, a secret language. For some of us, language is a homeland closer than the Southwest—for many Chicanos today live in the Midwest and the East. And because we are a complex, heterogeneous people, we speak many languages. Some of the languages we speak are:

1. Standard English
2. Working class and slang English
3. Standard Spanish
4. Standard Mexican Spanish
5. North Mexican Spanish dialect
6. Chicano Spanish (Texas, New Mexico, Arizona and California have regional variations)
7. Tex-Mex
8. *Pachuco* (called caló)

My "home" tongues are the languages I speak with my sister and brothers, with my friends. They are the last five listed, with 6 and 7 being closest to my heart. From school, the media and job situations, I've picked up standard and working class English. From Mamagrande Locha and from reading Spanish and Mexican literature, I've picked up Standard Spanish and Standard Mexican Spanish. From *los recién llegados,* Mexican immigrants, and *braceros,* I learned the North Mexican dialect. With Mexicans I'll try to speak either Standard Mexican Spanish or the North Mexican dialect. From my parents and Chicanos living in the Valley, I picked up Chicano Texas Spanish, and I speak it with my mom, younger brother (who married a Mexican and who rarely mixes Spanish with English), aunts and older relatives.

With Chicanas from *Nuevo México* or *Arizona* I will speak Chicano Spanish a little, but often they don't understand what I'm saying. With most California Chicanas I speak entirely in English (unless I forget). When I first moved to San Francisco, I'd rattle off something in Spanish, unintentionally embarrassing them. Often it is only with another Chicana *tejana* that I can talk freely.

Words distorted by English are known as anglicisms or *pochismos.* The *pocho* is an anglicized Mexican or American of Mexican origin who speaks Spanish with an accent characteristic of North Americans and who distorts and reconstructs the language according to the influence of English.[3] Tex-Mex, or Spanglish, comes most naturally to me. I may switch back and forth from English to Spanish in the same sentence or in the same word. With my sister and my brother Nune and with Chicano *tejano* contemporaries I speak Tex-Mex.

From kids and people my own age I picked up *Pachuco.* Pachuco (the language of the zoot suiters) is a language of rebellion, both against Standard Spanish and Standard English. It is a secret language. Adults of the culture and outsiders cannot understand it. It is made up of slang words from both English and Spanish. *Ruca* means girl or woman, *vato* means guy or dude, *chale* means no, *simón* means yes, *churro* is sure, talk is *periquiar, pigionear* means petting, *que gacho* means how nerdy, *ponte águila* means watch out, death is called *la pelona.* Through lack of practice and not having others who can speak it, I've lost most of the *Pachuco* tongue.

Chicanos, after 250 years of Spanish/Anglo colonization, have developed significant differences in the Spanish we speak. We collapse two adjacent vowels into a single syllable and sometimes shift the stress in certain words such as *maíz/maiz, cohete/cuete.* We leave out certain consonants when they appear between vowels: *lado/lao, mojado/mojao.* Chicanos from South Texas pronounce *f* as *j* as in *jue (fue).* Chicanos use "archaisms," words that are no longer in the Spanish language, words that have been evolved out. We say *semos, truje, haiga, ansina,* and *naiden.* We retain the "archaic" *j,* as in *jalar,* that derives from an earlier *h* (the French *halar* or the Germanic *halon* which was lost to standard Spanish in the 16th century), but which is still found in several regional dialects such as the one spoken in South Texas. (Due to geography, Chicanos from the Valley of South Texas were cut off linguistically from other Spanish speakers. We tend to use words that the Spaniards brought over from Medieval Spain. The majority of the Spanish

---

[3]R. C. Ortega, *Dialectologia Del Barrio,* trans. Hortencia S. Alwan (Los Angeles: R. C. Ortega Publisher & Bookseller, 1977), p. 132.

colonizers in Mexico and the Southwest came from Extremadura—Hernán Cortés was one of them—and Andalucía. Andalucians pronounce *ll* like a *y,* and their *d*'s tend to be absorbed by adjacent vowels: *tirado* becomes *tirao.* They brought *el lenguaje popular, dialectos y regionalismos.*)[4]

Chicanos and other Spanish speakers also shift *ll* to *y* and *z* to *s.*[5] We leave out initial syllables, saying *tar* for *estar, toy* for *estoy, hora* for *ahora (cubanos* and *puertorriqueños* also leave out initial letters of some words.) We also leave out the final syllable such as *pa* for *para.* The intervocalic *y,* the *ll* as in *tortilla, ella, botella* gets replaced by *tortia* or *tortiya, ea, botea.* We add an additional syllable at the beginning of certain words: *atocar* for *tocar, agastar* for *gastar.* Sometimes we'll say *lavaste las vacijas,* other times *lavates* (substituting the *ates* verb endings for the *aste*).

We use anglicisms, words borrowed from English: *bola* from ball, *carpeta* from carpet, *máchina de lavar* (instead of *lavadora*) from washing machine. Tex-Mex argot, created by adding a Spanish sound at the beginning or end of an English word such as *cookiar* for cook, *watchar* for watch, *parkiar* for park, and *rapiar* for rape, is the result of the pressures on Spanish speakers to adapt to English.

We don't use the word *vosotros/as* or its accompanying verb form. We don't say *claro* (to mean yes), *imagínate,* or *me emociona,* unless we picked up Spanish from Latinas, out of a book, or in a classroom. Other Spanish-speaking groups are going through the same, or similar, development in their Spanish.

Linguistic Terrorism

Deslenguadas. Somos los del español deficiente. *We are your linguistic nightmare, your linguistic aberration, your linguistic mestisaje, the subject of your burla. Because we speak with tongues of fire we are culturally crucified. Racially, culturally and linguistically somos huérfanos—we speak an orphan tongue.*

Chicanas who grew up speaking Chicano Spanish have internalized the belief that we speak poor Spanish. It is illegitimate, a bastard language. And because we internalize how our language has been used against us by the dominant culture, we use our language differences against each other.

Chicana feminists often skirt around each other with suspicion and hesitation. For the longest time I couldn't figure it out. Then it dawned on me. To be close to another Chicana is like looking into the mirror. We are afraid of what we'll see there. *Pena.* Shame. Low estimation of self. In childhood we are told that our language is wrong. Repeated attacks on our native tongue diminish our sense of self. The attacks continue throughout our lives.

---

[4]Eduardo Hernandéz-Chávez, Anderew D. Cohen, and Anthony F. Beltramo, *El Lenguaje de los Chicanos: Regional and Social Characteristics of Language Used by Mexican Americanas* (Arlington, VA: Center for Applied Linguistics, 1975), p. 39.

[5]Ibid., p. xvii.

Chicanas feel uncomfortable talking in Spanish to Latinas, afraid of their censure. Their language was not outlawed in their countries. They had a whole lifetime of being immersed in their native tongue; generations, centuries in which Spanish was a first language, taught in school, heard on radio and TV, and read in the newspaper.

If a person, Chicana or Latina, has a low estimation of my native tongue, she also has a low estimation of me. Often with *mexicanas y latinas* we'll speak English as a neutral language. Even among Chicanas we tend to speak English at parties or conferences. Yet, at the same time, we're afraid the other will think we're *agringadas* because we don't speak Chicano Spanish. We oppress each other trying to out-Chicano each other, vying to be the "real" Chicanas, to speak like Chicanos. There is no one Chicano language just as there is no one Chicano experience. A monolingual Chicana whose first language is English or Spanish is just as much a Chicana as one who speaks several variants of Spanish. A Chicana from Michigan or Chicago or Detroit is just as much a Chicana as one from the Southwest. Chicano Spanish is as diverse linguistically as it is regionally.

By the end of this century, Spanish speakers will comprise the biggest minority group in the U.S., a country where students in high schools and colleges are encouraged to take French classes because French is considered more "cultured." But for a language to remain alive it must be used.[6] By the end of this century English, and not Spanish, will be the mother tongue of most Chicanos and Latinos.

So, if you want to really hurt me, talk badly about my language. Ethnic identity is twin skin to linguistic identity—I am my language. Until I can take pride in my language, I cannot take pride in myself. Until I can accept as legitimate Chicano Texas Spanish, Tex-Mex and all the other languages I speak, I cannot accept the legitimacy of myself. Until I am free to write bilingually and to switch codes without having always to translate, while I still have to speak English or Spanish when I would rather speak Spanglish, and as long as I have to accommodate the English speakers rather than having them accommodate me, my tongue will be illegitimate.

I will no longer be made to feel ashamed of existing. I will have my voice: Indian, Spanish, white. I will have my serpent's tongue—my woman's voice, my sexual voice, my poet's voice. I will overcome the tradition of silence.

> *My fingers*
> *move sly against your palm*
> *Like women everywhere, we speak in code . . .*
>
>   Melanie Kaye/Kantrowitz[7]

²⁶Irena Klepfisz, "Secular Jewish Identity Yidishkayt in America," in *The Tribe of Dina,* eds. Kaye/Kantrowitz and Klepfisz, p. 43.

⁷Melanie Kaye/Kantrowitz, "Sign," in *We Speak in Code: Poems and Other Writings* (Pittsburgh: Motheroot Publications, 1980), p. 85.

Feeding the Ancestors

James W. Earl

James W. Earl is a professor of medieval literature at the University of Oregon. He wrote this essay to present at a meeting of the local Friends of the Library group, and it was subsequently published in The Chronicle of Higher Education.

When I was ten or so, I took a book from the living room shelf, and took it outside to read. I think my mother said, "That one's not for you," but she didn't stop me. I think it was one of those turning points in my life—one of the ones you don't realize is a turning point until long afterwards.

No, this isn't the story of discovering *that* inappropriate book. This one was just a Book-of-the-Month Club selection that I'd seen in the living rooms of all our friends and relatives, next to James Thurber and Anne Morrow Lindbergh and James Michener, and the six little volumes of Ogden Nash's poetry that I loved, and that I knew I could escape into in almost any house we visited. As for this book, I forget who wrote it, but it had a catchy title, *Where Did You Go? Out. What Did You Do? Nothing.* It was a popular book in a more innocent age, long before that other catchy title, *Everything You Always Wanted to Know About Sex but Were Afraid to Ask,* showed up on the same shelves.

The Fifties weren't really a more innocent age, of course. There were the McCarthy hearings and the Korean War and hydrogen bombs; in books, it was also the age of Sartre's *Nausea,* Burroughs's *Naked Lunch,* and Ginsberg's *Howl.* But the Book-of-the-Month Club was holding the line against the obscenity of beatniks and the despair of existentialists, and I'm glad it did. I was sheltered during my tenderest years by the Book-of-the-Month Club. I never had the chance to be a ten-year-old existentialist, like today's kids.

Where Did You Go? Out. What Did You Do? Nothing. was a book of advice for parents—more innocent, perhaps, than Dr. Reuben's, but equally subversive in my case. The only part I still remember told parents that sometimes kids just want to lie on the grass for hours watching the clouds. So it's all right if you ask your kid, *What did you do?* and he just answers vacantly, *Nothing.* . . . He's just taking time to look at clouds. He's a kid. He doesn't always have to be *doing* something.

My ten-year-old self thought, *Well, maybe I haven't spent enough time just lying on the grass looking at clouds.* Or if I had, I wasn't aware of it, or that it was so good for me. So, armed with this unexpected adult advice, I went outside and lay on the grass in front of our apartment building and read the book, occasionally looking up at the clouds. I thought, rather pretentiously, *This is good. This is what being a kid is all about.*

And it *was* good, though there was something a little awkward about it—like I was secretly hoping my parents might notice, so they'd ask, *What were you doing?*

I had my answer all ready—*Nothing . . .*—but they never noticed. To be honest, the book made me a little self-conscious about my habitual solitary idleness. It didn't just recommend that children *play,* you see, it actually recommended that they *daydream, alone.* This only licensed me to do what I think I did best anyway. Perhaps in making me so conscious about it, it spoiled my innocence a little, broke that bond of Wordsworthian immediacy between me and those clouds, me and that grass, and turned goofing off into something of a pose.

On the other hand, it did make me enjoy my laziness in a new way, from an adult perspective—very Wordsworthian, now that I think about it. And now, after almost half a century, when I fall into a certain kind of reverie, when I turn my back on work for a few minutes—or a few hours—that afternoon sometimes comes back to me like a "spot in time," and I excuse my laziness by saying, *This is good; I don't* have *to be* doing something.

Attitudes toward daydreaming are likely to be pretty conflicted, but I think we all know *in theory* that daydreaming isn't really a waste of time. When we're children, it's one of the ways we learn to *think.* Looking at clouds is really a way of looking into yourself. They resemble our moods, which also come in cumulus, nimbus, stratus and cirrus forms, and also drift, unpredictably, blown by invisible winds. Wordsworth saw this reflection of ourselves in nature; obviously I was to find in him a kindred soul. In any case, I remember learning important things from clouds—for example, *that things change slowly, without your noticing;* also, *clouds* do *have silver linings.*

I still watch clouds, in a pinch; but grown-ups find lots of other means to the same end, other things we can give ourselves over to with this same sort of passive but open attentiveness. There's gardening or fishing, of course, though I don't do those; but even the slowest game in the world, baseball, is good at slowing you down and letting you think about nothing in particular. On the more refined side, there's classical music: the four cloud types are there in every symphony, in the four movements of the sonata form, and the best listening is a kind of willing surrender to their shifting moods. Doesn't *your* mind drift at the concert-hall, even when you're listening intently? I've decided this isn't really a lack of attention. We may feel guilty about it, but in fact it is a *form* of attention, the open, evenly-suspended attention of free association.

My point, however—the focus of *my* wandering attention here—is that this sort of thinking, or meditating, or free association, from cloud-watching to baseball to concert-going, requires us to slow down to do it. Sometimes I fall into a reverie right at my desk, staring out the window at the clouds, or at the Coburg hills. And when that happens I sometimes remember my Greek Philosophy professor back in college, Dr. Fell. He'd stare out the window as the class sat waiting for an answer to a question. I remember wondering if that too might be a pose. Perhaps he was playing Socrates, who could stand on the street corner for hours, staring vacantly at the sky. Pose or not, though, here was a professor who managed to turn cloud-watching into a high vocation! He actually got paid for it! He could just say, *Excuse me, I'm thinking.*

The anthropologist Dan Sperber, in a book about the Dorze tribe of Ethiopia, tells a little story of his childhood that I like. He says,

> A scene marked my childhood: my father was seated in an armchair in the lounge, completely motionless, his hands empty, his eyes fixed on nothing. My mother whispered to me: "Don't bother your father, he's working." This worked on me. Later, I too became a scholar, I went to Ethiopia as an ethnographer and I heard a Dorze mother whisper to her son: "Don't bother your father, he's feeding the ancestors."

That's a better anecdote than my homely one of lying on the grass with a Book-of-the-Month Club selection. My parents weren't professors, but the lesson's the same. Like Sperber, I too was obviously destined to become a professor, though not a philosophy or anthropology professor. I became an English professor, so my reveries tend to take the form they did on that day I first took that book outside to read. Most of the clouds I stare at, now as then, are in books. Like many of you, I can sit quietly, alone, for hours, over a book. In our accelerated age, this aspect of reading—its solitary quietness—seems to me to have an important value in itself, quite independent of what you're reading. And yet, the way I've been telling this story makes me think that even though I'm a professor it's still something of a *guilty* pleasure, a practice I have to defend, and I'd like to know why.

The real oddity of reading, like cloud-watching, is that it's so solitary—so still, quiet, private, unsocial, and self-indulgent. Of course, we excuse ourselves by claiming we *are* doing something—we're learning—and of course we can share the experience afterwards—but really only partly, because there's a lot in the reading experience we can never share. In the end, there's something about the activity, or nonactivity, of reading that seems a little . . . un-American.

Now, Evelyn Wood's Speed-Reading: *there's* an American activity; and I know it's always possible to read on an exercise bike, or a stairmaster, or to listen to novels on tape while jogging or driving. But I'm talking about that old-fashioned, inefficient, time-consuming, antisocial, self-indulgent practice of reading alone, sitting quietly. This is the guilty pleasure. I should write a book for our fast-paced lives called *Where Did You Go? The Library. What Did You Do? I Read—You Got a Problem with That?*

This book wouldn't be aimed at the general public, though, which actually seems to find plenty of time to read, judging from the growth of bookstores. I have a more particular audience in mind: the subculture of professors and students, the very people you might think would be the last in the world to need my avuncular advice on the value of books. It's an irony professors share among themselves daily—even English professors, or perhaps particularly English professors—that somehow we just don't get the time anymore to read books. We became English majors and we became professors precisely because we were readers. I imagined, I think, a lifetime of sitting quietly in a book-lined study, with a cup of coffee or a glass of sherry, stopping periodically to discuss the books I'd read with loved ones, friends, and students. Now we have houses full of books, and classes full of students, but all the professors I know complain constantly that there's just no time any more to read. Why is that?

I dream of reading the way Machiavelli described it during the boom years of Italian humanism in the sixteenth century. He writes,

> Evenings I return home and enter my study; and at its entrance I take off my everyday clothes, full of mud and dust, and don royal and courtly garments. Decorously reattired, I enter into the ancient sessions of ancient men. Received amicably by them, I partake of such food as is mine only, and for which I was born. There, without shame, I speak with them and ask them about the reasons for their actions, and they in their humanity respond to me.

Oh, I've known that feeling. Twenty-five years ago, for example, when I got my first sabbatical leave, I spent my time reading Plato and Kant and Shakespeare and Milton and Shelley and the *Tao te ching* and the *Upanishads* and the *Bhagavad Gita* and Leibnitz and Bacon and Montaigne and Whitehead and Bergson and Cassirer and Freud and Shaw and Yeats and Wells and Powys and Auden and Heidegger and Heisenberg and Levi-Strauss—and Dan Sperber. I read everything I could, everything I hadn't gotten to in school. I read and I read . . . instead of *writing that book I was supposed to be writing.* Oh, that was a *very* guilty pleasure. And when the time came, the university asked me, *What did you do?* and I finally got to use my prepared answer: *Nothing. . . .*

In those days, when I got up from the desk at night, often at two or three in the morning, I felt . . . electric. I'd been wrestling with the angel. I should have been saying with Ecclesiastes, *Of making many books there is no end, and much study is a weariness of the flesh;* but instead, I felt like Ezekiel, when God said, "Mortal, eat what is offered to you; eat this book; fill your stomach with it." *And I ate it, and in my mouth it was as sweet as honey.*

Nights like that are fewer and farther between now, partly because I've changed. I can see now that Machiavelli's account of his reading, and my nightly electric wrestling-matches with the angel, were grossly egoistic. Machiavelli's so *confident* he can just chat with Plato and Livy and Cicero, as their equal. There's something in the act of reading itself that can give you this heady, false impression: once we come to understand a writer, we mistakenly think we're his equal. It's like looking at a modern painting, and thinking "*I* could have done *that!*" The fact is, we *didn't* do it, and couldn't even have *dreamed* of it until that moment.

I look back at the notes I took in those days—scores of yellow sheets crammed with dizzying profundities—I look at them now with amused and amazed embarrassment. I cringe when I run into my marginal notes. It seems I discovered the meaning of life, and the secrets of the universe! I don't read like that any more, but I certainly don't regret having gone through the experience. I read differently now, and I'll tell you how. But I do wonder: Why do so few of my *students* have that electricity, that wonderful, youthful, egomaniacal passion for reading?

At the beginning of the year, I tell the 250 students in my Introduction to the English Major class,

> The most important work of this course doesn't take place in the classroom, and it doesn't take place in a group, or even aloud; it takes place at home, or somewhere else where you can be alone, and quiet, and undisturbed and undistracted; perhaps the library, way back in a corner of the fourth floor, or some other spot

you can make your own. You need at least a comfortable chair and good light. If you don't have such a place, find one. You can't be a good student without it, and you shouldn't be an English major unless you really enjoy being there. This is where you can read. For me, as for many of you, it'll be at home, late at night. I usually sit at my desk. There, when the rest of the house is dark and quiet at last, I sit with my book in a magic circle of light: just me and the book—or me and the author of the book, with the book in between. The most important work of this course is your reading; and it doesn't take place here in the classroom, it can only take place there, where you can enter into that magic circle of light.

My graduate students, I should mention, get quite a different speech, about how to *live* in the Knight Library instead of in their English offices; how to wrestle with the angel, and eat books like Ezekiel; I also tell them, *Of making many books there is no end, and much study is a weariness of the flesh*—but I spare my freshmen this frightening prospect. Many of them are frightened enough already by the prospect of reading at all.

It's amazing how many students today—even English majors—will unashamedly confess to their professors, "I don't like to read." Reading must seem like work, compared with movies, TV, music, or even the computer. Reading's so damned *slow!* These kids, after all, complain about the speed of their computers! What they also don't like, of course, is the quiet and the solitude. For all their precious self-esteem, they don't much like being alone with themselves, and they don't much like just listening to others. And reading is first of all *listening*. At least this is what I tell them. In that same speech, I say,

> In that magic circle of light, you're not there to conquer the book, or tame the book, or criticize it, or even analyze it. You're not even there to *like* it or *dislike* it. You're not there to approve or disapprove, or to prove you're smarter than the author. You're there, first of all, just to *listen*, and to *hear* what he or she is trying to tell you. Don't take an attitude until you've listened.

That's my newer attitude. It's a much less egoistic approach than Machiavelli's, or my godlike reading as a young professor. The person who taught me this more patient kind of reading was, of all people, Freud. In his advice for new psychoanalysts on how to listen to patients, I found the connection between reading and the cloud-watching of my childhood, the art of doing nothing. The method, he says,

> consists simply in not directing one's notice to anything in particular and in maintaining the same "evenly-suspended attention" (as I have called it) in the face of all that one hears. In this way . . . we avoid a danger which is inseparable from the exercise of deliberate attention. For as soon as anyone deliberately concentrates his attention to a certain degree, he begins to select from the material before him. . . . This, however, is precisely what must not be done. In making the selection, if he follows his expectations he is in danger of never finding anything but what he already knows. . . . The rule for the doctor may be expressed: . . . "He should simply listen, and not bother about whether he is keeping anything in mind."

It's extremely difficult for a psychoanalyst to learn how to sit quietly and just listen to his or her patients in this totally open fashion, instead of leaping to interpretations, drawing premature conclusions, and interrupting with advice; and it's just as difficult for students to learn how to listen to a book. At first they're impatient, judgmental, intolerant of any voice but their own. They actually have to be *taught*—taught to do nothing.

It's ironic that this *art of doing nothing,* which I've worked so hard to perfect since childhood, is not well understood, much less appreciated, by the university, where, as I said before, professors like myself complain unceasingly that they no longer have time to read books. I hate to set aside the whimsical tone I've adopted for such a pleasant occasion, but I just have to say that I'm . . . annoyed . . . that the university—even this university—seems to have forgotten that so much of the work that scholars and intellectuals have to do, especially in the Humanities, takes the form that we smile at in Dan Sperber's little anecdote about his father.

It must sound odd to university administrators, who have to worry more and more about funding and legislation, budgets and bottom lines, accountability and productivity, market forces and competition, technology and change, that professors—and students too, and everyone else, in and out of the academy—need time just to sit quietly and read. This too is work, though it may not *look* like work.

Look at this campus, with all of its broad green spaces. In Latin *campus* means "field," and the practice of building universities in this form, with all these open, spacious lawns, rather than in the form of, say, shopping-malls or corporate office-buildings (which are much more efficient and effective uses of space), these lawns are a conscious evocation of the pastoral tradition. The campus has been set aside, purposely, from the hustle-bustle world of daily commerce and the demands of ordinary life. It's been set aside specifically as a place where one can slow down to read, to listen, and to learn. But in the thirty years I've been a professor, there's been a gradual sea-change in the institution—another example of what the clouds taught me, that *things change slowly, without your noticing.*

Now we're being told that history is accelerating, that society is changing faster every day, that we have to race faster and faster to keep up with it. If we rest for a moment, the future will zoom out of sight, and the university will be left behind! We have to be on the cutting edge, the university of the future, the university of the computer age, the university of the 21st century!

Do those who are running America's universities really believe this? Could they really have forgotten that the present and the future are firmly anchored in the past, in history and tradition, and that change has *always* felt like this? Or is the university letting itself be manipulated by political and commercial forces that would turn us into a kind of well-run, even profitable corporation?

The university doesn't have to catch up with the future, like a dog chasing a mechanical rabbit. "Keeping up with the future" sounds like an advertising jingle— which in fact it is. The university has begun to market itself, and for some reason it's decided that America wants it to be a fast-paced, cutting-edge, technological, efficient, corporate institution that will land its graduates (now thought of as *customers,* or *consumers*) high-paying jobs in the computer age.

I think America knows better. What America wants is not faster and faster change; that's only what the *marketplace* wants, to keep customers thirsty for new products. What America wants right now is some continuity with the past, some stability of social and ethical values. What America wants is a university it can count on *not* to change every year with the fashions. I don't think we're moving too slow, I think we're moving too fast! I want a university that *creates* the future, not one that has to run to keep up with it.

Ah, but now it's easy to see why professors have so little time to read, isn't it, and why reading has become a guilty pleasure. Can you imagine a well-run business that actually *encourages* its employees to *slow down*—to sit quietly, alone, for hours on end, watching clouds or something? How will we catch up with the future by sitting in magic circles of light, or chatting with the ancients? By just listening quietly? By feeding the ancestors?

There's a new magic *rectangle* of light, and there's an information highway running right through this green campus now, and there's an on-ramp on every desk where people used to sit and read. The damn thing actually *beeps* every time it wants your attention:

> *Beep!* Committee meeting! *Beep!* Committee meeting! *Beep!* Committee meeting! *Beep!* Advising meeting! *Beep!* Overload teaching again! *Beep!* Bigger classes next year! *Beep!* Read these files! *Beep!* Technology training class! *Beep!* "Process for Change"! *Beep!* Senate meeting! *Beep!* Working lunch tomorrow! *Beep!* Working *breakfast* tomorrow! *Beep!* Committee meeting! *Beep!* Turn in your book orders; your syllabi; your evaluations; your updated curriculum vitae; your activity report, your post-tenure review materials! *Beep!* Lunch with the Provost! *Beep!* Department meeting! *Beep!* Oh, and don't forget to write that book! *Beep! Beep!* Retirement Planning Workshop!

Whoa! The Retirement Planning Workshop sounds like a great exit line. . . . But the fact is, I love my work, and I do a good job. I teach my students how to read books. I teach them how to respect the past, to listen patiently to the voices of the ancestors, even as we sail into the future. I tell them: *If we don't remember and respect the past, we have no reason to hope the future will respect us*—and I think we all hope that future generations will remember the world we've lived in, the things we've cared about, the efforts we've made, the books we've written.

The future may be in computers, but the past is in books. So, bless the Knight Library for still caring about them, and bless the Friends of the Library for helping to preserve book culture for the future. I may be annoyed with the university's drift, but I'm hardly depressed. I'd just like us to come up with a new marketing approach. How about this?

> The University of Oregon
> Because We'll Never Outgrow
> Our Need for Books.

(Now you can see why they don't ask English professors to do the marketing.) Or, how about this?

> Stop.
> Listen.
> Feed the Ancestors.

Issues about Privacy and Biological Science

The Right to Privacy

Samuel D. Warren and Louis D. Brandeis

Louis D. Brandeis (1856–1941) was an American lawyer who served on the Supreme Court from 1916 to 1939. He coauthored this influential article with his Boston law partner, Samuel D. Warren (1817–1888). It was published in the Harvard Law Review *in 1890. It originally appeared with lengthy footnotes, which have been omitted from this reprinting. Consult your college library to see how in the original text citations of legal precedent are used to support the authors' claims.*

It could be done only on principles of private justice, moral fitness, and public convenience, which, when applied to a new subject, make common law without a precedent; much more when received and approved by usage.

Willes, J., In *Millar v. Taylor*, 4 Burr. 2303, 2312.

That the individual shall have full protection in person and in property is a principle as old as the common law; but it has been found necessary from time to time to define anew the exact nature and extent of such protection. Political, social, and economic changes entail the recognition of new rights, and the common law, in its eternal youth, grows to meet the demands of society. Thus, in very early times, the law gave a remedy only for physical interference with life and property, for trespasses *vi et armis*. Then the "right to life" served only to protect the subject from battery in its various forms; liberty meant freedom from actual restraint; and the right to property secured to the individual his lands and his cattle. Later, there came a recognition of man's spiritual nature, of his feelings and his intellect. Gradually the scope of these legal rights broadened; and now the right to life has come to mean the right to enjoy life,—the right to be let alone; the right to liberty secures the exercise of extensive civil privileges; and the term "property" has grown to comprise every form of possession—intangible, as well as tangible.

Thus, with the recognition of the legal value of sensations, the protection against actual bodily injury was extended to prohibit mere attempts to do such injury; that is, the putting another in fear of such injury. From the action of battery grew that of assault. Much later there came a qualified protection of the individual against offensive noises and odors, against dust and smoke, and excessive vibration. The law of nuisance was developed. So regard for human emotions soon extended the scope of personal immunity beyond the body of the individual. His reputation, the standing among his fellow-men, was considered, and the law of slander and libel arose. Man's family relations became a part of the legal conception of his life, and the alienation of a wife's affections was held remediable. Occasionally the law halted,—as in its refusal to recognize the intrusion by seduction upon the honor of the family. But even here the demands of society were met. A mean fiction, the action *per quod servitium amisit*, was resorted to, and by allowing damages for injury to the parents' feelings, an adequate remedy was ordinarily afforded. Similar to the expansion of the right to life was the growth of the legal conception of property. From corporeal property arose the incorporeal rights issuing out of it; and then there opened the wide realm of intangible property, in the products and processes of the mind, as works of literature and art, goodwill, trade secrets, and trademarks.

This development of the law was inevitable. The intense intellectual and emotional life, and the heightening of sensations which came with the advance of civilization, made it clear to men that only a part of the pain, pleasure, and profit of life lay in physical things. Thoughts, emotions, and sensations demanded legal recognition, and the beautiful capacity for growth which characterizes the common law enabled the judges to afford the requisite protection, without the interposition of the legislature.

Recent inventions and business methods call attention to the next step which must be taken for the protection of the person, and for securing to the individual what Judge Cooley calls the right "to be let alone." Instantaneous photographs and newspaper enterprise have invaded the sacred precincts of private and domestic life; and numerous mechanical devices threaten to make good the prediction that "what is whispered in the closet shall be proclaimed from the house-tops." For years there has been a feeling that the law must afford some remedy for the unauthorized circulation of portraits of private persons; and the evil of the invasion of privacy by the newspapers, long keenly felt, has been but recently discussed by an able writer. The alleged facts of a somewhat notorious case brought before an inferior tribunal in New York a few months ago, directly involved the consideration of the right of circulating portraits; and the question whether our law will recognize and protect the right to privacy in this and in other respects must soon come before our courts for consideration.

Of the desirability—indeed of the necessity—of some such protection, there can, it is believed, be no doubt. The press is overstepping in every direction the obvious bounds of propriety and of decency. Gossip is no longer the resource of the idle and of the vicious, but has become a trade, which is pursued with industry as well as effrontery. To satisfy a prurient taste the details of sexual relations are spread broadcast in the columns of the daily papers. To occupy the indolent, column upon column is filled with idle gossip, which can only be procured by intrusion upon the domestic circle. The intensity and complexity of life, attendant upon advancing civilization, have rendered necessary some retreat from the world, and man, under the refining influence of culture, has become more sensitive to publicity, so that solitude and privacy have become more essential to the individual; but modern enterprise and invention have, through invasions upon his privacy, subjected him to mental pain and distress, far greater than could be inflicted by mere bodily injury. Nor is the harm wrought by such invasions confined to the suffering of those who may be made the subjects of journalistic or other enterprise. In this, as in other branches of commerce, the supply creates the demand. Each crop of unseemly gossip, thus harvested, becomes the seed of more, and, in direct proportion to its circulation, results in a lowering of social standards and of morality. Even gossip apparently harmless, when widely and persistently circulated, is potent for evil. It both belittles and perverts. It belittles by inverting the relative importance of things, thus dwarfing the thoughts and aspirations of a people. When personal gossip attains the dignity of print, and crowds the space available for matters of real interest to the community, what wonder that the ignorant and thoughtless mistake its relative importance. Easy of comprehension, appealing to that weak side of human nature which is never wholly cast down by the misfortunes and frailties of our neighbors, no one can be surprised that it usurps the place of interest in brains capable of other things. Triviality destroys at once robustness of thought and delicacy of feeling. No enthusiasm can flourish, no generous impulse can survive under its blighting influence.

It is our purpose to consider whether the existing law affords a principle which can properly be invoked to protect the privacy of the individual; and, if it does, what the nature and extent of such protection is.

Owing to the nature of the instruments by which privacy is invaded, the injury inflicted bears a superficial resemblance to the wrongs dealt with by the law of slander and of libel, while a legal remedy for such injury seems to involve the treatment of mere wounded feelings, as a substantive cause of action. The principle on which the law of defamation rests, covers, however, a radically different class of effects from those for which attention is now asked. It deals only with damage to reputation, with the injury done to the individual in his external relations to the community, by lowering him in the estimation of his fellows. The matter published of him, however widely circulated, and however unsuited to publicity, must, in order to be actionable, have a direct tendency to injure him in his intercourse with others, and even if in writing or in print, must subject him to the hatred, ridicule, or contempt of his fellow men,—the effect of the publication upon his estimate of himself and upon his own feelings not forming an essential element in the cause of action. In short, the wrongs and correlative rights recognized by the law of slander and libel are in their nature material rather than spiritual. That branch of the law simply extends the protection surrounding physical property to certain of the conditions necessary or helpful to worldly prosperity. On the other hand, our law recognizes no principle upon which compensation can be granted for mere injury to the feelings. However painful the mental effects upon another of an act, though purely wanton or even malicious, yet if the act itself is otherwise lawful, the suffering inflicted is *damnum absque injuria*. Injury of feelings may indeed be taken account of in ascertaining the amount of damages when attending what is recognized as a legal injury; but our system, unlike the Roman law, does not afford a remedy even for mental suffering which results from mere contumely and insult, from an intentional and unwarranted violation of the "honor" of another.

It is not however necessary, in order to sustain the view that the common law recognizes and upholds a principle applicable to cases of invasion of privacy, to invoke the analogy, which is but superficial, to injuries sustained, either by an attack upon reputation or by what the civilians called a violation of honor; for the legal doctrines relating to infractions of what is ordinarily termed the common-law right to intellectual and artistic property are, it is believed, but instances and applications of a general right to privacy, which properly understood afford a remedy for the evils under consideration.

The common law secures to each individual the right of determining, ordinarily, to what extent his thoughts, sentiments, and emotions shall be communicated to others. Under our system of government, he can never be compelled to express them (except when upon the witness-stand); and even if he has chosen to give them expression, he generally retains the power to fix the limits of the publicity which shall be given them. The existence of this right does not depend upon the particular method of expression adopted. It is immaterial whether it be by word or by signs, in paintings, by sculpture, or in music. Neither does the existence of the right depend upon the nature or value of the thought or emotion, nor upon the excellence of the means of expressions. The same protection is accorded to a casual letter or an entry in a diary and to the most valuable poem or essay, to a botch or daub and to a masterpiece. In every such case the individual is entitled to decide whether that which is his shall be given to the public. No other has the right to publish his productions in any form, without his consent. This right is wholly independent of the material on which, or the means by which, the thought, sentiment, or emotion is expressed. It may exist independently of any corporeal being, as in words spoken, a song sung, a drama acted. Or if expressed on any material, as a poem in writing, the author may have parted with the paper, without forfeiting any proprietary right in the composition itself. The right is lost only when the author himself communicates his production to the public,— in other words, publishes it. It is entirely independent of the copyright laws, and their extension into the domain of art. The aim of those statutes is to secure to the author, composer, or artist the entire profits arising from publication; but the common-law protection enables him to control absolutely the act of publication, and in the exercise of his own discretion, to decide whether there shall be any publication at all. The statutory right is of no value, *unless* there is a publication; the common-law right is lost *as soon as* there is a publication.

What is the nature, the basis, of this right to prevent the publication of manuscripts or works of art? It is stated to be the enforcement of a right of property; and no difficulty arises in accepting this view, so long as we have only to deal with the reproduction of literary and artistic compositions. They certainly possess many of the attributes of ordinary property: they are transferable; they have a value; and publication or reproduction is a use by which that value is realized. But where the value of the production is found not in the right to take the profits arising from publication, but in the peace of mind or the relief afforded by the ability to prevent any publication at all, it is difficult to regard the right as one of property, in the common acceptation of that term. A man records in a letter to his son, or in his diary, that he did not dine with his wife on a certain day. No one into whose hands those papers fall could publish them to the world, even if possession of the documents had been obtained rightfully; and the prohibition would not be confined to the publication of a copy of the letter itself, or of the diary entry; the restraint extends also to a publication of the contents. What is the thing which is protected? Surely, not the intellectual act of recording the fact that the husband did not dine with his wife, but that fact itself. It is not the intellectual product, but the domestic occurrence. A man writes a dozen letters to different people. No person would be permitted to publish a list of the letters written. If the letters or the contents of the diary were protected as literary compositions, the scope of the protection afforded should be the same secured to a published writing under the copyright law. But the copyright law would not prevent an enumeration of the letters, or the publication of some of the facts contained therein. The copyright of a series of paintings or etchings would prevent a reproduction of the paintings as pictures; but it would not prevent a publication of a list or even a description of them. Yet in the famous case of Prince Albert *v.* Strange, the court held that the common-law rule prohibited not merely the reproduction of the etchings which the plaintiff and Queen Victoria had made for their own pleasure, but also "the publishing (at least by printing or writing), though not by copy or resemblance, a description of them, whether more or less limited or summary, whether in the form of a catalogue or otherwise." Likewise, an unpublished collection of news possessing no element of a literary nature is protected from piracy.

That this protection cannot rest upon the right to literary or artistic property in any exact sense, appears the more clearly when the subject-matter for which protection is invoked is not even in the form of intellectual property, but has the attributes of ordinary tangible property. Suppose a man has a collection of gems or curiosities which he keeps private: it would hardly be contended that any person could publish a catalogue of them, and yet the articles enumerated are certainly not intellectual property in the legal sense, any more than a collection of stoves or of chairs.

The belief that the idea of property in its narrow sense was the basis of the protection of unpublished manuscripts led an able court to refuse, in several cases, injunctions against the publication of private letters, on the ground that "letters not possessing the attributes of literary compositions are not property entitled to protection"; and that it was "evident the plaintiff could not have considered the letters as of any value whatever as literary productions, for a letter cannot be considered of value to the author which he never would consent to have published." But these decisions have not been followed, and it may now be considered settled that the protection afforded by the common law to the author of any writing is entirely independent of its pecuniary value, its intrinsic merits, or of any intention to publish the same, and, of course, also, wholly independent of the material, if any, upon which, or the mode in which, the thought or sentiment was expressed.

Although the courts have asserted that they rested their decisions on the narrow grounds of protection to property, yet there are recognitions of a more liberal doctrine. Thus in the case of Prince Albert *v.* Strange, already referred to, the opinions both of the Vice-Chancellor and of the Lord Chancellor, on appeal, show a more or less clearly defined perception of a principle broader than those which were mainly discussed, and on which they both placed their chief reliance. Vice-Chancellor Knight Bruce referred to publishing of a man that he had "written to particular persons or on particular subjects" as an instance of possibly injurious disclosures as to private matters, that the courts would in a proper case prevent; yet it is difficult to perceive how, in such a case, any right of property, in the narrow sense, would be drawn in question, or why, if such a publication would be restrained when it threatened to expose the victim not merely to sarcasm, but to ruin, it should not equally be enjoined, if it threatened to embitter his life. To deprive a man of the potential profits to be realized by publishing a catalogue of his gems cannot *per se* be a wrong to him. The possibility of future profits is not a right of property which the law ordinarily recognizes; it must, therefore, be an infraction of other rights which constitutes the wrongful act, and that infraction is equally wrongful, whether its results are to forestall the profits that the individual himself might secure by giving the matter a publicity obnoxious to him, or to gain an advantage at the expense of his mental pain and suffering. If the fiction of property in a narrow sense must be preserved, it is still true that the end accomplished by the gossip-monger is attained by the use of that which is another's, the facts relating to his private life, which he has seen fit to keep private. Lord Cottenham stated that a man "is entitled to be protected in the exclusive use and enjoyment of that which is exclusively his," and cited with approval the opinion of Lord Eldon, as reported in a manuscript note of the case of Wyatt *v.* Wilson, in 1820, respecting an engraving of George the Third during his illness, to the effect that "if one of the late king's physicians had kept a diary of what he heard and saw, the court would not, in the king's lifetime, have permitted him to print and publish it"; and Lord Cottenham declared, in respect to the acts of the defendants in the case before him, that "privacy is the right invaded." But if privacy is once recognized as a right entitled to legal protection, the interposition of the courts cannot depend on the particular nature of the injuries resulting.

These considerations lead to the conclusion that the protection afforded to thoughts, sentiments, and emotions, expressed through the medium of writing or of the arts, so far as it consists in preventing publication, is merely an instance of the enforcement of the more general right of the individual to be let alone. It is like the right not to be assaulted or beaten, the right not to be imprisoned, the right not to be maliciously prosecuted, the right not to be defamed. In each of these rights, as indeed in all other rights recognized by the law, there inheres the quality of being owned or possessed—and (as that is the distinguishing attribute of property) there may be some propriety in speaking of those rights as property. But, obviously, they bear little resemblance to what is ordinarily comprehended under that term. The principle which protects personal writings and all other personal productions, not against theft and physical appropriation, but against publication in any form, is in reality not the principle of private property, but that of an inviolate personality.

If we are correct in this conclusion, the existing law affords a principle which may be invoked to protect the privacy of the individual from invasion either by the too enterprising press, the photographer, or the possessor of any other modern device for recording or reproducing scenes or sounds. For the protection afforded is not confined by the authorities to those cases where any particular medium or form of expression has been adopted, nor to products of the intellect. The same protection is afforded to emotions and sensations expressed in a musical composition or other work of art as to a literary composition; and words spoken, a pantomime acted, a sonata performed, is no less entitled to protection than if each had been reduced to writing. The circumstance that a thought or emotion has been recorded in a permanent form renders its identification easier, and hence may be important from the point of view of evidence, but it has no significance as a matter of substantive right. If, then, the decisions indicate a general right to privacy for thoughts, emotions, and sensations, these should receive the same protection, whether expressed in writing, or in conduct, in conversation, in attitudes, or in facial expression.

It may be urged that a distinction should be taken between the deliberate expression of thoughts and emotions in literary or artistic compositions and the casual and often involuntary expression given to them in the ordinary conduct of life. In other words, it may be contended that the protection afforded is granted to the conscious products of labor, perhaps as an encouragement to effort. This contention, however plausible, has, in fact, little to recommend it. If the amount of labor involved be adopted as the test, we might well find that the effort to conduct one's self properly in business and in domestic relations had been far greater than that involved in painting a picture or writing a book; one would find that it was far easier to express lofty sentiments in a diary than in the conduct of a noble life. If the test of deliberateness of the act be adopted, much casual correspondence which is now accorded full protection would be excluded from the beneficent operation of existing rules. After the decisions denying the distinction attempted to be made between those literary productions which it was intended to publish and those which it was not, all considerations of the amount of labor involved, the degree of deliberation, the value of the product, and the intention of publishing must be abandoned, and no basis is discerned upon which the right to restrain publication and reproduction of such so-called literary and artistic works can be rested, except the right to privacy, as a part of the more general right to the immunity of the person,—the right to one's personality.

It should be stated that, in some instances where protection has been afforded against wrongful publication, the jurisdiction has been asserted, not on the ground of property, or at least not wholly on that ground, but upon the ground of an alleged breach of an implied contract or of a trust or confidence.

Thus, in Abernethy *v.* Hutchinson, 3 L. J. Ch. 209 (1825), where the plaintiff, a distinguished surgeon, sought to restrain the publication in the "Lancet" of unpublished lectures which he had delivered at St. Batholomew's Hospital in London, Lord Eldon doubted whether there could be property in lectures which had not been reduced to writing, but granted the injunction on the ground of breach of confidence, holding "that when persons were admitted as pupils or otherwise, to hear these lectures, although they were orally delivered, and although the parties might go to the extent, if they were able to do so, of putting down the whole by means of short-hand, yet they could do that only for the purposes of their own information, and could not publish, for profit, that which they had not obtained the right of selling."

In Prince Albert *v.* Strange, 1 McN. & G. 25 (1849), Lord Cottenham, on appeal, while recognizing a right of property in the etchings which of itself would justify the issuance of the injunction, stated, after discussing the evidence, that he was bound to assume that the possession of the etchings by the defendant had "its foundation in a breach of trust, confidence, or contract," and that upon such ground also the plaintiff's title to the injunction was fully sustained.

In Tuck *v.* Priester, 19 Q. B. D. 639 (1887), the plaintiffs were owners of a picture, and employed the defendant to make a certain number of copies. He did so, and made also a number of other copies for himself, and offered them for safe in England at a lower price. Subsequently, the plaintiffs registered their copyright in the picture, and then brought suit for an injunction and damages. The Lords Justices differed as to the application of the copyright acts to the case, but held unanimously that independently of those acts, the plaintiffs were entitled to an injunction and damages for breach of contract.

In Pollard *v.* Photographic Co., 40 Ch. Div. 345 (1888), a photographer who had taken a lady's photograph under the ordinary circumstances was restrained from exhibiting it, and also from selling copies of it, on the ground that it was a breach of an implied term in the contract, and also that it was a breach of confidence. Mr. Justice North interjected in the argument of the plaintiff's counsel the inquiry: "Do you dispute that if the negative likeness were taken on the sly, the person who took it might exhibit copies?" and counsel for the plaintiff answered: "In that case there would be no trust or consideration to support a contract." Later, the defendant's counsel argued that "a person has no property in his own features; short of doing what is libellous or otherwise illegal, there is no restriction on the photographer's using his negative." But the court, while expressly finding a breach of contract and of trust sufficient to justify its interposition, still seems to have felt the necessity of resting the decision also upon a right of property, in order to bring it within the line of those cases which were relied upon as precedents.

This process of implying a term in a contract, or of implying a trust (particularly where the contract is written, and where there is no established usage or custom), is nothing more nor less than a judicial declaration that public morality, private justice, and general convenience demand the recognition of such a rule, and that the publication under similar circumstances would be considered an intolerable abuse. So long as these circumstances happen to present a contract upon which such a term can be engrafted by the judicial mind, or to supply relations upon which a trust or confidence can be erected, there may be no objection to working out the desired protection through the doctrines of contract or of trust. But the court can hardly stop there. The narrower doctrine may have satisfied the demands of society at a time when the abuse to be guarded against could rarely have arisen without violating a contract or a special confidence; but now that modern devices afford abundant opportunities for the perpetration of such wrongs without any participation by the injured party, the protection granted by the law must be placed upon a broader foundation. While, for instance, the state of the photographic art was such that one's picture could seldom be taken without his consciously "sitting" for the purpose, the law of contract or of trust might afford the prudent man sufficient safeguards against the improper circulation of his portrait; but since the latest advances in photographic art have rendered it possible to take pictures surreptitiously, the doctrines of contract and of trust are inadequate to support the required protection, and the law of tort must be resorted to. The right of property in its widest sense, including all possession, including all rights and privileges, and hence embracing the right to an inviolate personality, affords alone that broad basis upon which the protection which the individual demands can be rested.

Thus, the courts, in searching for some principle upon which the publication of private letters could be enjoined, naturally came upon the ideas of a breach of confidence, and of an implied contract; but it required little consideration to discern that this doctrine could not afford all the protection required, since it would not support the court in granting a remedy against a stranger; and so the theory of property in the contents of letters was adopted. Indeed, it is difficult to conceive on what theory of the law the casual recipient of a letter, who proceeds to publish it, is guilty of a breach of contract, express or implied, or of any breach of trust, in the ordinary acceptation of that term. Suppose a letter has been addressed to him without his solicitation. He opens it, and reads. Surely, he has not made any contract; he has not accepted any trust. He cannot, by opening and reading the letter, have come under any obligation save what the law declares; and, however expressed, that obligation is simply to observe the legal right of the sender, whatever it may be, and whether it be called his right of property in the contents of the letter, or his right to privacy.

A similar groping for the principle upon which a wrongful publication can be enjoined is found in the law of trade secrets. There, injunctions have generally been granted on the theory of a breach of contract, or of an abuse of confidence. It would, of course, rarely happen that any one would be in the possession of a secret unless confidence had been reposed in him. But can it be supposed that the court would hesitate to grant relief against one who had obtained his knowledge by an ordinary trespass,—for instance, by wrongfully looking into a book in which the secret was recorded, or by eavesdropping? Indeed, in Yovatt *v.* Winyard, 1 J. & W. 394 (1820), where an injunction was granted against making any use of or communicating certain recipes for veterinary medicine, it appeared that the defendant, while in the plaintiff's employ, had surreptitiously got access to his book of recipes, and copied them. Lord Eldon "granted the injunction, upon the ground of there having been a breach of trust and confidence"; but it would seem to be difficult to draw any sound legal distinction between such a case and one where a mere stranger wrongfully obtained access to the book.

We must therefore conclude that the rights, so protected, whatever their exact nature, are not rights arising from contract or from special trust, but are rights as against the world; and, as above stated, the principle which has been applied to protect these rights is in reality not the principle of private property, unless that word be used in an extended and unusual sense. The principle which protects personal writings and any other productions of the intellect or of the emotions, is the right to privacy, and the law has no new principle to formulate when it extends this protection to the personal appearance, sayings, acts, and to personal relation, domestic or otherwise.

If the invasion of privacy constitutes a legal *injuria,* the elements for demanding redress exist, since already the value of mental suffering, caused by an act wrongful in itself, is recognized as a basis for compensation.

The right of one who has remained a private individual, to prevent his public portraiture, presents the simplest case for such extension; the right to protect one's self from pen portraiture, from a discussion by the press of one's private affairs, would be a more important and far-reaching one. If casual and unimportant statements in a letter, if handiwork, however inartistic and valueless, if possessions of all sorts are protected not only against reproduction, but against description and enumeration, how much more should the acts and sayings of a man in his social and domestic relations be guarded from ruthless publicity. If you may not reproduce a woman's face photographically without her consent, how much less should be tolerated the reproduction of her face, her form, and her actions, by graphic descriptions colored to suit a gross and depraved imagination.

The right to privacy, limited as such right must necessarily be, has already found expression in the law of France.

It remains to consider what are the limitations of this right to privacy, and what remedies may be granted for the enforcement of the right. To determine in advance of experience the exact line at which the dignity and convenience of the individual must yield to the demands of the public welfare or of private justice would be a difficult task; but the more general rules are furnished by the legal analogies already developed in the law of slander and libel, and in the law of literary and artistic property.

1. The right to privacy does not prohibit any publication of matter which is of public or general interest.

In determining the scope of this rule, aid would be afforded by the analogy, in the law of libel and slander, of cases which deal with the qualified privilege of comment and criticism on matters of public and general interest. There are of course difficulties in applying such a rule; but they are inherent in the subject-matter, and are certainly no greater than those which exist in many other branches of the law,—for instance, in that large class of cases in which the reasonableness or unreasonableness of an act is made the test of liability. The design of the law must be to protect those persons with whose affairs the community has no legitimate concern, from being dragged into an undesirable and undesired publicity and to protect all persons, whatsoever; their position or station, from having matters which they may properly prefer to keep private, made public against their will. It is the unwarranted invasion of individual privacy which is reprehended, and to be, so far as possible, prevented. The distinction, however, noted in the above statement is obvious and fundamental. There are persons who may reasonably claim as a right, protection from the notoriety entailed by being made the victims of journalistic enterprise. There are others who, in varying degrees, have renounced the right to live their lives screened from public observation. Matters which men of the first class may justly contend, concern themselves alone, may in those of the second be the subject of legitimate interest to their fellow-citizens. Peculiarities of manner and person, which in the ordinary individual should be free from comment, may acquire a public importance, if found in a candidate for political office. Some further discrimination is necessary, therefore, than to class facts or deeds as public or private according to a standard to be applied to the fact or deed *per se*. To publish of a modest and retiring individual that he suffers from an impediment in his speech or that he cannot spell correctly, is an unwarranted, if not an unexampled, infringement of his rights, while to state and comment on the same characteristics found in a would-be congressman could not be regarded as beyond the pale of propriety.

The general object in view is to protect the privacy of private life, and to whatever degree and in whatever connection a man's life has ceased to be private, before the publication under consideration has been made, to that extent the protection is to be withdrawn. Since, then, the propriety of publishing the very same facts may depend wholly upon the person concerning whom they are published, no fixed formula can be used to prohibit obnoxious publications. Any rule of liability adopted must have in it an elasticity which shall take account of the varying circumstances of each case,—a necessity which unfortunately renders such a doctrine not only more difficult of application, but also to a certain extent uncertain in its operation and easily rendered abortive. Besides, it is only the more flagrant breaches of decency and propriety that could in practice be reached, and it is not perhaps desirable even to attempt to repress everything which the nicest taste and keenest sense of the respect due to private life would condemn.

In general, then, the matters of which the publication should be repressed may be described as those which concern the private life, habits, acts, and relations of an individual, and have no legitimate connection with his fitness for a public office which he seeks or for which he is suggested, or for any public or quasi public position which he seeks or for which he is suggested, and have no legitimate relation to or bearing upon any act done by him in a public or quasi public capacity. The foregoing is not designed as a wholly accurate or exhaustive definition, since that which must ultimately in a vast number of cases become a question of individual judgment and opinion is incapable of such definition; but it is an attempt to indicate broadly the class of matters referred to. Some things all men alike are entitled to keep from popular curiosity, whether in public life or not, while others are only private because the persons concerned have not assumed a position which makes their doings legitimate matters of public investigation.

2. The right to privacy does not prohibit the communication of any matter, though in its nature private, when the publication is made under circumstances which would render it a privileged communication according to the law of slander and libel.

Under this rule, the right to privacy is not invaded by any publication made in a court of justice, in legislative bodies, or the committees of those bodies; in municipal assemblies, or the committees of such assemblies, or practically by any communication made in any other public body, municipal or parochial, or in any body quasi public, like the large voluntary associations formed for almost every purpose of benevolence, business, or other general interest; and (at least in many jurisdictions) reports of any such proceedings would in some measure be accorded a like privilege. Nor would the rule prohibit any publication made by one in the discharge of some public or private duty, whether legal or moral, or in conduct of one's own affairs, in matters where his own interest is concerned.

3. The law would probably not grant any redress for the invasion of privacy by oral publication in the absence of special damage.

The same reasons exist for distinguishing between oral and written publications of private matters, as is afforded in the law of defamation by the restricted liability for slander as compared with the liability for libel. The injury resulting from such oral communications would ordinarily be so trifling that the law might well, in the interest of free speech, disregard it altogether.

4. The right to privacy ceases upon the publication of the facts by the individual, or with his consent.

This is but another application of the rule which has become familiar in the law of literary and artistic property. The cases there decided establish also what should be deemed a publication,—the important principle in this connection being that a private communication of circulation for a restricted purpose is not a publication within the meaning of the law.

5. The truth of the matter published does not afford a defence. Obviously this branch of the law should have no concern with the truth or falsehood of the matters published. It is not for injury to the individual's character that redress or prevention is sought, but for injury to the right of privacy. For the former, the law

of slander and libel provides perhaps a sufficient safeguard. The latter implies the right not merely to prevent inaccurate portrayal of private life, but to prevent its being depicted at all.

6. The absence of "malice" in the publisher does not afford a defence.

Personal ill-will is not an ingredient of the offence, any more than in an ordinary case of trespass to person or to property. Such malice is never necessary to be shown in an action for libel or slander at common law, except in rebuttal of some defence, *e.g.*, that the occasion rendered the communication privileged, or, under the statutes in this State and elsewhere, that the statement complained of was true. The invasion of the privacy that is to be protected is equally complete and equally injurious, whether the motives by which the speaker or writer was actuated are, taken by themselves, culpable or not; just as the damage to character, and to some extent the tendency to provoke a breach of the peace, is equally the result of defamation without regard to the motives leading to its publication. Viewed as a wrong to the individual, this rule is the same pervading the whole law of torts, by which one is held responsible for his intentional acts, even though they are committed with no sinister intent; and viewed as a wrong to society, it is the same principle adopted in a large category of statutory offences.

The remedies for an invasion of the right of privacy are also suggested by those administered in the law of defamation, and in the law of literary and artistic property, namely:—

1. An action of tort for damages in all cases. Even in the absence of special damages, substantial compensation could be allowed for injury to feelings as in the action of slander and libel.
2. An injunction, in perhaps a very limited class of cases.

It would doubtless be desirable that the privacy of the individual should receive the added protection of the criminal law, but for this, legislation would be required. Perhaps it would be deemed proper to bring the criminal liability for such publication within narrower limits; but that the community has an interest in preventing such invasions of privacy, sufficiently strong to justify the introduction of such a remedy, cannot be doubted. Still, the protection of society must come mainly through a recognition of the rights of the individual. Each man is responsible for his own acts and omissions only. If he condones what he reprobates, with a weapon at hand equal to his defence, he is responsible for the results. If he resists, public opinion will rally to his support. Has he then such a weapon? It is believed that the common law provides him with one, forged in the slow fire of the centuries, and today fitly tempered to his hand. The common law has always recognized a man's house as his castle, impregnable, often, even to its own officers engaged in the execution of its commands. Shall the courts thus close the front entrance to constituted authority, and open wide the back door to idle or prurient curiosity?

Privacy and Intimate Information

Ferdinand Schoeman

The author is a professor of philosophy at the University of South Carolina. He edited Philosophical Dimensions of Privacy *in 1984, in which this essay appeared.*

I knew the mass of men conceal'd
Their thought, for fear that if reveal'd
They would by other men be met
With blank indifference, or with blame reproved;

Matthew Arnold's "The Buried Life"

Privacy itself is suspect as a value. It makes deception possible and provides the context for concealing things about which we may feel ashamed or guilty. Embarrassed by this feature, defenders of privacy often argue that privacy is a necessary response to a social and political world that is insufficiently understanding, benevolent, respecting, trustworthy, or caring. I shall call this rationale for privacy "reactive." This response assumes that we would no longer care who knows the most intimate facts about ourselves were the world morally improved. Some have even suggested that, divorced from its prudential motivation, a proclivity for privacy should be seen as an attitude that impedes the realization of a sense of community and at the same time makes the individual more vulnerable to selective disclosures on the part of others. [If everything about a person is already known by others, that person need not fear revelations. If he (or she) discovers that others are more like him than he first suspected, he is less subject to the intimidations engendered by a sense of comparative inferiority.]

Philosophers and legal theorists have discussed privacy as valuable independent of its effectiveness in protecting persons from a morally harsh world. Charles Fried,[1] Robert Gerstein,[2] James Rachels,[3] and Richard Wasserstrom,[4] have elaborated the ways in which the intimate qualities of some interpersonal relationships would not be possible outside the context of privacy. Ruth Gavison,[5] Jeffrey Reiman,[6] Richard Wasserstrom,[7] Robert Gerstein,[8] and Stanley Benn[9] have pointed out how certain intimate dimensions of the self (having to do with the creation or discovery of moral character) would be truncated or debased without respect accorded to the individual's claim to control personal information. In the vein of these theorists, I would like to add to the discussion of the place of privacy as a value independent of its feature of protecting people from an imperfect social world. In this chapter I will elaborate themes others have introduced as well as suggest some new ones. Essentially I hope to show that on balance, outside of special contexts, revelation of self is not to be thought of as desirable in itself and may be detrimental. I hope to persuade readers that respect for privacy marks out something morally significant about what it is to be a person and about what it is to have a close relationship with another. Put abstractly, I shall argue that respect for privacy reflects a realization that not all dimensions of self and relationships gain their moral worth through their promotion of independently worthy ends.

I

I shall begin by discussing the question of whether revelation of self is good, except in those special contexts when it enables others to injure one's interests. Let me begin with the presumption that, prudent mistrust aside, more knowledge about a person is better. One implication of this view, a view entertained by Richard Wasserstrom[10] and endorsed by Richard Posner,[11] is that it is a better state of the world, other things being equal, if when I go to the dry cleaners to pick up my pants the attendant and I also share our innermost feelings and attitudes, despite the fact that we have no close relationship. The claim is that even outside the context of an especially close relationship, it is somewhat better for people to know more about one another than it is for them to know less. This attitude strikes me as most implausible but enlightening. It can be used to illustrate how much of what is good about people sharing and knowing one another intimately is contextually dependent.

As things now stand, people generally reveal intimate parts of their lives only to persons in contexts in which some special involvement is anticipated. It is, accordingly, very awkward to be going about one's business and be confronted with a plea or expectation for personal involvement which, by hypothesis, is unoccasioned by the relationship. Although sometimes welcome, generally such pleas are disturbing for they seem to give us less control over where we will expend our emotional resources. The reason for being reserved in these situations is not fear of being harmed by the content of one's revelations, but rather a realization that such situations call for something personally important to be given without first assuring that it is given freely. It does not seem plausible to suggest that it would be better if people generally revealed intimacies without really caring about the emotional attachments normally associated with such revelations; the very intimacies such revelations characteristically promote would have a harder time surfacing if they were deprived of their social and personal significance.

Three exceptions to this position should be noted and explained. First, there are times when a person so desperately needs the concern of others that something like an insistence on intimacy is legitimized. (Crisis may occasion temporary intimacy.) This concession in no way goes to showing that in normal situations such revelations are appropriate. Second, the publication of personal diaries, autobiographies, poems, confessions, and the like, though revealing of personal intimacies, hardly seems to warrant moral disapproval, as the position here advocated about reserve would seem to suggest. In response, we can observe that unlike personal disclosure, the publication of personal information leaves others completely free emotionally to take whatever attitude they want toward the writer. Even though the point of the writing may be to affect others in a personal way, there is still the distance that publication imposes that differentiates this communication from person-to-person revelations. Third, it may be pointed out that we often talk to complete strangers about intimate matters and that the frequency with which this occurs suggests that something important is being missed in the analysis presented. In considering this argument, it is important to notice that a stranger is someone uninvolved in the web of one's ordinary social relationships and someone one expects to stay uninvolved. Thus to a certain extent, revelations to a complete stranger are largely equivalent to publication because the expectation of involvement is so remote. The stranger provides an objective perspective—a perspective people admittedly find very useful to confront. The fact that one is in a position to tell a stranger things of an intimate nature does not suggest that it would be good to tell the same things to someone with whom one has an ongoing relationship. Our relationship with these people would become very different if intimate sharing were made a part of it. (Below I take up the question of the desirability of redefining relationships so as to include such intimacy.)

The emphasis in discussion of these exceptions has been on the demands revelations place upon the listener. Now, I shall discuss in detail difficulties for the person who is doing the revealing. Essentially, I shall argue that what is revealed in abstract contexts may not be at all what the revealer intends to convey.

What makes information private or intimate for a person is not just a function of the content of the information; it is also a function of the role the information plays for the person. One facet of this role is that the information is to be regarded as special and thus only revealed in certain contexts—contexts in which the very giving of the information is valued as a special act, and where the information so given will be received sympathetically. We tend to think of private information as pertaining to primarily embarrassing or wrongful conduct or thoughts. I think that what makes things private is in large part their importance to our conceptions of ourselves and to our relationships with others. To entrust another with intimate information is not primarily to provide the other with an arsenal that could prove detrimental to ourselves if revealed to the world. Perhaps the most significant aspect of what the revealer of intimate information has to convey is *that the information matters deeply to himself.* Typically, this involves a trust that the other will not regard the revelation as inconsequential, as it would be to the world at large. What is conveyed to someone uninvolved is different in an essential way from what is intimately conveyed. Selective self-disclosure provides the means through which people envalue personal experiences which are intrinsically or objectively valueless.

Perhaps the closest analogy to what I am trying to express about intimate information is our attitude toward a holy object—something that is appropriately revealed only in special circumstances. To use such an object, even though it is a humble object when seen out of context, without the idea of its character in mind is to deprive the object of its sacredness, its specialness. Such an abuse is regarded as an affront, often requiring ritual procedures to restore the object's sacred character. (Note that there are certain uses which are permitted even though not devotional in nature: use for educational purposes, for example.)

Supportive of this analogy between the private and the sacred are some literary treatments of privacy invasions. Incursions into one's privacy, one finds, are described as *pollutions* or *defilements*. In Henry James's novel *The Reverberator* we find Gaston Probert trying to explain to his fiancée, Francie Dosson, just what her revelations of family matters to, and the subsequent publication in, a society newspaper has meant to his family. Gaston puts it this way: "They were the last, the last people in France, to do it to. The sense of excruciation—or pollution."[12] We also find the theme of privacy invasion as defilement explored in Athol Fugard's play, *A Lesson from Aloes*. The South African secret police have ransacked Piet and Gladys Bezuidenhout's house. They discover Gladys's diary and read it, despite the fact that there is nothing significant in it to anybody but Gladys. Gladys, trying to explain to her husband just how defiling the experience was, speaks as follows:[13]

> There, I've cancelled those years, I'm going to forget I ever lived them. They weren't just laundry lists, you know. There were very intimate and personal things in those diaries, things a woman only talks about to herself. Even then it took me a lot of trust and courage to do that. I know I never had much of either, but I was learning. (*Her hysteria begins to surface again*) You were such a persuasive teacher, Peter! "Trust, Gladys. Trust yourself. Trust Life." There's nothing left of that. (*She brandishes her diary*) Must I tell you what I've been trying to do with this all day? Hide it. It's been behind the dressing table . . . under the mattress.
>
> Can you think of somewhere really safe? Where nobody would find it, including yourself? There isn't is there? Do you know what I would really like to do with this? Make you eat it and turn it into shit . . . then maybe everybody would leave it alone. Yes, you heard me correctly. Shit! I've learned how to use my dirty words. And just as well, because there's no other adequate vocabulary for this country. Maybe I should do that in case they come again. A page full of filthy language. Because that is what they were really hoping for when they sat down with my diaries. Filth . . . !
>
> If you were to tell me once more that they won't come again . . . ! To start with, I don't believe you, but even if I did, that once was enough. You seem to have a lot of difficulty understanding that, Peter. It only needs to happen to a woman once, for her to lose all trust she ever had in anything or anybody. They violated me, Peter. I might just as well have stayed in that bed, lifted up my nightdress and given them each a turn. I've shocked you. Good! Then maybe now you understand.

Not only is it a violation of an individual if intimate information is forced or tricked out of the person, or if a confidence is betrayed, as the literary examples here illustrate, but even the person himself who feels something special about this information may be insufficiently sensitive to the role of this information in his own mind. (Perhaps we should say that a person can violate his own privacy.) Probably every person has had the experience of telling another something very important, something that is unappreciated as special by the listener. This information, we learn, is really only meant for those who will treat it as something that matters *because it matters to the speaker*. Otherwise the most we have is a good or interesting story; often not even that. By being shared with others who cannot really appreciate the personal significance of certain information, such information loses some of its special character for the revealers. The kind of connectedness that is a prerequisite for intimate sharing must be present for this kind of appreciation to emerge. Otherwise the effort at communicating will misfire.

I have been arguing that the revelation of intimate information should be regarded as appropriate only in certain contexts, and that indeed, in a sense this kind of revelation *cannot* take place outside such a context. When it does take place outside the proper setting, a sense of violation is occasioned, whether the revelation was voluntary or not. Let me now address the question: Would the world be a better place if everyone shared the kind of relationship in which it was appropriate to make private disclosures? In response, let me begin by noting that different kinds of relationships require different qualities of persons. For instance, qualities which make persons good friends may make them unsuitable for a supervisor–supervisee relationship. There need not be any defect in the persons either as friends or as workers; qualities required in each relationship may be mutually exclusive. For a host of reasons, personal characteristics may determine that a person feels more comfortable in, and gains more out of, certain personal settings than others. Such concerns cannot be irrelevant to the capacity and desirability for intimacy. It is worth noting that in many of our important relationships emotional distance between the parties is crucial. For instance in a lawyer–client relationship, a psychotherapist–patient relationship, or even a student–teacher relationship it is not ideal that there be unbounded emotional involvement between the parties. These relationships require an objectivity of judgment that would be counterproductive to eliminate. Conversely, such professional detachment would be inappropriate in relationships in which identification with the other is a central feature of the relationship, as in parent–child relationships, friendships, and marriages.

People have, and it is important that they maintain, different relationships with different people. Information appropriate in the context of one relationship may not be appropriate in another. Such observations have been captured by sociological notions such as "audience segregation," "role," and "role credibility."[14] Such notions have been introduced to help describe or explain how the effectiveness of our relationships to various people in diverse contexts depends on limited access to persons or, more precisely, on access to limited dimensions of persons. Though some of our important relationships and aspirations involve intimacy with others, some are focused on really quite limited and objective interactions. As Ruth Gavison has argued,[15] part of our capacity to work with others in professional contexts may depend on remaining uninvolved in personal, political, moral, and religious aspects of the other. Accordingly, if a person finds the discussion of his own or anyone else's intimate life inappropriate in many contexts, it is not necessarily because he has anything to be ashamed about or anything for which he should feel guilty. It is that there are various dimensions of a person which it is important to develop, only some of which may involve intimate sharing. The integrity of different spheres of a person, and the ultimate integrity of the person, depends on that person's capacity to focus on one dimension at a time. This defense of privacy has nothing to do with lack of trust or good will generally, or with any fact about the moral imperfections of the world.

Some writers have equated nondisclosure of self to others as tantamount to fraud, hypocrisy, deceit.[16] Keeping people ignorant about what one is like in spheres they are not part of, or have no reasonable claim to knowledge about, is in no way morally tainted behavior. Generally, so long as a person does not misrepresent himself to those who, within the relevant domain, reasonably rely on his projected image, that person is not acting deceptively.

Related to the concern that role segregation is deceptive or hypocritical is the claim that it would be better if people exhibited coherence across the different roles they maintain. For instance, what one is like as a professional would in relevant ways be indicative of what one is like as a family member, as a citizen, as a friend, as an athlete, and so on. Though what I shall have to say here is admittedly sketchy and speculative, there does seem to be evidence of a psychological nature that relates to this issue. Different conceptions of what it is to be a person do bear on the issue of an individual's personality coherence and the role of privacy. According to the commonsense view, there is a core personality that is integrated but puts on various guises (for various purposes) in particular contexts. The picture is of a character standing behind various masks, none of which is really the actor, with the ability of discarding all the personae and revealing the true core. From this view, we can distinguish authentic responses of an individual from those that are role-governed, context-dependent, and inauthentic. On this account, privacy serves to protect a person's intimate self through concealment. Privacy permits pretense.

There is another view according to which there may be no unified core personality that exhibits authentic or inauthentic responses to circumstances. Instead there are diverse facets of personality that are brought into play in various contexts. These facets of self are not personae that some central self dons in its inauthentic mode. Rather these selves actually constitute the person. A person is something like a corporation of context-dependent characters. Any coherence between dimensions is something achieved and not something naturally implicit in the person.

On this second view it is still possible for people to be deceptive or inauthentic. The reference self is simply not the central core; it is the particular dimension of self that is specific to the prevailing context. Roles are not the masks of personality but the very medium within which personality is attributable to people. Privacy from this perspective supplies the condition for the expression and fulfillment of different dimensions of self, all of which may be equally real. It is important to emphasize that the attribution of dimensionality to individuals does not mean that people are multiple personalities in a clinical sense. Rather this view states that one may operate with different values and sensitivities in these different modes without being either schizophrenic or deceptive.

Psychologists who have advanced this second view of the self have done so on the basis of clinical and experimental findings.[17] Their most dramatic evidence is that certain consequences that would be anticipated on the basis of the commonsense view of self are frequently not what is found. On the commonsense view an individual's behavior in one setting should be quite predictable on the basis of his behavior in other settings. This is not the case. What is found is that knowledge about a person in one context is of little predictive value when anticipating behavior in dissimilar contexts. Instead, what proves to be a better predictor of behavior is knowledge of how others, however varied in personality, have behaved in the particular context at issue. Knowing the context of behavior and knowing how others have responded to this context prove to be more reliable indicators of behavior than does knowing how an individual has behaved in other contexts. There is more uniformity in behavior among different individuals in the same context than there is in the same person over a range of different contexts.

This evidence may suggest that there is no core self; one of the key functions that the core self is supposed to serve is to account for the consistency of behavior through diverse contexts and times. If the effect is not present, there is less reason to posit the cause. The results of the experiments cited above suggest there is some basis for thinking that privacy may play a central role in personality development. Privacy may provide the contexts in which various facets of personality can develop.

There are situations which require unusually high coherence between roles or even require that there be only one role in the agent's life. Someone who joins a monastic order has apparently committed himself to leading only a monastic life, or at least to doing only things consistent with that life. People who present themselves in such roles indicate to others that all their dimensions can be expected to conform to the ideals of their self-proclaimed ideal self. Such roles may preclude much of what would normally count as private domains. Although there are obviously things to admire about such choices, it is also apparent that there are costs in terms of aspects of the self that must be foregone.

II

Are there domains of life which are inherently private? Several positions have been developed in the literature in answer to this question. According to some, what it is that is regarded as private is culturally determined and respect for a person's privacy is primarily symbolic in significance.[18] According to a related position, what is private is determined by each particular relationship.[19] Relationships define which parts of another's life one can legitimately inquire into and which are beyond one's legitimate ken. According to still others, what is private is determined by what area of one's life does not, or tends not to, affect the significant interests of others.[20]

The last criterion is subject to the following difficulty. Whatever one might claim as private can cease being such if others manage to generate a stake in that state of affairs. With such a criterion one no longer maintains control over what would otherwise seem a private part of one's life. For instance, so long as one is in a position to make a large bet on any matter relating to another's life, that matter ceases to be private because of the interest one acquires in uncovering this facet of another's life. Additionally, if we think of the large investments certain institutions have in tracking down intimate details of various people's lives, we should have to concede that these details are not really private after all. While we may want to be somewhat utilitarian in considering how much weight to give to individual privacy claims, I think that there is little persuasive about the position that the "self-regarding" aspects of life are at the same time the private aspects.

A related criterion of the private, it could be suggested, is that it be the domain of a person's life which the individual is generally in the best position to manage well. Assigning rights over this area to anyone else, the suggestion continues, would result in lower overall benefits. One may concede the point that individuals should control those parts of their lives which they can best manage without thinking that this constitutes a criterion of the private. Although a physician might be in the best position to regulate how we should care for our bodies, this remains a private matter.

Although there are many things that we regard as private, some of these things seem essentially private because they are central to us—because they define what we are emotionally, physically, cognitively, and relationally. We might say about these categories that we consider information relating to them presumptively private. Other values may offset our interest in protecting an individual's privacy in any particular context, nonetheless, roughly speaking, one's private sphere in some sense can be equated with those areas of a person's life which are considered intimate or innermost. Though categories like parent, poet, and patriot have the meaning they do in a social context, it is their centrality to identity which makes these roles part of a person's private dimension.

This view is my basis for rejecting the second criterion of the private mentioned above: the view that each relationship defines what is private to it. It may be true that depending on our relationship we will regard some pieces of information appropriate for some to inquire into and others not. This fact does not settle what it is that is private. Even if we think that it is appropriate for a psychiatrist or a spouse to ask us about various things, this does not mean that such topics are not private matters. It is just that the norms permit some people access to our private domains.

The position advocated here might be challenged by observing that qualities such as age, race, family status, profession, and general appearance are central to us even though we do not generally regard these as private. And other characteristics are taken as private even though they do not have much to do with what is central to our lives or with the integrity of our intimate selves, for example, annual income. The qualities that I mention as central but which are not regarded generally as private are those that would be either very difficult to conceal if one were to have any social existence at all, or else central to one's public role and thus counterproductive to keep private for that reason. With respect to those things that are not central to people but about which people feel a sense of privacy, these might generally be regarded as sensitive topics because of the reactive concerns we all share or because of socially conditioned norms. In any event, in saying that the realm of the intimate is essentially private or marks off what is the private realm, I am not saying that there are not other bases for people feeling private about certain matters. Everyone would concede that much of what people regard as private is a culturally conditioned sensitivity. The issue is whether culturally distinctive norms determine all of what is regarded as private, and I am arguing that the answer to this is no.

Numerous lawyers and philosophers have accused those who introduce privacy terminology when discussing state regulation of birth control and abortion as confused.[21] Still, if one thinks that whether a married couple uses birth control is a *private matter* and for that reason not within the proper domain of state regulation, the sense of privacy I am advocating is vindicated. Even if some pressing need legitimized state involvement with such decisions, they would remain private decisions in the sense that they related to intimate elements of life. (They would cease to be private in the sense of answering who had final legal authority to make decisions here.)[22] The centrality of decisions concerning birth control and abortion to intimate relationships and intimate aspects of oneself *makes* such issues privacy issues.

One might ask how am I differentiating the notion of the private from the notion of the intimate. Although I have regarded the intimate as a criterion of the private, labeling something as part of one's private realm indicates that there are norms of nonintrusion which apply to that area of a person's life. Labeling an area one of intimacy does not carry the same normative associations. The relationship between the two is, however, internal.

III

I have argued that respect for privacy enriches social and personal interaction by providing contexts for the development of varied kinds of relationships and multiple dimensions of personality. I have also suggested that while one can usually share informational aspects of oneself without apparent limit, sharing what is significant to one about this information is effectively limited to special kinds of relationships, and that we have independent reasons for not taking as an ideal the generalization of such special relationships to encompass all our interactions with others. Let me now move on.

The general point I wish to advance in this section is that respect for privacy signifies our recognition that not all dimensions of persons or relationships need to serve some independently validated social purpose. A private sphere of valuation must be morally recognized. My position involves two arguments. First, part of what is meant by respecting persons as persons is the acknowledgment that what has meaning for one individual thereby gains presumptive moral value independent of its promotion of socially valuable ends. Second, the personal basis of value is best kept located in the private realm generally; otherwise it will atrophy and be subsumed by public standards of value.

I start with the thesis that the individual is a source of value. A number of considerations are important to keep in mind. First, if the only morally recognizable point of a person's activities were to consist in the degree to which his activities assisted other people's projects, we would have a self-defeating and groundless situation. Some things must be good for persons, independent of their effects on others, or else there would be no point to helping others in the first place. Second, what is important to a person about pursuing goals is not only the objective relevance of the goals themselves but also their personal relevance—the fact that they are his goals.[23] It would be wrong to say of a person that his attachment to his objective should not count in assessing whether it is worth his while to pursue that end. And it would be wrong to say that his attachment should have no independent bearing on others' evaluations and pursuits. Without an individual's capacity to create value in something by valuing it, what we are left with is respect for values but no respect for persons as such. The respect for persons would be derivative only to the extent to which persons happened to value what was really and independently valuable. On such a view persons would have only instrumental or incidental value insofar as they promoted the right objectives. This is not to say that the fact that a person forms an objective is to be taken by others as a decisive reason for valuing and facilitating that objective. It is only to say that this valuation by the individual must be accorded moral weight independent, to a certain degree, of its overall consequences for society.

One could object to this position on the ground that what is valuable in an individual's idiosyncratic objectives is not the object of his or her loyalties as such, which may be neutral or detestable, but rather the *process through which the individual exercises autonomy*. Focusing on the desirability of autonomous choice provides sufficient basis for respect for individuals without having to further suppose that individuals add value to the objectives themselves by valuing them.[24] In response, one can observe that the values or loyalties one adheres to may not reflect autonomous choice in a direct sense and insofar as the agent sees it. For instance, a person may think that it is only through subjection to something over which he has no legitimate choice that he satisfies important objectives, for example, subjection to moral principles and rules or to divine commands. (One could then respond that even such first-order subjection reflects autonomy but at a higher level; the problem can be reiterated at each level.) Why should we judge that it is because a value reflects autonomous choice, and not inner meaning, that a person's objectives gain presumptive value? It seems much more plausible to suggest that whatever value autonomy has derives from its provision of prospects for meaningful existence than to say that the value of inner meaning derives from its reflection of autonomy.

It is no accident that some of our institutions that protect people's loyalties to ends which are potentially antagonistic to social well-being (such as testimonial privileges generally and the protection against self-incrimination specifically) generally were secured in a context of freedom of conscience,[25] which is an aspect of protection of intimacy. The essence of such struggles is the argument that there is within each individual some part that is not to be exploited even for socially or politically worthy ends. The medieval notion of *subsidiarity* can be usefully applied here. Subsidiarity involves regarding the political state as limited in its scope to certain domains of a person's life. This view specifically regards the state as not being competent to involve itself with determinations in matters of conscience or inner meanings generally. This position need not imply that the state does not have the ability or capacity to be effective in such areas. More pertinent to our concern is the theory's insistence that whatever the state's ability or capacity to mold consciences, it is violative of a person to do so.

Privacy, I wish to suggest, insulates individual objectives from social scrutiny. Social scrutiny can generally be expected to move individuals in the direction of the socially useful. Privacy insulates people from this kind of accountability and thereby protects the realm of the personal. When in conflict with social aims, private objectives tend to be devalued. For example, discussing parent–child relationships, nearly all the vast literature cites the best interest of the child as the sole basis for legitimizing parental control over the child. These discussions leave out entirely the interest parents and children alike have in maintaining intimate involvement (except as it promotes the child's well-being). This interest in intimacy must be taken into account when characterizing the moral basis for family autonomy. It is in such contexts that important aspects of personality develop. Something important is obscured when the family is seen as having primarily social, rather than personal, objectives.[26]

I believe it is important in a society for there to be institutions in which people can experience some of what they are without excessive scrutiny. Privacy is such an institution. Privacy involves norms that allow the pursuit and development of aims and relationships that count simply because the people involved find meaning in them. Privacy, I want to argue, provides the context for personal objectives being respected. I have suggested there is nothing wrong with people pursuing personally validated objectives, even though these do not serve the interest of everyone or enhance the autonomous status of others.

I have argued in this chapter that from a number of perspectives privacy is important independent of its *reactive* function of protecting people from the morally unscrupulous, or merely suboptimal, qualities of others. Privacy is important with respect to the multidimensionality of persons and with respect for the personal or inner lives of people. Dimensionality and inner meaning together provide the primary bases for defending the nonreactive importance of privacy.

Notes

For helpful comments and discussions I am indebted to Herbert Fingarette, Kent Greenawalt, Teri Bell, Michael Gardner, Sara Schechter-Schoeman, Evelyn B. Pluhar, and Linda Weingarten.

1. Charles Fried, "Privacy," 77 *Yale Law Journal* (1968) 475–93.
2. Robert Gerstein, "Intimacy and privacy," 89 *Ethics* (1978) 76–81.
3. James Rachels, "Why privacy is important," 4 *Philosophy and Public Affairs* (1975) 323–33.
4. Richard Wasserstrom, "Privacy: some arguments and assumptions," in Richard Bronaugh, ed., *Philosophical Law,* Westport, Conn.: Greenwood Press, 1978.
5. Ruth Gavison, "Privacy and the limits of law," 89 *Yale Law Journal* (1980) 421–71.
6. Jeffrey Reiman, "Privacy, intimacy, and personhood," 6 *Philosophy and Public Affairs* (1976) 26–44.
7. Richard Wasserstrom, "Privacy: some arguments and assumptions," in Richard Bronaugh, ed., *Philosophical Law,* Westport, Conn.: Greenwood Press, 1978.
8. Robert Gerstein, "Privacy and self-incrimination," 80 *Ethics* (1970) 87–101.
9. Stanley Benn, "Privacy, freedom and respect for persons," in J. R. Pennock and W. Chapman, eds., *Nomos XIII: Privacy,* New York, Atherton Press, 1971.
10. Richard Wasserstrom, "Privacy: some arguments and assumptions," in Richard Bronaugh, ed., *Philosophical Law,* Westport, Conn.: Greenwood Press, 1978.
11. Richard Posner, "The right to privacy," 12 *Georgia Law Review* (1978) 393–422.
12. Henry James, *The Reverberator,* New York: Grove Press, 1979, p. 190. See also Helen Lynd, *On Shame and the Search for Identity,* New York: Harcourt, Brace & Co., 1958.
13. Athol Fugard, *A Lesson from Aloes,* New York: Random House, 1981, pp. 27–28.
14. Erving Goffman, *The Presentation of Self in Everyday Life,* Garden City: Double-day, 1959.
15. Ruth Gavison, "Privacy and the limits of law," 89 *Yale Law Journal* (1980) 87–101.
16. See the works of Posner, Wasserstrom, and Goffman already cited for expressions to this effect.
17. Walter Mischel, *Personality and Assessment,* New York: John Wiley, 1968, chapter 5.
18. Charles Fried, "Privacy," 77 *Yale Law Journal* (1968) 475–93.
19. James Rachels, "Why privacy is important," 4 *Philosophy and Public Affairs* (1975) 323–33.
20. H. J. McCloskey, "The political ideal of privacy," 21 *Philosophical Quarterly* (1971) 303–14, and "Privacy and the right to privacy," 55 *Philosophy* (1980) 17–38.
21. Louis Henkin, "Privacy and autonomy," 74 *Columbia Law Review* (1974) 1410–33; Ruth Gavison, "Privacy and the limits of law" 89 *Yale Law Journal* (1980) 421–71, esp. 438 ff.; Hyman Gross, "Privacy and autonomy," in J. R. Pennock and J. W. Chapman, eds., *Nomos XIII: Privacy,* New York: Atherton Press, 1971; and Hyman Gross, "The concept of privacy," 42 *New York University Law Review* (1967) 35–54.
22. Stanley I. Benn and Gerald Gaus, "The Public and the private: concepts and action," in Stanley I. Benn and Gerald Gaus, eds., *The Public and the Private in Social Policy,* London: Croon Helm and St. Martin's Press, 1983, pp. 3–27.

23. See Thomas Nagel, "The Limits of Objectivity," in Sterling McMurren, ed., *The Tanner Lectures on Human Values,* Salt Lake City: University of Utah Press, 1980, pp. 75–140; Bernard Williams, "Persons, character and morality," in Amelie Rorty, ed., *Identity of Persons,* Berkeley: University of California Press, 1976, pp. 197–216; and Samuel Scheffler, *The Rejection of Consequentialism,* Oxford: Oxford University Press, 1982, especially chapter 2.

24. Evelyn Pluhar suggested this problem in her "Commentary on 'privacy and intimate information,' " presented at the 1983 American Philosophical Association, Western Division, meetings.

25. See Leonard Levy, *Origins of the Fifth Amendment,* Oxford: Oxford University Press, 1968. Interestingly, even Jeremy Bentham, who was hostile to testimonial privileges generally, acknowledged the priest-penitent privilege since it recognized a Catholic's institutionally defined duty to confess transgressions, and thus was a requirement of religious freedom.

26. For an extensive defense of this claim see two works by Ferdinand Schoeman: "Rights of children, rights of parents, and the moral basis of the family," 91 *Ethics* (1980) 6–19, and "Childhood competence and autonomy," 12 *The Journal of Legal Studies* (1983) 267–87.

NIH, the Modern Wonder

Bernadine Healy

The author composed this essay when she was Director of the National Institutes of Health. She delivered it as a speech for the City Club Forum of Cleveland, Ohio, in 1992.

Certain discoveries—America, electricity, the atom, DNA—transcend their time by redefining our world. But the exact nature of the transformation is never known with certainty at the outset. Such has been the case with the biological revolution and how it is transforming medicine and influencing our economy. The National Institutes of Health, now a $9 billion enterprise, has spearheaded this revolution through its investment in biomedical research over the past 40 years, emerging as a wonder of the modern world. Unlike the ancient wonders, NIH is alive, vibrant, and relevant to the life of everyone in this country. Not a monument to the past, but a searchlight on the future.

The Biological Revolution and Molecular Medicine

First, what is this biological revolution that NIH has wrought? The ability to define, recombine, and express genes of virtually all living organisms, has enabled us to begin to understand the fundamental basis of life processes. What was "effectively science fiction" only a couple of decades ago, is now becoming science fact. And NIH's efforts have been undertaken for entirely the right reasons: to protect and help those who suffer an

"unjust throw of the genetic dice"

and to attain a more profound knowledge about facts

"which underlie the subtleties of human existence."

The health benefits that are derived from this explosion of knowledge in the life sciences and, specifically, in molecular biology, have only just begun.

It has been said that

"The quick harvest of pure science is the useable
process, the medicine, the machine."

The lush harvest of the biological revolution is the understanding, prevention, and treatment of human disease. It has brought us to a key time of transition. We are crossing the bridge from the conventional medicine of our ancestors to the medicine—the molecular medicine—of tomorrow. We are acquiring new tools, raising new practical questions, creating new possibilities for both life and for livelihood. And, with world tensions reduced, we are at a point in history where, after many decades of worldwide anguish and conflict, it finally may be possible to turn science to the permanent service of life itself.

For the next few minutes let me back up those large claims with some practical examples.

In 1951, Watson and Crick discovered that the "staff of life," DNA, has a double helical structure—a six-foot-long coiled thread of heredity that resides in our every cell. In 1961, Marshall Nirenberg at the NIH campus in Bethesda decoded the DNA, giving us the recipes of life—its Rosetta stone—the "proteins that are us." In the 1970's, NIH grantees discovered enzymes that snip DNA at specific locations, and devised methods to synthesize and insert new information into the genes. Cloning genes has made possible the production of human insulin, growth hormone, blood-clot dissolving substances, and other previously rare natural substances for the treatment of a wide range of diseases.

Today, NIH researchers French Anderson and Steven Rosenberg have begun gene therapy, replacing or suppressing faulty pieces of genetic information that are recipes for disaster—not life. Genetically engineered vaccines are already a reality in preventing hepatitis—and a real possibility in combatting heart disease, Alzheimer's disease, AIDS, and other human afflictions. Less than a year ago, the NIH undertook the first test of a genetically engineered cancer vaccine. Tumor cells were removed from a number of patients, and an immune strengthening gene was added. We are, of course, only at the beginning. But unlike some cancer treatments you often read about which are all too often acts of desperation, this kind of genetic work is an act of exploration and promise.

On a still more sweeping scale, so is NIH's Human Genome Project. It just may be the most ambitious medical research pursuit ever undertaken. It involves government, universities, industrial, and the latest technology to crack the human genetic code: the human genome. An elongated molecule of DNA is made up of some 50,000 to 100,000 genes located on 23 pairs of chromosomes. The genome contains all the information necessary to make a human being. *How* remains a mystery, and, in all likelihood, the most profound discovery in the 21st Century will be the mechanisms that enable a single-cell fertilized egg to become a complex human being.

The term "mapping" is instructive. The 50,000 to 100,000 genes are made up of more than 3 billion base pairs. If there were three billion people on the face of the earth—there are actually 5.3 billion—the genome project would be roughly the equivalent of knowing precisely where each person is, mapping each person's exact location. It is estimated that some 5,000 genes cause human disease. One of the aims is to identify the location of genes that cause disease, and to solve the combinations among genes that cause other diseases. Once we know what the genes are, where they are, and how they work, we will be much further on the way to understanding why and how they fail.

We have already made amazing progress in isolating disease genes. Recent examples include cystic fibrosis, Duchenne muscular dystrophy, familial polyposis (which predisposes to colon cancer), and the fragile X syndrome. Let me expand briefly on the fragile X syndrome, a recent discovery which offers but one example of the power of this kind of knowledge to transform medicine.

Fragile X syndrome is the most common form of mental retardation in males, affecting about one in 1,250. Females have a lower prevalence, because they are blessed with two X chromosomes, and have only a 50 percent chance of expressing the diseased gene if they inherit it. Although the fragile X chromosome has seemingly been in the human gene pool for a long time, it possesses the devastating characteristic of becoming worse with each successive generation. In other words, the abnormality in the chromosome becomes more marked, and that results in increasingly severe mental retardation. The discovery of the gene on the X chromosome responsible for this syndrome has led to the development of a diagnostic test for the condition. The discovery also uncovered a novel type of mutation never seen before by geneticists. Within a few months of the discovery of the Fragile X mutation, two other genetic neurologic diseases (myotonic dystrophy and spinal bulbar muscular atrophy) were shown also to be caused by a similar mutation. Both of these diseases also have the devastating characteristic of increasing in severity in each succeeding generation.

In many other diseases, the pattern of inheritance involves multiple genes rather than a single mutation on a single gene. For example, various forms of cancer and cardiovascular disease have a clear genetic component, but the genetic basis is complex. Analysis of complex genetic inheritance, so far, has led to little success. The creation of complete human chromosomal maps could make analysis of complex genetic diseases possible. It could, in short, bring the genetic determinants of asthma, heart attacks, vulnerability to alcoholism, and susceptibility to environmentally induced diseases within our grasp.

Once a gene has been identified, we can move more quickly to an understanding of the mechanism of gene action, control of gene expression, the function played by the expressed gene product in normal biological processes, and the dysfunctional effects of an abnormal gene product in disease. Gene discovery—its mapping on a given chromosome and its sequencing which deciphers its code—is at the heart of molecular medicine, the medicine that will transform how we understand, prevent and treat all manner of human disease.

Ethical, Legal and Social Implications

At the NIH, this powerful human genomic information is being gathered to benefit humankind. Science itself, however, does not provide the answers to all the many questions about how society will use the information when it is available. NIH is dedicated to exploring the legal, ethical, and social implications of the work it does and to handling the expected and the unexpected in a socially responsible way. Let me again illustrate concretely two major issues that are of immediate concern to the NIH: one is genetic privacy, the other is patent protection.

First, genetic privacy information about the genetic makeup and predisposition of individuals and groups is powerful in many ways. It is also highly personal, as it describes the biological essence of an individual human being. Genetic information may be of interest to others who for a variety of reasons—not all good—can make use of such information. Thus, we firmly believe that individuals must have control over the acquisition and disclosure of their own personal genetic information. Genetic information can identify health risks we inherit from our families. Genetic information almost always has implications for close relatives who share genes. It also raises issues for children and at how early an age we should identify long-term future risks—like for cancer or heart disease—in the interest of modifying lifetime behavior. At the same time, contrary to popular belief, genetic analyses are not foolproof predictors; they are not crystal balls. They always involve uncertainties and cannot predict how individuals will surely experience the possibilities they face. As physicians and scientists, we believe it is the right of individuals and their families to determine the relative value of this information for their own lives, and to control its acquisition as well as its disclosure to others.

We must also be sensitive to concerns about possible discrimination on the basis of genotype. I wager that the most time honored form of discrimination has been genetic—namely, against people who are born without a Y chromosome. For example, there appears to be a relationship between *not* having a Y chromosome and not being able to get a line of credit. Clearly,

"Genetics *is the* science of differences."

Genetic information has the potential to be used to categorize people. Genetic information about individuals can expose them to discrimination and loss of access to social and economic opportunities. For example, consider the current efforts to unravel the molecular genetics of disorders such as Alzheimer's disease, schizophrenia, or alcoholism: conditions that carry a stigma in our society. Discrimination on the basis of genotype is ethically no different from discrimination based on other biological traits or genetic facts such as gender, skin color, or disability. Protection from such discrimination must be a right.

Issues of privacy, of potential discrimination in the job market, of insurability, and the handling of information when science permits us to identify the potential victim of a disease in the absence of any known treatment or cure for it—these and related concerns will accompany us all the days of the Human Genome Project. NIH's Human Genome Center sets aside five percent of its funding to explore the ethical, social, and legal implications of its research and the pursuit of mechanisms for dealing with these issues. For example, the program established an Insurance Task Force, a group representing the insurance industry, consumer groups, geneticists, health policy analysts, and insurance policy makers, which has set for itself the task of establishing industry guidelines and public policy options regarding insurer use of genetic information. The NIH Program Advisory Committee has also communicated with the Equal Employment Opportunity Commission on the issues of discrimination based on genetic tests for disease in the workplace. We are committed to taking these concerns seriously, to seeking the best thinking we can find, and to educating and soliciting the views of the public, who are the ultimate arbiter of social change in a democratic society.

Gene Patenting

And finally, gene patenting—another matter of broad societal concern that has received some recent attention. It is a matter which has generated more heat than light, so let me put the issue in context.

Recently, scientists at NIH developed rapid gene sequencing technology which has made it possible to identify in a few months' time thousands of previously unknown genes. The so-called cDNA approach to gene discovery is not a new concept, but rather a major and important technological breakthrough using newly developed instrumentation, powerful computers, and advanced robotics. New genes or gene fragments are discovered by direct sequencing of human-made, edited copies of natural genes and then searching the NIH maintained computer bank of known genes to see if the sequence is novel. This approach uncovers large quantities of new genes, but provides limited knowledge of the function of each gene. One knows that a given gene is expressed in a certain tissue, for example, brain or heart; one knows that a given gene can be used as a probe to map the gene to a chromosome; and by comparing the sequence of a given gene or gene fragment to other known genes in humans and other organisms, possible biologic function or disease causing potential are suggested. The technology does not, however, provide the specific biologic function or the reason the gene is being expressed in the given tissue. This approach differs from the more traditional—and slower—method of gene discovery which starts with a known protein, like a hormone, or a genetic trait, and works back to clone the gene.

The cDNA approach "rediscovers" some known genes—sometimes finding them expressed in unexpected places—which leads to provocative and potentially important information. Similarly, with rapid sequencing discovering thousands of new genes, the more classical gene-by-gene approach will "rediscover" genes that have already been discovered by sequencing. These two approaches are complementary and—used in tandem—will greatly accelerate the pace of mapping and sequencing the entire human genome, which brings us to the current patenting dilemma. Over the past ten to twelve years, intellectual property protection of the many discoveries stemming from the biological revolution, including genes, has fostered the development of the biotechnology industry. The biotechnology industry is the "quick harvest of pure science" in that it has produced the useable processes, the medicine and the machines that have transferred scientific knowledge into products to benefit the public. Through a broad portfolio of legislation, NIH has the mandate to ensure that its basic discoveries are transferred into the commercial sector. For NIH, our primary goal is to ensure that new therapies and new pharmaceuticals reach patients. NIH has provided the scientific base and the brainpower for the new biotechnology industry. NIH has been the "silent partner" in creating the biotech industry and now finds itself in a new role: that of contributing to the nation's economy.

The President's Council on Competitiveness recently noted that the biotechnology industry has the potential to surpass the computer industry in size and importance. Last year it had $4 billion in sales; by the year 2000 it is estimated to approach 50 billion. Today the biotechnology industry employs 70,000 Americans; in the future it may employ millions. This, however, is a fragile industry, and the United States, at the moment, enjoys a fragile lead. American firms dominate in the biotechnology fields—as we did in the early years of electronics. We own between 70 and 80 percent of biotech patents. The industry shows a positive U.S. trade balance. Its commercial benefits extend beyond medicine into agriculture, the environment, and chemical production.

Some have suggested that the information based economy of today will give way to a "bioeconomy" in the next century. It is not surprising that Japan, France, Britain, and many of the less developed countries have identified biotechnology as among their highest national priorities. With this backdrop, exactly how we handle technology transfer, including the matter of intellectual property rights is no small matter—and it is a matter that goes well beyond the NIH.

Applying existing patent law to the fruits of molecular biology has had a short but rocky history. Back in the late 1970s, it took a series of court decisions and finally the Supreme Court in *Diamond v. Chakrabarty*, in a 5 to 4 vote, to declare genetically engineered microorganisms patentable. Some argued that living organisms should not be patented, and the debate was noisy and intense. Similar contention surrounded the issuance of the Boyer-Cohen Patent, which protected the use of the method for making recombinant DNA. You may remember the furor that the patenting of the Harvard transgenic mouse generated in the mid 1980s. Over this time, human and other genes have also been patented. Patents have become important to the growth and survival of the biotechnology industry.

So, by trial and error, by debate and split decision, with some fear and trepidation, we have trekked along the sometimes parallel, sometimes intersecting paths of evolving science, evolving patent law, evolving technology transfer policy and evolving new industry. In this context, the recent, sometimes hot, debate surrounding NIH's patent filing for human gene sequences is not really new.

Let me explain precisely how NIH ended up at the center of this debate. No one, including a vast array of patent lawyers, knew a year ago, or knows today, whether novel genes sequences for which biological function is still unknown can be patented. In the face of uncertainty, NIH filed for patent protection on more than 2,000 novel gene sequences discovered by Dr. Craig Venter and his colleagues at the NIH. The filing enabled Dr. Venter to immediately release his data to the public. Here I would like to emphasize that NIH's goal in patenting any discovery, including a gene, is not to make money but rather to promote and encourage the rapid development and commercialization of products to improve human health, and to do so in a socially responsible way. The filing—which NIH must make public but which other entities including industry, universities or foreign governments do not have to make public—sparked an important debate. The debate was inevitable—but as is often the case, the inevitable came too soon.

There are numerous pros and cons to seeking patent protection for gene sequences. I will briefly touch on them:

1. *A major issue is whether one should claim rights to the discovery of a novel molecule when biological function is limited*—an incomplete discovery if you will. The fact remains that there are scientific and legal ambiguities here. Because the gene is expressed, say in a human brain, it is *de facto* important; it has some utility as a probe and may eventually prove useful as a therapeutic. But how much utility must be demonstrated when one has defined novel composition of matter is not known. Patents have been awarded for discovery of novel biological molecules for which the full range of function—or even most important function—is not known.

2. Another issue that is raised is *a moral/philosophical one, should we patent our "universal heritage?"* In a recent editorial entitled "Don't Patent Human Genes," the French science minister Curien is quoted as saying a patent should not be granted

> "for something that is part of our universal heritage."

This view is inconsistent with the policy of the French government which holds that it *is* alright to patent a gene if function is known and commercial importance assured.

3. *Some fear that if patents are issued they will be too broad and too plentiful.*
The concern about broadness—that a patent would automatically grant rights to
the functional protein, antibodies, and all uses—may well be overstated. Patent
law clearly states that one can only claim protection for that which one can produce without the need for further undue experimentation. Concern about patent
clutter is real, and already plagues the biotechnology field because of the rapid
pace of discovery. In my view, this provides all the more reason to have a test case.

4. One of the most important issues is *whether patenting is likely to help or
hinder product development.* NIH is only interested in patenting if it will facilitate
product development—facilitate the movement of basic discoveries out of the
laboratories into the commercial sector to develop new products and technolo-
gies to benefit the public. NIH cannot do this without industry. I have met with
numerous leaders of biotechnology and pharmaceutical companies—large and
small—and I have found that the industry itself is not at all certain. Not surprisingly, the Industrial Biotechnology Association and the American Biotechnology
Association, which together represent virtually all of the U.S. biotechnology industry, have taken positions in support of NIH's filing as an appropriate action

"to preserve the Government's options with respect
to protecting potentially patentable subject matter while the
technology transfer policy issues are being resolved."

5. Another issue is *whether the U.S. government—the federal government—
should be filing for patents on these potentially powerful "informational molecules."*
One leading pharmaceutical firm says no—but in their view it is OK if individual scientists do so under the rubric of academic freedom. I've found little support either in industry or academia for this view. In any case, NIH has a mandate
from both the President and the Congress to seek patents on discoveries made
with NIH support—and taxpayers' money.

6. *Yet another matter has to do with the international community.* Whatever
is done in the patent arena must take into account the global marketplace. As
in the United States, views within foreign countries differ. Some foreign scientists have publicly stated they will not seek patents; others have privately indi-
cated they have and or will. Several foreign countries have criticized the U.S.
filing but have not officially embraced a uniform policy of full disclosure or of
patenting. The British kept their cDNA sequences secret for a year and now
have stated that they will file because we have—as a defensive move. The very
level of discussion seems to acknowledge that some kind of intellectual property value may exist.

The NIH believes that American discoveries must be published for the benefit of all including the international community. But, it also believes that intellectual property rights in the interests of American taxpayers and U.S. industry
cannot be ignored. Some kind of international agreement—and harmony—must
be achieved, but we are simply not there yet.

7. Finally, *an area of great uncertainty is what would happen if for the time being we were NOT to file for patents.* The dumping of the first wave of thousands of novel genes from the human brain into the open literature makes those specific sequences unpatentable, and immediately forfeits international rights. It is also likely to make the sequences unpatentable by anyone. The alternative to molecular or product patents—so called composition of matter patents—are *use patents.* The problem that industry leaders know well is that many foreign countries—including Japan—do not honor use patents.

Another concern is that, until we know what is patentable and what uniform practice can be achieved, it would be chaotic if some of the genome were patented and other parts not. The parts with no patent protection would be less likely to be developed commercially, however important they may be to preventing or treating human disease.

NIH's Modern Wager

And so, in the face of many uncertainties, NIH has adopted an *interim policy* that protects its options—and those of the taxpayers—by filing. We did it to hold our place. We did it so that we could publish immediately. We reaffirmed the filing in the interest of resolving the matter. And while it is being resolved through the patent office and through policy discussions and decisions, patent filing protects U.S. interests.

As we look ahead, NIH and the Department of Health and Human Services are actively participating with other components of the federal government to explore policy options and their consequences, whatever the patent office decides. These include exploration of the issues I've raised. Also, consideration as to whether "use patents" need to be strengthened for this class of molecules; how licensing policies should be defined; and whether new legislation may be needed, as was the case for plant varieties developed in the agricultural sector. New systems also became necessary for protection of semiconductor chip products in the computer industry. The new systems generally gave a defined but narrower protection.

It is important to note that no outcome is forced by NIH's interim decision to file for patents. If, after thorough evaluation, it is decided that these cDNA sequences should not be patented, NIH could withdraw its patents or dedicate them to the public. In any event, we have a 200 year old patent system established by Thomas Jefferson for the express purpose of making sure that

"both individuals and society reap the benefits
of human industry and creativity."

Surely Thomas Jefferson could never have predicted what a quandary his highly successful patent system would face over Mother Nature's secrets.

In conclusion, the National Institutes of Health is at the center of much change: change in the way we live and in the work we do. Standing alone, it is world famous for excellence. Involved in biotechnology, it is a world leader.

At NIH we are often walking on paths that have no footprints, encountering much that is new—but never forgetting our core mission—a noble mission to decrease the ravages of death and disability through the discovery of new knowledge and the application of that knowledge for public good. Let me recall the words of Napoleon to his men as they stood in Egypt. He reminded them

"from the heights of these pyramids, forty centuries are watching."

In the shadow of a wonder of the ancient world, he spoke of civilizations linked by conquest and war. Today, we have the chance to link civilizations by working, thinking, discovering, and striving to extend and enrich human life.

And that truly *IS* a wonder of the *modern* world.

Thank you.

FORUM ON CLONING FROM *NATURE*

Following the publication of Axel Kahn's essay in the magazine *Nature,* which begins these selections, the magazine ran a continuing discussion of the issues raised by Kahn's argument and the successful cloning of a sheep by British researchers. The following selections from this discussion were all contributed by scientists working in genetic research.

Clone Mammals . . . Clone Man?

Axel Kahn

The experiments of I. Wilmut *et al.* (*Nature* 385, 810; 1997) demonstrate that the sheep embryonic eggs (oocytes) can reprogramme the nuclei of differentiated cells, enabling the cells to develop into any type. The precise conditions under which this process can occur remain to be elucidated; the factors determining the success of the technique, and the long-term prospects for animals generated in this way, still need to be established. But, of course, the main point is that Wilmut *et al.* show that it is now possible to envisage cloning of adult mammals in a completely asexual fashion.

The oocyte's only involvement is the role of its cytoplasm in reprogramming the introduced nucleus and in contributing intracellular organelles—mainly mitochondria—to the future organism. This work will undoubtedly open up new perspectives in research in biology and development, for example, in understanding the functional plasticity of the genome and chromatin during development, and the mechanisms underlying the stability of differentiated states. Another immediate question is to ask whether a species barrier exists. Could an embryo be produced, for example, by implanting the nucleus of a lamb in an enucleated mouse oocyte? Any lamb born in this way would possess a mouse mitochrondrial genome.

The implications for humans are staggering. One example is that the technique suggests that a woman suffering from a serious mitochondrial disease might in the future be able to produce children free of the disease by having the nucleus of her embryo implanted in a donor oocyte (note that this process is not the same as "cloning").

Would Cloning Humans Be Justified?

But the main question raised by the paper by Wilmut *et al.* is that of the possibility of human cloning. There is no *a priori* reason why humans should behave very differently from other mammals where cloning is possible, so the cloning of an adult human could become feasible using the techniques reported.

What medical and scientific "justification" might there be for cloning? Previous debates have identified the preparation of immunocompatible differentiated cell lines for transplantation, as one potential indication. We could imagine everyone having their own reserve of therapeutic cells that would increase their chance of being cured of various diseases, such as cancer, degenerative disorders and viral or inflammatory diseases.

But the debate has in the past perhaps paid insufficient attention to the current strong social trends toward a fanatical desire for individuals not simply to have children but to ensure that these children also carry their genes. Achieving such biological descendance was impossible for sterile men until the development of ICSI (intracytoplasmic sperm injection), which allows a single sperm to be injected directly into the oocyte.

But human descendance is not only biological, as it is in all other species, but is also emotional and cultural. The latter is of such importance that methods of inheritance where both parents' genes are not transmitted—such as adoption and insemination with donor sperm—are widely accepted without any major ethical questions being raised.

But today's society is characterized by an increasing demand for biological inheritance, as if this were the only desirable form of inheritance. Regrettably, a person's personality is increasingly perceived as being largely determined by his or her genes. Moreover, in a world where culture is increasingly internationalized and homogenized, people may ask themselves whether they have anything else to transmit to their children apart from their genes. This pressure probably accounts for the wide social acceptance of ICSI, a technique which was widely made available to people at a time when experimental evidence as to its safety was still flimsy. ICSI means that men with abnormal sperm can now procreate.

Going further upstream, researchers have now succeeded in fertilizing a mouse oocyte using a diploid nucleus of a spermatogonium: apparently normal embryonic development occurs, at least in the early stages. But there are also

severe forms of sterility—such as dysplasia or severe testicular atrophy—or indeed lesbian couples, where no male germ line exists. Will such couples also demand the right to a biological descendance?

Applying the technique used by Wilmut *et al.* in sheep directly to humans
would yield a clone "of the father" and not a shared descendant of both the father and mother. Nevertheless, for a woman the act of carrying a fetus can be as
important as being its biological mother. The extraordinary power of such "ma-
ternal reappropriation" of the embryo can be seen from the strong demand for
pregnancies in post-menopausal women, and for embryo and oocyte donations
to circumvent female sterility. Moreover, if cloning techniques were ever to be
used, the mother would be contributing something—her mitochondrial genome.
We cannot exclude the possibility that the current direction of public opinion will
tend to legitimize the resort to cloning techniques in cases where, for example,
the male partner in a couple is unable to produce gametes.

The creation of human clones solely for spare cell lines would, from a philosophical point of view, be in obvious contradiction to an ethical principle expressed by Emmanuel Kant: that of human dignity. This principle demands that
an individual—and I would extend this to read human life—should never be
thought of only as a means, but always also as an end. Creating human life for
the sole purpose of preparing therapeutic material would clearly not be for the
dignity of the life created.

Analysing the use of cloning as a means of combating sterility is much
more difficult, as the explicit goal is to create a life with the right to dignity.
Moreover, individuals are not determined entirely by their genome, as of course
the family, cultural and social environment have a powerful "humanizing" influence on the construction of a personality. Two human clones born decades
apart would be much more different psychologically than identical twins raised
in the same family.

Threat of Human "Creators"

Nonetheless, part of the individuality and dignity of a person probably lies in the
uniqueness and unpredictability of his or her development. As a result, the uncertainty of the great lottery of heredity constitutes the principal protection
against biological predetermination imposed by third parties, including parents.
One blessing of the relationship between parents and children is their inevitable
difference, which results in parents loving their children for what they are, rather
than trying to make them what they want. Allowing cloning to circumvent sterility would lead to it being tolerated in cases where it was imposed, for example,
by authorities. What would the world be like if we accepted that human "creators" could assume the right to generate creatures in their own likeness, beings
whose very biological characteristics would be subjugated to an outside will?

The results of Wilmut *et al.* undoubtedly have much merit. One effect of
them is to oblige us to face up to our responsibilities. It is not a technical barrier

that will protect us from the perspectives I have mentioned, but a moral one, originating from a reflection of the basis of our dignity. That barrier is certainly the most dignified aspect of human genius.

Cloning for Research "Should Be Allowed"

Meredith Wadman

[Washington] The British leader of the research team that cloned Dolly the sheep has strongly endorsed US moves to outlaw the cloning of human beings. But he said that he has no ethical objection to the use of his technique to create for research purposes human embryos that are not implanted.

Ian Wilmut of the Roslin Institute near Edinburgh said it is "entirely appropriate" to decide that cloning human beings is "not socially acceptable and for a law to be passed." Wilmut was speaking last week at a seminar sponsored by the American Association for the Advancement of Science.

His comments came three days after leaders of the world's eight major industrial nations issued a communiqué after their summit meeting in Denver, Colorado, stating agreement on "the need for appropriate domestic measures and close international cooperation to prohibit the use of somatic cell nuclear transfer to create a child."

The heads of government who agreed to the statement came from Canada, France, Germany, Italy, Japan, Russia, the United Kingdom and the United States.

President Bill Clinton has already sent to Congress a bill that would penalize anyone attempting "to create a human being using somatic cell nuclear transfer cloning" (see *Nature* 387, 644 & 748; 1997). But antiabortion advocates have complained that the proposed law—as reflected in the Denver communiqué—would not penalize the use of the cloning technology to create human embryos where such work stops short of implantation.

Wilmut said he would have no ethical difficulties with such research. But he would have a practical objection: "There are a very limited number of oocytes available for research with human embryos. For the foreseeable future this technology would be much more appropriately developed in a laboratory animal."

His comments coincided with reports that many animals pregnant with clones in research laboratories in the United States and Europe are miscarrying, and that some of the surviving fetuses show evidence of subtle genetic abnormalities. Others are growing abnormally large in the womb.

Other speakers at last week's seminar were less sanguine than Wilmut about the prospect of a law banning cloning. Maxine Singer, president of the Carnegie Foundation, warned of a "slippery slope" that could eventually lead to Congress banning other kinds of research. "To make a precedent like this, to have national legislation that would govern what people can do in labs, would be a very, very big step," said Singer.

Gillian Woollett, assistant vice-president of biologics and biotechnology at Pharmaceutical Research and Manufacturers of America, said one concern is that the Clinton bill and the report from the National Bioethics Advisory Commission on which it is based contain between them "three different definitions of a somatic cell."

The bill defines a somatic cell as "any cell of the body other than germ cells (egg or sperm)." The bioethics commission's 110-page report, published on 9 June, defines a somatic cell in its glossary as "any cell of an embryo, fetus, child or adult not destined to become a sperm or egg cell." And on the first page of the report, the commission defines a somatic cell as "any cell of the embryo, fetus, child or adult which contains a full complement of two sets of chromosomes; in contrast with a germ cell, i.e., an egg or sperm, which contains only one set of chromosomes."

One influential member of the biotechnology industry argued that federal action to prevent the cloning of human beings would be preferable to a patchwork of state laws. "If there is not a sufficient national response you will find very, very unfavourable, awkward and in some cases very misinformed legislation cropping up in the states," said Carl Feldbaum, president of the Biotechnology Industry Organization.

He cited a bill introduced in the Florida state legislature, which would have inadvertently banned the "cloning" of human DNA through *in vitro* replication.

But Feldbaum, a criminal lawyer, said that the Clinton bill still needs "enormous work," partly because of its lack of a declaration that it would pre-empt state law. He warned that the bill proposed "draconian" penalties and an indistinct intent clause that could deter legitimate research.

Jeff Smith, the executive director for policy at the White House's Office of Science and Technology Policy, said that the White House had received assurances from James Sensenbrenner (Republican, Wisconsin), chairman of the House Science Committee, that he would produce anticloning legislations. "Whether it will be an exact clone of the president's bill is not clear," Smith said. The purpose behind the Clinton bill, he said, was to frame the debate and "get the president's position out in front."

European Biotech Industry Plans Ethics Panel

Declan Butler

[Paris] Europe's biotechnology industry is seeking to improve its image by setting up a committee of independent experts to advise it on ethical issues and to draft a code of conduct for its members.

The committee is the initiative of EuropaBio, an industry association representing about 600 biotechnology companies and 11 national biotechnology industry associations. Andrew Dickson, the secretary general of the organization, says that the industry felt it "needed not just to be acting responsibly but to be seen to be acting responsibly."

EuropaBio has not yet decided on the final form of the committee. It says it would provide a secretariat but that the eight to ten members of the committee would need to be—and to be seen to be—independent of industry with complete freedom in their activities. Dickson says EuropaBio is contemplating asking neutral bodies to help to nominate the members, who would be paid only expenses.

The ethics committee would be modelled on the European Commission's expert advisory group on biotechnology ethics, which is chaired by Noelle Lenoir, a member of the French constitutional council.

EuropaBio last week issued a draft "core set of ethical values," which it has made available for public comment (website: http://www.europa-bio.be) and to which its member companies will be expected to adhere. This would be revised regularly to take into account scientific progress and changes in public perception.

Dickson says it is important for the industry to take the temperature of "the boundaries which society believes are acceptable" and to act within these if it is to win public acceptance.

The current draft of the code of ethics rejects the use of cloning to reproduce human beings, arguing that this reflects the current consensus. But Jurgen Drews, chairman of EuropaBio and president of research at Hoffmann-La Roche, points out that this consensus may change.

The code also commits member companies not to work on genes of human sperm, eggs or germline cells. It proposes a moratorium on work on the genes of human embryos "until the medical, ethical, and societal issues that may arise from this kind of therapy have been publicly discussed, clarified and resolved and, if applicable, put into legislation."

Calls for Human Cloning Ban "Stem from Ignorance"

Declan Butler

[Paris] The recent flood of calls for an international ban on the use of human cloning techniques for reproduction appear, at least in some quarters, to be slowly giving way to recognition that such practices may be justified in certain circumstances.

There is also a growing feeling that advocates of a ban have so far failed adequately to substantiate their claims that cloning would be either harmful or unethical.

A report published this month by a working group on cloning set up by the World Health Organization (WHO), for example, argues that much of the opposition to human cloning stems from "science fiction accounts" which have resulted in "fear and ignorance on the part of the public."

The report says that this has prompted legislators and other policy-makers to act from "moral panic" rather than considered deliberation. It says that the cloning debate involves many issues that still need to be discussed in detail, and concludes that introducing an immediate international ban on cloning would be "unwise and counterproductive."

The report adds that a ban or moratorium may be "most incautious," as a hasty prohibition could result in loss of actual and potential benefits. But its conclusion that WHO should proceed more carefully appears to have gone unheeded by the organization's General Assembly, a political body representing WHO's member states. Last week, the assembly adopted a resolution affirming that "the use of cloning for the replication of human individuals is ethically unacceptable and contrary to human integrity and morality."

The assembly's resolution follows similar calls for an international ban from political leaders such as Jacques Chirac, the French president, and Jürgen Rüttgers, Germany's research minister (see *Nature* 387, 111; 1997). Such opposition appears to be based on a perception that the benefits of human cloning would be few, whereas the risks of abuse could be large. But critics argue that the benefits are being underestimated and the risks overstated.

"A sense of proportion is needed," says David Shapiro, executive secretary of the UK Nuffield Council on Bioethics, who points out that there is plenty of time for debate, given the enormous technical hurdles to be overcome before human cloning could even be authorized on safety grounds.

Any demand for cloning would also be relatively small and could be tightly regulated, predicts Shapiro, arguing that, from an ethical point of view, the technique is not significantly different from many accepted forms of medically assisted procreation.

John Robertson, professor of law at the University of Texas in Austin, last week told a meeting of the International Bioethics Committee of the United Nations Educational, Scientific, and Cultural Organization that "initial repugnance has given way to the recognition that there may be some benefits to infertile couples and others from human cloning."

He added that there was also a growing awareness that "the harms alleged to flow from cloning are too vague and speculative to justify a ban on all possible uses of cloning or on cloning research."

Indeed, the widespread political opposition to cloning is causing concern among many scientists and bioethicists. Considered discussion is falling victim to emotion and politics, says Guiseppe Benagiano, director of WHO's programme on research on human reproduction.

"The president or prime minister stands up and says you have to ban human cloning; everybody applauds, he gets more votes, and the arguments play no role," says Benagiano. The fact that the assembly also requested WHO to assess fully the ethical, scientific and social implications of human cloning is "the only thing that is keeping the door open," he adds.

David Griffin, the secretary of WHO's working group on cloning, says the arguments are highly complex, while attitudes to applications of human cloning differ widely between cultures. He argues that a "lack of information" has obscured the debate.

The WHO report points out, for example, that while producing a cloned twin child for spare organs and tissues would clearly be ethically unacceptable, individuals in some cultures might not object to producing clones of early human embryos as a source of spare parts—via the production of embryonic stem cells, perhaps (see *Nature* 387, 218).

Infertile couples are also likely to be a source of demand for cloning. In couples where both partners lack gametes, cloning could provide an alternative to the current practice of embryo donation. It could also be used by couples where the male partner lacks gametes, as it might be considered preferable to using sperm from donors.

Couples undergoing *in vitro* fertilization may also wish to use cloning to generate extra embryos and increase the chances of fertilization in cases where the female partner has few oocytes. Robertson recently told a panel of the US National Bioethics Advisory Commission that if this was essential to reproducing, the couple might have a legal right to the technique under US law, as it would fall under the fundamental freedom to reproduce.

Robertson argues that for most realistic applications of cloning, it is "difficult to see harm for either children, families or society." A ban on cloning for reproduction or on research that might lead to it, "is imprudent and unjustified," he asserts. "Science fiction should not guide science policy."

Is Cloning an Attack on Human Dignity?

John Harris

Sir—Appeals to human dignity, and to the moral obligation to protect it, have been a feature of responses to the cloning of Dolly the sheep (*Nature* 385, 810–813; 1997). Dr. Hiroshi Nakajima, director general of the World Health Organization (WHO), said: "WHO considers the use of cloning for the replication of human individuals to be ethically unacceptable as it would violate some of the basic principles which govern medically assisted procreation. These include respect for the dignity of the human being."

The European Parliament rushed through a resolution banning cloning, which stated as part of the rationale (clause 6) that the parliament "believes it is essential to establish ethical standards, based on respect for human dignity, in the areas of biology, biotechnology and medicine." Neither of these august authorities provided a scrap of argument as to how the idea of human dignity is relevant to the ethics of cloning.

A first question to ask when the idea of human dignity is invoked is: whose dignity is attacked and how? Is it the duplication of a large part of the genome that is supposed to constitute the attack on human dignity? If so, we might legitimately ask whether and how the dignity of a natural twin is threatened by the existence of the other twin. The notion of human dignity is often also linked to Kantian ethics. A typical example, and one that attempts to provide some basis for objections to cloning based on human dignity, is Axel Kahn's invocation of this principle in his Commentary on cloning (*Nature* 386, 119; 1997).

But the Kantian principle, which is generally interpreted as demanding that "an individual should never be thought of as a means but always also as an end," crudely invoked, as it usually is, without any qualification or gloss, is seldom helpful in a medical or bioscience context. It would outlaw blood transfusions and abortions carried out to protect the life or health of the mother. It would also outlaw one form of cloning, embryo splitting, which could allow genetic and other screening by embryo biopsy. One embryo could be tested to ascertain the health and genetic status of the remaining clones, and then destroyed. To this it is objected, *pace* Kahn, that one twin would be destroyed for the sake of another.

It is bizarre and misleading to marshal the Kantian principle as an objection either to using cell mass division to create clones for screening purposes, or to creating clones by nuclear substitution to generate spare cell lines. It is surely ethically dubious to object to one embryo being killed for the sake of another, but not to object to it being killed for nothing. In *in vitro* fertilization (IVF), for example, it is, in the United Kingdom, regarded as good practice to store spare embryos for future use by the mother or for disposal at her direction, either to other women who require donor eggs, or for research, or simply to be destroyed. It cannot be morally worse to an embryo to provide information about its sibling than to use it for more abstract research or simply to destroy it. If it is permissible to use early embryos for research or to destroy them, their use in genetic and other health testing is surely also permissible. The same would surely go for their use in creating cell lines for therapeutic purposes.

A moral principle that has at least as much intuitive force as that recommended by Kant is that it is better to do some good than to do no good. It cannot, from the ethical point of view, be better or more moral to waste human material that could be used for therapeutic purposes than to use it to do good. If it is right to use embryos for research or therapy then it is surely also right to produce them for such purposes, as is usual in IVF. Kant's prohibition does after all refer principally to use. Of course some will think that the embryo is a full member of the moral community with all the rights and protections possessed by Kant himself. Although this is a tenable position, it cannot consistently be held by any society that permits abortion, post-coital contraception or research with human embryos.

Cloning, Dignity, and Ethical Revisionism

Axel Kahn

Sir—Several texts published in *Nature,* notably a leading article devoted to the opinion of the French Consultative Ethics Committee (*Nature* 387, 321 & 324; 1997) and John Harris's letter (*Nature* 387, 754; 1997), discuss the argument that application to man of asexual reproduction and cloning represents an affront to human dignity.

However, the two main arguments I set out in my Commentary (*Nature* 386, 119; 1997), and which were expanded in the French ethics committee opinion, were not accurately reported.

One of the components of human dignity is undoubtedly autonomy, the indeterminability of the individual with respect to external human will. No man or woman on Earth exists exactly as another has imagined, wished or created.

The birth of an infant by asexual reproduction would lead to a new category of people whose bodily form and genetic make-up would be exactly as decided by other humans. This would lead to the establishment of an entirely new type of relationship between the "created" and the "creator," which has obvious implications for human dignity.

Harris contests the validity of arguments based on the Kantian principle. But Kant did not say that respect for human dignity requires that an individual is *never* used as a means, but that an individual must never be used *exclusively* as a means. The word "exclusively" makes all the difference between idle talk and one of the fundamental principles of modern bioethical thought.

The workman is indeed the means for doing work, the person who donates an organ is the means for saving the patient, but they are never exclusively a "means," but also ends in themselves.

The creation of human embryos exclusively as a means, uniquely as a source of therapeutic material, would therefore seem in contradiction of Kant's principle, whose universality is far superior to that which Harris dismisses by omitting the word "exclusively."

In reality, the debate is about the status of the human embryo and its rights as a human individual, and the answers to this question differ greatly both between and within nations. In general, however, all those who would le-gitimize *de novo* creation of human embryos for research or preparation of ther-apeutic material base their position on their belief that the embryo is not a human individual, without calling Kant's principle into question.

Is Harris announcing the emergence of a revisionist tendency in bioethical thinking?

Don't Leave Dignity Out of the Cloning Debate

Karim Labib

Sir—John Harris clearly doubts that the idea of human dignity is relevant to the ethics of human cloning (*Nature* 387, 754; 1997). He questions how the inten-tional creation of a cloned embryo might contravene the notion of human dig-nity, in a society that accepts both abortion and research on early human embryos. But, although he rightly illustrates the potential hypocrisy of accepting abortion and embryo research at the same time as opposing cloning on the grounds of human dignity, this is hardly a justification for conveniently leaving the question of human dignity out of the debate.

The complex moral issues raised by the prospect of human cloning go to the heart of our self-understanding, our ideas of what it is to be a human being. To deny this would itself be a moral view, and one that would need to be supported by convincing arguments. There really is a fundamental difference between a naturally occurring identical twin, and a child that would be the clone of the per-son it would look to as its father or mother, and the genetic progeny of the people it would consider to be its grandparents.

Most people would surely agree that an individual should be treated as an "end" in its own right, and never as simply as a means. I disagree with Harris that this principle "is seldom helpful in a medical or bioscience context," or that "it would outlaw blood tranfusions or abortions carried out to protect the life of the mother." People who give blood find the act of donating to be something that en-riches their lives, rather than simply reducing them to being the means to some-one else's health. And those who value others as ends in their own right are not therefore bound to oppose abortion when essential to preserve a mother's life, since to do so would be treating the mother as a "means," as much as valuing the child as an end.

Surely it is reasonable to argue that society must debate seriously the impli-cations of human cloning for the individuals who would be created, rather than simply treating the issue as just another potential form of infertility treatment. And in such a debate, the question of human dignity will hardly be inappropriate.

Cloning and Bioethical Thinking

John Harris

Sir—Axel Kahn reminds us, rightly, that Kant's famous principle states: "Respect for human dignity requires that an individual is never used . . . exclusively as a means," and suggests that I have ignored the crucial use of the term "exclusively" (*Nature* 388, 320; 1997).

I did not, of course, and I am happy with Kahn's reformulation of the principle. It is not that Kant's principle does not have powerful intuitive force but that it is so vague and open to selective interpretation, and its scope for application is consequently so limited, that its utility as one of the "fundamental principles of modern bioethical thought," as Kahn describes it, is virtually zero.

Kahn himself rightly points out that debates about the moral status of the human embryo are debates about whether embryos fall within the *scope* of Kant's or any other moral principles concerning persons; so the principle itself is not illuminating in this context. Applied to the creation of individuals which are, or will become, autonomous, it has limited application. True, it rules out slavery, but so do other principles based on autonomy and rights.

If you are interested in the ethics of creating people, then, so long as existence is in the created individual's own best interests, and so long as the individual will have the capacity for autonomy like any other, the motives for which the individual was created are either morally irrelevant or subordinate to other moral considerations.

So even where, for example, a child is engendered exclusively to provide "a son and heir" (as in many cultures), it is unclear how or whether Kant's principle applies. Either other motives are also attributed to the parent to square parental purposes with Kant, or the child's eventual autonomy, and its clear and substantial interest in or benefit from existence, take precedence over the comparatively trivial issue of parental motives. Either way, the "fundamental principle of modern bioethical thought" is unhelpful.

I am therefore at a loss to know why Kahn invokes it with such dramatic assurance or how he thinks it applies to the ethics of human cloning. It comes down to this: either the ethics of human cloning turn on the creation or use of human embryos, in which case, as Kahn himself says, "in reality the debate is about the status of the human embryo" and Kant's principle must wait upon the outcome of that debate; or it is about the ethics of producing clones that will become autonomous human persons.

In the latter case, as David Shapiro rightly comments (*Nature* 388, 511; 1997), the ethics of their creation are, from a Kantian perspective, not dissimilar to that of other forms of assisted reproduction or indeed to the ethics of the conduct of parents concerned exclusively with producing an heir or preserving their genes or, as is sometimes alleged, making themselves eligible for public housing—and debates about whether these are *exclusive* intentions are sterile or irresolvable.

When Kahn asks: "Is Harris announcing the emergence of a revisionist tendency in bioethical thinking?," the answer must be rather that I am pleading for the emergence of "bioethical thinking" as opposed to empty rhetoric of invoking resonant principles with no conceivable or coherent application to the problem at hand.

The Evening and the Morning and the Night

Octavia Butler

Octavia Butler is a distinguished author of science fiction. This short story first appeared in Omni Magazine *in 1987 and later in Butler's 1996 book,* Bloodchild.

When I was fifteen and trying to show my independence by getting careless with my diet, my parents took me to a Duryea-Gode disease ward. They wanted me to see, they said, where I was headed if I wasn't careful. In fact, it was where I was headed no matter what. It was only a matter of when: now or later. My parents were putting in their vote for later.

I won't describe the ward. It's enough to say that when they brought me home, I cut my wrists. I did a thorough job of it, old Roman style in a bathtub of warm water. Almost made it. My father dislocated his shoulder breaking down the bathroom door. He and I never forgave each other for that day.

The disease got him almost three years later—just before I went off to college. It was sudden. It doesn't happen that way often. Most people notice themselves beginning to drift—or their relatives notice—and they make arrangements with their chosen institution. People who are noticed and resist going in can be locked up for a week's observation. I don't doubt that that observation period breaks up a few families. Sending someone away for what turns out to be a false alarm. . . . Well, it isn't the sort of thing the victim is likely to forgive or forget. On the other hand, not sending someone away in time—missing the signs or having a person go off suddenly without signs—is inevitably dangerous for the victim. I've never heard of it going as badly, though, as it did in my family. People normally injure only themselves when their time comes—unless someone is stupid enough to try to handle them without the necessary drugs or restraints.

My father had killed my mother, then killed himself. I wasn't home when it happened. I had stayed at school later than usual, rehearsing graduation exercises. By the time I got home, there were cops everywhere. There was an ambulance, and two attendants were wheeling someone out on a stretcher—someone covered. More than covered. Almost . . . bagged.

The cops wouldn't let me in. I didn't find out until later exactly what had happened. I wish I'd never found out. Dad had killed Mom, then skinned her completely. At least that's how I hope it happened. I mean I hope he killed her first. He broke some of her ribs, damaged her heart. Digging.

Then he began tearing at himself, through skin and bone, digging. He had managed to reach his own heart before he died. It was an especially bad example of the kind of thing that makes people afraid of us. It gets some of us into trouble for picking at a pimple or even for daydreaming. It has inspired restrictive laws, created problems with jobs, housing, schools. . . . The Duryea-Gode Disease Foundation has spent millions telling the world that people like my father don't exist.

A long time later, when I had gotten myself together as best I could, I went to college—to the University of Southern California—on a Dilg scholarship. Dilg is the retreat you try to send your out-of-control DGD relatives to. It's run by controlled DGDs like me, like my parents while they lived. God knows how any controlled DGD stands it. Anyway, the place has a waiting list miles long. My parents put me on it after my suicide attempt, but chances were, I'd be dead by the time my name came up.

I can't say why I went to college—except that I had been going to school all my life and didn't know what else to do. I didn't go with any particular hope. Hell, I knew what I was in for eventually. I was just marking time. Whatever I did was just marking time. If people were willing to pay me to go to school and mark time, why not do it?

The weird part was, I worked hard, got top grades. If you work hard enough at something that doesn't matter, you can forget for a while about the things that do.

Sometimes I thought about trying suicide again. How was it I'd had the courage when I was fifteen but didn't have it now? Two DGD parents—both religious, both as opposed to abortion as they were to suicide. So they had trusted God and the promises of modern medicine and had a child. But how could I look at what had happened to them and trust anything?

I majored in biology. Non-DGDs say something about our disease makes us good at the sciences—genetics, molecular biology, biochemistry. . . . That something was terror. Terror and a kind of driving hopelessness. Some of us went bad and became destructive before we had to—yes, we did produce more than our share of criminals. And some of us went good—spectacularly—and made scientific and medical history. These last kept the doors at least partly open for the rest of us. They made discoveries in genetics, found cures for a couple of rare diseases, made advances against other diseases that weren't so rare—including, ironically, some forms of cancer. But they'd found nothing to help themselves. There had been nothing since the latest improvements in the diet, and those came just before I was born. They, like the original diet, gave more DGDs the courage to have children. They were supposed to do for DGDs what insulin had done for diabetics—give us a normal or nearly normal life span. Maybe they had worked for someone somewhere. They hadn't worked for anyone I knew.

Biology school was a pain in the usual ways. I didn't eat in public anymore, didn't like the way people stared at my biscuits—cleverly dubbed "dog biscuits" in every school I'd ever attended. You'd think university students would be more creative. I didn't like the way people edged away from me when they caught sight of my emblem. I'd begun wearing it on a chain around my neck and putting it down inside my blouse, but people managed to notice it anyway. People who don't eat in public, who drink nothing more interesting than water, who smoke nothing at all—people like that are suspicious. Or rather, they make others suspicious. Sooner or later, one of those others, finding my fingers and wrists bare, would fake an interest in my chain. That would be that. I couldn't hide the emblem in my purse. If anything happened to me, medical people had to see it in time to avoid giving me the medications they might use on a normal person. It isn't just ordinary food we have to avoid, but about a quarter of a *Physicians' Desk Reference* of widely used drugs. Every now and then there are news stories about people who stopped carrying their emblems—probably trying to pass as normal. Then they have an accident. By the time anyone realizes there is anything wrong, it's too late. So I wore my emblem. And one way or another, people got a look at it or got the word from someone who had. "She *is!*" Yeah.

At the beginning of my third year, four other DGDs and I decided to rent a house together. We'd all had enough of being lepers twenty-four hours a day. There was an English major. He wanted to be a writer and tell our story from the inside—which had only been done thirty or forty times before. There was a special-education major who hoped the handicapped would accept her more readily than the able-bodied, a premed who planned to go into research, and a chemistry major who didn't really know what she wanted to do.

Two men and three women. All we had in common was our disease, plus a weird combination of stubborn intensity about whatever we happened to be doing and hopeless cynicism about everything else. Healthy people say no one can concentrate like a DGD. Healthy people have all the time in the world for stupid generalizations and short attention spans.

We did our work, came up for air now and then, ate our biscuits, and attended classes. Our only problem was housecleaning. We worked out a schedule of who would clean what when, who would deal with the yard, whatever. We all agreed on it; then, except for me, everyone seemed to forget about it. I found myself going around reminding people to vacuum, clean the bathroom, mow the lawn. . . . I figured they'd all hate me in no time, but I wasn't going to be their maid, and I wasn't going to live in filth. Nobody complained. Nobody even seemed annoyed. They just came up out of their academic daze, cleaned, mopped, mowed, and went back to it. I got into the habit of running around in the evening reminding people. It didn't bother me if it didn't bother them.

"How'd you get to be housemother?" a visiting DGD asked.

I shrugged. "Who cares? The house works." It did. It worked so well that this new guy wanted to move in. He was a friend of one of the others, and another premed. Not bad looking.

"So do I get in or don't I?" he asked.

"As far as I'm concerned, you do," I said. I did what his friend should have done—introduced him around, then, after he left, talked to the others to make sure nobody had any real objections. He seemed to fit right in. He forgot to clean the toilet or mow the lawn, just like the others. His name was Alan Chi. I thought Chi was a Chinese name, and I wondered. But he told me his father was Nigerian and that in Ibo the word meant a kind of guardian angel or personal God. He said his own personal God hadn't been looking out for him very well to let him be born to two DGD parents. Him too.

I don't think it was much more than that similarity that drew us together at first. Sure, I liked the way he looked, but I was used to liking someone's looks and having him run like hell when he found out what I was. It took me a while to get used to the fact that Alan wasn't going anywhere.

I told him about my visit to the DGD ward when I was fifteen—and my suicide attempt afterward. I had never told anyone else. I was surprised at how relieved it made me feel to tell him. And somehow his reaction didn't surprise me.

"Why didn't you try again?" he asked. We were alone in the living room.

"At first, because of my parents," I said. "My father in particular. I couldn't do that to him again."

"And after him?"

"Fear. Inertia."

He nodded. "When I do it, there'll be no half measures. No being rescued, no waking up in a hospital later."

"You mean to do it?"

"The day I realize I've started to drift. Thank God we get some warning."

"Not necessarily."

"Yes, we do. I've done a lot of reading. Even talked to a couple of doctors. Don't believe the rumors non-DGDs invent."

I looked away, stared into the scarred, empty fireplace. I told him exactly how my father had died—something else I'd never voluntarily told anyone.

He sighed. "Jesus!"

We looked at each other.

"What are you going to do?" he asked.

"I don't know."

He extended a dark, square hand, and I took it and moved closer to him. He was a dark, square man—my height, half again my weight, and none of it fat. He was so bitter sometimes, he scared me.

"My mother started to drift when I was three," he said. "My father only lasted a few months longer. I heard he died a couple of years after he went into the hospital. If the two of them had had any sense, they would have had me aborted the minute my mother realized she was pregnant. But she wanted a kid no matter what. And she was Catholic." He shook his head."Hell, they should pass a law to sterilize the lot of us."

"They?" I said.

"You want kids?"

"No, but—"

"More like us to wind up chewing their fingers off in some DGD ward."

"I don't want kids, but I don't want someone else telling me I can't have any."

He stared at me until I began to feel stupid and defensive. I moved away from him.

"Do you want someone else telling you what to do with your body?" I asked.

"No need," he said. "I had that taken care of as soon as I was old enough."

This left me staring. I'd thought about sterilization. What DGD hasn't? But I didn't know anyone else our age who had actually gone through with it. That would be like killing part of yourself—even though it wasn't a part you intended to use. Killing part of yourself when so much of you was already dead.

"The damned disease could be wiped out in one generation," he said, "but people are still animals when it comes to breeding. Still following mindless urges, like dogs and cats."

My impulse was to get up and go away, leave him to wallow in his bitterness and depression alone. But I stayed. He seemed to want to live even less than I did. I wondered how he'd made it this far.

"Are you looking forward to doing research?" I probed.

"Do you believe you'll be able to—"

"No."

I blinked. The word was as cold and dead a sound as I'd ever heard.

"I don't believe in anything," he said.

I took him to bed. He was the only other double DGD I had ever met, and if nobody did anything for him, he wouldn't last much longer. I couldn't just let him slip away. For a while, maybe we could be each other's reasons for staying alive.

He was a good student—for the same reason I was. And he seemed to shed some of his bitterness as time passed. Being around him helped me understand why, against all sanity, two DGDs would lock in on each other and start talking about marriage. Who else would have us?

We probably wouldn't last very long, anyway. These days, most DGDs make it to forty, at least. But then, most of them don't have two DGD parents. As bright as Alan was, he might not get into medical school because of his double inheritance. No one would tell him his bad genes were keeping him out, of course, but we both knew what his chances were. Better to train doctors who were likely to live long enough to put their training to use.

Alan's mother had been sent to Dilg. He hadn't seen her or been able to get any information about her from his grandparents while he was at home. By the time he left for college, he'd stopped asking questions. Maybe it was hearing about my parents that made him start again. I was with him when he called Dilg. Until that moment, he hadn't even known whether his mother was still alive. Surprisingly, she was.

"Dilg must be good," I said when he hung up. "People aren't usually . . . I mean . . ."

"Yeah, I know," he said. "People don't usually live long once they're out of control. Dilg is different." We had gone to my room, where he turned a chair backward and sat down. "Dilg is what the others ought to be, if you can believe the literature."

"Dilg is a giant DGD ward," I said. "It's richer—probably better at sucking in the donations—and it's run by people who can expect to become patients eventually. Apart from that, what's different?"

"I've read about it," he said. "So should you. They've got some new treatment. They don't just shut people away to die the way the others do."

"What else is there to do with them? With us."

"I don't know. It sounded like they have some kind of . . . sheltered workshop. They've got patients doing things."

"A new drug to control the self-destructiveness?"

"I don't think so. We would have heard about that."

"What else could it be?"

"I'm going up to find out. Will you come with me?"

"You're going up to see your mother."

He took a ragged breath. "Yeah. Will you come with me?"

I went to one of my windows and stared out at the weeds. We let them thrive in the backyard. In the front we mowed them, along with the few patches of grass.

"I told you my DGD-ward experience."

"You're not fifteen now. And Dilg isn't some zoo of a ward."

"It's got to be, no matter what they tell the public. And I'm not sure I can stand it."

He got up, came to stand next to me. "Will you try?"

I didn't say anything. I focused on our reflections in the window glass—the two of us together. It looked right, felt right. He put his arm around me, and I leaned back against him. Our being together had been as good for me as it seemed to have been for him. It had given me something to go on besides inertia and fear. I knew I would go with him. It felt like the right thing to do.

"I can't say how I'll act when we get there," I said.

"I can't say how I'll act, either," he admitted. "Especially . . . when I see her."

He made the appointment for the next Saturday afternoon. You make appointments to go to Dilg unless you're a government inspector of some kind. That is the custom, and Dilg gets away with it.

We left L.A. in the rain early Saturday morning. Rain followed us off and on up the coast as far as Santa Barbara. Dilg was hidden away in the hills not far from San Jose. We could have reached it faster by driving up I-5, but neither of us were in the mood for all that bleakness. As it was, we arrived at one P.M. to be met by two armed gate guards. One of these phoned the main building and verified our appointment. Then the other took the wheel from Alan.

"Sorry," he said. "But no one is permitted inside without an escort. We'll meet your guide at the garage."

None of this surprised me. Dilg is a place where not only the patients but much of the staff has DGD. A maximum security prison wouldn't have been as potentially dangerous. On the other hand, I'd never heard of anyone getting chewed up here. Hospitals and rest homes had accidents. Dilg didn't. It was beautiful—an old estate. One that didn't make sense in these days of high taxes. It had been owned by the Dilg family. Oil, chemicals, pharmaceuticals. Ironically, they had even owned part of the late, unlamented Hedeon Laboratories. They'd had a briefly profitable interest in Hedeonco: the magic bullet, the cure for a large percentage of the world's cancer and a number of serious viral diseases— and the cause of Duryea-Gode disease. If one of your parents was treated with Hedeonco and you were conceived after the treatments, you had DGD. If you had kids, you passed it on to them. Not everyone was equally affected. They didn't all commit suicide or murder, but they all mutilated themselves to some degree if they could. And they all drifted—went off into a world of their own and stopped responding to their surroundings.

Anyway, the only Dilg son of his generation had had his life saved by Hedeonco. Then he had watched four of his children die before Doctors Kenneth Duryea and Jan Gode came up with a decent understanding of the problem and a partial solution: the diet. They gave Richard Dilg a way of keeping his next two children alive. He gave the big, cumbersome estate over to the care of DGD patients.

So the main building was an elaborate old mansion. There were other, newer buildings, more like guest houses than institutional buildings. And there were wooded hills all around. Nice country. Green. The ocean wasn't far away. There was an old garage and a small parking lot. Waiting in the lot was a tall, old woman. Our guard pulled up near her, let us out, then parked the car in the half-empty garage.

"Hello," the woman said, extending her hand. "I'm Beatrice Alcantara." The hand was cool and dry and startlingly strong. I thought the woman was DGD, but her age threw me. She appeared to be about sixty, and I had never seen a DGD that old. I wasn't sure why I thought she was DGD. If she was, she must have been an experimental model—one of the first to survive.

"Is it Doctor or Ms.?" Alan asked.

"It's Beatrice," she said. "I am a doctor, but we don't use titles much here."

I glanced at Alan, was surprised to see him smiling at her. He tended to go a long time between smiles. I looked at Beatrice and couldn't see anything to smile about. As we introduced ourselves, I realized I didn't like her. I couldn't see any reason for that either, but my feelings were my feelings. I didn't like her.

"I assume neither of you have been here before," she said, smiling down at us. She was at least six feet tall, and straight.

We shook our heads. "Let's go in the front way, then. I want to prepare you for what we do here. I don't want you to believe you've come to a hospital."

I frowned at her, wondering what else there was to believe. Dilg was called a retreat, but what difference did names make?

The house close up looked like one of the old-style public buildings—massive, baroque front with a single domed tower reaching three stories above the three-story house. Wings of the house stretched for some distance to the right and left of the tower, then cornered and stretched back twice as far. The front doors were huge—one set of wrought iron and one of heavy wood. Neither appeared to be locked. Beatrice pulled open the iron door, pushed the wooden one, and gestured us in.

Inside, the house was an art museum—huge, high ceilinged, tile floored. There were marble columns and niches in which sculptures stood or paintings hung. There were other sculptures displayed around the rooms. At one end of the rooms there was a broad staircase leading up to a gallery that went around the rooms. There more art was displayed. "All this was made here," Beatrice said. "Some of it is even sold from here. Most goes to galleries in the Bay Area or down around L.A. Our only problem is turning out too much of it."

"You mean the patients do this?" I asked.

The old woman nodded. "This and much more. Our people work instead of tearing at themselves or staring into space. One of them invented the p.v. locks that protect this place. Though I almost wish he hadn't. It's gotten us more government attention than we like."

"What kind of locks?" I asked.

"Sorry. Palmprint-voiceprint. The first and the best. We have the patent." She looked at Alan. "Would you like to see what your mother does?"

"Wait a minute," he said. "You're telling us out-of-control DGDs create art and invent things?"

"And that lock," I said. "I've never heard of anything like that. I didn't even see a lock."

"The lock is new," she said. "There have been a few news stories about it. It's not the kind of most people would buy for their homes. Too expensive. So it's of limited interest. People tend to look at what's done at Dilg in the way they look at the efforts of idiots savants. Interesting, incomprehensible, but not really important. Those likely to be interested in the lock and able to afford it know about it." She took a deep breath, faced Alan again. "Oh, yes, DGDs create things. At least they do here."

"Out-of-control DGDs."

"Yes."

"I expected to find them weaving baskets or something—at best. I know what DGD wards are like."

"So do I," she said. "I know what they're like in hospitals, and I know what it's like here." She waved a hand toward an abstract painting that looked like a photo I had once seen of the Orion Nebula. Darkness broken by a great cloud of light and color. "Here we can help them channel their energies. They can create something beautiful, useful, even something worthless. But they create. They don't destroy."

"Why?" Alan demanded. "It can't be some drug. We would have heard."

"It's not a drug."

"Then what is it? Why haven't other hospitals—?"

"Alan," she said. "Wait."

He stood frowning at her.

"Do you want to see your mother?"

"Of course I want to see her!"

"Good. Come with me. Things will sort themselves out."

She led us to a corridor past offices where people talked to one another, waved to Beatrice, worked with computers. . . . They could have been anywhere. I wondered how many of them were controlled DGDs. I also wondered what kind of game the old woman was playing with her secrets. We passed through rooms so beautiful and perfectly kept it was obvious they were rarely used. Then at a broad, heavy door, she stopped us.

"Look at anything you like as we go on," she said. "But don't touch anything or anyone. And remember that some of the people you'll see injured themselves before they came to us. They still bear the scars of those injuries. Some of those scars may be difficult to look at, but you'll be in no danger. Keep that in mind. No one here will harm you." She pushed the door open and gestured us in.

Scars didn't bother me much. Disability didn't bother me. It was the act of self-mutilation that scared me. It was someone attacking her own arm as though it were a wild animal. It was someone who had torn at himself and been restrained or drugged off and on for so long that he barely had a recognizable human feature left, but he was still trying with what he did have to dig into his own flesh. Those are a couple of the things I saw at the DGD ward when I was fifteen. Even then I could have stood it better if I hadn't felt I was looking into a kind of temporal mirror.

I wasn't aware of walking through that doorway. I wouldn't have thought I could do it. The old woman said something, though, and I found myself on the other side of the door with the door closing behind me. I turned to stare at her.

She put her hand on my arm. "It's all right," she said quietly. "That door looks like a wall to a great many people."

I backed away from her, out of her reach, repelled by her touch. Shaking hands had been enough, for God's sake.

Something in her seemed to come to attention as she watched me. It made her even straighter. Deliberately, but for no apparent reason, she stepped toward Alan, touched him the way people do sometimes when they brush past—a kind of tactile "Excuse me." In that wide, empty corridor, it was totally unnecessary. For some reason, she wanted to touch him and wanted me to see. What did she think she was doing? Flirting at her age? I glared at her, found myself suppressing an irrational urge to shove her away from him. The violence of the urge amazed me.

Beatrice smiled and turned away. "This way," she said. Alan put his arm around me and tried to lead me after her.

"Wait a minute," I said, not moving.

Beatrice glanced around.

"What just happened?" I asked. I was ready for her to lie—to say nothing happened, pretend not to know what I was talking about.

"Are you planning to study medicine?" she asked.

"What? What does that have to do—?"

"Study medicine. You may be able to do a great deal of good." She strode away, taking long steps so that we had to hurry to keep up. She led us through a room in which some people worked at computer terminals and others with pencils and paper. It would have been an ordinary scene except that some people had half their faces ruined or had only one hand or leg or had other obvious scars. But they were all in control now. They were working. They were intent but not intent on self-destruction. Not one was digging into or tearing away flesh. When we had passed through this room and into a small, ornate sitting room, Alan grasped Beatrice's arm.

"What is it?" he demanded. "What do you do for them?"

She patted his hand, setting my teeth on edge. "I will tell you," she said. "I want you to know. But I want you to see your mother first." To my surprise, he nodded, let it go at that.

"Sit a moment," she said to us.

We sat in comfortable, matching upholstered chairs—Alan looking reasonably relaxed. What was it about the old lady that relaxed him but put me on edge? Maybe she reminded him of his grandmother or something. She didn't remind me of anyone. And what was that nonsense about studying medicine?

"I wanted you to pass through at least one workroom before we talked about your mother—and about the two of you." She turned to face me. "You've had a bad experience at a hospital or a rest home?"

I looked away from her, not wanting to think about it. Hadn't the people in that mock office been enough of a reminder? Horror film office. Nightmare office.

"It's all right," she said. "You don't have to go into detail. Just outline it for me."

I obeyed slowly, against my will, all the while wondering why I was doing it. She nodded, unsurprised. "Harsh, loving people, your parents. Are they alive?"

"No."

"Were they both DGD?"

"Yes, but . . . yes."

"Of course, aside from the obvious ugliness of your hospital experience and its implications for the future, what impressed you about the people in the ward?"

I didn't know what to answer. What did she want? Why did she want anything from me? She should have been concerned with Alan and his mother.

"Did you see people unrestrained?"

"Yes," I whispered. "One woman. I don't know how it happened that she was free. She ran up to us and slammed into my father without moving him. He was a big man. She bounced off, fell, and . . . began tearing at herself. She bit her own arm and . . . swallowed the flesh she'd bitten away. She tore at the wound she'd made with the nails of her other hand. She . . . I screamed at her to stop." I hugged myself, remembering the young woman, bloody, cannibalizing herself as she lay at our feet, digging into her own flesh. Digging. "They try so hard, fight so hard to get out."

"Out of what?" Alan demanded.

I looked at him, hardly seeing him.

"Lynn," he said gently. "Out of what?"

I shook my head. "Their restraints, their disease, the ward, their bodies . . . "

He glanced at Beatrice, then spoke to me again. "Did the girl talk?"

"No. She screamed."

He turned away from me uncomfortably. "Is this important?" he asked Beatrice.

"Very," she said.

"Well . . . can we talk about it after I see my mother?"

"Then and now." She spoke to me. "Did the girl stop what she was doing when you told her to?"

"The nurses had her a moment later. It didn't matter."

"It mattered. Did she stop?"

"Yes."

"According to the literature, they rarely respond to anyone," Alan said.

"True." Beatrice gave him a sad smile. "Your mother will probably respond to you, though."

"Is she? . . ." He glanced back at the nightmare office.

"Is she as controlled as those people?"

"Yes, though she hasn't always been. Your mother works with clay now. She loves shapes and textures and—"

"She's blind," Alan said, voicing the suspicion as though it were fact. Beatrice's words had sent my thoughts in the same direction. Beatrice hesitated. "Yes," she said finally. "And for . . . the usual reason. I had intended to prepare you slowly."

"I've done a lot of reading."

I hadn't done much reading, but I knew what the usual reason was. The woman had gouged, ripped, or otherwise destroyed her eyes. She would be badly scarred. I got up, went over to sit on the arm of Alan's chair. I rested my hand on his shoulder, and he reached up and held it there.

"Can we see her now?" he asked.

Beatrice got up. "This way," she said.

We passed through more workrooms. People painted; assembled machinery; sculpted in wood, stone; even composed and played music. Almost no one noticed us. The patients were true to their disease in that respect. They weren't ignoring us. They clearly didn't know we existed. Only the few controlled-DGD guards gave themselves away by waving or speaking to Beatrice. I watched a woman work quickly, knowledgeably, with a power saw. She obviously understood the perimeters of her body, was not so dissociated as to perceive herself as trapped in something she needed to dig her way out of. What had Dilg done for these people that other hospitals did not do? And how could Dilg withhold its treatment from the others?

"Over there we make our own diet foods," Beatrice said, pointing through a window toward one of the guest houses. "We permit more variety and make fewer mistakes than the commercial preparers. No ordinary person can concentrate on work the way our people can."

I turned to face her. "What are you saying? That the bigots are right? That we have some special gift?"

"Yes," she said. "It's hardly a bad characteristic, is it?"

"It's what people say whenever one of us does well at something. It's their way of denying us credit for our work."

"Yes. But people occasionally come to the right conclusions for the wrong reasons." I shrugged, not interested in arguing with her about it.

"Alan?" she said. He looked at her.

"Your mother is in the next room."

He swallowed, nodded. We both followed her into the room.

Naomi Chi was a small woman, hair still dark, fingers long and thin, graceful as they shaped the clay. Her face was a ruin. Not only her eyes but most of her nose and one ear were gone. What was left was badly scarred. "Her parents were poor," Beatrice said. "I don't know how much they told you, Alan, but they went through all the money they had, trying to keep her at a decent place. Her mother felt so guilty, you know. She was the one who had cancer and took the drug. . . . Eventually, they had to put Naomi in one of those state-approved, custodial-care places. You know the kind. For a while, it was all the government would pay for. Places like that . . . well, sometimes if patients were really troublesome—especially the ones who kept breaking free—they'd put them in a bare room and let them finish themselves. The only things those places took good care of were the maggots, the cockroaches, and the rats."

I shuddered. "I've heard there are still places like that."

"There are," Beatrice said, "kept open by greed and indifference." She looked at Alan. "Your mother survived for three months in one of those places. I took her from it myself. Later I was instrumental in having that particular place closed."

"You took her?" I asked.

"Dilg didn't exist then, but I was working with a group of controlled DGDs in L.A. Naomi's parents heard about us and asked us to take her. A lot of people didn't trust us then. Only a few of us were medically trained. All of us were young, idealistic, and ignorant. We began in an old frame house with a leaky roof. Naomi's parents were grabbing at straws. So were we. And by pure luck, we grabbed a good one. We were able to prove ourselves to the Dilg family and take over these quarters."

"Prove what?" I asked.

She turned to look at Alan and his mother. Alan was staring at Naomi's ruined face, at the ropy, discolored scar tissue. Naomi was shaping the image of an old woman and two children. The gaunt, lined face of the old woman was remarkably vivid—detailed in a way that seemed impossible for a blind sculptress.

Naomi seemed unaware of us. Her total attention remained on her work. Alan forgot about what Beatrice had told us and reached out to touch the scarred face.

Beatrice let it happen. Naomi did not seem to notice. "If I get her attention for you," Beatrice said, "we'll be breaking her routine. We'll have to stay with her until she gets back into it without hurting herself. About half an hour."

"You can get her attention?" he asked.

"Yes."

"Can she? . . ." Alan swallowed. "I've never heard of anything like this. Can she talk?"

"Yes. She may not choose to, though. And if she does, she'll do it very slowly."

"Do it. Get her attention."

"She'll want to touch you."

"That's all right. Do it."

Beatrice took Naomi's hands and held them still, away from the wet clay. For several seconds Naomi tugged at her captive hands, as though unable to understand why they did not move as she wished.

Beatrice stepped closer and spoke quietly. "Stop, Naomi." And Naomi was still, blind face turned toward Beatrice in an attitude of attentive waiting. Totally focused waiting.

"Company, Naomi."

After a few seconds, Naomi made a wordless sound.

Beatrice gestured Alan to her side, gave Naomi one of his hands. It didn't bother me this time when she touched him. I was too interested in what was happening. Naomi examined Alan's hand minutely, then followed the arm up to the shoulder, the neck, the face. Holding his face between her hands, she made a sound. It may have been a word, but I couldn't understand it. All I could think of was the danger of those hands. I thought of my father's hands.

"His name is Alan Chi, Naomi. He's your son." Several seconds passed.

"Son?" she said. This time the word was quite distinct, though her lips had split in many places and had healed badly. "Son?" she repeated anxiously. "Here?"

"He's all right, Naomi. He's come to visit."

"Mother?" he said.

She reexamined his face. He had been three when she started to drift. It didn't seem possible that she could find anything in his face that she would remember. I wondered whether she remembered she had a son.

"Alan?" she said. She found his tears and paused at them. She touched her own face where there should have been an eye, then she reached back toward his eyes. An instant before I would have grabbed her hand, Beatrice did it.

"No!" Beatrice said firmly.

The hand fell limply to Naomi's side. Her face turned toward Beatrice like an antique weather vane swinging around. Beatrice stroked her hair, and Naomi said something I almost understood. Beatrice looked at Alan, who was frowning and wiping away tears.

"Hug your son," Beatrice said softly.

Naomi turned, groping, and Alan seized her in a tight, long hug. Her arms went around him slowly. She spoke words blurred by her ruined mouth but just understandable.

"Parents?" she said. "Did my parents . . . care for you?" Alan looked at her, clearly not understanding.

"She wants to know whether her parents took care of you," I said.

He glanced at me doubtfully, then looked at Beatrice.

"Yes," Beatrice said. "She just wants to know that they cared for you."

"They did," he said. "They kept their promise to you, Mother."

Several seconds passed. Naomi made sounds that even Alan took to be weeping, and he tried to comfort her.

"Who else is here?" she said finally.

This time Alan looked at me. I repeated what she had said.

"Her name is Lynn Mortimer," he said. "I'm . . ." He paused awkwardly. "She and I are going to be married."

After a time, she moved back from him and said my name. My first impulse was to go to her. I wasn't afraid or repelled by her now, but for no reason I could explain, I looked at Beatrice.

"Go," she said. "But you and I will have to talk later."

I went to Naomi, took her hand.

"Bea?" she said.

"I'm Lynn," I said softly.

She drew a quick breath. "No," she said. "No, you're . . ."

"I'm Lynn. Do you want Bea? She's here."

She said nothing. She put her hand to my face, explored it slowly. I let her do it, confident that I could stop her if she turned violent. But first one hand, then both, went over me very gently.

"You'll marry my son?" she said finally.

"Yes. "

"Good. You'll keep him safe."

As much as possible, we'll keep each other safe. "Yes," I said.

"Good. No one will close him away from himself. No one will tie him or cage him." Her hand wandered to her own face again, nails biting in slightly.

"No," I said softly, catching the hand. "I want you to be safe, too."

The mouth moved. I think it smiled. "Son?" she said.

He understood her, took her hand.

"Clay," she said. Lynn and Alan in clay. "Bea?"

"Of course," Beatrice said. "Do you have an impression?"

"No!" It was the fastest that Naomi had answered anything. Then, almost childlike, she whispered. "Yes."

Beatrice laughed. "Touch them again if you like, Naomi. They don't mind."

We didn't. Alan closed his eyes, trusting her gentleness in a way I could not. I had no trouble accepting her touch, even so near my eyes, but I did not delude myself about her. Her gentleness could turn in an instant. Naomi's fingers twitched near Alan's eyes, and I spoke up at once, out of fear for him.

"Just touch him, Naomi. Only touch."

She froze, made an interrogative sound.

"She's all right," Alan said.

"I know," I said, not believing it. He would be all right, though, as long as someone watched her very carefully, nipped any dangerous impulses in the bud.

"Son!" she said, happily possessive. When she let him go, she demanded clay, wouldn't touch her old-woman sculpture again. Beatrice got new clay for her, leaving us to soothe her and ease her impatience. Alan began to recognize signs of impending destructive behavior. Twice he caught her hands and said no. She struggled against him until I spoke to her. As Beatrice returned, it happened again, and Beatrice said, "No, Naomi." Obediently Naomi let her hands fall to her sides.

"What is it?" Alan demanded later when we had left Naomi safely, totally focused on her new work—clay sculptures of us. "Does she only listen to women or something?"

Beatrice took us back to the sitting room, sat us both down, but did not sit down herself. She went to a window and stared out. "Naomi only obeys certain women," she said. "And she's sometimes slow to obey. She's worse than most—probably because of the damage she managed to do to herself before I got her." Beatrice faced us, stood biting her lip and frowning. "I haven't had to give this particular speech for a while," she said. "Most DGDs have the sense not to marry each other and produce children. I hope you two aren't planning to have any—in spite of our need." She took a deep breath. "It's a pheromone. A scent. And it's sex-linked. Men who inherit the disease from their fathers have no trace of the scent. They also tend to have an easier time with the disease. But they're useless to use as staff here. Men who inherit from their mothers have as much of the scent as men get. They can be useful here because the DGDs can at least be made to notice them. The same for women who inherit from their mothers but not their fathers. It's only when two irresponsible DGDs get together and produce girl children like me or Lynn that you get someone who can really do some good in a place like this." She looked at me. "We are very rare commodities, you and I. When you finish school you'll have a very well-paying job waiting for you."

"Here?" I asked.

"For training, perhaps. Beyond that, I don't know. You'll probably help start a retreat in some other part of the country. Others are badly needed." She smiled humorlessly. "People like us don't get along well together. You must realize that I don't like you any more than you like me."

I swallowed, saw her through a kind of haze for a moment. Hated her mindlessly—just for a moment.

"Sit back," she said. "Relax your body. It helps."

I obeyed, not really wanting to obey her but unable to think of anything else to do. Unable to think at all. "We seem," she said, "to be very territorial. Dilg is a haven for me when I'm the only one of my kind here. When I'm not, it's a prison."

"All it looks like to me is an unbelievable amount of work," Alan said.

She nodded. "Almost too much." She smiled to herself. "I was one of the first double DGDs to be born. When I was old enough to understand, I thought I didn't have much time. First I tried to kill myself. Failing that, I tried to cram all the living I could into the small amount of time I assumed I had. When I got into this project, I worked as hard as I could to get it into shape before I started to drift. By now I wouldn't know what to do with myself if I weren't working."

"Why haven't you . . . drifted?" I asked.

"I don't know. There aren't enough of our kind to know what's normal for us."

"Drifting is normal for every DGD sooner or later."

"Later, then."

"Why hasn't the scent been synthesized?" Alan asked. "Why are there still concentration-camp rest homes and hospital wards?"

"There have been people trying to synthesize it since I proved what I could do with it. No one has succeeded so far. All we've been able to do is keep our eyes open for people like Lynn." She looked at me. "Dilg scholarship, right?"

"Yeah. Offered out of the blue."

"My people do a good job keeping track. You would have been contacted just before you graduated or if you dropped out."

"Is it possible," Alan said, staring at me, "that she's already doing it? Already using the scent to . . . influence people?"

"You?" Beatrice asked.

"All of us. A group of DGDs. We all live together. We're all controlled, of course, but . . ." Beatrice smiled. "It's probably the quietest house full of kids that anyone's ever seen."

I looked at Alan, and he looked away. "I'm not doing anything to them," I said. "I remind them of work they've already promised to do. That's all."

"You put them at ease," Beatrice said. "You're there. You . . . well, you leave your scent around the house. You speak to them individually. Without knowing why, they no doubt find that very comforting. Don't you, Alan?"

"I don't know," he said. "I suppose I must have. From my first visit to the house, I knew I wanted to move in. And when I first saw Lynn, I . . ." He shook his head. "Funny, I thought all that was my idea."

"Will you work with us, Alan?"

"Me? You want Lynn."

"I want you both. You have no idea how many people take one look at one workroom here and turn and run. You may be the kind of young people who ought to eventually take charge of a place like Dilg."

"Whether we want to or not, eh?" he said.

Frightened, I tried to take his hand, but he moved it away. "Alan, this works," I said. "It's only a stopgap, I know. Genetic engineering will probably give us the final answers, but for God's sake, this is something we can do now!"

"It's something *you* can do. Play queen bee in a retreat full of workers. I've never had any ambition to be a drone."

"A physician isn't likely to be a drone," Beatrice said.

"Would you marry one of your patients?" he demanded. "That's what Lynn would be doing if she married me—whether I become a doctor or not."

She looked away from him, stared across the room. "My husband is here," she said softly. "He's been a patient here for almost a decade. What better place for him . . . when his time came?"

"Shit!" Alan muttered. He glanced at me. "Let's get out of here!" He got up and strode across the room to the door, pulled at it, then realized it was locked. He turned to face Beatrice, his body language demanding she let him out. She went to him, took him by the shoulder, and turned him to face the door. "Try it once more," she said quietly. "You can't break it. Try."

Surprisingly, some of the hostility seemed to go out of him. "This is one of those p.v. locks?" he asked.

"Yes."

I set my teeth and looked away. Let her work. She knew how to use this thing she and I both had. And for the moment, she was on my side.

I heard him make some effort with the door. The door didn't even rattle. Beatrice took his hand from it, and with her own hand flat against what appeared to be a large brass knob, she pushed the door open.

"The man who created that lock is nobody in particular," she said. "He doesn't have an unusually high I.Q., didn't even finish college. But sometime in his life he read a science-fiction story in which palmprint locks were a given. He went that story one better by creating one that responded to voice or palm. It took him years, but we were able to give him those years. The people of Dilg are problem solvers, Alan. Think of the problems you could solve!"

He looked as though he were beginning to think, beginning to understand. "I don't see how biological research can be done that way," he said. "Not with everyone acting on his own, not even aware of other researchers and their work."

"It *is* being done," she said, "and not in isolation. Our retreat in Colorado specializes in it and has—just barely—enough trained, controlled DGDs to see that no one really works in isolation. Our patients can still read and write—those who haven't damaged themselves too badly. They can take each other's work into account if reports are made available to them. And they can read material that comes in from the outside. They're working, Alan. The disease hasn't stopped them, *won't* stop them." He stared at her, seemed to be caught by her intensity—or her scent. He spoke as though his words were a strain, as though they hurt his throat. "I won't be a puppet. I won't be controlled . . . by a god-damn smell!"

"Alan—"

"I won't be what my mother is. I'd rather be dead!"

"There's no reason for you to become what your mother is."

He drew back in obvious disbelief.

"Your mother is brain damaged—thanks to the three months she spent in that custodial-care toilet. She had no speech at all when I met her. She's improved more than you can imagine. None of that has to happen to you. Work with us, and we'll see that none of it happens to you."

He hesitated, seemed less sure of himself. Even that much flexibility in him was surprising. "I'll be under your control or Lynn's," he said.

She shook her head. "Not even your mother is under my control. She's aware of me. She's able to take direction from me. She trusts me the way any blind person would trust her guide."

"There's more to it than that."

"Not here. Not at any of our retreats."

"I don't believe you."

"Then you don't understand how much individuality our people retain. They know they need help, but they have minds of their own. If you want to see the abuse of power you're worried about, go to a DGD ward."

"You're better than that, I admit. Hell is probably better than that. But . . ."

"But you don't trust us."

He shrugged.

"You do, you know." She smiled. "You don't want to, but you do. That's what worries you, and it leaves you with work to do. Look into what I've said. See for yourself. We offer DGDs a chance to live and do whatever they decide is important to them. What do you have, what can you realistically hope for that's better than that?"

Silence. "I don't know what to think," he said finally.

"Go home," she said. "Decide what to think. It's the most important decision you'll ever make."

He looked at me. I went to him, not sure how he'd react, not sure he'd want me no matter what he decided.

"What are you going to do?" he asked.

The question startled me. "You have a choice," I said. "I don't. If she's right . . . how could I not wind up running a retreat?"

"Do you want to?"

I swallowed. I hadn't really faced that question yet. Did I want to spend my life in something that was basically a refined DGD ward? "No!"

"But you will."

". . . Yes." I thought for a moment, hunted for the right words. "You'd do it."

"What?"

"If the pheromone were something only men had, you would do it."

That silence again. After a time he took my hand, and we followed Beatrice out to the car. Before I could get in with him and our guard-escort, she caught my arm. I jerked away reflexively. By the time I caught myself, I had swung around as though I meant to hit her. Hell, I did mean to hit her, but I stopped myself in time. "Sorry," I said with no attempt at sincerity.

She held out a card until I took it. "My private number," she said. "Before seven or after nine, usually. You and I will communicate best by phone."

I resisted the impulse to throw the card away. God, she brought out the child in me.

Inside the car, Alan said something to the guard. I couldn't hear what it was, but the sound of his voice reminded me of him arguing with her—her logic and her scent. She had all but won him for me, and I couldn't manage even token gratitude. I spoke to her, low voiced.

"He never really had a chance, did he?"

She looked surprised. "That's up to you. You can keep him or drive him away. I assure you, you *can* drive him away."

"How?"

"By imagining that he doesn't have a chance." She smiled faintly. "Phone me from your territory. We have a great deal to say to each other, and I'd rather we didn't say it as enemies."

She had lived with meeting people like me for decades. She had good control. I, on the other hand, was at the end of my control. All I could do was scramble into the car and floor my own phantom accelerator as the guard drove us to the gate. I couldn't look back at her. Until we were well away from the house, until we'd left the guard at the gate and gone off the property, I couldn't make myself look back. For long, irrational minutes, I was convinced that somehow if I turned, I would see myself standing there, gray and old, growing small in the distance, vanishing.

Afterword

"The Evening and the Morning and the Night" grew from my ongoing fascinations with biology, medicine, and personal responsibility.

In particular, I began the story wondering how much of what we do is encouraged, discouraged, or otherwise guided by what we are genetically. This is one of my favorite questions, parent to several of my novels. It can be a dangerous question. All too often, when people ask it, they mean who has the biggest or the best or the most of whatever they see as desirable, or who has the smallest and the least of what is undesirable. Genetics as a board game, or worse, as an excuse for the social Darwinism that swings into popularity every few years. Nasty habit.

And yet the question itself is fascinating. And disease, grim as it is, is one way to explore answers. Genetic disorders in particular may teach us much about who and what we are.

I built Duryea-Gode disease from elements of three genetic disorders. The first is Huntington's disease—hereditary, dominant, and thus an inevitability if one has the gene for it. And it is caused by only one abnormal gene. Also Huntington's does not usually show itself until its sufferers are middle-aged.

In addition to Huntington's, I used phenylketonuria (PKU), a recessive genetic disorder that causes severe mental impairment unless the infant who has it is put on a special diet.

Finally, I used Lesch-Nyhan disease, which causes both mental impairment and self-mutilation.

To elements of these disorders, I added my own particular twists: a sensitivity to pheromones and the sufferers' persistent delusion that they are trapped, imprisoned within their own flesh, and that that flesh is somehow not truly part of them. In that last, I took an idea familiar to us all—present in many religions and philosophies—and carried it to a terrible extreme.

We carry as many as 50,000 different genes in each of the nuclei of our billions of cells. If one gene among the 50,000, the Huntington's gene, for instance, can so greatly change our lives—what we can do, what we can become—then what are we?

What, indeed?

For readers who find this question as fascinating as I do, I offer a brief, unconventional reading list: *The Chimpanzees of Gombe: Patterns of Behavior* by Jane Goodall, *The Boy Who Couldn't Stop Washing: The Experience and Treatment of Obsessive-Compulsive Disorder* by Judith L. Rapoport, *Medical Detectives* by Berton Roueché, *An Anthropologist on Mars: Seven Paradoxical Tales* and *The Man Who Mistook His Wife for a Hat and Other Clinical Tales* by Oliver Sacks.

Enjoy!

Credits